SAFETY
WAS NO
ACCIDENT

SAFETY WAS NO ACCIDENT

History of the UK
Civil Aviation Flying Unit

CAFU

1944 -1996

by
JAMES FULLER

Order this book online at www.trafford.com
or email orders@trafford.com

Most Trafford titles are also available at major online book retailers.

© Copyright 2012 James Fuller.

All rights reserved. No part of this publication may be reproduced, stored in a retrieval system, or transmitted, in any form or by any means, electronic, mechanical, photocopying, recording, or otherwise, without the written prior permission of the author.

Printed in the United States of America.

ISBN: 978-1-4669-6892-9 (sc)
ISBN: 978-1-4669-6894-3 (hc)
ISBN: 978-1-4669-6893-6 (e)

Library of Congress Control Number: 2012921706

Trafford rev. 03/20/2013

www.trafford.com

North America & international
toll-free: 1 888 232 4444 (USA & Canada)
phone: 250 383 6864 ♦ fax: 812 355 4082

CONTENTS

Accident Statistics vii
Foreword ix
Preface xi
Acknowledgements xv
Introduction xix

Chapter 1   1944-1949 1
Chapter 2   1950-1959 61
Chapter 3   1960-1969 130
Chapter 4   1970-1974 191
Chapter 5   1975-1979 232
Chapter 6   1980-1989 282
Chapter 7   1990-1996 337

Conclusion 361
Afterword 365

Appendix A   ICAO International Civil Aviation Organisation ... 373
Appendix B   NAVIGATIONAL AIDS 375
Appendix C   ILS and VOR inspection procedures 395
Appendix D   Leeds Letter 400
Appendix E   CAFU FACTS 402
Appendix F   Papers by A. C. Marchant 407

Bibliography 423
Abbreviations 425

ACCIDENT STATISTICS

One of the attempts at recording the safety of transport flights used by *Flight* magazine was the number of crashes per million flights. *Flight* thought that if it cannot be zero, then there should be no more than one fatal crash per million flights.

The table below records world and UK transport accident rates:

World Accident Rate Crashes per Million Flights	UK Accident Rate Crashes per Million Flights
1930-35 = **15**	1936 = **67**
1963-72 = **2.5**	1960 = **04**
	1970 = **3.6**
1973-78 = **2.1**	1977 = **1.2**

Source: *Flight* 25 Jan. 1951 p. 112 & 21 Oct. 1978 p. 1492-1504

As can be seen from the table above, in 1970, the UK rate of 3.6 was still above the world rate of around 2.1. By 1978, the UK rate plummeted below the world rate.

However, there are many ways of attempting to record aviation safety. What is apparent is that however the statistics are shown, accident rates have fallen.

Year	Fatal Accidents per 100 Million Miles Flown	Fatality Rate per 100 Million Passenger Miles
1950	3.02	3.15
1955	1.82	1.07
1960	1.76	1.29
1965	0.98	0.56
1970	0.72	0.28
1972	0.92	0.35

Source: *Flight* 1973 18 Jan p. 94 & 1985 26 Jan p. 29-35

FOREWORD

by Charles Marchant, CAFU Superintendent, 1950-1970

One interpretation of Jim Fuller's clever title to this book is that the word "safety" in the civil aviation context should ideally be associated with an accident-free record. Clearly this is an impossible target to achieve in our imperfect world, but the story told by Jim illustrates the hard and dedicated work of the Civil Aviation Flying Unit (CAFU) over decades as a part of the worldwide effort to improve the safety of civil aviation.

The statistics showing the ratio of aviation accidents to number of flights per year are impressive evidence of the success of this endeavour.

Anyone working at CAFU had the satisfaction of knowing that they belonged to an organisation that was at the leading edge of an effort by the United Kingdom to promote safety in commercial aviation. It was a worthy and rewarding target compared with so many other employments on offer.

Inevitably from the beginning of civil aviation, there was a conflict between the aims of achieving financial profit and those of safety. Too little of the latter would ultimately set a limit to profitability—but too much spent on developing "safety" would be unnecessarily expensive. So the cost of CAFU's contribution to safety was always under review in a technically fast developing world.

Thus developments arising from the invention of semiconductors and computers led to improvements in reliability, accuracy, and integrity of navigational systems. This eventually dispensed with the need for frequent flight inspections by CAFU and its elements of research and development. So in the mid-nineties, CAFU was closed.

With the abolition of CAFU came the realisation that the record of its work and significance existed only in the memories of ageing people—there was an urgent need for a record to be written. But the prospect of the work involved in doing so was very daunting and would involve a great deal of research and dedication. Not an attractive prospect for most older people.

Therefore Jim Fuller is to be congratulated in now undertaking this mammoth task.

From his firsthand experience in the CAFU Operations Section, Jim was able to appreciate the complexities of safely running a flying programme. But this book, with its history of CAFU evolution, embraces a wide-ranging research into the history of UK Civil Aviation.

The book will be of great interest to all CAFU veterans—and perhaps some of the pilot "examinees" from the early days! It will be an essential reference source for those with an interest in aviation history.

Congratulations, Jim, for your energy, drive, and dedication.

PREFACE

Although essential to aviation safety, flight calibration is a service that does not have a high profile outside of the aviation industry. Even within it, many are not aware of a service that ensures that important navigation aids, including instrument landing systems, are working correctly. Yet these are aids that allow airlines to operate services, particularly in poor weather conditions, that their customers virtually take for granted.

This story is only one of the threads or strands of work undertaken by the UK government immediately after World War II. Telling of the beginning of the Civil Aviation Flying Unit (CAFU) that, among many other tasks, was initially set up to flight inspect UK civil aviation radio, navigational and landing aids, test candidates for the issue of a commercial pilot's licence, and inspect post-airline training captains delegated to act on the Ministry's behalf.

It is not so much a history of CAFU but perhaps more of a diary of events in which CAFU was involved. In the main, it has been written by others and assembled by me and placed between aviation events for the period 1944 to 1996.

After my retirement, I rediscovered an old magazine, the *Hunting Group Review*, which had an article on my old workplace, and realised that CAFU had had some importance in the role of post-war civil aviation within the United Kingdom and beyond. The more I searched, the more I pondered as to why, immediately following World War II, the British government would want to spend money—be allowed to spend money—in the most austere period of time in post-war Britain. How did it come about? From whom and where were the policies being driven?

The article in the *Hunting Group Review* told that the Civil Operations Fleet (COF—forerunner of CAFU) was started in 1944. But why during wartime? Exactly when? And how? From this juncture, I found, much to my surprise, very little had been written about the work of the unit. From this point, I set about researching.

Finding many people within the CAA Retired Staff Association, I began to record their memories. The only difficulty was finding a date for many of these events.

The Internet provided a homely method of research, using such sites as the National Archives, *Hansard*, *Aeroplane Monthly*, *Flight* magazine, to name the best. Importantly, the CAA provides a database of aircraft registrations, which was also invaluable.

The CAA's in-house paper, *Airway*, together with the CAA's Safety Regulation Groups (SRG) Central Library at Gatwick hold a vast amount of data from many of their publications. These and other books, which helped to confirm dates and many technical facts, are listed in the bibliography section.

A great source of information came about when I created a web site (cafuhistory.com). This provided contact with CAA staff, ex-CAA staff, and total strangers from the United Kingdom and abroad. I have had e-mails and snail mail sent from Canada, Ireland, Norway, and Spain. All have provided a source of guidance, contact, and comfort in my slow research.

At least three families have allowed me access to private collections of memorabilia, including photographs.

Having found sources of information, I realised there could be several ways to display the work; should it be separated by the type of work undertaken, i.e., flight inspection, examining, company inspection, communication, and other tasks such as ordnance survey? However, although the work was separate, the aircrew, particularly the pilots, shared all of the tasks, at least until 1988.

What I felt was required was to endeavour to collate and display each period of time, with its civil aviation happenings, in order to provide an explanation as to how and why CAFU had evolved and, where CAFU sat within the aviation world, to show not just the important role it played but how it responded to those events that were happening at the time. I also hoped my research would explain how it came about that CAFU was broken apart in the 1980s. So within these pages, the reader will find a host of snippets of aviation events running concurrent and merging with the work of CAFU.

Finally, what seems to emerge is that the whole period from 1946 to 1996 was a period of continuing change. Necessary government changes were brought about by a never-ending requirement to reduce costs; nothing could ever remain the same because the aviation industry is ever evolving. Advance in aviation rapidly took place during the First World War, slowing during the interwar period, and sped up again during the Second World War—not only with developments in aircraft design, performance, and instrumentation, but also in the shape of new and better navigational and landing aids. Improvements were so rapid that even during WWII, the allies were beginning to think of the future, a future causing the UK Air Ministry to form a tiny unit, first called the Civil Operations Fleet and later CAFU, which now forms the basis of this book.

ACKNOWLEDGEMENTS

One of the two main contributors has been Mr. A. C. Marchant, who joined the Civil Aviation Flying Unit (CAFU) in the fifties, becoming deputy signals officer and later the telecommunications superintendent of CAFU. He is joined by Captain G. B. Gurr, a pilot who also joined in the fifties, later becoming commander of the fleet.

To assist in some factual aircraft registration dates, I have used the Civil Aviation Authority's own aircraft registration database named GINFO.

In order to provide additional factual information over the period, I have resorted to the Internet, where, among a number of sites, I have found *Flight* magazine, the National Archives, and *Hansard* web sites to be very comprehensive. *Flight* wrote on the "Work of CAFU" both in the fifties and sixties, recording articles on "The Men from the Ministry" (my terminology), as well as other topics, such as navigational aids and any number of other interesting articles over the period.

My first thanks should be to Captain Gurr, a commander in the 1970s, who donated to me his biography, *A Testing Time*, which has been a great provider of events and policy decisions from the fifties to the seventies (the section on CAFU was written by Sidney Pritchard).

Equally important are technical paper(s) written by the telecommunications superintendent of the 1950s and 1960s, Charles Marchant, who wrote in *Flight* magazine in the mid-1960s, as well as a lecture he delivered in the new millennium to the Institute of

Navigation. I am also indebted to a second superintendent from the 1970s, Eddy Harris, who has been both enthusiastic and helpful with his memories, producing articles and a great many old photographs. Sadly, he died in November 2011, his son Geoff presenting me with much of his CAFU memorabilia and photographs.

Two navigators, Sidney Pritchard, who wrote the chapter on CAFU in Geoff Gurr's *A Testing Time*, and Derek Carruthers (Derek introduced me to the Charles Marchant papers)—both later becoming pilots. Also a radio operator, Iain Smith, all three having joined CAFU in the 1940s. Iain went on to much higher work with the Ministry in later life.

Numerous pilots helped; Hugh McDowall recalled MLS trials, as did Dick Hawkes. John Robinson and Paddy Carver remembered events in the seventies and eighties and are still involved with aviation. David Gray, an ex-examiner at Stansted in the eighties, is now retired and living in Canada. Peter Ray, a telecommunications pilot who saw the last throes of CAAFU before it moved to Teesside in the 1990s, has passed ideas and memories of CAFU. Captain Don Hale, ex-CAFU flight manager and an All Weather Ops member, provided assistance with his recall of events. Another source of photographs, some of which were taken by Peter Moon, has been Jean "Jan" Jenkins, who worked with the calibration unit right up until the work of flight inspection was contracted out. Late contacts have been Capt. Brian Morgan and Capt. John Oliver, who (both reluctant and ever modest) provided me with details from their logbooks. Capt. Scott Anderson of the FCU and FCS also passed advice, memories, and videos right through until 1996.

I am also indebted to Steve Rees, son of Captain J. I. "Dai" Rees, who loaned me one of his father's personal flying logbooks.

Several books have helped in my search for items about Stansted, all mentioned in the bibliography, as well as numerous Internet sites. Many telecommunications staff assisted in the technical aspects of the work; in particular Alan Richardson, ex-CAFU NAI, who ensured the appendix on navaids is near to being correct. Iain Smith, who joined in the forties; Ted Pillinger, a principal and now secretary of the CAA Retired Staff Association; Jim Lawson, a deputy director in the seventies; David Lacey, with explanations, facts, and memories; Ken

Chapel; Doug Durrant; Ian Miles; and so many more—all provided much required assistance.

Anne Noonan, the CAA Retired Staff Association chairman and ex-editor of the CAA staff paper, *Airway,* introduced me to Tony Doyle, an ex-CAA chief librarian who assisted me with finding policy papers and provided research tips and did my proofreading. Aside from proofreading and research, Tony used his vast knowledge of aviation to correct my own limited knowledge and many inaccuracies. Tony Doyle in turn introduced me to John Havers, ex-ARB (Air Registration Board). Both have been a great source of information and encouragement.

Steve Dench from the CAA found much of my *Airway* articles, ably assisted by CAA Library staff, Vagn Pedersen and Brendan Hennessy.

My Internet site cafuhistory.com solicited many interested observers to make interesting and encouraging comments. Not least were two Norwegians, Kjell Haug and Per Aarkvik, who remembered CAFU in the 1970s.

Thanks also to Richard J. Church, who provided details of the HS748 aircraft.

A friend's wife, Margaret Reynolds, who directed me to photos and story in the Stansted Experience.

A nurse at my local surgery, Hazel Harris—who turned out to be the daughter of Captain C. M. James "Jimmy" Joy, who was a senior principal training inspector and manager of the HS125 operation at CAFU Stansted. Sadly her father had died, but she found a number of artefacts belonging to him, in her loft, which enabled me to ascertain facts and dates.

Finally, of course, not forgetting my own wife, Kay, who has allowed me to neglect our garden, house, and herself, at the same time encouraging me by putting up with my absence (study/computer room) while I have attempted to record and place items in some semblance of order—my sincere thanks to all of them.

INTRODUCTION

During the Second World War, the UK Coalition Government made plans for the rigorous development of civil aviation.

In 1942, it set up a committee, under the chairmanship of Lord Brabazon of Tara, to make recommendations on suitable civil transport aircraft for immediate post-war development.

Later in 1942, there was an independent committee set up under Captain A. G. Lamplugh to investigate post-war civil aviation. One of the recommendations of this committee was for a post-war London airport. This was followed by articles in the press and debate in the House of Commons. It seems hardly credible there should have been, at this time, so much discussion as to what should happen post-war; the evil of "monopolies"; opportunities for competition; the United Kingdom disadvantaged in the types of aircraft available; airport creation, particularly in London, which "might have ten thousand passengers a day, requiring a movement every ten minutes"!

In 1943, the UK Westminster Parliament discussed post-war civil aviation; Mr. W. R. D. Perkins (Conservative, Stroud) asked Clem Atlee, the deputy prime minister, to consider the appointment of an additional permanent undersecretary of state to the Air Ministry to take charge of civil aviation.

Others sought a different solution: the setting up of a new Ministry of Civil Aviation. Alan J. Cobham, KBE, AFC (nicknamed the Apostle of Civil Aviation), wrote an article in the February *Flight*:

It is far too big and virile an industry to be tacked onto an existing Ministry, and the very nature of its ever-changing developments, inventions and progress would make collaboration with another Ministry unworkable. Therefore, let us start off by having a new Ministry of Civil Aviation.

Chapter One
1944-1949

1944

For several weeks in 1944, delegates of fifty-two nations met in Chicago to consider the problem of post-war international civil aviation.

The most important result of the conference, known as the Chicago Convention, included provision for an organisation to foster and encourage international civil aviation. The permanent body, subsequently charged with the administration of the principles of the convention, became known as the International Civil Aviation Organisation (ICAO).

The United Kingdom had still not decided on the best way forward, and there were many who did not want to see the Air Ministry (AM) given responsibility for civil aviation. Viscount Swinton, in charge of civil aviation at the Air Ministry, attended Commonwealth Civil Aviation discussions on post-war empire routes, held in Montreal, October 22 to 27. This was in preparation for attending the Chicago conference, to be held between November 1 and December 7.

It wasn't until late October that it was announced, in Parliament, that Viscount Swinton would be the new minister of Civil Aviation (MCA) for the United Kingdom. There was much criticism in the House of Commons at the little available time for him to prepare for the conference, which was only a few weeks away. It was noticed that the government had taken such a high view of the importance of post-war civil aviation; they had appointed a minister of cabinet rank to control it.

His appointment did create a stir in Parliament; Viscount Rothermere welcomed the appointment of a minister for civil aviation, but he said,

"It was obvious that he was going to be nothing but a planning Minister. So far we had had nobody whatever who had paid any attention to planning anything in the direction of civil aviation."

Perhaps due to disquiet in Westminster about the fate, or rather start-up, of civil aviation in the United Kingdom, the Air Ministry (AM), in June 1944, set up a small fleet of aircraft, based at Croydon Airport, under the supervision of an RAF officer, squadron leader A. D. L. "Dan" Carroll (later OBE). Derek Carruthers, a navigator who joined the unit in 1947, says his understanding was that S/L Carroll was, at one time, commanding officer (CO) of an Advanced Flying Unit of the RAF.

Thus it was, during this activity in 1944, what would later become the Civil Aviation Flying Unit (CAFU), which was first spawned when Squadron Leader Carroll was seconded from the Royal Air Force. The fleet at this time was first called the Civil Operations Fleet (COF) by the AM and was inaugurated with the objective of providing facilities for operational trials, etc.; Refresher flying by qualified pilots among the Operational, Control, and Signals staff; radio development work and monitoring of ground aids; instructional and communication flying; practical flying tests for issue of a "B" pilot's licence.

Much of this information was found in a Ministry 1944/45 report discovered by Tony Doyle, which continued to say that the availability of aircraft gave little choice in the matter of types, but to meet these requirements as far as possible, the fleet was to be equipped with seven aircraft of the most suitable types obtainable:

- one Anson Mark XI, for operational trials, radio development and VIP communication work;

- two Proctors, for operational trials, general communication work, and refresher flying;
- two Austers for short communication work, refresher, and instructional flying;
- two Tiger Moths for "B" licence testing and refresher flying.

The above report shows seven aircraft, but in 1944, the Air Ministry only had two Autocrat Austers, one Percival Proctor, and one Avro Anson, all placed on the civil register between August and October 1944.

Air Ministry COF Aircraft:
REGISTERED

Auster	G-AGLK	AM	AUG 1944
Auster	G-AGLL	AM	AUG 1944
Proctor	G-AGLJ	AM	AUG 1944
Anson	G-AGLM	AM	OCT 1944

The Austers were three-seat, single-engine, high-wing aircraft, the Proctor another single, but low-wing monoplane with four seats, and the Anson a six to ten-seater, twin-engine low-wing monoplane with retractable undercarriage. All four were tail draggers.

The Avro Anson was used by the RAF in various roles from coastal command to communication and ferrying duties, and it was intended that this Anson XI, an early ex-RAF type, would be later exchanged for the later Avro XIX, when the latter became available. A further five Avro XIXs were ordered by the Air Ministry to meet additional commitments in the radio development and monitoring programme and an expected increase in demand for communication work, consequent upon the expanding duties of the Ministry.

The numbers were not made up to seven until a further Proctor and two Tiger Moths were registered in August 1945. All four aircraft were based at Croydon, with maintenance conducted at the British Overseas Airways Corporation (BOAC) overhaul base.

Croydon Airport had become a fighter station at the commencement of war, but they departed in 1944, given over to

RAF Transport Command. This may have been the reason for calling the Air Ministry's small fleet of aircraft, the Civil Operation Fleet, distinguishing it as separate from RAF Transport Command. When civil flying activities were resumed at Croydon, it had both internal and international operations with a number of companies: KLM, Air France, Swissair, SABENA, as well as Transport Command, using the field. However, the grass runways were somewhat short for large modern-for-the-period aircraft; about 1,100 yards, with the longest only 1,250 yards and with a one-hundred-foot chimney on the centreline of the approach to the longest runway. Additionally, there was little room for expansion on the airfield due to a housing development. The general administration of the airport was the responsibility of the new MCA, but traffic handling arrangements for most of the airline companies was undertaken by BOAC, and certain specialist facilities, such as flying control and telecommunications, were still the responsibility of the RAF.

In the middle of October 1944, the government announced a white paper on civil aviation as well as the setting up of a new Ministry of Civil Aviation.

In response to an invitation from the US government, representatives of fifty-two nations met in Chicago from November 1 to December 7, 1944, to "make arrangements for the immediate establishment of provisional world air routes and services," and "to set up an interim council to collect, record and study data concerning international aviation and to make recommendations for its improvement." The conference was also invited to "discuss the principles and methods to be followed in the adoption of a new aviation convention."

Having accepted the invitation, extended to them by the Government of the United States of America, to be represented at an International Civil Aviation Conference, the United Kingdom sent the following delegates:

Lord Swinton, minister of civil aviation, chairman of the delegation

Sir Arthur Street, permanent undersecretary, Air Ministry

Sir George London, Government of Newfoundland
W. P. Hildred, director of civil aviation, Air Ministry
J. H. Magowan, minister, British Embassy, Washington
W. C. G. Cribbett, assistant undersecretary, Air Ministry
G. G. Fitzmaurice, legal adviser, Foreign Office
A. J. Walsh, Newfoundland.

After the conference had finished, Lord Swinton and party returned to England via Bermuda in an aircraft of RAF Transport Command.

Before WWII, from 1919, the Department of Civil Aviation had formed part of the Air Ministry. That organisation remained, even after the first Ministry of Civil Aviation was created in 1944, until the Ministry of Civil Aviation was formed as a separate government department in April 1945. This all happened in the same month as the Air Ministry Anson was given its civil registration, G-AGLM.

Air Ministry COF Aircraft Registered 1944. Total = 04

Auster V	2	G-AGLK, G-AGLL
Proctor	1	G-AGLJ
Anson	1	G-AGLM

1945

By the Ministry of Civil Aviation (MCA) Act 1945, responsibility for the control of civil aviation was transferred to the new Ministry. The MCA was formed as a separate government department in April 1945 and introduced its first white paper on civil aviation, which envisaged, among many other ideas, ownership of airports by the MCA. Upon the formation of the MCA, the Safety and General Group was formed to deal with safety in the air and on the ground by means of training, licensing of aircraft and crew, and the control of operating standards.

The Chicago convention, held in November and December the previous year, turned out to be one of the most successful, productive, and influential conferences ever held. If there was one thing that came out of this conference, it was the need to set up a body that would advise countries on civil aviation requirements and standards that would need to be adopted.

In March 1945, this Convention on International Civil Aviation set up a body, the Provisional International Civil Aviation Organisation (PICAO), signed by fifty-two of the participating nations, including the United Kingdom, which, by April 1947, became known as the International Civil Aviation Organisation (ICAO), the sole universal institution of international public aviation rights, superseding the Paris Convention of 1919 and the Havana Convention of 1928.

It would be the start of countries adopting common practices that would ensure aviation standardisation; for the first time in the history of international aviation, an authority would facilitate the order in the air, introduce maximum standardisation in technical matters to unify the methods of exploitation, and settle any differences that might occur.

At the end of March the MCA minister, Viscount Swinton, used his official visit to Heathrow to announce future plans for the airfield. Three things emerged: the runway system would be eventually expanded to provide three pairs of parallel runways, permanent terminal buildings to be constructed in the centre of the pattern, and there would be no extension north of the Bath Road. It was expected to be started before 1950. The minister also took the opportunity (as *Flight* quoted) to *"baptize"* the airport, with words if not with wine, with its new name, "The London Airport." The reason was, apparently, because this long-range empire terminal had caused difficulty in pronunciation with its previous local name (Heathrow).

MCA OPERATIONS FLEET Aircraft:
REGISTERED

Proctor	G-AGPA	MCA	June 1945
T.Moth	G-AGRB	MCA	June 1945
T.Moth	G-AGRA	MCA	Aug 1945
Anson	G-AGPB	MCA	Sept 1945
Anson	G-AGWE	MCA	Dec 1945
Anson	G-AGWF	MCA	Dec 1945

In June 1945, the new Ministry of Civil Aviation (MCA) had its first civil aircraft directly registered to them; one was the second Percival Proctor, G-AGPA, and the first of two de Havilland DH82 Tiger Moths, G-AGRB and in August, the second Tiger Moth, G-AGRA, was also registered. The Tiger Moths were to be used for commercial pilot licence "B" tests and refresher flying.

When it became clear that the AM were no longer going to look after civil aviation, due to the creation of the MCA, they had the two Austers, Proctor and Anson, placed under the control of the newly created MCA in July 1945. It was likely that this was when S/L Dan Carroll was seconded from the RAF allowing him to be commander, no longer of the Air Ministry Civil Operations Fleet, but what now became known as the Ministry of Civil Aviation Operations Fleet. This name then carried through into the move to Gatwick in January 1946.

In August 1945, Lord (Viscount) Swinton, the first minister of Civil Aviation, was replaced due to a change of government. Clement Atlee, the previous deputy prime minister under the coalition, and now leader of the Labour Party, asked Lord Winster to be his new minister of Civil Aviation.

In September came the first of a batch of Ansons, G-AGPB, which was delivered to Croydon, followed by G-AGWE and GWF, both in late December and delivered to Gatwick. The interesting point to note here is that the Anson G-AGPB was registered as being at Croydon in September 1945, whereas Ansons G-AGWE and WF were registered in very late December as being at Gatwick, so one must assume that delivery was most likely in the New Year, which therefore ties in with the fleet move reported as being in 1946.

The 1944/5 report also revealed there were thirty-three members of staff who were qualified pilots, piloting themselves on their various duties. The report also stated that the fleet was staffed with three seconded officers from the RAF. They were required to undertake flying in connection with radio development, monitoring "B" licence (commercial) flying tests and VIP communication work.

Indeed, while it was previously thought that operations for the MCA did not properly start until 1946, what we discover in the report is that the total hours flown in 1945 amounted to 1,425, which made up as follows:

- 595 hours: operational trials and refresher flying
- 300 hours: radio development and monitoring
- 518 hours: communication and VIP flying
- 12 hours: "B" licence day and night flying tests

As the RAF officers were involved in all of the tasks, including the radio development trials and communications, it can be seen that they were flying around three hundred hours each in 1945, remembering, of course, that during the first half of 1945, the COF only had one Anson and one Proctor, as the second Proctor did not arrive until at least June, while the second Anson was not available before September.

The amount of communication flying is also surprising. It covered visits by ministerial staff on inspection (airports perhaps), or for the purpose of attending meetings or conferences. In fact most of the important airports throughout the United Kingdom were visited this year. There were several visits to Dublin and two visits to the continent, which included a survey flight over the air routes to the Northern European capitals.

VIP passengers carried were the minister and parliamentary secretary (on numerous occasions), the chancellor of the Exchequer, Lord Pakenham, Sir William Hildred, previously the director of civil aviation at the Air Ministry, Dr. Warner and several important foreign visitors.

MCA OPS FLEET Aircraft at the end of 1945. Total = 10

Auster	2	G-AGLK, G-AGLL
Proctor	2	G-AGLJ, G-AGPA
Tiger Moth	2	G-AGRA, G-AGRB
Anson	4	G-AGLM, GPB, GWE, GWF

1946

A Labour White Paper of 1945 argued for full nationalisation, with no participation by private interests in international services. These recommendations were embodied in the Civil Aviation Act of 1946. The act led to the reorganisation of two divisions of the British Overseas Airways Corporation (BOAC) to form three separate corporations.

On January 1, all flight restrictions that were imposed on UK civil flying during the war were lifted; and on the same date, the Air Ministry handed over London Heathrow airfield to the new Ministry of Civil Aviation. At the same time, British European Airways (BEA) was established to take over the European services of BOAC.

It is not surprising that immediately after WWII had finished in Europe, the new MCA Fleet would want to establish themselves, perhaps at an airport both away from its links with the Air Ministry and the increasingly busy airport of Croydon, and selected Gatwick Airport as the new home for their MCA Operations Fleet.

Gatwick at this time was still a small grass airfield, like Croydon, set to expand. It was also in use by the RAF during the war and, by 1946, retained under requisition and operated for civilian use by the MCA, with a small number of charter airlines also using the airport. It was warmly, I believe, remembered for the two wartime Nissen huts that housed the telecommunications staff and for the Faraday cages (chicken wire) where ground equipment testing was performed. There were separate cages for GEE, Rebecca, and ILS (the ILS used was thought to be SR14 [Localiser] and SR15]Glide Path]).

One of the prime requirements for the setting up of the Fleet, foreseen by the MCA in its earliest days, would be the responsibility for the provision of all telecommunications services for civil aviation throughout the United Kingdom, and although many of the navigational aids at the time could be checked on the ground, there would also be a requirement to ensure an aids accuracy and quality that would, increasingly, require them to be checked from the air.

A reminder, at this point, that the second of the primary functions of the fleet would be the testing of candidates requiring a commercial licence, but more of that later.

The pilots participated in all of the functions of the operations fleet, but the navigational aids inspecting function was seen, at least by the Telecommunication side, to be separate from the communication flying and the testing of candidates for commercial licences. Once operations began in 1946, it isn't too surprising that the Telecommunication side should want to be recognised as performing an important function, the flight checking of navigational aids, and adopted the name of CATFU (Civil Aviation Telecommunications Flying Unit), which was one step towards the later adoption of the all-encompassing name of Civil Aviation Flying Unit (CAFU) of both telecommunications and licensing, which lasted until the late 1980s.

The unit as a whole was headed by the fleet commander, Captain A. D. L. Carroll, while the telecommunications staff was headed by the signals officer, Ted Luff. Initially, in this first year of operations, the aircrew engaged on the telecommunications side consisted of just a pilot, and signals or radio officer.

Navigation and landing aids requiring checking and/or calibration were MFDF (medium frequency direction finders, which were Morse code-operated ground-based "homers"), RDF (radio direction finders), and VDF (very high frequency direction finders).

Additionally, there were approach aids (see appendix B): BABS (Blind Approach Beacon System); SBA (Standard Beam Approach), which was known to be at Heathrow at this time; and GCA (Ground Controlled Approach). BABS had no glide path, and SBA was principally used for approaches at civil airports at this time. GCA, another approach to landing aid, was radar that required control experts on the ground directing the aircraft.

Later in the decade, the Germans, not being allowed to fly, had CAFU undertake some flight inspection work in the British Occupied Zone.

While the MCA had set up operations for the calibration of civil aids in the United Kingdom, the Royal Air Force were at the same time setting up their own Inspectorate of Radio Services (IRS) with HQ90 (signals) Group at Medmenham, Berkshire. The RAF had many more resources than the MCA and were able to use Lancaster, Anson, and Mosquito aircraft, all based at RAF Watton, location of the Central Signals Establishment (CSE), coordinating the calibration of radio and navigational aids airborne equipment, including Rebecca, BABS, SBA, Loran, GEE, radio altimeters, and radio compass.

At this time, Pye were developing an instrument landing system (ILS) after experience supporting the RAF BABS, and this was adopted by the Royal Air Force in 1946.

Early in 1946, a meeting convened by the Radio Technical Division of the Provisional International Civil Aviation Organisation, after considering all available navigational aids, agreed that the system that should be standardised along the world's air routes must determine distance and bearing from a predetermined point and present it directly to the pilot. This functional requirement was supplemented by the decision to adopt distance-measuring equipment, or DME as it is now usually termed, as a fundamental component of any such system for short-range navigational purposes. At that time, only the overall characteristics of the required DME had been worked out; a long and detailed study was required before an internationally agreed specification could be laid down. This study was later carried out, and the results discussed, at international aviation meetings during the succeeding years.

In February 1946, representatives from most European countries met with the Ministry of Civil Aviation in the United Kingdom in order to begin a fortnight of discussion on radio and radar navigational aids and their application to international civil aviation. The latest types of radar equipment, previously on the "Top Secret" list throughout the war, were viewed, and technical lectures and films demonstrated to the delegates the secrets of our wartime navigational developments. The first two days of the conference were occupied by papers, given by the Ministry of Supply and Aircraft Production, on GEE, Loran, Rebecca, BABS, Consol, and the Decca navigation system, ACR (see appendix B), and Communications for Civil Aviation.

There was also a paper by the MCA on *"Special Problems of Airfield Control."* The papers were well illustrated by films and slides. The remainder of the last week was spent by the delegates at

RAF station Bassingbourn, where various aids were demonstrated in actual flying conditions by RAF Transport Command aircraft.

Following the negotiations at the Chicago conference in 1944, and subsequent discussions, which had taken place in both Paris and London in 1945, it was realised that there would be important changes to the licensing arrangements in civil aviation. Throughout 1946, the MCA were bringing into force an updating of the licensing requirements for aircrew—both pilots and navigators. In the 1930s, the licensing of pilots and navigators was much less stringent in its requirement, as can be seen by the two following items:

> *CIVIL AVIATION NEWS*
> *At present, Annex I requires that the rating should be held by pilots who manipulate the flight controls of an aircraft when under IFR conditions. It applies, therefore, equally to co-pilots as well as to pilots-in-command. Since it was not the intention that this general requirement should apply to co-pilots, a re-wording of the regulations was recommended, which makes it quite clear that the general requirement to hold an instrument rating under IFR (Instrument Flight Rules) applies only to pilots in-command.*
> *. . . after a Hillman Airways Rapide accident in 1934 it was disclosed that the pilot did not have a navigators Licence, had not taken a blind-flying course and was inexperienced in Radio Communications. This led to far stricter regulations for the award of the "B" Licence.*

In February 1946, it was announced that there would now be four classes of pilot licence, which were expected to replace the existing "A" and "B" licence system. The intention was to differentiate clearly between the qualifying standards expected from private owners, commercial pilots, and from regular airline pilots. The following were the four types of licence envisaged:

1. Provisional—for pupil (student) pilots under training (SPL)
2. Class A—for private pilots (PPL)

3. Class B—for commercial pilots (CPL)
4. Class C—for airline transport pilots (ATPL)

No pilot would be allowed to undertake regular airline transport flying without first obtaining the C licence, but the new class "B" licence would cover all commercial and normal flying other than regular airline work.

In order to give an indication of how busy the fleet had already become, here are the statistics for the number of licences held during the full prewar year, 1938, and the post-war years of 1945 and 1946; 1938 and 1945 were still with the Air Ministry and 1946 with the new MCA Operations Fleet. The year 1946, it will be noted, had an almost 80 percent increase in the number of "B" licence holders:

	Dec-38	**Dec-45**	**Dec-46**
Pilot's A	5,352	649	2,510
Pilot's B	952	917	1,637
Navigators	533	600	917
Operational Engineers	(Did not exist)		147
Maintenance Engineer	1,984	2,044	2,593
Total, all types	**8,821**	**4,210**	**7,804**

On 31 May, 1946, Heathrow was officially handed over to the MCA in January and officially renamed as "London Heathrow Airport." It was also the date for the commencement of regular international services at Heathrow. BOAC, operating from Bournemouth, were so keen to move to Heathrow that they accepted the use of tents to accommodate passenger handling, although more permanent structures became available in August. CATFU would now have a major international airfield, with up-to-date navigational and landing aids to flight inspect.

MCA OPS FLEET (Flying Wing) Staff

Pilots	05	
Navigators	00	
Signals Officers	01	
Asst. Sig. Officers	01	
Radio Officers	22	
Clerical Staff	04	2 staff side & 2 Tels

It can be seen that in the first year of operation, there were no navigators, but this was already being addressed. The pilots were called "staff pilots," and it is noteworthy that the clerical staff were split, working for either the flying wing or the telecommunications side, which was already seen as a Telecommunications Flying Unit (TFU), though this name was going to cause a problem, which I will come back to later.

A total of 1,455 hours were flown this year, including 140 hours in testing and calibrating 16 ground stations; 195 hours in testing 243 applicants for "B" licences; and 1,120 hours in operational trials, air communications, etc.

MCA OPS FLEET Aircraft:
DEREGISTERED

Anson	G-AGLM	AM/MCA	FEB 1946

REGISTERED

Anson	G-AGWA	MCA	May 1946
Anson	G-AGZS	MCA	May 1946
Anson	G-AGZT	MCA	May 1946
Gemini	G-AIRS	MCA	Oct 1946

In February, the original Anson XI first registered to the Air Ministry, G-AGLM, was returned to the RAF, and replaced with one of the newer Avro XIX aircraft. This now completed the order for five Ansons plus a replaced aircraft.

One Anson, G-AGWD, although appearing as being registered to the MCA between December 1945 and February 1946, was in fact never used by the operations fleet. Its registration papers do show ownership to the MCA, but John Havers, an ex-Air Registration Board (ARB) employee, was able to explain that this aircraft was actually delivered to Egyptian airline Misr-Air, with a "C of A" (Certificate of Airworthiness) on January 10, 1946, and left Croydon on delivery on February 23, 1946, as VN889, becoming SU-DAN. It was bent in a collision in January 1947. So hopefully, G-AGWD can be discounted as ever being with the MCA Operations Fleet.

In May, three new Ansons were registered to the MCA, Avro XIX 652A G-AGWA, G-AGZS, and its sister ship G-AGZT, and noted on the registration forms as having eleven seats! Although these aircraft could clearly be used for communications, they could also be adapted for the flight checking of navigational equipment at that time. So some, if not all of these Ansons, were allocated to the duties of "flight inspection of navigational aids" and fitted with a variety of receivers inherited from wartime work. This was when flight inspection duties truly began.

When the Ansons were registered to the MCA Operations Fleet, they were officially known as the Avro XIX series 652A, which was the civil version of the military Anson. However, the type was best known for its military name, Anson, and this name stuck, even in its civilian role. In the civil role, it could be used as a feeder-liner or for charter flying and survey work as part of its many capabilities. It had all-metal wings and tail, hydraulically operated undercarriage, and increased headroom for passengers. It was said to cruise at 164 mph at five thousand feet, had a Sperry A3 automatic pilot, and was equipped with Marconi radio. Some of the Fleet Ansons were specially fitted for flight inspection work and were unsuitable for communication tasks. The rest were capable of all the tasks of communication flying, some part of Tels flying, continuation flights, and training for headquarter staff. It is remembered that most of the Ansons were dark blue.

In October, a new aircraft type was added to the fleet, a twin-engine Miles Gemini, G-AIRS. This would be flown on communication flying by the Operations staff from HQ. Based at Gatwick, it was delivered on May 14.

MCA OPS FLEET aircraft at the end of 1946. Total = 13

Auster	02	GAGLK, G-AGLL
Tiger Moth	02	G-AGRA, G-AGRB
Proctor	02	G-AGLJ, G-AGPA
Anson	06	G-AGPB, GWA, GWE, GWF, GZS & GZT
Gemini	01	G-AIRS

Here we see that the MCA fleet had as many as thirteen aircraft, although many of the light singles would have been for HQ staff and used for refresher and communication flying, yet the number of fleet pilots was only five, and surprisingly, there were no navigators at this stage.

You may have noticed that there are now six Ansons at the end of 1946, when the MCA had ordered five of the later Mark XI back in 1945. Well, these include the five plus the replacement for Anson G-AGLM, which was returned to the RAF back in February.

Just because an aircraft was registered to the MCA did not necessarily mean that it was destined for CAFU; for instance, the Gemini G-AIRS, although registered to the MCA in October 1946, was at first thought to be destined for the use of the Civil Air attaché in Washington, Peter Masefield. It is not known if it was delivered to the USA and returned at a later date. What is known about this aircraft is that it was first flown in December 1946, delivered on May 5, 1947, to Gatwick where it was based, and later moved to Stansted, allegedly for licence testing, which I believe to be incorrect, as they were only intended for HQ staff for continuation training and communication flights. It is possible it was used by CAFU; on the other hand, perhaps it was used by Peter Masefield and simply kept with the other MCA aircraft at Stansted. As with all of this information, I gain the impression that sometimes a report suggests an aircraft is with the operations fleet when in fact it was used in other areas of the MCA.

1947

ICAO Guide—Arbiter of Civil Aviation. This is the wording of the preamble to the Convention on International Civil Aviation, which was signed by fifty-two allied and neutral countries in Chicago on December 7, 1944, and in which the present International Civil Aviation Organisation (ICAO) had its origin. ICAO actually came into force on April 4, 1947, and the Provisional ICAO, which had been preparing the ground, was replaced by the substantive body. In succeeding years, many other nations joined ICAO:

WHEREAS the future development of international civil aviation can greatly help to create and preserve friendship and understanding among the nations and peoples of the world, yet its abuse can become a threat to the general security; and
WHEREAS it is desirable to avoid friction and to promote that co-operation between nations and peoples upon which the peace of the world depends;
THEREFORE, the undersigned governments having agreed on certain principles and arrangements in order that international civil aviation may be developed in a safe and orderly manner and that international air transport services may be established on the basis of equality of opportunity and operated soundly and economically;
Have accordingly concluded this convention to that end.

By October, the instrument landing system (ILS) was "recommended" as the ICAO standard approach aid.

ICAO was already influencing civil aviation. The telecommunications team was taking their instruction on the calibration of equipment by following the guidelines of ICAO annexe 10 (see appendix A). These would be the standards and recommendations the new UK MCA were set to adopt.

It could not be unnoticed that the formation of ICAO had made heavy demands on the Ministry as it was now responsible for

- airborne radio navigational aids,
- air traffic control services,
- aeronautical information service (AIS),
- communication services,

to name but a few. To this end, the minister of Civil Aviation made three appointments to advise him on important aspects of civil aviation:

> Professor George Temple, who was to be the chief scientific adviser;
> Mr. Leslie Gamage, chief business adviser to the Ministry;
> Lord D. U. K. Weston, chief adviser on Industrial Relations.

The responsibilities of the minister of Civil Aviation in the technical field in the years 1946 and 1947 involved a problem having three elements:

> to build up an adequate operational and technical staff;
> take over services and responsibility transferred from the RAF to civil aviation;
> apply new lessons learned during the war to civil requirements.

Notice to Airmen (NOTAM) no. 270 of 1947 laid down that Area Controls serving Flight Information Regions (FIRs) should be responsible for alerting Search and Rescue (SAR) services for aircraft known to be in distress.

While the government expenditure on Aviation for the eleven-month period ending on March 31, 1946, was £6,792,058, the next twelve-month period ending on March 31, 1947, had risen to £15,513,510 18s 7d for the year. Even so, the latter was substantially less than estimated, owing mainly to expenditure on civil aircraft, works, and equipment that were incurred slower than expected. (I wonder what added the extra eighteen shillings and seven pence.)

In 1947, the government announced a policy of acquisition. In practice, however, the policy was slow to develop, and subsequently the Conservatives followed a policy of selling off airports acquired under the labour government.

At this time, both Croydon and Gatwick airport had 100, 87, and 73 octane fuel for resale, whereas Aldermaston and Stansted provided only 100 octane.

The "B" licence was the pre-war commercial pilot's licence, and most of the demobbed service pilots could obtain them by passing some written examinations and showing logbook evidence of sufficient pilot flying time. There was only a rudimentary flying test required for ex-military pilots.

When the commercial pilot's licence (CPL) and ATPL (airline transport pilot's licence) came out, the "B" licence was converted to one of these new licences, provided that the applicant had enough of the right kind of flying experience at the time. The "B" test was now more thorough; it included a general flight test, a cross-country flight, and a night test. There were to be some concessions, however, as the new rules endeavoured to show a more realistic approach to the practical needs of commercial flying. The previous examination that required all captains to commit to memory rules and regulations, which were seldom needed, now only required them to memorize details and knowledge of where the regulations might be found. For new applicants, however, a much tougher regime of examination and training was required.

Captain B. E. E. (Basil—but best known simply as "Bee") Marshall, later to be commander, joined the fleet in 1947, and three months later went on an Instrument Flying Examiner course with the RAF at Hullavington, passing with special distinction. He became the unit's first instrument rating (IR) examiner. Together with his colleagues, they had considerable influence in designing and developing the instrument rating flying tests, instituting a pass-or-fail criterion for every one of a series of tests.

During the year, the MCA employed four navigators for duties with the fleet, in particular duties for the Civil Aviation Telecommunications Flying Unit (CATFU). Sid Pritchard, who joined the Ministry in 1947 as a navigator, remembers that he had obtained a second-class navigators' licence "on the strength of my RAF Nav. flying and by passing some written and oral examinations. However, when the new Licences were introduced I found that to keep my job I had to sit the new exams for the Flight Navigator Licence, and to obtain that Licence. (Gulp!)"

MCA OPERATIONS (Fleet Wing) Staff

Staff Pilots	17	Increase of 10
Navigators	04	Increase of 4
Signals Officers	01	
Asst. Sig. Officers	02	
Radio Officers	05	
Radio Mechanics	05	
Clerical staff	08	4 staff side & 4 Tels

The terms radio operator (RO), wireless Telegraphist (WT), or airborne signal officer (ASO) were all used for the same job according to Iain Smith, a radio operator himself in the forties and fifties. Among a selection of names that Iain remembered was "Queeny" Green, one of the few (only) female ASOs from Headquarters. Another notable name was an ASO called Wilkinson who was blind, and another wireless operator that Iain recalled was a man named Humphries.

Statistics of UK Licences held:

Yr End	1938	1945	1946	1947	Women 1947
Pilots A	5,352	649	2,510	3	22
Pilots B	952	917	1,637	2,517	5
Navs.	533	600	917	2,027	3
Total	**6,837**	**2,166**	**5,064**	**4,547**	**30**

By the end of 1947, the total number of hours flown in the MCA Fleet aircraft was 5,103, a staggering 250 percent increase on the previous year. On the licensing side, the number of candidates requiring their "B" licence had increased by over 53 percent.

The telecommunications side figures were no less dramatic. The number of ground stations to be checked had increased from sixteen to fifty, and the number of hours testing and flight checking them from 140 to 1,609, all this with the addition of only one more Anson, although the number of these aircraft was now up to seven. CATFU had truly got into its stride, achieved with only two extra pilots together with the introduction of navigators and radio operators, and a doubling of clerical staff.

Due to criticism at the lack of GCA (Ground Controlled Approach) radar at Heathrow, the MCA were loaned, by the Air Ministry, a unit from Prestwick, which became operational on February 27. However, it was not until the RAF had started a training programme for civil crews that Heathrow was able to take over complete operations in July. By autumn, the MCA had sufficient civilian staff trained to be able to set up their own GCA school at Aldermaston.

By the end of 1947, it was thought essential there should be as many as four different landing aids at some international airports. London, for instance, now had BABS (Beam Approach Beacon System—for Rebecca fitted aircraft), SBA (Standard Beam Approach), GCA, and SCS51 (a form of ILS—when it was serviceable), which was modified to be equivalent to the ILS. The use of ILS was dependent upon British manufacturers, and most aircraft at this time were using SBA as an aid to landing.

The most valuable navigational aid, for general orientation and holding purposes, was, without a doubt, the radio compass or ADF (automatic direction finder). This aid was often used in conjunction with BABS, SBA, or ILS, with the final stages of the approach being monitored by GCA.

By the end of 1947, the MCA had detailed plans for the provisional control of air traffic within the United Kingdom.

MCA OPS FLEET Aircraft:
REGISTERED

Dove	G-AJLV	MCA	Apr 1947
Consul	G-AJXE	MCA	June 1947
Consul	G-AJXF	MCA	June 1947
Consul	G-AJXG	MCA	June 1947
Consul	G-AJXH	MCA	June 1947
Consul	G-AJXI	MCA	June 1947
Gemini	G-AJZL	MCA	Sept 1947
Gemini	G-AKDD	MCA	Sept 1947
Anson	G-AGVA	MCA	Oct 1947

DEREGISTERED

Proctor	G-AGPA	Crashed	Aug 1947

The de Havilland Dove, a post-war design, was selected as the new twin-engine aircraft to be used by the MCA Fleet; and in April 1947, G-AJLV was the first DH104 (Dove) registered to the MCA and destined for flight inspection work. It had a refined aerodynamic design and supercharged Gypsy Queen engines providing an exceptional standard of single-engine performance. It could cruise at 170 mph and with full standard tanks would give a still-air range of 800 miles. Doves at this time were fitted with Marconi lightweight radio as standard. One can imagine there was a period of trials of new equipment to be fitted, as well as a requirement for pilots to be rated on the new aircraft type before it could be fully operational in its new role. For instance, it would eventually be fitted out with a camera hatch in the floor to enable vertical photographs of the ground for exact positioning during flight inspections.

The fleet was then further expanded with the registrations in June of five twin-engine Airspeed Consuls, G-AJXE to G-AJXI, to be used for the testing of candidates for the new commercial pilot licence and, in addition, could be used in a communications role. They would remain in service with the MCA/MTCA until 1956. The Consul was a civilian version of the proven military Oxford trainer with twin Armstrong Siddeley Cheeter X engines, having an inter-overhaul life of 1,250 hours. It was most familiar in the five—to six-seater modes but could be modified for photography, etc. It could cruise at 127 mph, with pilot and four passengers, and had a range of 870 miles. Although the Consuls were registered to the MCA in 1947, they were not remembered at Gatwick by Mr. Pritchard until about 1949. However, two of the Consuls were mentioned in the September issue of *Light Plane* as being used, together with the two Proctors, for taking Ministry officials about in the course of their duties, and the MCA Report for 1947 does say the total number of aircraft at the end of 1947 to be twenty-one, a number that tallies with my own findings. *Light Plane* magazine reported in its September issue that the MCA Operations Fleet had six Anson XIX, two Consuls, two Proctor Vs, and two tiger Moths. Whilst I agree with the number 21, I note that there was only one Proctor and seven Ansons. The seventh Anson was G-AGVA, and one of the Proctors, G-AGPA, had crashed. It was involved in an incident at Plympton St. Mary, Devon, on August 4, 1947; damaged beyond repair and eventually scrapped at Gatwick in July the following year, which was when it was eventually deregistered.

September saw the arrival of two more Gemini, G-AJZL and G-AKDD. Not a great deal of information is known about either of these two aircraft. In the following month, October, the seventh Anson, G-AGVA, was registered to the MCA.

Two Tiger Moths were correct. What it goes to show is how precarious it is to try and estimate the number, or even the type, of aircraft that the fleet had at any particular time.

Some of the Ansons were specifically fitted for DF and blind-approach beam and radar checking work for which they were fully equipped, having SCS51, VHF, and SBA. These aircraft though were unsuitable for communication tasks; the remainder were available for all duties, which included communications, continuation flights, and training for HQ staff.

The Gemini was used for HQ pilot continuation flying and communications.

One further anomaly with the aircraft types is that a Viking, G-AGRR, was registered to the MCA in December 1947. This was first registered to the Ministry of Supply (MoS) in 1946 and then went to BOAC (British European Division) though never actually used by

BEA. Because I have not found any other evidence of its use with the fleet at this time, I have noted it in my list, but not used it within my figures for the number of aircraft used by the fleet—but more on this a little later.

Tony Doyle, who gained information from the book *Early Ringway 1946 to 49*, noted that Captain Carroll was flying one of the first MCA Ansons, G-AGPB, on a communication flight from Liverpool to Ringway in June 1947.

Iain Smith mentioned to me that he remembered a Fieseler Storch Fi156 being flown by Captain Carroll around this period. "The Storch was such a fleeting period and I don't think it played any significant purpose on the Fleet. I think it stuck in my memory as it was a Storch which rescued Mussolini and returned him to the Axis side, albeit for only a short time."

Much later, Tony Doyle found a sheet in the SRG Library at Gatwick that showed a Storch aircraft, captured in May 1945, was impressed by the Air Ministry and passed to the Royal Aircraft Establishment (RAE) as VP546. It is possible that the RAE asked CAFU to assess this aircraft, which would account for Iain remembering it at Gatwick in the mid to late 1940s. Although it cannot be proven that VP546 was the Storch seen at CAFU, it is known there were a few being used in the United Kingdom, and this was the longest lasting one in the RAF/RAE. This particular one was maintained in flying condition at Farnborough until 1955 when it was grounded, due to lack of spare parts. It was used for a large variety of projects; including aircraft-carrier deck landings (on HMS *Triumph* in 1946, flown by "Winkle" Brown), formation flying with helicopters to allow air-to-air photography of rotor blade behaviour, glider towing, and routine communications flying. In 1948, another Fi156, used by Air Vice Marshal H. E. Broadhurst as a personal transport, was added to the RAF fleet (serial number VX154). This was flown for two years on similar duties, until it was grounded to act as a source of spares for the original aircraft.

MCA OPS FLEET Aircraft at the end of 1947. Total = 21

Auster	02	G-AGLK, G-AGLL
Tiger Moth	02	G-AGRA, G-AGRB

Proctor	01	G-AGLJ
Gemini	03	G-AIRS, JZL, KDD
Anson	07	G-AGPB, GWE, GWF, GWA, GZS, GZT, GVA
Consul	05	G-AJXE, JXF, JXG, JXH, JXI
Dove	01	G-AJLV

1948

On January 15, 1948, the MCA implemented their plans for the provisional control of UK air traffic with the segregation of traffic over London, and planned the introduction of what they called the "Metropolitan Control Zone."

No control areas would be established for the time being, but they could be introduced as and when facilities became available. Control areas (in the form of zones) and airways (connecting the airfield zones) were defined by radio ranges and MF beacons. These were being put in place, but there were insufficient MF (medium frequencies) to provide a complete system of checkpoints, so the latter would be defined throughout the country by VHF (very high frequency) fan markers. It was expected that the plans would probably begin to take effect in 1949 and would be completed in 1950-51.

A NOTAM (Notice to Airmen) 03/48, issued on January 15, advised that aircraft approaching London Airport would have to signal to the control centre the radio landing aid, such as ILS, SBA, etc., that they proposed to use.

Because of the introduction of controlled airspace, a new instrument rating was being prepared, a new requirement being introduced under what would be the 1949 Air Navigation Regulation.

Also from January 15, a form of aircraft "type rating" was required for all applicants for a pilot's "B" (commercial) licence, and those who wished to have a further type of aircraft entered on their "B" licence would be required to submit evidence of having carried out satisfactorily on that type, certain manoeuvres. The required manoeuvres included, for multiengine aircraft, by day at maximum landing weight, all manoeuvres used in normal flight, including take-off and landing, landing with one engine inoperative, and emergency manoeuvres including simulated engine failure after take-off, and approach to the stall in both level and banked attitudes.

All manoeuvres used in normal flight, including take-off and landing, were also required at night at the aircraft landing weight. Similar manoeuvres were required with one engine inoperative, with the exception of a take-off. At the maximum permissible all-up weight, one take-off had to be done by day or by night.

For single-engine aircraft, all manoeuvres used in normal flight, simulated forced landing, and recovery from stall from level and banked attitudes had to be flown by day. For certification, a qualified observer had to fly on board the aircraft and had to certify that the applicant was at the controls and that he witnessed these manoeuvres. The tests had to be made six months before each application but could be done in any order, on different flights, and could be certified by more than one observer. Certification would normally be accepted from the holder of a current "B" licence endorsed for the type of aircraft to which the application referred, and a form of application (MCA Form 528) when completed would be accepted as evidence that the requirements had been met. Applicants would also be required to pass an Air Registration Board examination on the type. The rather loose term "normal manoeuvres" was understood to include climbing, gliding, and the usual turns at various rates.

NOTAM no. 371/48 announced that the total number of hours flying experience required as a pilot for the new professional pilot's licence and instrument rating could be made up as hours in command and as co-pilot. Requirements were 200 hours for the commercial pilot's licence (CPL), 700 for the senior commercial pilot's licence (SCPL), and 1,200 for the airline transport pilot licence (ATPL). Flying time as co-pilot would be counted as only half. If, for example, a candidate for the airline transport pilot's licence had only the minimum of 250 hours in command and wished to make up the remaining 950 hours by co-pilot time, he would require 1,900 co-pilot hours to achieve it.

In February, with a view to extending ground-controlled radar facilities for covering the whole of the United Kingdom, the MCA made arrangements with the Air Ministry for eighteen sets of US Federal type GCA equipment to be transferred from the Royal Air Force for use as landing aids at civil airfields. Eight were to be allotted for operational use, including one for training, and the remainder for maintenance and development. In addition to those already established at London Airport and Prestwick, the equipment was planned to be installed at Aldermaston, Speke, Northolt, Belfast, and Bovingdon during the following six months. Although it was the original intention to include Renfrew (Glasgow), it was found that, owing to excessive permanent echo interference from local hills and buildings present, GCA was not suitable for this airport. In order to provide even greater GCA cover, it was hoped to arrange for integrated use of all existing equipment by both civil and military aircraft.

In the February issue of *Light Plane*, it was reported that the MCA Operations Fleet were due to move to a new base at Aldermaston Airport near Reading, Berkshire. First, it indicated that the name of the fleet had not changed thus far. Second, that there was to be a move away from Gatwick. It was expected that the new airport would provide better facilities in terms of accommodation for staff and aircraft, as well as having a hard surface runway with up-to-date aids. Another point mentioned was that the fleet would be taking to Aldermaston, in addition to their own fleet of aircraft, an Ercoupe, G-AKFC, a single-engine monoplane, registered to the Ministry of Supply (MoS) in August 1947, which was being used by the MCA and the Ministry of Supply (MoS) for technical development work. John Havers feels sure that it was never part of the MCA Operations Fleet, but purely being evaluated because of its unconventional flying controls. What is also indicated is that the fleet were not solely involved in licensing and telecommunications activities during this period, hence the mention of both the Viking and Ercoupe. As if to confirm that Aldermaston was in the offing, Anson G-AGZT was known to have flown from Gatwick to Aldermaston on March 11, 1948, while Anson G-AGPB was known to have flown from Aldermaston to Gatwick on July 13, noted by Ray Webb in his book *Early Ringway*.

Aldermaston, it should be explained, was the site of a former RAF airfield constructed during World War II and used by the Royal Air Force and the United States Army. It was selected by the UK government as a bomber unit in the early days of the war and provided with four hangars and three concrete runways, the main one having 1,800 metres (6,000 feet) length. The airport was relinquished to the Air Ministry in 1945, with many of the buildings refurbished and the runway lighting improved.

In 1947, the MCA designated the airfield as a temporary civil airport and possibly a third London airport; and in April, the facilities were further improved when a flying training school, Airways Training Ltd., was taken over by BOAC and BEA. But by the end of September 1948, the school had closed down.

It is unclear if the MCA planned the operations fleet to be at Aldermaston at the same time as the school was operating. It probably was, as the school would have had the MCA Operations Fleet Examiners on site at an airport with good-sized hangars, hard runways, and refurbished buildings available. Importantly, the airfield was well equipped with SBA, SCS51 (ILS), GCA, BABS, MF D/F, VHF D/F, and HF R/T. There was also a complete GEE and Decca coverage over the airfield and a radio range at Bovingdon.

But somehow it was not to be; the Atomic Weapons Research Establishment (AWRE) popped into the equation and, perhaps with greater priority and requiring isolation, was given this site over the needs and requirement of CAFU, which, after all, no longer had the school candidates on site.

Subsequently, the GCA training base was moved from Aldermaston to Bournemouth, Hurn Airport, and moved to WWII huts vacated by BOAC, providing another reason for CAFU not to be housed there.

It was reported that good progress was being made with the Decca Navigator System, a long-range navigational aid, during the past year, when trials had taken place more or less continuously.

The Royal Aircraft Establishment (RAE) at Farnborough had made a number of tests, including a long-range flight as far as five hundred miles west of the Azores. This, together with a flight to the north of Iceland, afforded the opportunity to demonstrate this system to the Portuguese Air Force and the Icelandic Ministry of Civil Aviation respectively. The French Air Force and other French authorities had completed over 1,500 hours of trial flights with this apparatus, and the results had proved satisfactory. Air France also found the Decca system to be very successful as an aid to navigation on the Paris-London route on which three Decca-equipped Dakotas were operating regularly for the past three months.

The fleet was involved with Decca in this period as G-AGWE, one of the Ansons registered to the MCA in December 1945 and given its C of A in June 1946, was noted to have flown from Gatwick to Squires Gate on the January 28, 1948, flight inspecting Decca.

Lord Pakenham replaced Lord Nathan as the minister of Civil Aviation.

After the government announced the nationalisation programme, it indicated their intention that Manchester airport should be nationalised. Manchester Corporation would be responsible for buildings and conversions, which were necessary, but the MCA, it was expected, would take over full responsibility.

Lorenz, another landing aid, had been installed at Manchester before the war in one direction only with airfield lighting also provided. The MCA installed interim G lighting with omni-directional contact lights at 300-foot intervals on the N-S and E-W runways, and at 100-foot intervals on the NE-SW. There was sodium lighting on all approaches, and both a civil airfield identification beacon and an RAF identification beacon flashed during the hours of darkness.

Communications, which included MF D/F W/T on two frequencies, VHF on two frequencies for communication only, HF R/T and Cathode Ray VHF D/F R/T (VHF direction finding radio telephone), was in process of calibration by the fleet.

Lengthening of the runways was possible in nearly every direction, and the corporation had shown considerable enterprise by purchasing surrounding land, making a possible landing area of six hundred acres. The perimeter, already built at the north end of the N-S runway was ready for an extension to nearly five thousand feet, but the immediate surrounding countryside was flat and extensions in all directions was thought to be a simple matter.

In October, for the first time, more passengers passed through London Airport than Northolt.

One additional pilot, the 1948 MCA Report tells us, joined the operations fleet. I am unsure that this is the man, but Tony Doyle, who has done quite a bit of research in this area, found a Captain Huggins, flying from Ringway to Gatwick in April 1948, conducting a calibration flight in G-AGZS. Then an interesting article came to light when John Havers sent me a cutting from a local paper reporting the death, in 2011, of a squadron leader Peter Huggins, DFC. He had joined the RAFVR in September 1938 and joined Bomber Command in 1942 until the end of the war. He then joined the MCA Operations Fleet based at Gatwick. It is likely that he joined earlier than 1948 and may have been one of those seconded from the RAF. It is most likely he was the pilot doing the reported calibration flight.

MCA OPS FLEET Aircraft:
REGISTERED

Anson	G-AHID	MCA	May 1948
Anson	G-AHIH	MCA	May 1948
Anson	G-AHIJ	MCA	May 1948
Anson	G-AGUD	MCA	July 1948
Anson	G-AHIC	MCA	July 1948
Dove	G-ALFT	MCA	Dec 1948
Dove	G-ALFU	MCA	Dec 1948

In researching these aircraft, it is sometimes difficult to ascertain whether these aircraft were actually used or flown by the MCA Fleet; most of the Ansons mentioned above for instance we do have photographs, including the four later registered in 1948, G-AHIC, HIH, and HIJ, even though they were initially not thought to be part of the CAFU fleet. Though there is not a picture of HID, there is evidence of it on a calibration flight when it diverted to Manchester later in November 1949.

The Ansons flown by the fleet were mostly painted dark blue, but one Anson was remembered as being all white. This aircraft was G-AHIJ. It was first registered in April 1946, to Railway Air Services Co. Ltd.; but then in August, the ownership was transferred to BEA Corporation. However, BEA had it re-registered to their BEA Flying

Club in July 1947, which may have explained the reason for this aircraft being painted white. Only five months later, it was registered to the MCA for use by the fleet, where it was known, by Tels staff at least, as the "White Elephant."

The other four Ansons registered to the MCA and destined for work with the fleet were G-AHID, G-AHIH, G-AGUD, and G-AHIC, all ex-BEA aircraft. These were the last Ansons to be registered to the MCA that were in use by CAFU until the 1950s.

Although the first DH Dove registered to the MCA, G-AJLV, was registered in April the previous year, it was ten months before it was given its Certificate of Airworthiness (C of A) on February 20 of this year and handed over to the operations fleet a few days later on the twenty-fifth.

In July, a Zaunkonig aircraft, VX190/G-ALUA, was sent from the RAE (Royal Aircraft Establishment) to CAFU for further testing. It was built in Germany in 1944 at Braunschweig by a university professor and his students as a very light short-landing aircraft. It is believed that this was done in association with the forerunner of the PFA/LAA (Private Flying Association/Light Aircraft Association), the Ultralight Aircraft Association (ULAA) with whom Peter Masefield had a connection, and thought working for the MCA at this time. It seems the aircraft was damaged soon after its arrival at Gatwick but was soon repaired. It was transferred from military to civil registration and flown by MCA and ULAA pilots. It was returned to the RAE on March 15, 1949.

Later in the year, December, two more Doves were registered to the MCA, G-ALFT and LFU. These later Doves did not have to wait so long to be handed over to the fleet after the issue of their C of A.

Up until this point, the aircraft and crew were known as the MCA Operation Fleet, but on the MCA Report for 1948/9, the MCA formally used the name MCA Flying Unit. The Tels side had adopted the name CATFU, but this had caused a problem because it clashed with a similar name, the Telecommunications Flying Unit (TFU) at RAF Defford, which later became the RAF Radar Research Flying Unit. With the introduction of controlled airspace and the consequent need for commercial licences with the new instrument rating, it was sensible for the MCA Fleet as a whole to be seen as one. It was obviously realised how relatively easy it would be to simply drop the "M" (of MCA) and the "CAT" (of CATFU) to enable a change to the more encompassing name of CAFU (Civil Aviation Flying Unit), the name best remembered and one that remained until 1976 when many more changes would take place.

CAFU Anson aircraft were fitted with calibration equipment and a camera hatch in the floor to enable vertical photography for exact positioning of the aircraft. Calibration could be a time-consuming task. Before the introduction of the VOR (VHF omni range) in the fifties, CAFU was calibrating VDF (VHF radio, voice-operated homers) as well as MFDF (medium frequency Morse code-operated homers), and all route and airfield communications were by W/T (wireless telegraphy "dits and dahs," tells Sid Pritchard), hence the MFDF.

Up to this point, the principal landing aid for the RAF, and most civil airports in the United Kingdom, was the Standard Beam Approach (SBA). SBA aircraft had an instrument displaying field strength to assist determining distance from the runway. In addition, there was BABS in conjunction with Rebecca (Transponder) and GCA (Ground Controlled Approach) using radar.

Using GCA was very flexible; the aircraft only had to be equipped with VHF radio, while a ground controller then guided the pilot on to its final three-dimensional path on course to the runway by advising altitude and direction corrections. As for the GCA ground equipment, it could be positioned near any runway in use. The air traffic control ground controllers liked this tool, especially when there was poor visibility. Heathrow was equipped with GCA in 1947, but its major disadvantage was that it could handle only one aircraft at a time, and the pilot had to use his own eyes to complete the last two miles before the runway.

Now that the UK airways system was about to be constructed, en route aids such as radio ranges, non-directional beacons (NDBs), and marker beacons were also being flight checked. Non-directional beacons operated in the medium frequency (MF) band. Non-directional meant that the beacon was not limited to fixed beams, but emitted radio waves equally to all points of the compass. Radio ranges were installed at a number of places such as Epsom, Dunsfold, Maidstone, Watford, and Prestwick and could be used as part of the landing phase at an airfield.

A radio range at London Airport was brought into operation. The equipment was originally sited at Dorking and then withdrawn from service on October 29, but reinstalled on a site one hundred yards from the Bath Road, near the entrance to Heston. The call sign was "MYR," operating on a frequency of 362.5 mc/s. The Northolt Radio Range and the HF Aeronautical Communications and Approach Control Service, operating at Blackbushe, were now withdrawn.

It is interesting to note that on March 14, Wing Commander Reginald Brie received the first helicopter licence to be issued by the Royal Aero Club.

MCA CAFU Aircraft at the end of 1948. Total = 28

Auster	02	G-AGLK, G-AGLL
Tiger Moth	02	G-AGRA, G-AGRB
Proctor	01	G-AGLJ
Gemini	03	G-AIRS, JZL, KDD
Anson	12	G-AGPB, GWE, GWF, GWA, GZS, GZT, GVA, HID, HIH, HIJ, GUD, HIC
Consul	05	G-AJXE, JXF, JXG, JXH, JXI
Dove	03	G-AJLV, G-ALFT, G-ALFU

1949

Minister of Civil Aviation Lord Packenham

The MCA made a general statement of policy to provide a warning of new regulations regarding the carriage of radio equipment and allow sufficient time for the production and installation of equipment to meet the minimum scale to be carried in all aircraft flying under IFR (Instrument Flight Rule) conditions when standardisation of approved navigational systems was agreed. It was expected that the minimum scale of equipment required in aircraft would be VHF R/T, MF receiving equipment and associated DF facilities, and VHF receiving equipment for the 75 mc/s fan marker signals.

Basic navigational services would be provided by employing the available medium frequencies for the increased use of radio ranges and MF beacons. Aids to the final approach and landing at airports were not yet finalised.

On Monday, March 14, 1949, there came into force the revised edition of the British civil aviation code of law known as the Air Navigation Order (ANO) 1949 and Regulations. This was to replace the Air Navigation (Consolidation) Order 1923 and Air Navigation Directions 1936, and all amendments. The new order and regulations provided for the introduction, on April 1, of the new pilot's licence announced in NOTAM (Notices to Airmen) nos. 255/48 and 358/48. In order to allow a pilot time to comply with the new requirement, holders of "B" licences would be able to renew them up to June 30, 1950.

A report was published by the committee formed to inquire into the provision of qualified staff for civil aviation. The committee, under the chairmanship of Group Captain C. A. B. Wilcock, MP, issued its report on the recruitment, training, and licensing of personnel for civil aviation. Included in the terms of reference were the review of present licensing arrangements and the recommendation of amendments, if necessary.

The committee was also briefed to consider and make recommendations with regard to steps that could be taken to ensure an adequate flow of aircrew and ground personnel into the industry. Comparison was to be made between the standard required of all categories of personnel for service and civil aviation purposes, with a view to making them available for civil aviation from service sources, after as little additional training as possible. Other sources of recruitment were also to be considered.

The long expected new classes of licence were introduced in April, bringing into line the United Kingdom's responsibility to comply, as a member state, with ICAO recommendations. The major change was that for the commercial pilot's licence (CPL); replacing the old "B" licence with a graduated system that related more closely with an individual's flying experience.

Along with the new licence, the new UK instrument rating (IR) was introduced, a qualification required of pilots wishing to fly inside the newly introduced controlled airspace (airways and control zones) when weather conditions were such that flight by visual reference alone was not possible and instrument flight rules (IFR) applied. CAFU would now be using the five Airspeed Consuls that were fitted with two-staged amber equipment to simulate blind-flying conditions, for the testing of the many candidates that would materialise. In fact, the unit's examiners tested 349 candidates (600 hours) at Gatwick and other UK airfields in this first year of the requirement for an IR.

The new instrument rating (IR), when passed, would require an annual renewal. Although the number of staff pilot examiners had grown to almost a score at CAFU, it was not possible to keep pace with the growing number of tests that would later require the renewal of their IR. For this reason, it was necessary for the MCA to authorise certain company pilots to conduct the renewal test on behalf of the Ministry. These pilots would become known as delegated examiners (DEs) and later to be called authorised examiners (AEs). From the 1948/9 MCA Report, we are told that "a number of Corporation pilots were tested for approval to act as Delegated Examiners within the Corporations (BEA and BOAC)."

In June 1949, *Flight* magazine gave a comprehensive overview of the new instrument rating test, which is interesting reading:

IN the curriculum of the Ministry of Civil Aviation the new British Instrument Rating is at least one examination which is 100 per cent practical and useful and in which the syllabus covers only those points which are of vital everyday use to the commercial pilot. An account of a candidate's experience may be of some interest to others.

Briefly, the syllabus is divided into five sections and failure in any one of them may mean a further examination, though only in that section. The five can be listed as follows:—

(1) General instrument work.
(2) Limited panel.
(3) Asymmetric power.
(4) QDM approach, let-down.
(5) SBA, ILS, Babs or Radio Range approach and letdown (the aid used to be specified by the candidate).

On reporting to Gatwick one is immediately engaged in a friendly chat with one's examiner, who provides a very adequate pre-flight briefing with emphasis on the theme "Don't worry if you make a silly mistake, we expect you to be suffering from examination-itis."

Stress is also laid on the fact that the tolerances specified in MCA Pamphlet 56 are treated only as a guide and failure to fly within these limits over some brief period in the test will not automatically disqualify a candidate.

Due note is taken of the examinee's past experience on the Consul or Anson and, if necessary, a brief familiarization flight can be carried out before the test. In this connection it should be mentioned that pre-flight checks which have no part in the test are not a subject for examination.

After this briefing—which also serves as a means of familiarizing examiner with candidate and vice-versa—both repair to the aircraft, which is suitably equipped with amber screens and the necessary radio equipment.

As soon as the machine is approached the test is commenced and one is expected to check such items as the pitot-head heater, radio aerials for security and any other items which have a direct bearing on the safety of flight under IFR conditions. Similar checks are carried out inside the aircraft both before and after starting engines and great importance is attached to them. Radio equipment must also be tested, even though, in the case of blind-approach aids, no complementary aid equipment exists at Gatwick.

FLIGHT TRIALS. The Rating test does not call for a "blind" take-off but it does require the candidate to fly on instruments as soon as a height of 100 ft is attained. The candidate takes off with helmet and blue goggles in position, but with a clear-vision panel in the amber screens. At 100 ft this panel is closed, so one is well advised to be on instruments before this moment. Throughout the test all aircraft, engine and radio controls have to be operated by the candidate, although information as to power settings, speeds and rates of descent or climb is given by the examiner.

Having obtained the necessary control instructions by R/T the pupil takes-off and is examined on his general instrument-flying during the climb and in level flight. This part includes the manoeuvre of reducing speed to 85 mph and returning to the recommended cruising speed of 140 mph without alteration of height or heading.

Next comes, "limited panel" work, in the writer's opinion the section most likely to give trouble to the average pilot. In this test the artificial horizon and the directional gyro are screened, which means that all turns have to be made with the aid of a clock, since normal compass errors do not permit a sufficiently rapid indication of one's course to be obtained. A standard Rate 1 turn requires a change of heading of three degrees per second, i.e., a 90-degree turn requires an elapsed time of 30 seconds. The rate of turn is measured by a "needle and ball" instrument and it is advisable to check this rate against a turn over a known time-interval in order to gauge the needle position for a Rate 1 turn.

Having established the "rate" of the instrument one is required to fly straight and level at constant air-speed and then carry out Rate 1 turns on to predetermined headings. A period of 30 seconds is allowed for the final adjustment on to the required course within +10 deg.

After the successful conclusion of this manoeuvre the candidate is required to recover from a sustained 45-deg bank turn and also from a steep descending spiral. In this connection, "recovery" means a return to straight, level flight on any suitable heading.

The final item in this section is an approach to the stall and return to normal flight, particular attention being paid to throttle and stick movements in the initial stages of the recovery.

The sequence of the five tests probably varies with the instructor, but in the writer's case the next test was the SBA let-down. This was attempted at Bovingdon under actual QBI (instrument flight rules compulsory on approach to this airfield) *conditions, but, due to traffic density and a VHF snag, the let-down there had to be abandoned and the test carried out at Dunsfold. Pilots who have had VHF troubles due to continual interference from other aircraft and ground stations will be relieved to hear that the MCA has a special frequency for these tests which is relatively uninterrupted by extraneous noises.*

CRITICISM. One of two possible criticisms of the rating examination concerns the SBA section. At the moment, the minimum height required for the final approach over the inner marker is 500 ft. In view of the fact that SBA is essentially an "approach-to-land" aid this seems unnecessarily high and it would be preferable if the approach was continued down to 150 ft. This would not only require a somewhat higher standard of instrument flying but would introduce a psychological effect akin to that which might be expected under conditions of a bad-weather SBA.

APPROACH. Apart from this, one had no fault to find with the SBA test. We were passed a homing QDM (magnetic heading to steer) *by the examiner and given complete freedom in our selection of method of homing on to the beam; apart from the R/T procedure (which would normally be done by a co-pilot, but which in the examination had to be done by the candidate) the SBA test was straightforward.*

At 500 ft we were given instructions to overshoot, and here, again, particular attention was paid to throttle opening—it should be fully open—and other cockpit routine to do with landing gear and flaps. Candidates are, of course, required to maintain the SBA QDM up to the required height and make necessary power adjustments to normal power after the initial climb.

On the return home we launched into the "asymmetric power" test, which was initiated when the aircraft was climbing at maximum power at the single-engine-safety speed of 85 mph. One throttle was pulled back smartly and, after the initial corrections had been made, the "dud" engine was restored to partial power to improve the single-engine characteristics. Great attention was paid to yaw control and a maximum initial deviation of 15 deg was allowed. In the writer's opinion it is a mistake to emphasize this point, since, under actual conditions of engine failure as opposed to the simulated, the maintaining of a steady heading is not nearly so important as is the checking of air speed, the readjustment of power output and the maintenance of altitude. An involuntary alteration of course is relatively insignificant and, anyway, is probably inevitable after an engine failure on a light twin under IFR conditions. What is far more important is the regaining of the original heading after all the other details have been attended to.

After dealing with the initial circumstances of the engine failure, the candidate is required to fly straight and level at 95 mph and carry out Rate 1 turns to the right and left, followed by a straight descent, descending turns and then a straight climb. This completes the asymmetric syllabus.

By this time the candidate may be getting tired, since simulated instrument flying with amber screens is more exhausting than is flight under actual instrument conditions. If this should occur he is allowed to rest for a time while the instructor handles the machine. All that remains to be done then, is the QDM let-down, and here again the procedure is quite normal. Some pilots, however, especially those who normally operate large aircraft with correspondingly large crews, may find a certain amount of difficulty in handling the R/T side as well as the actual flying, especially as the Consul is, by some standards, rather "mushy." Here again no rigid procedures are called for and, provided the candidate can demonstrate his ability to position himself over the airfield on the required heading at the required height in a reasonable period of time his performance will be acceptable. As with the SBA test, the required height before overshoot is 500 ft.

That completes the syllabus for the British Instrument Rating. The test, one feels, was fairly conducted and a general attitude of "we want to pass you, not fail you" persisted throughout. Normally the test occupies between two and three hours, and afterwards a debriefing chat covers the whole examination in retrospect, and any strong or weak points in one's IF (instrument flying) *are discussed.*

No one at Gatwick attempted to be dogmatic and all conversations were conducted with a frank interest in the candidate's point of view. Realizing that many aspects of instrument flying are open to discussion, the examiners are receptive to new ideas and, if some applicant has a new idea which works, no one will fail him because it has not been done before. Such an attitude might well be commended to all bodies connected with the examining of aviation candidates.

The MCA not only had CAFU requiring a move but also had put in place a policy of decentralisation during the two years of review, 1948 and 1949. There were now to be four divisions located at Heston (southern), Bristol (west), Liverpool (northern), and Prestwick

(Scottish). These four divisions would now assume increased responsibility for their areas.

Appointments to these divisions were

> A.V.M. V.B. Callaway, divisional controller, south-western;
> Captain A. B. L. Huskisson, RN, northern division;
> Air Marshal Sir Roderick Carr, London and south-eastern division;
> Commodore J. G. Murray, controller, Scottish division.

In reply to a question in the House of Commons by a Commodore Harvey on October 18, Mr. Lindgren said that he was aware of the fact that pilots and navigators employed in the MCA "Communication Flight" at Gatwick received salaries far below those paid by the corporations or charter operators, and that the pension rates paid on their behalf were also below those advocated by the minister himself for commercial firms; he stated that the matter was now under consideration.

The MCA decentralisation policy was probably one of the reasons why, in the early months of 1949, CAFU sent a small detachment of aircraft to Prestwick, under the operational control of the Scottish division, for the purpose of inspection and calibration of navigational and landing aids in Scotland. Prestwick was by now a busy international airport as many transatlantic airlines chose to stop there in order to "tank up" with maximum fuel. Probably for this reason, the main runway and taxiways at Prestwick were strengthened to withstand landings by aircraft of Stratocruiser weight.

This small detachment consisted of three Anson aircraft and crews. The crew consisted of pilot, navigator, and radio officer, together with a ground engineer. The three pilots, it is believed, were Capt. Jock Keir—later to become commander of the CAFU Fleet—Capt. Sandy Powell, and a pilot known as "Trader Horn." The provision of aircraft and engineering was the only responsibility retained by CAFU at Gatwick.

Not all of the aircraft sent on detachment were to be used for just the flight inspection task, however, as one of the Ansons was used in a communication role; carrying divisional officers, such as G. F. K. Donaldson, Scottish regional operations officer—later to become commander of the fleet at Stansted—to the remote highland and island facilities for which they now had overall responsibility. Sid Pritchard, one of the navigators sent on detachment, who had joined the unit at Gatwick in 1947 explained that "flying Ansons, which had a limited performance and no deicing, was an interesting exercise in a Scottish winter!"

With the object of carrying out radio experiments in VHF R/T, MCA signals technicians and members of the Mountain Rescue Unit from RAF station Kinloss were to spend a weekend on the summit of Ben Nevis (4,406 feet). It was intended they carry packs of mobile radio equipment and establish a VHF R/T transmitter and receiver station on the mountain in order to test, with the assistance of the MCA Ansons operating from Prestwick ("Flying Wing" detachment), coverage over North and West Scotland. Communications with aircraft and ground stations were to be tried at ranges of more than one hundred miles. Effective VHF R/T coverage was important in Northern Scotland, particularly in the Moray Firth area, where there was considerable Service and civil flying activity. A further aim of the exercise was to strengthen the liaison between the MCA and the RAF Mountain Rescue Unit.

It was this year that the Council of ICAO approved the ILS and GCA for international use. ILS was specified as the aid for all regular international airports where a blind-landing system was required and GCA approved as a supplementary device wherever it would materially assist air traffic control, or elsewhere for aircraft not fitted with ILS.

A long-range navigational aid was not yet approved, as there was not a system that was considered suitable for adoption as a standard. The council did recommend, however, that research and development should continue on this problem and that, in the meantime, present types of long-distance aids should be maintained.

Aeronautical telecommunications standards would be effective as of March 1, 1950, unless previously disapproved by a majority of ICAO members. Authority for establishing standards came from the Convention on International Civil Aviation concluded at Chicago in 1944, and a set of standards became annexes to the convention, when adopted by the ICAO Council.

Step by step, with the increase in complexity of ground installations, aircraft equipment had grown from a single MF transmitter/receiver, which was considered adequate for pre-war civil airliners, to the elaborate installations of the current period. A typical example of a modern (1949) installation, BOAC was shortly putting into service Canadair (American Douglas DC4s with four Rolls-Royce Merlin engines), and Handley Page Hermes (a British post-war commercial aircraft with four Bristol Centaurus engines and tricycle undercarriage), with the following radio and navigational equipment:

- HF transmitter/receiver (Marconi AD 107/108) in duplicate
- VHF transmitter/receiver (Standard Telephones and Cables STR23)
- Intercom system (Ultra UL 17)
- Automatic D/F (radio compass) (Marconi AD 7092), in duplicate or single twin installation
- Rebecca II
- ILS (glide-path and localiser receivers) might be added.

When the de Havilland DH106 Comet was doing its test flying, it had, in 1949, the following equipment installed:

- MF/HF Com VHF R/T
- ADF (duplicated)
- ILS
- DME
- LORAN

Even though these aircraft had ILS, *Flight* had reported that the installation of ILS equipment at airports was not proceeding very rapidly outside of the USA. It was additionally reported that in the United Kingdom, ILS equipment was being developed by Pye, STC, and GEC.

In order to give some appreciation of the task of the calibration unit at this time, here is a list of the aids that were installed at London Heathrow Airport in 1949. It was extracted from a Notice to Airmen (NOTAM) and covers only facilities available to aircraft:
London Airport Aids:

- MF D/F bearings and aeronautical communications
- HF D/F bearings and aeronautical communications
- Meteorological broadcast service
- HF R/T airfield control
- VHF R/T airfield control and universal guard
- VHF R/T approach control
- VHF D/F
- SCS51 main beacon and glide path
- SCS51 boundary marker, middle marker, and outer marker
- BABS Mk. II beacon
- SBA main beacon, inner marker, and outer marker
- MF non-directional beacon
- GCA radar search system
- GCA radar precision-landing system
- VHF R/T GCA control
- HF R/T GCA control

Mr. Pritchard was able to advise that SCS51 was the device that became ILS when the name and specification for "ILS" was internationally accepted.
Navigational Aids (also seen in appendix B):

- Direction-Finding MF Beacons (associated with NDBs), HF DF, VHF DF
- HF DF
- BABS (Blind Approach Beacon System)
- SBA (Standard Beam Approach)

- ILS (instrument landing system, a modification of the wartime SCS51)
- GEE, a hyperbolic fixing system, was a position-finding system developed to enable aircraft and ships to find their position by radio means. (Incidentally, installation of the Scottish GEE chain was now complete).
- Decca, by the Decca Navigator Co. Ltd.
- Consol, by Marconi.
- DME (distance-measuring equipment) associated with VOR

The VHF omni-directional beacon (VOR) was developed under government contract by Marconi. Both the two equipment, DME and VOR, would eventually provide the necessary range and bearing information for use in a computer so that any desired track could be flown.

ACR (airfield controlled radar) and ASMI (airfield surface movement indicator) were a development of radar.

GCA (ground-controlled approach), recommended as a standby landing aid used for monitoring ILS. No British-made GCA equipment was available at this time, but STC (Standard Telephones and Cables) were to have a complete system ready in the near future. Some details of this were

- Frequency 0080 mc/s
- Peak power output 50 kW
- Maximum range 60,000 feet
- Minimum range . . . 10,000 feet
- Range accuracy . . . ± 1 percent of range from maximum range to 12,000 feet. From 12,000 feet to 1,000 feet ± 20 feet.
- Elevation accuracy ± 10 feet at 4,500 feet from the vehicle.

Features of the GCA British equipment were its mobility, pan climatic operation, and ease of maintenance. A radio link between the vehicle on the airfield and the tower provided remote display control and monitoring. The equipment had been designed with a view to requiring the minimum of personnel necessary to operate the station. See the full list in appendix B.

It should be noted that by 1949, the Ministry was able to publish exactly where they were with regard to
- air traffic control and its further expansion,
- ground navigation equipment, and the
- carriage of equipment they expected to be carried by aircraft within the United Kingdom.

This would enable the expansion and expertise of CAFU to be developed, both on the telecommunications and licensing side.

The number of air traffic control officers employed by the MCA was 375, and ATC facilities were provided at thirty-six airports. Extensive operational research was carried out into problems relating to air-traffic control, particularly at London and Northolt airfields.

At the end of 1949, the MCA Interdepartmental Aircraft Control Committee was engaged on long-term planning for a common air traffic control system on United Kingdom and Empire routes. It was also in 1949 that, along with the GCA training base, the Ministry also set up standardised Aerodrome and Approach Control training for air traffic controllers at Bournemouth, Hurn Airport.

The following is an article from the August 11 edition of *Flight* magazine that indicates the policies rapidly being devised for this new era in civil aviation:

> *THE Ministry of Civil Aviation has outlined the policy upon which basic traffic control and navigational services will be developed in the United Kingdom during the next two to three years, and upon which regulations governing the carriage of radio equipment in aircraft will be based.*
>
> *This general statement of policy provides a warning of the new regulations, so allowing sufficient time for the production and installation of equipment to meet the minimum scale to be carried in all aircraft flying under IFR (Instrument Flight Rules) when Standardisation of approved navigational systems has been agreed.*

The use of the medium-frequency band for air-to-ground communications will contract rapidly in the near future as a result of the implementation, during 1950, of the new international frequency allocation plans. The first ground stations to be withdrawn will be those in South-Eastern England and then progressively in the North and South-West of England, followed by Scotland. The D/F facilities associated with this frequency band will also be withdrawn. Basic navigational services will be provided by employing the available medium frequencies for the increased use of Radio Range and the MF non-directional beacons. Control areas in the form of Airways—defined by radio ranges and MF beacons—are being set up, but there will not be sufficient medium frequencies to provide a complete system of check points, so the latter will be defined throughout the country by VHF Fan Markers. VHF D/F would continue to be available at many airfields, but the ability to use this facility alone would not continue to be sufficient for air-traffic control purposes under IFR in control areas, and in control zones associated with major airports.

It is intended progressively to extend the system of positive control of air traffic throughout the country. With the growth of air traffic needing IFR clearance in control areas and zones it will probably become necessary by 1950 to require each aircraft to carry a minimum scale of equipment in the form of VHF R/T, MF receiving equipment and associated D/F facilities, and VHF receiving equipment for the 75 Mc/s fan marker signals. The use of GEE and Decca will continue to be acceptable for traffic control.

For international flying it is thought probable that full operational flexibility will be achieved only if aircraft are capable of communicating on at least 19 VHF R/T frequencies. In the United Kingdom full use of airfield, approach and en route facilities will be achieved only if communication is possible on ten frequencies. In the interests of safety it is anticipated that aircraft having less than the full facilities will be restricted to those routes on which their equipment will allow communications to be maintained. Since the MF band is being used more for navigational facilities, great importance is attached to the incorporation of better selectivity characteristics in new airborne MF receivers.

The Ministry of Civil Aviation announced that the Civil Aviation Act 1949, which had received royal assent, would be effective from November 24, 1949.

It was in 1949 that the MCA, having to find a new site for CAFU, realised there were adequate facilities at Stansted; long hard runways with a wartime T2 hangar. Other facilities though were not so hot: the accommodation would be the WWII Nissen huts, airfield lighting was the wartime "gooseneck" (a paraffin can with a wick in the spout) and the landing aid was SBA.

The decision to move to Stansted, when it came, was not soon enough, as for some months, it had been a very wet period at the grass airfield at Gatwick; staff with any outside duties needing to wear gum boots for much of the time, remembered Eddy Harris. There was also a deteriorating hole in the hangar roof to dampen spirits, which hardly helped matters. Perhaps the thought of the conditions at Stansted: gooseneck runway lighting and draughty Nissen huts, made the idea of a "temporary" home there more one of resignation than hope. Finally, the move happened just before Christmas.

Having started out at Croydon with the Air Ministry in 1944, then transferred to the newly created MCA and moving to Gatwick soon after the war in late 1945, it may seem difficult to understand why CAFU was required to move again. I believe it needs to be seen in context of what was happening in the United Kingdom at that time. From about 1947 or 1948, the MCA were endeavouring to have Gatwick nominated as the second London Airport—although it was not to be finally announced until 1952—when the government finally gave approval for the proposed development of the airport as a "bad weather" airfield for Heathrow. It has to be assumed that the MCA, probably as early as 1948, could see that in the longer term, CAFU required an airfield with updated radio facilities and the latest landing aids and equipment in order to be able to carry out the new licensing tests that ICAO was endeavouring to put into place. It was in 1949 that the UK instrument rating (IR) was introduced and airline pilots would be requiring initial instrument ratings, as well as future renewals, and required these tests to be conducted at an airfield with a modicum of modern facilities. In addition to the new Dove aircraft that CAFU was acquiring, even the Consuls and Ansons would benefit from hard runways rather than grass that would not, during take-off and landing, shake delicate equipment, required for the calibration of the many navigational and landing aids that would be coming into service throughout the country. In short, CAFU required something better than its present home; the grass airfield at Gatwick, an airfield that would, anyway, most likely be closed during any period of future development.

Perhaps that is why in March 1949, Stansted was under discussion in the House of Commons, when £30,000 was allocated for conversion work in certain areas of the airport buildings. However, the main expenditure was to be used in the installation of VHF (very high frequency) voice communication radio and general reorganisation of the control tower, as well as having some remedial work carried out on the runways and taxiways.

Finally, at only thirty-four miles from London, Stansted would still provide easy access for the Headquarters staff in London to do their training and refresher flying. Stansted, which already had a six-thousand-foot runway, was being brought up to date in order to provide that requirement.

A total of almost eighty-four thousand aircraft movements were reported at civil airports in the United Kingdom for the month of June, of which eighteen thousand were attributed to civil transport. The number of passengers handled was 205,336 at all reporting airports, more than half of this figure being accounted for by London Airport and Northolt. Average daily traffic at Northolt was over two thousand passengers.

Approximately 1,800 tons of freight was flown into, and out of, the London area. Renfrew was again the third-busiest passenger terminal; it handled nearly 14,000 passengers and 1,200 air transport movements.

Evidence, collated from statistical reports sent in by member airlines to the IATA head office, indicated that the international airline safety factor in 1949 showed a continuation of the trend towards improvement, which had been observed in the two previous years. The classical index of airline safety (i.e., passenger miles per passenger fatality) was found to stand at 34.84 million miles in 1949, as compared with 30.49 million in 1948 and 21.184 million in 1947. The evidence was gathered from forty-two reporting airlines that, during the year, carried some 17.801 million passengers in the course of 543 million miles of flying. Nineteen accidents occurred, involving 306 passenger deaths for a total passenger mileage of 10.68 billion. Translation of these statistics into a more popular idiom shows that the amount of service involved in the 1949 passenger-mileage figure was the equivalent of a mass airlift of the entire population of the Benelux countries to Norway.

Because of the varying number of airlines reporting in each year, the IATA figures can only be regarded as rough, though reasonably accurate, comparisons. The forty-two companies that reported in 1949 carried, in all, about 85 percent of the traffic lifted by all members of the organisation. It is gratifying to notice, however, that in spite of the rapid growth of air transport since the end of WWII, there had nevertheless been a constant improvement in the safety record—a fact that received too little recognition in the popular press.

In April, the Civil Estimates revealed that for the period 1949-1950, the MCA would be costing the taxpayer £22 million, even with a reduction of spending of £3 million. Even so, there was an effort to economise in the matter of personnel; the total number to be employed would fall from 8,588 in the previous year to 8,550! In the Ministry itself, Headquarters staff reductions went from 1,786 to 1,720. It was hoped that these "drastic" reductions would not seriously affect the efficiency of the Ministry!

Savings at the MCA Headquarters were made reducing certain staff, including twenty staff pilots; twenty navigators; sixty-two assistant signals officers. While at the outstations, another forty-three assistant signals officers were dispensed with.

During the next financial year, airports were expected to require the following amounts:

- Belfast (Nutts Corner), £40,000; Blackbushe, £2,500;
- Bovingdon, £124,000; Croydon, £33,000;
- Edinburgh (Turnhouse), £16,000; Hurn £35,000;
- Kirkwall (Hatston), £47,000; Liverpool (Speke), £7,000;
- London Airport, £3,205,000; Manchester (Ringway), £104,000; Northolt, £115,000; Prestwick, £113,000;
- Renfrew, £208,000; Scilly Isles, £8,500;
- Southampton Water Marine Base, £5,000; and Stansted, £30,000.

By September 1949, *Flight* reported that the Ministry employed a total of 7,687 persons.

G-ALFT was spotted at Ringway departing for Heathrow at the end of April 1949. In August, the first Dove registered to the MCA, G-AJLV, was seen at Ringway piloted by Captain Powell, returning to Gatwick. In August, G-ALFU, not registered to the MCA until December 1948, appeared to be doing a post-accident flight check of the SBA at Ringway after a BEA Dakota, G-AHCY, had an accident in poor weather conditions on a flight from Belfast a few days before.

Two of the Gemini were seen at Ringway: G-AIRS 25/01/49, G-AKDD 26/04/49, and G-AGLJ, the Proctor, on 30/08/49, all on communication flights.

MCA CAFU Aircraft:
REGISTERED

| Dove | G-ALVS | MCA | Oct 1949 |

In October, DH Dove, G-ALVS, was registered to the MCA. It was the first of five Doves intended for IR tests, communication and refresher flying roles. It is believed that the aircraft was not delivered to CAFU until April in the following year.

It is unclear exactly when the man in charge of the Telecommunications section was called superintendent, but it is thought that the position of the original signals officer, Ted Luff, had now moved to a new man, Mr. W. R. Denis.

The MCA report for 1949 shown in *Flight* provided the following information:

> *MCA FLYING UNIT*
> *During the years 1948 and 1949 nine new aircraft were added to the MCA Flying Unit (formerly the MCA Operations Fleet). These were, two Gemini, one Avro XIX, and one Dove in 1948, and three Avro XIX's and two Doves in 1949. One Proctor and one Auster were withdrawn from service, and at the end of 1949 the total number operational was 27.*

In 1949, there are a few minor discrepancies in the numbers of aircraft that I have found. For instance, the "apparent" 1948/49 report says that there were nine new aircraft in 1948/9. My findings show only eight. I found the MCA flying Unit had twenty-one aircraft in 1947; and by the end of 1949, the number had increased to twenty-nine.

The report also says that one Auster and one Proctor were withdrawn from service at the end of 1949. The Auster, GLL, although not deregistered until 1950, did have an accident, damaged beyond repair at Gatwick, says John Havers, in 1949, while the Proctor had actually crashed in 1947, though not deregistered until August 1948.

They also show three Doves, where I show four. This may be because the last one, G-ALVS, registered in October 1949 was probably not delivered until the following year.

Hours flown for the two years were as follows:—

Hours Flown	**1948**	**1949**
Telecommunications Flying	2,800	3,186
"B" Licence Tests	450	200

Instrument Rating	000	630
Communications, Operational Trials, and Headquarters Staff Refresher Flying	4,030	2,863
GCA Crew Training	1,320	1,160
Totals	**8,600**	**8,039**

The Flying Unit's staff, at the end of 1949, comprised:
MCA CAFU (Fleet Wing) Staff

Staff Pilots	20	Increase of 10
Navigators	10	Increase of 6
Signals Officers	01	
Asst. Sig. Officers	02	
Radio Officers	08	
Radio Mechanics	13	Increase of 8
Maintenance Overseer	01	
Clerical staff	—	Not Recorded

One additional pilot joined the unit in 1948, and six officers from Headquarters were seconded as pilots to the unit in 1949.

One further point of interest to note is that the number of hours flown in total for 1949 was about 6.5 percent lower than the previous year. The hours flown on GCA work at Bournemouth (hours spent radar training for air traffic controllers) reduced by 12 percent, but this was possibly due to greater attention being given to the provision of the new ATC services.

"B" licence testing was reduced drastically due to the changes for a commercial licence. However, the introduction of controlled airspace in 1949 was being taken seriously by commercial airlines, as can be seen by the number of instrument ratings taken. However, although the total number of hours flown in 1949 was down, the fleet telecommunications hours flying increased by just over 13.5 percent, no doubt due to the introduction of the new airway system.

So to end the decade, the unit was at long last getting in to its stride with both the telecommunications and licence testing work; for although the "B" licence testing reduced considerably, the introduction of the new IR tests caused the fleet examining pilots to be extremely busy.

MCA CAFU Aircraft at the end of 1949. Total = 27

Auster	01	G-AGLK, (GLL crashed 1949)
Tiger Moth	02	G-AGRA, G-AGRB
Proctor	01	G-AGLJ
Gemini	03	G-AIRS, JZL, KDD
Anson	12	G-AGPB, GWE, GWF, GWA, GZS, GZT, GVA, GUD, HIC, HID, HIH, HIJ
Consul	05	G-AJXE, JXF, JXG, JXH, JXI
Dove	03	G-AJLV, G-ALFT, G-ALFU, (LVS arrived Stansted in 1950)

If you simply counted the number of CAFU aircraft still registered to the MCA, it totals twenty-nine: two Austers, one Proctor, twelve Ansons, two tiger Moths, five Consuls, four Doves and three Gemini.

However, in spite of a few differences—the one Auster GLL and IR Dove LVS—we both have the same count of twenty-seven aircraft, which is the number of aircraft said to depart for Stansted at the very end of 1949.

Auster at Croydon. Registered to Air Ministry Aug 1944, passed to MCA June 1945
Photo: Eddy Harris/JF

de Havilland Tiger Moth at Croydon. Registered to MCA June 1945
Photo: Eddy Harris/JF

Percival Proctor, Registered to MCA June 1945
Photo: John Havers Collection

Avro Anson, Registered to MCA May 1946
Photo: Late Gerald Lawrence via Tony Clark/David Whitworth

Airspeed Consul, Registered June 1947—used for IR tests
Photo: Late Gerald Lawrence via Tony Clark/David Whitworth

Tels. De Havilland Dove, Registered April 1947
Photo: Eddy Harris/JF

Gemini Registered 1947
Photo: John Havers collection

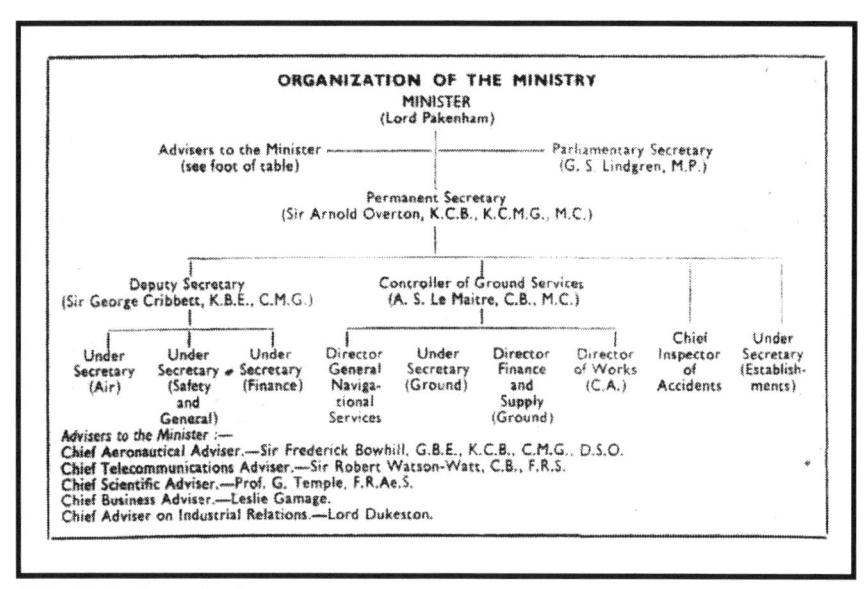

1949 MCA Organisation
Photo: Flight, April 29, 1949, p. 508

Chapter Two
1950-1959

With three homes in the first six years, CAFU could only hope for a more stable period in a decade when the airways system would kick-off, commercial licences and instrument ratings would be in demand, and new and improved navigational and landings aids would increase throughout the United Kingdom.

1950

Stansted had been constructed as part of a wartime agreement between Winston Churchill and President Roosevelt and handed over to the United States on a ninety-nine-year lease. Construction was started in July 1942 by the 817th Engineer Army Battalion (EAB) of the US Army, and the work was taken over by the 825th EAB. A WWII bomber base, with a typical wartime construction of three 60-degree runways: 13/31, 18/36, and the main runway of around six thousand feet with headings of 230/050. After the war, the airfield, originally handed over to the Air Ministry in 1947, was, in turn, handed over to the Ministry of Civil Aviation on January 3, 1949.

It had recently had its runways and standing ground resurfaced, and there were rumours that it might be used by BOAC as a Comet flight testing base. It was said that Stansted might be the main alternate to Northolt instead of Bovingdon and the MCA had hoped that it would be the centre of charter companies' operations, but seen by them as being too far from London for commercial operations.

It was thought, at the time, that one of the airport's advantages was that it was outside of the Metropolitan Control Zone and off the "beaten track" of air routes; one of the reasons seen as useful to the MCA Flying Unit for the testing of pilots.

NOTAM 18, dated January 18, allowed the MCA to announce a postponement of the issue of instrument ratings due to a conclusion that adherence to the date of April 1 might entail "considerable curtailment in commercial air services . . ." and accordingly decided to amend the date to October 1, 1950.

It was believed that the instrument rating (IR) would only result in the desired all-round improvement in safety when a similar standard was enforced by all foreign operators. And in order to attempt coordination of traffic control and navigational facilities in the European area, meetings of airline authorities, sponsored by the International Air Transport Association (IATA) were now in progress.

When the Civil Aviation Flying Unit moved from Gatwick, at the end of December 1949 and the beginning of January 1950, they moved all of the aircraft, at least those not on detachment, to their new home at Stansted Airport.

Although the Consul aircraft were acquired for the purpose of conducting instrument rating tests, they were occasionally used for communication flights. The Tiger Moths were used for pilot licence tests and refresher flying; the proctor for operational trials, general communication, and refresher flying; while the Gemini appeared to be used solely by headquarter pilots for continuation and communication flying.

The second Gemini, G-AJZL, did have a Certificate of Airworthiness Renewal, including some modifications, incorporated in January 1950. It was spotted in March having flown from Stansted to Manchester Ringway, probably to refuel, departing for Liverpool Speke. In July, the Proctor GLJ also flew into Ringway, refuelled, and returned to Stansted. While in August, Gemini KDD arrived at Manchester from Stansted, then continued on a communication flight to Prestwick.

Other Ansons found to be registered to the MCA in May 1950—but not with CAFU—were all ex-BEA, and not remembered at either Gatwick or Stansted. These are simply recorded here to advise future investigators that they have been noted but not used by CAFU.

These were

MCA ANSONS NOT REGISTERED TO CAFU
G-AHIB registered to MCA 14.05.48 until 20.03.50
G-AHIE registered to MCA 14.05.48 until 20.03.50
G-AHIF registered to MCA 14.05.48 until 20.03.50
G-AHIG registered to MCA 14.05.48 until 13.07.50

It is a slight mystery as to why the MCA should have so many aircraft registered to them. One theory, put forward by Tony Doyle, is that the MCA, as the government representative, took over various aircraft from the nationalised corporations when they were surplus. This is probably what happened with these Ansons. They were originally operated by Railway Air Services and nominally went to BEA, who then probably declared them as surplus to requirement in August 1947. Over a period of time, the MCA then probably found homes for them, and it probably suited their purpose to move some towards CAFU in May to July 1948, which is likely how CAFU came to have G-AHIC, HID, HIH, and HIJ. The others were sold in this country and abroad, so the fact that they appeared registered to the MCA name was simply a matter of convenience, nothing to do initially with CAFU, even though some of them ended there.

The CAFU aircraft were all installed in the large WWII T2 hangar at Stansted, while staff were ensconced in old draughty WWII Nissen huts, painted blue and heated by coke-burning stoves, which, as Charles Marchant recalled, "struggled to cope with the bitter East winds of an Essex winter."

Finally, in November, G-AGPB, one of the first Ansons, was retired after joining the MCA Operation Fleet in September 1945.

Just to further muddy the waters in the numbers and types of aircraft with CAFU, in *Hansard* for the July 26, 1950, under the heading "Communications Flight," a question was asked of the parliamentary secretary to the Ministry of Civil Aviation, on "the types of aircraft, and how many, the Department's 'Communication Flight' had?" (As early as this, it can be seen that politicians were concerned about cost yet did not appreciate the role of CAFU, thinking of them as one simply for "Communication.")

The answer, for April 1, 1950, was almost exactly as my figures show for the end of 1949, except that the Doves were not four but three, most likely accounted by the fact that G-ALVS, although registered in October 1949, was probably not delivered before April 1.

Then there is the Viking. You may remember the Viking was registered to the MCA in 1947 through until March 1951, but not properly remembered as being used by CAFU, although thought so by *Flight* magazine. Well, the *Hansard* report showed no Viking being with the fleet on April 1, 1950 (so where was it?), but noted that a Viking had been added to the fleet after that date! As if to confirm the existence of the MCA Viking, in a September issue of *Flight*, they reported that the "Flying Unit" had staged an air traffic control exercise at Bournemouth, Hurn Airport, using an assortment of its aircraft, which included the Viking, G-AGRR. This aircraft had, it said, been recently acquired from BOAC's development flight. In fact, this Viking was originally registered to the Ministry of Supply in 1946, as a medium range, general transport twenty-eight-seat aircraft, later passed to BOAC, BEA division, in June of 46, but never actually taken up by them. Eventually it was registered to the MCA in December 1947 until March 1951, when it was taken on by Britavia Ltd. Tony Doyle did find a photograph of this aircraft dated, he believes, April 1950 and showing no ownership markings, which explains why it was difficult to ascertain who was using it in any particular period.

The exercise at Hurn airport in 1950 was a demonstration of various ways of arranging holding stacks and letdown procedures, which were put to practical test. One of the CAFU navigators, Sidney Pritchard, did tell me that the Viking was vaguely remembered but could not recall it belonging to, or used by them (CAFU) operationally. It was thought that although not taken up by BEA, BOAC were given use of this MCA aircraft for various trials.

Safety Was No Accident

Although work had barely commenced for the unit, either on the licensing or flight inspection side, considerations of cost were already being realised. In September, questions were asked in Parliament as to whether CAFU could be more economical by subcontracting work to charter firms. The parliamentary secretary gave a firm *no,* when he said that he believed that a study of the unit's work, and appreciation of the complications involved in the variety of different tasks in all parts of the United Kingdom, would, he believed, satisfy any outside assessor that the Ministry needed its own aircraft. What the Ministry had done, he further reported, was to subcontract the maintenance and overhaul of its aircraft ever since it started immediately after WWII to Airwork.

The Dove, G-ALFU, was later known in the sixties for VOR flight inspection work, but it was reported by *Flight* magazine as having flown an urgent VIP flight to Llandow, Glamorgan. On March 12, a Tudor V of Fairflight Ltd. crashed on approach to landing, and CAFU was asked, at short notice, to carry Lord Packenham to the airport.

The fact that LFU was carrying passengers, and perhaps not used for telecommunications work at this time, might explain the early photograph of G-ALFU with the new examining test screens (probably being tested), designed by Captain Marshall. Much later in this decade, LFU was kitted out to calibrate VORs.

Up until this time, Capt. Dan Carroll, the original RAF officer who in 1944 was asked to set up the AM Civil Operations Fleet, before it was transferred to the MCA Operations Fleet in 1945, had been commander. But sometime in the early fifties, the Ministry, for some reason known only to itself, found a need to replace him with a new commander. This was an ex-RAF group captain, G. F. K. Donaldson, a senior Ministry operations officer, previously a Scottish regional operations officer in the late forties. One theory was that Dan Carroll did not fit into the mould; he was not an "Ops Manual" pilot but flew by the seat of his pants, seen perhaps as somewhat contemptuous of Ministry regulations. It was known that Captain Carroll had fallen out with the unit signals officer (who himself was to leave—later involved in some scandal!).

Yet in spite of this apparent demotion, Captain Carroll seemed to accept his fate, was given his own office, and continued as a most respected examiner and telecommunications pilot right up until his retirement in the early years of the 1960s. He was a slight, small man, a relaxed, almost nonchalant leader, known for the use of a silver cigarette case and, when walking out to the Tels aircraft, carrying his white leather gloves, striding ahead of his crew.

Until now, the air space within the United Kingdom was divided up into five flight information regions (FIRs), within each of which, around each terminal airport, there existed areas known as control zones. The Air Traffic Control Centre (ATCC) at Uxbridge provided an "Informative" Control Service for all aircraft in the south-eastern flight information region (FIR) and for all aircraft above five thousand feet in the south-western FIR. Zone boundaries were provided with traffic separation and flight information. This service was dependent, however, upon the number of aircraft using it as it was only voluntary.

To augment this service, on February 22, 1950, a long-range London radar service was put into operation. Flight plans using the information service would be coordinated with flights visible on the radar, although the area covered would be dependent upon the height of individual aircraft. As an additional safety measure, aircraft visible on the radar screens would be continuously monitored.

Although intended as long-range radar, it could also be used within the Metropolitan Control Zone (London) and would also work in contact with the GCA installations of both London and Northolt airports and was expected to be able to provide an improved landing rate. It was emphasised, however, that the system was not intended as a navigational guide and that pilots were expected to be able to navigate without aid from the service. It was, in effect, an avoidance service in virtually the whole of the south-eastern area. As an additional safety measure, the type of radar used would also be able to provide a weather warning service.

Phase I of the UK airways system came in to force on August 1, 1950. Green One, from Strumble in the west to Dover in the east, was the first airway, followed shortly after by five more.

Safety Was No Accident

The calibration unit at CAFU was going to be seriously busy. Already there were radio ranges at Dunsfold and Epsom. In addition, marker beacons (75 mc/s, otherwise called fan markers) were used to provide a known position on the airway. Marker beacons were also used in conjunction with landing aids such as SBA and ILS, though these beacons were not nearly as powerful as the airway beacons, which were required to be identified at altitudes up to ten thousand feet or more. Maidstone and Watford Ranges also served the Metropolitan Inner and Outer Control Zone of the London Area, as it was known at that time.

As a result of the implementation of the new international frequency allocation plans, it was expected that the use of the medium frequency (MF) band for air-ground communications would contract rapidly, because the provision of very high frequency (VHF) radio-telephony equipment for airfield and approach communications at MCA airfields was now almost complete. The direction-finding (D/F) facilities associated with this frequency band would also be withdrawn.

British equipment undergoing development at this time, were landing aids such as ILS and GCA, and navigational aids such as DME, cloud-warning radar, and various types of search radar.

Installation of the Scottish GEE chain was now complete, and the introduction of new semiautomatic equipment begun. The MCA Operational Research Section, together with workers loaned by the corporations, carried out extensive research into problems relating to air-traffic control, particularly at London and Northolt. Control facilities were provided at thirty-six airports.

Somewhere around this time, Mr. M. "Mike" F. Whitney, aged about thirty-one, was made the signals officer (SO) at CAFU, taking over from Mr. R. W. Davis. This position of signals officer at CAFU later became known as superintendent.

Mike Whitney was possibly one of the leading figures in the success of CAFU in the field of setting standards of calibration, not only for the United Kingdom but also towards influencing ICAO in setting standards of practice that were in use by the British. Nearly three decades later, he would be part of the British team in support of the Plessey Doppler microwave landing system proposal to ICAO. One of his first initiatives was to create a new post for a deputy, with particular responsibility for flight inspection.

In the year ended March 31, 1950, *Hansard* reported that £157,741 was spent in maintaining the flying unit on essential technical and operational work. The average cost per flying hour was £18.16s 0d (£18.80).

There were twenty-six aircraft, and staff numbers employed at CAFU was one hundred.

CAFU tasks noted by *Hansard*:

- Calibration of radio and radar aids throughout the British Isles
- Examination of candidates for the instrument ratings and CPL licence
- Operational trials of ATC and airway procedures
- Development and trials of new airborne equipment
- Flight testing of airfield lighting aids
- Training of ATC GCA crews
- Departmental communication and the maintenance of flying standards of HQ personnel
- VIP communications

CAFU had flown 8,620 hours in the twelve-month period up to May 31, 1950. A 3,836 went on checking aids, and 3,427 hours on checking pilots. The remaining 1,357 hours were divided between "general purpose" flying, including demonstration and development flying for prototype radio and radar aids as well as other tasks.

In the early fifties, only the more important airfields had VHF radio telephone (R/T); apart from this, all route and airfield communications were by wireless telegraphy (W/T), hence MFDF and CAFUs need for an airborne radio operator. At first, it was thought wise to routinely check all navigational aids, but with experience, it was later possible to abandon routine checks on such items as non-directional beacons (NDBs) and direction finders.

Before the introduction of the VHF omni range (VOR) as a navigational aid, CAFU was flight-inspecting MFDF and very high frequency DF (VDF) direction finders, VDF (VHF radio voice-operated "homers"), as well as MFDF (medium frequency Morse code-operated "homers.") But once countrywide VHF radio-telephony was introduced, there was little or no requirement for the wireless Telegraphist. This position in the CAFU aircraft would then be replaced by a more senior technician with experience of the radio navigation systems that were to be inspected. These technicians were given the title of navigational aid (navaid) inspectors (NAIs).

Radio aid calibration was extended to the new instrument landing system (ILS) that was being installed at all the larger airports around the world. In addition, there were non-directional beacons (NDBs) and fan markers associated with both ILS and en route aids.

By 1950, factors emerged that clearly influenced subsequent flight inspection developments:

First was the publication by ICAO (of which the United Kingdom was a member state) of annexe 10 to the Convention of International Civil Aviation, titled "International Standards and Recommended Practices (SARP) for Aeronautical Telecommunications," prescribing which systems were to be used for air navigation and what the accuracies should be. ICAO also issued an advisory document on the ground and air testing of navigation aids known as Doc 8071. It was, therefore, recognised that CAFU should evolve methods of flight inspection that had accuracies that were demonstrably appropriate for the ICAO prescribed tolerances and that produced recorded results to confirm and justify the findings of a flight inspection (FI).

The instrument landing system (ILS), recommended as the ICAO standard approach aid in 1946, with the guiding standard (annexe 10), that appeared in June 1949, became effective from March 1, 1950.

Decca (long wave) was being trialled by the MCA (CAFU). It was becoming recognised in the United Kingdom as both a potential long—and short-range navigational aid, possibly in preference to the American VOR.

MCA CAFU Aircraft
DEREGISTERED

| Auster | G-AGLL | AM/MCA | Jan 1950 |
| Anson | G-AGPB | MCA | Nov 1950 |

As mentioned earlier, the Auster, G-AGLL, lost its registration (PWFU) in January, while the Anson, G-AGPB, was deregistered in November because, reports Tony Doyle, it was damaged beyond repair at Bovingdon in an overshoot on September 22 of this year. Apparently, it overshot the runway, crossed a road, and ended up in a hedge, according to Lloyds. Interestingly, the pilot's name was Stallibrass. Could this be Geoffrey (later Sir Geoffrey) Stallibrass who became controller of National Air Traffic Services (CNATS) and later still a board member of the CAA? He was well known as a very pleasant person to work with and wearing a buttonhole to work.

MCA CAFU Aircraft at the end of 1950. Total = 26

Auster	01	G-AGLK
Tiger Moth	02	G-AGRA, G-AGRB
Proctor	01	G-AGLJ
Gemini	03	G-AIRS, JZL, KDD
Anson	10	G-AGUD, GWA, GWE, GWF, GZS, GZT, GVA, HIC, HIH, HIJ
Consul	05	G-AJXE, JXF, JXG, JXH, JXI
Dove	04	G-AJLV, G-ALFT, G-ALFU, LVS

1951

Lord Ogmore replaced Lord Pakenham as the minister of Civil Aviation.

Another task soon added to the unit's growing list was to participate in the Ordnance Survey Department's countrywide photographic resurvey of the United Kingdom. This work, carried out using the Decca navigator system for accuracy, took place during summer months when cloud conditions and visibility permitted high-quality photography. Ansons, with a hole cut into the nose for a large camera, were first used, later came the Dove, usually G-ANAP.

CAFU was known to be checking UK airfield lighting, normally completed by operations staff from London. Consul G-AJXE was seen at Manchester Ringway in January of this year doing a lighting inspection before going on to Liverpool Speke. Ten days later, Consul G-AJXF did another lighting check before departing for Heathrow.

Also recorded during the year were a number of Anson flights nominated as GCA Testing: G-AHIH in January, G-AGVA and G-AGWA in June, and G-AGZT in September. Similarly, all three Tels Doves, JLV, LFT, and LFU, were on flight inspection duties at Manchester throughout the year.

In a published summary of air transport movements at United Kingdom airfields during 1950, the MCA revealed that traffic generally increased by nearly 10 percent.

Over 2.25 million passengers passed through reporting airfields—an increase of more than 16 percent—while the total of freight handled (30,634 tons) represented a rise of 20 percent. London Airport handled over half-a-million passengers and Northolt nearly three-quarters of a million—increases of 32 and 19 percent, respectively, over the totals for the previous year. Glasgow was third in order of importance, with 138,146 passengers, followed by Belfast, Prestwick, and Manchester. Stansted did not have any figures reported.

An interesting paper was presented to the 1951 Radio Convention, held at Southampton, under the auspices of the British Institution of Radio Engineers and given by Mr. G. W. Stallibrass of the MCA's Directorate of Navigational Service (Control and Navigation), later to be a director of Aerodromes Standards (DAS), and by the eighties, a board member of the CAA. In the paper, he discussed the application of radio to certain navigational and air traffic control problems, referring to the economic difficulties and international tension that were, he said, responsible for creating the delay in the spread of modern navigational aids that were in need of replacement in 1947. He believed the failure to reach the standard of development of new equipment was brought about by the realisation of the high costs involved in the introduction of numerous new installations that had combined to bring about an element of uncertainty, both by member states and the airlines, in the economical justification of the installation of certain ground and airborne equipment.

> *So far* (continued Mr. Stallibrass), *I have dwelt more on problems arising from the present situation and the limitations of existing equipment. It would be a mistake to infer from this either that the existing facilities were bad in themselves or that the overall situation was unsatisfactory. In fact, although much more needs to be done, particularly in certain parts of Europe, the airways system recently introduced in the UK worked very much better than anything available before, and landing rates in bad visibility at the more important airports were increasing steadily.*
>
> *The first basic requirement [in solving en route problems] was for a navigational system that would provide aircraft with continuous information of their position, presented in such a form that they could make good any track laid down without the need for careful calculation, and without requiring the presence of a specialist navigator among the crew.*

The US Airborne Instruments Laboratory, Long Island, was evaluating VOR/DME, stating that, currently, the accuracy of airborne VOR receivers appeared to be directly related to their size, weight, and cost. The total spreads in VOR ground-station errors at flat, mountainous, and valley sites were given as 3 degrees, 3.1 degrees, and 4.4 degrees, respectively.

Of DME, it is said that small errors of a fraction of a mile could sometimes be increased to as much as four miles at extreme range, but that this was chiefly a matter of improving the equipment.

The article also stated that the most favourable evidence of future potentialities of VOR was that "despite the many types of errors affecting the course indication, the actual resulting off-course displacement of the aircraft was never more than four degrees, and was usually very much smaller."

According to a *Flight* magazine calculation, a four-degree error at a range of fifty miles (the nominal maximum of a VOR station) would place an aircraft 3.5 miles off course; and if the error was only two degrees, then the aircraft would be 1.75 miles off-course.

By the end of June this year, the US CAA intended to have 415 VOR stations in operation with an ultimate total of 466, plus sixty-four two-course VHF visual-aural ranges (VAR), which would subsequently be converted to VOR. The article concluded with the statement that within two or three years DME and the course-line computer will enable a pilot to fly a straight line to any destination he wanted and not have to stick to established controlled airways. It seems there would, eventually, be in America a navaid system that, subject to some limitations, would do what the British system, Decca, already did with greater ease and accuracy.

The US authorities had generously agreed to supply VOR installations free of charge to the following ICAO member countries:

Britain, 2; France, 2; Italy, 4; Belgium, 1; Holland, 1.

Perhaps it is unmannerly to suggest, wrote a *Flight* article, *that this offer was not altogether unconnected with the fact that US airlines are operated through these countries. The fact remains that VOR is extremely expensive, and its operational limitations are such that, to obtain anything approaching general coverage, a large number of sets per country is required.*

Lord Brabazon's report on relative responsibilities in bad-weather take-offs and landings was published as a white paper: "How to Make Air Transport Pay."

On 15 February, 1951, phase 2 of the UK airways system became operational. It included the extension of Green One and three new airways: Blue One, Red One, and Red Two.

The present Metropolitan "Inner" Control Zone was replaced by the London Control Zone (LCZ), and the Metropolitan "Outer" Control Zone replaced by the London Control Area.

Then in the spring of 1951, phase 3 of the UK airways system came into force.

In order to comply with the new airway system, aircraft flown on the airways would have to carry VHF R/T and have minimum radio navigation equipment: MF receivers associated with ADF (manually operated D/F loop) and a VHF receiver capable of receiving signals from 75,000 kc/s marker beacons, or Decca or GEE.

Although Norway, Sweden, and the US zone of Germany had airway systems in operation, it was reported at an ICAO progress meeting at the Palais de Chaillot, Paris, in October 1951, that the most complex airway system existing in Europe was that in Great Britain (incidentally, at this time, CAFU was still checking aids in Germany).

But although the rest of Europe were being encouraged to set up airway systems, it was thought likely that some of the smaller states would find difficulties in meeting the implementation date of September 1, 1952. One of the major problems, attendant upon the establishment of a European network of airways, was finding a common standard altimeter setting. It was agreed, however, that the QNH (regional altimeter setting) system should be used as from August 1, 1952.

Another recommendation tabled was that SBA should be withdrawn in favour of ILS, the latter now being the standard ICAO recommended aid. Whilst not disagreeing with this recommendation, the UK delegation asked that implementation should be delayed as British European Airways employed SBA and would have the greatest difficulty in re-equipping their aircraft for ILS sufficiently quickly.

Examination was given to the relative merits of Decca and VOR, and it was pointed out that Decca coverage of some two million square miles of Europe already existed. IATA tabled a demonstration plan of about eighty-five VOR stations, but during an examination, these were reduced to thirty-three, twenty of which were, however, the subject of reservations or statements of intention by a number of the states concerned.

What was really required was an evaluation of VOR and Decca. The Ministry of Civil Aviation had already made a preparatory evaluation of Decca, and in practice, this would be very considerably amplified by the practical use of Decca by BEA. A full and reliable evaluation of the system should, therefore, be available within the comparatively near future, it was said. However, it was thought doubtful if a corresponding evaluation of VOR would appear in a similar time frame.

In June 1951, the Fourth Session of the Communications Division of ICAO agreed the full specification for DME that was proposed should be installed along the international air routes. It might be supposed that, with the international specification agreed only in the previous June, the development of equipment to meet the specification could be delayed for many months. In fact, the progress made towards the implementation of DME was such that the MCA sponsored the temporary installation of a prototype DME at Rome and Cairo to assist in establishing when to commence an aircraft descent from cruise when used by BOAC's Comet aircraft. Beacons were being installed at each stopping point, the London installation being directly associated with the VHF omni-directional range (VOR), which would provide the bearing component of the complete system. The Comet's equipment, developed and manufactured by Ferranti, Ltd., had been subjected to a series of flight trials over the previous two years involving 240 hours of operation in the air.

As if the calibration unit of CAFU was not already being pushed to the limit, it was then further stretched on May 10 as the United Kingdom National Airways system came into full operation with the airways extended to Scotland. This would involve additional navigational aids to be checked by the calibration section, as well as the probability of an increased requirement for the examining side to test those candidates requiring the necessary qualifications to fly these routes.

Lord Ogmore replaced by Hon. John Maclay as the new minister of Civil aviation.

A Stratocruiser flight-simulator for BOAC was demonstrated by Redifon Ltd.

The MCA Interdepartmental Helicopter Committee published its report, in which ten/twelve-passenger helicopters were visualized as possibly being in service by 1954.

MCA CAFU Aircraft:
DEREGISTERED

Proctor	G-AGLJ	AM/MCA	Feb 1951
Gemini	G-AJZL	MCA	Mar 1951
Anson	G-AGWF	MCA	Nov 1951
Anson	G-AHIJ	MCA	Nov 1951

During February, the single-engine Percival Proctor G-AGLJ was removed from the register as belonging to the MCA. It was subsequently reregistered to a consortium of named owners on March 15, but by April 1, 1951, it was permanently withdrawn from use, it being noted that the aircraft had "disappeared during a cross-channel flight"! According to Lloyd's, it was on a flight from Southend to Le Touquet when it disappeared.

Meanwhile, Gemini G-AJZL was sold to Shackleton, the broker, and subsequently sent abroad to Australia to be registered as VHALJ, ending its days when it belly-landed at Rockhampton, Queensland, and was burnt in 1963.

MCA CAFU Aircraft:
REGISTERED

Prince	G-AMKW	MCA	Aug 1951
Prince	G-AMKX	MCA	Aug 1951
Prince	G-AMKY	MCA	Aug 1951

In August, three Percival Princes were registered to the MCA: G-AMKW, MKX, and MKY.

These aircraft were required for the additional calibration work undertaken by the Telecommunications section. These aircraft would stay on the register until 1971.

The standard blurb on the Prince aircraft read

Percival Prince, roominess and versatility are accentuated in the all-metal, high-wing Prince, which was powered by two Alvis Leonides radial engines of 550 hp. By virtue of its nose-wheel undercarriage, the Prince rests at such an angle that the low cabin-floor is parallel with the ground.
The standard version offers a still-air range of 800 miles, carries eight passengers, a crew of two, and 400 lb of baggage. Indicative of the roominess of the cabin is the unobstructed height of 6 ft.
Opposite the large main entry door is a toilet compartment, and aft of this, a baggage space with 12.7 sq ft of floor area. Removal of the toilet bulkhead and fittings allows two additional passenger seats to be installed.
As a freighter, the Prince offers possibilities unrivalled among aircraft of its class and is provided with unobtrusive lashing-down fixtures. The adjustable chairs are upholstered in PVC-coated glass cloth and Dunlopillo padding. Radio is by Marconi.

In spite of this generous appraisal of the Prince aircraft by *Flight* magazine, Captain Gurr, in his biography, *A Testing Time,* was more critical:

The prototype was overweight and underpowered, he wrote, *and it did have three basic faults:*
1. *the nose wheel could develop a violent shimmy.*
2. *the wing was set at too low an angle of incidence in relation to the fuselage, causing unnecessary drag.*
3. *if left out in very cold weather the boiler supplying cabin heating could freeze, causing boiling water and steam to spray out in all directions.*

September saw the first MCA de Havilland DHC1 Chipmunk registered, G-AMMA. This was the first of two Chipmunks to be delivered to CAFU that were to replace the biplane Tiger Moths for the testing of candidates for the commercial pilot's licence (CPL), a daytime test known as the general flying test (GFT), as well as being used by CAFU pilots for refresher flying, and instructor rating renewal training and renewal tests.

Finally, in November, both G-AGWF and G-AHIJ, the white Anson, were sold by the MCA to Sperry Gyroscope Co. Ltd. Interestingly, both these two Ansons, G-AGWF and G-AHIJ (known as the white Elephant by Tels staff), were not retired from the register until November 1951, even though the advert (see attached photo) shows that their Certificate of Airworthiness (CoA) expired well before this date.

What is apparent from this advert is that the MCA were still calling the unit the MCA Civil Operations Fleet, in spite of the 1948 MCA Report calling it the MCA Flying Unit. Rather similar to the 1947 MCA report when the word "Operations" is dropped and the unit is simply called the MCA Fleet. With such confusion, it is hardly surprising that in 1952, the unit is called, by *Flight* magazine, the MCA "Flying Wing," and why I shall continue to call the unit CAFU.

MCA CAFU Aircraft at the end of 1951. Total = 26

Auster	01	Communication, Refresher
Tiger Mth	02	CPL tests, Refresher flying
Gemini	02	Communication. Refresher

Anson	08	Tels, VIP, Comm, O/S
Consul	05	I/R, Comm, Refresher, VIP
Dove	04	3 Tels & 1 I/R, Comm, Ref
Prince	03	Tels flight Inspection
Chipmunk	01	CPL, Instructor Rat & Ref

1952

In January 1952, there was a fatal aircraft accident involving CAFU. The CAA register database simply shows that Anson, owned by the MCA, G-AGZS, was taken off the register, having been "Destroyed—Crashed"! Ian Smith, a Tels officer at the time, remembered the accident, as did Derek Carruthers (navigator), involving a CAFU Anson flying one evening to Bournemouth, Hurn airport. The accident happened at Bell Hill, Petersfield on January 4 on its way to carry out evaluation trials on the Decca flight log in the Hampshire area.

The crew, Alec A. Betts, AFC, aged thirty-four, an MCA staff pilot since 1949, and Pat V. Meyer, aged thirty, a navigator with the MCA since 1948 at both Stansted and Prestwick. The third member of the MCA crew was Mr. A. S. Crisp, aged thirty-two, the signals officer.

The fourth occupant, Mr. J. B. Copping, had been employed by the Decca Navigator Company since December 1945. He was associated from its inception with the air section of which he ultimately became manager. His particular achievement was the conception of the flight log of which he had figured largely. The Accident Court of Enquiry was uncertain as to the cause of the accident.

Although there were other known "incidents" involving CAFU, this would be the only fatal accident that occurred with CAFU aircrew in a CAFU aircraft.

Tony Doyle did find for me an accident that happened to the newly received Prince, G-AMKW, that had a wing tip and aileron damaged by a lorry at Luton on June 9, 1952.

Even as early as 1952, there was much debate as to why ICAO was unable to choose a global standard navigational aid. The following letter was in the February *Flight* magazine:

> *I read with great interest your leader in the January 25th issue concerning navigational aids, and would endorse your viewpoint that it is very necessary to reach an early decision on short-range navigational aid policy.*

You state, however, in connection with the controversial question of VOR/DME or Decca, that "America is lined up against Europe, and particularly Britain, on this subject."
To the best of my knowledge and belief this is not according to the facts and it would be truer to say that an influential body of opinion in this country is lined up against the rest of the world, which is consequently delaying the introduction of the VOR/DME system internationally. I am sure that an approach to any of the major European airlines would confirm the correctness of this view.
London, WC2 W. GREGSON, Ferranti Ltd.

One of the pilots mentioned on detachment to Scotland was "Trader Horn." Trader, previously a telecommunications officer, had flown in the maritime navy and was later seconded to the unit. Apparently, he was not admired by one of the commanders for his alleged "slaphappy" flying and was subsequently "got rid of"! By 1952, the detachment, sent to Scotland in 1949, was gradually reduced to just one Anson, but now under the control of CAFU at Stansted. This heralded the end of the detachment altogether.

The first attempts at change in the way flight inspections were to be conducted would bring fundamental improvements that would eventually lead to the United Kingdom leading the way in enabling zero tolerance landings. Some of the immediate changes, or improvements, that the new signals officer, Mike Whitney, introduced at CAFU were

- New deputy post responsible for flight inspection;
- Aircraft (a/c) to be fitted with pen recorders;
- 35 mm camera to record a/c instruments, with a synchronised F24 camera for ground recordings;
- Decca navigator receivers to assist position fixing;
- Modifications made to commercially available airborne receivers to provide measurements of field strength and other component parts of navigational aid systems (all flight inspection equipment to be isolated from the

aircraft operational radio installation to avoid conflict with airworthiness requirements);
- A photographic laboratory to be created.
- A Tels laboratory was created where ILS and VOR signals were simulated in order to develop modifications and provide a calibration source (CAFU Calibration [CAL] BAY) for the airborne installation;
- Document systems were introduced to prescribe flight inspection procedures and the tolerances to be met. A system for reporting and certifying flight inspection results was also established.

For a description of the tasks that an ILS flight inspection entailed, see appendix C.

In July 1952, approval was given by the government for the proposed development of Gatwick as a "bad weather" alternative to Heathrow.

On September 13, the Bishop's Stortford Royal Air Force Association held an Open Day at Stansted. Aircraft seen were American F84 fighters and RAF twin-engine Meteor aircraft.

In October 1952, *Flight* magazine wrote an article on Radio Aids. What is obvious here is that the United Kingdom still had high expectations that DECCA would be accepted by ICAO as a major navigational aid. The two most likely contenders for selection as the new navigational system were the VHF omni-directional range (VOR) on 112-118 mc/s, together with distance measuring equipment (DME) on 1,000 mc/s, and the Decca system of hyperbolic navigation incorporating the automatic flight log and operating on low frequencies (100 kc/s).

VOR was recommended by ICAO as a standard aid "in localities where conditions of traffic density and low visibility necessitated a short-distance aid to navigation for the efficient exercise of air traffic control."

The United Kingdom dissented from this recommendation, as it doubted the adequacy of VOR for this purpose, and these doubts had since been confirmed, wrote *Flight,* by the inaccuracies disclosed by extensive trials in the United States, and by examination of the cost of providing VOR/DME on the scale required in Europe. For these reasons, at the recent meeting of the ICAO, COM (Communication) division, the United Kingdom took a leading part in discussing the advances made in the development and application of Decca. This resulted in a recommendation that the system should be further examined and evaluated operationally, preferably in the European region where so much cover already existed.

Broadly speaking, the advantages offered by Decca were greater accuracy and cover, pictorial presentation, about two-thirds of the cost to authorities supplying ground installations and availability for shipping purposes. On the airborne side, it was about half the cost and a little over half the weight of corresponding equipment for VOR/DME.

In addition, *Flight* also had an article on CAFU, or "*Flying Wing*" as they named it. The article is particularly worthy of printing here, though I have removed some of the least interesting parts or comments. It is probably the first time that the flight inspection work of the Civil Aviation flying unit had been described, which is why I have printed it (almost) in full:

WORK OF THE MCA FLYING WING
It is doubtful if any other factor has been of such great assistance to the development of safe and regular air transport as the world-wide acceptance of ground radio aids, so wrote *Flight* on October 3, 1952. *America favoured the DC3 for calibration work, but in Great Britain the MCA have shown that calibration can be undertaken with much smaller, and more economical, aircraft; the Percival Prince and the de Havilland Dove being the types used by the MCA—with complete success—and it is worth examining their equipment in some detail.*

The MCA navigational installations in the United Kingdom are now checked in all weathers to maintain the prescribed tolerances. Checking is also required in the investigation of complaints, or to provide data for post-accident inquiries.

The MCA Flying Wing is based at Stansted Airport, Essex, under the command of G/C. G. F. K. Donaldson, DFC, AFC (who has raced Helliwells Globe Swift during the past season). Helliwells are under contract to the MCA and have carried out the entire task of equipping the newest calibration aircraft; the design-work is done at the company's Walsall division to MCA specification.

In the Dove, G-ALFU, the following has been introduced without difficulty:

MF/HF W/T and R/T, 140-channel VHF R/T; intercom, Radio compass, SBA, ILS, Decca; radio range receiver, Radio altimeter, Autopilot, Two instrument recorders, one pen and one photographic, Drift sight; F-24 camera and—awaiting installation—Zero Readers and Decca Flight Log.

All the main flight instruments are duplicated in the cabin, where four seats are provided, although work normally requires a crew of two only.

Additional ground equipment may also be involved where extreme accuracy is required, such as long-focus cameras—F-24 with a 20 in lens—or a recording theodolite, used in conjunction with index marks on the aircraft.

The actual equipment used is as follows:

Standard STR9, STR12C (duplicated), SBA193A, Ultra intercom, SR14-15 ILS, AD709, STR30, AD86, Decca with one set of standard Decometers, Lane Identification and Flight Log (pilot type), and, soon to be installed, Ferranti DME.

The pen-recorder is an Esterline Angus product, with DC amplifier. This unit hails from Indianapolis, and it appears that no English equipment is suitable for airborne work. Signals to any instrument can be jacked into it. The instrument camera is an F.73, and the box in which it is mounted is fitted to receive suitable combinations of instruments, feeder counter, and a clock. Its use is primarily intermittent—as, for example, during bad-weather VOR calibration, when the camera might be used to tie up the VOR indication with the Decometers every 10 seconds.

In service, all the equipment is carefully checked before and after each calibration. For ILS measurement, the aircraft makes numerous approaches down the beam and the pen recorder is used to keep an accurate record of field strength while the position of the aircraft is checked; the usual instruments for the latter purpose are the Decometers for range and the radio altimeter for height.

These (and sometimes other) instruments are photographically recorded and the results analysed on the ground. It is the ultimate intention of the MCA to equip the calibration aircraft with a mobile dark-room for air-processing film. With such a facility, the ground personnel responsible for the radio aid could be given instructions to effect an adjustment within a few minutes of the initial calibrating runs; the amended emission could then be re-checked at once.

The ILS indicator cross-pointers and other instruments are also, of course, involved in ILS work but, as we saw during a recent "job," the pilot and observer can conduct an efficient calibration without being overworked. Accurate flying is essential but error in the aircraft position—perhaps due to false radio signals—can be accurately measured by the several position-recording aids previously mentioned. The autopilot is usually engaged when the aircraft is flying down an ILS beam. DME and VOR equipment is not yet in large-scale use outside the USA but British equipment is available and will be introduced when necessary; the VOR will be linked with the ILS by approach coupling, which will provide a further means of checking air calibration.

The MCA are necessarily taking radio calibration very seriously. They are, after all, the landlords at British civil airfields and to them flows revenue collected in the form of landing fees from all aircraft using their facilities. It is of far-reaching importance that, of all scheduled flights using airfields in Southern England, something less than 35 per cent are British. There is always a delicate situation when foreign traffic uses an airport and, in this country at least, no preference is given to flights by United Kingdom operators—

in fact, if there is any discrimination, the foreign aircraft is the one which benefits.

In such a sphere, the MCA are forced to admit that they are "always wrong" until they are proved right. And, if a foreign captain reports poor field-strength, or a wandering beam, it is up to the MCA Flying Wing either to confirm or refute the complaint. They are, in this country, the final air-measuring tool, capable of checking any aid or facility offered. And they are understandably interested in obtaining ICAO approval for international use of their methods and equipment.

This leads us to an even more advanced development. At the recent ICAO conference it was made mandatory that all ground aids should reach a specified standard. It was also ruled that they should be checked at regular intervals to ensure that this tolerance was maintained.

This leads to the final, and unexpected, development. The MCA are "working themselves out of a job" in that they are confident that air calibration will eventually be rendered unnecessary. Constant, regular checking of every radio facility is bound to lead to a precise knowledge of the variation of these aids and the ultimate goal is the achievement of accurate forecasting of expected variation—or, alternatively, the knowledge that the aid in question does not vary at all. When this ideal state is reached, all ground adjustment will be effected from previously determined data and the elimination of air checking will be reflected in a suitably revised ministerial budget.

As a final point, it is worth recording that the present calibration aircraft are kept as "normal" as possible, and ARB (Air Registration Board) approval is sought before any intended modification is made. The Doves and Princes have normal unrestricted C of A., and are frequently called upon to undertake passenger transport.

So there we have it, in 1952, CAFU was *"the final air measuring tool"*! And it was particularly interesting to note how the MCA (CAFU) were "working themselves out of a job"!

It is also interesting to note how *Flight* referred to CAFU as the "MCA Flying Wing," even though by now they were already known as CAFU. It also confirmed that G/C Donaldson had taken over from S/L ADL Carroll as commander by 1952.

The *Aeroplane* magazine also reported on the work of the MCA Flying Unit this year, recording that two-stage Amber screens were used in the Consuls and fitted with VHF, ADF, SBA, and ILS. The unit, it reported, was headed by the commander, G. F. K. Donaldson, DFC, AFC. In charge of A Flight, Flight Captain Carroll, license and instrument rating tests, communication and other flying. In charge of B Flight, Flight Captain Keir, telecommunications calibration, test and development flying, and Senior Navigator Officer E. "Eric" Jenkins. In charge of the Telecommunications section was Signals Officer M. F. Whitney whose duties were the organisation of unit telecommunications and experimental flying tasks, maintenance of airborne radio, and development of calibration policy. The operations officer was Mr. A. F. White (possible Allen White, an operations officer from HQ known to fly the Dove from time to time). Helliwells of Walsall were the maintenance contractor and made a speciality of designing and manufacturing, to Ministry specification, the equipment carried by the calibration aircraft. (See the photo at the end of this chapter of the aerials of the Tels Dove in 1952).

The Doves, Princes, and later the HS748s, all used the F24 camera, which photographed marker boards on the ground. This camera was synchronised with an F73 35 mm camera in the cockpit, which took simultaneous photos of the instrument panel in order to help with the assessment of the calibration. These photos were five inches by five inches.

The following year when Dove G-ANAP arrived, it was often used for ordnance survey work using an F49 camera, which was located in the floor of the fuselage. These images were nine by nine inches.

The UK original flight plan form was abolished when the MCA accepted the new ICAO recommendation of a new European standardisation with the introduction, via Information Circular no. 114/1952, of a revised Form 48.

Minister of Civil Aviation is now Mr. A. T. Lennox-Boyd.

Finally, or perhaps curiously, on December 10, a decision was made not to proceed with an extension to London Heathrow Airport.

Iain Smith, who had joined CATFU in 1947 as a radio operator was promoted and posted to Preston.

The mention previously by the *Aeroplane* of pilots in charge of A and B Flight now changes to the first mention of "deputies," when at the end of 1952, *Flight* magazine reported there were fourteen pilots, including the two "deputies" and commander. This number most likely did not include the six seconded from Headquarters in 1949.

The CAFU Pilots' Union, the Institute of Professional Civil Servants (IPCS), was negotiating with the Ministry to increase the salary of CAFU pilots. The original claim was

COMMANDER	£2,400
DEPUTY	£2,275
STAFF PILOT	£1,535-£2,115

After negotiations had failed, IPCS agreed to go to a Civil Service Arbitration Tribunal, and the union finally had to settle with

COMMANDER	£1,600
DEPUTY	£1,475
STAFF PILOT	£1,200-£1400

The increase was to be backdated to November 1, 1951.

MCA CAFU Aircraft:
DEREGISTERED

Anson	G-AGZS	MCA	Crashed
Auster	G-AGLK	AM/MCA	Aug 1952
T. Moth	G-AGRA	MCA	Aug 1852

| T. Moth | G-AGRB | MCA | Aug 1952 |
| Gemini | G-AIRS | MCA | Oct 1952 |

After the crash of the Anson in January, in August 1952 both the Tiger Moths, G-AGRA and G-AGRB, were deregistered, along with the Auster G-AGLK. Both the Moths went to the brokers of W. S. Shackleton, later to be sold abroad—GRA going to the Republic of Ireland and GRB to Belgium. The Auster, GLK, which was originally registered with the Air Ministry in 1944, also went to the brokers (more on GLK a little further on).

October saw the departure of the first Miles Gemini registered to the MCA back in 1946, G-AIRS, which almost immediately was sold on to East Anglian Flying Services Ltd., Southend, before ending up a year later with the mayor, aldermen, and burgesses of the County Borough of Southend-on-Sea. This aircraft crashed on Oxhey golf course, Watford, in March 1956, its remains broken up at Elstree.

Aeroplane for October 24, 1952, had reported that CAFU had eighteen aircraft: the Princes, Chipmunk, Consuls, and Gemini were the same as below. But they inexplicably report only three Doves, which they reported as for calibration work, so somehow they missed the single IR Dove, LVS, that was registered in October 1949 and surely with the unit by 1952. They then reported the number of Avro 19s or Ansons to be five, which could well be correct, as two of the Ansons, GWE and GZT, were deregistered in January 1953 and had probably stopped flying when *Aeroplane* visited Stansted.

MCA CAFU Aircraft at the end of 1952, Total = 21

Anson	07	Tels, Comm, O/S, VIP
Consul	05	I/R, VIP, Comm, Ref flying
Gemini	01	Communication, Ref flying
Dove	04	3 Tels & 1 I/R, Comm, Ref
Prince	03	Tels Flight Inspection
Chipmunk	01	CPL, Instructor Ratings, Ref

1953

Mr. A. C. "Charles" Marchant—who had spent six years with the Royal Navy working on radio and radar equipment and after the war worked in the Wireless Development Branch of the Post Office—joined the MCA's Telecommunications Branch and was soon moved to CAFU at Stansted Airport, where he was taken on as Mike Whitney's deputy ASO (assistant signals officer). Mr. Marchant later became superintendent himself when Mike Whitney was further promoted to Headquarters later in the 1950s.

MCA CAFU Aircraft:

DEREGISTERED

Anson	G-AGWE	MCA	Jan 1953
Anson	G-AGZT	MCA	Jan 1953

REGISTERED

Dove	G-ANAP	MCA	July 1953

At the very beginning of the year, two more Ansons were retired—G-AGWE, going to The Decca Navigation Co. Ltd., and G-AGZT, going to Jersey with Channel Air Services Ltd.

However, in July, CAFU had another Tels Dove, the fourth, registered G-ANAP, although this was principally remembered as being used for Ordnance Survey work and GCA Target Training at Bournemouth, Hurn Airport.

This year, one of the flight inspection Doves from CAFU, G-ALFT, was exhibited at Farnborough. It was one of two Doves in the static park, the other a more conventional six-seater showing the versatility of the type.

Occasional VIP flights were flown, most likely in the Consul or Anson, carrying ministers around the country. The sole IR Dove at this time would have been far too busy to release.

According to the Civil Aviation Ensign Order 1937, the "Ensign may be 'flown' by any aircraft registered in the UK at any licensed aerodrome in the UK and at an air transport operators place of business," and can still be seen on some civil aircraft today. It is first seen on the fin of the MCA aircraft in photographs of the first two Austers and Tiger Moths used by the COF. What is intriguing, were they put on by the Air Ministry or not until taken over by the MCA? I think it was the Air Ministry, as at Croydon in 1944, they did need to indicate that they were not military. In which case, the MCA, when handed the aircraft, simply carried on the tradition. Certainly the photographs do show most of the aircraft with the Ensign, though it was never seen on the Gemini or Consuls.

The flag, the Civil Air Ensign, a light (Royal Air Force) blue flag with a darker blue cross edged with white providing four quarters: the port side of the fin held the Union flag within the top left quarter and the starboard side of the fin had the Union flag in the top right quarter.

Although the silver, white, and black aircraft displayed this flag, it did appear on every aircraft that later had the red, white, and black livery.

The question of the flying unit's cost and efficiency was always an issue. At the Lords, in January, questions were now being asked as to what duties were carried out by the MCA flying Unit, and were told,

> *My Lords, the Minister of Civil Aviation is responsible for the safety of civil air transport in these islands. This entails, among other things, providing and operating the radio and radar services and the ground lighting required. It also entails licensing civil aircrew. The aircraft of the Ministry of Civil Aviation Flying Unit are employed on work essential to these two duties.*
> *On navigational services My Lords, the Minister of Civil Aviation is responsible for the safety of civil air transport in these islands.*
> *On navigational services, this work consists of continuous Flight testing and calibration of aids; and of operational trials of procedures and development flying.*

The Flying Unit is also used for training ground control approach crews and for maintaining flying standards of operations officers at Headquarters.

As regards civil aircrew, the Flying Unit examines candidates for instrument rating certification and commercial pilot's licences.

The Unit is not provided for the transport of Ministers and officials. Commercial operators are available for this. It is, however, occasionally used for departmental communications where these can be combined with the programme of specialist duties.

At the beginning of this year, there were thirteen pilots and seventeen aircraft, shortly to be reduced to fourteen.

Having learnt that the flying unit had cost £210,000 in the fiscal year 1951-1952, Lord Balfour then asked if the minister would examine if some of the functions, such as the testing of pilots and calibration of tests, could be carried out more economically and just as successfully, by delegating them to other air operational bodies, in the same way that the safety of aircraft was made the responsibility of the Air Registration Board.

The Earl of Selkirk replied:

My Lords, I am sure that my right honourable friend will examine anything which might reasonably be an economy in the administration of his Department and that he will examine carefully what the noble Lord, who speaks with such great experience on this question, has said. I must point out, however, that the duties of this Unit are of a highly technical character, requiring very special equipment to be carried in the aircraft, and these aircraft cannot be used easily for alternative purposes. May I also point out, in regard to this work of calibration, which closely relates to safety, that the Minister would be most reluctant to delegate any of his duties in this field? At the same time, I am sure the Minister will look carefully at what the noble Lord has said to see whether anything can be done on the lines he has suggested.

Lord Ogmore then replied:

My Lords, would the noble Earl also refer his right honourable friend to the fact that this is a most efficient Unit, and that if there is any attempt to break it up, the result will undoubtedly be a falling off of efficiency and an increase in the danger to air communication in this country?

The Earl of Selkirk then "entirely endorsed" what the noble Lord had just said and further stated:

The Ministry of Civil Aviation Flying Unit is a very efficient unit, and I can say quite definitely that there is not the slightest intention to break it up. What I have said is that there may be certain duties which conceivably could be parted with; but at the present time it appears, from the duties carried out by the Unit, that a very fair utilisation of the more modern aircraft is, in fact, achieved.

As early as this, it can be noted that changes at CAFU could and would be made at an appropriate time.

This year was to see the further development of the main runway at Stansted airport. The United States Air Force was negotiated to lengthen and widen the main 05/23 runway from its present 6000 feet by 150 feet to over 10,000 feet (10,016) by 200 feet wide. The purpose of this was to facilitate a modern American jet bomber base, in order to be a main standby base for the NATO forces' heavy bomber fleet. This extension work to the runway was expected to take three years. During the extension to runway 05/23, all flights would use taxiway two for take-off and landing, situated between the main runway and the (then) control tower.

ATC told the story of Dan Carroll, one-time commander of CAFU, now examining candidates for CPL and IR tests, when making a landing always referring to the taxiway/runway as either "finals for 23 right" or "05 left"!

Also in 1953, Mr. Alan Lennox-Boyd, now the minister for Transport and Civil Aviation, announced Gatwick as London's second airport. The old airport was then closed for major redevelopment. This would have explained the necessity for CAFU to relocate when it did back in 1950.

Group Captain George Donaldson was due to retire. He had "held the fort" during various changes to the administrative structure, and he now appointed Capt. "Jock" Keir as the new commander. Captain Keir had a very good wartime record as a bomber pilot who was absolutely fearless. It was a surprise, I was told, as he was more in the style of Dan Carroll, again not the scientific pilot that would perhaps have been best suited to the job. Captain B. E. E. "Bee" Marshall was now appointed as Jock's deputy, who supervised the unit's examining standards.

In 1953, the MCA, in order to meet the demands of companies and crews wishing to fly commercially, as well as use the new airway structure set up within the United Kingdom and Europe, began taking on more staff. At CAFU, there were two grades in the staff pilot class: grade I pilots were those who held flying instructor qualifications and were trained to be the examiners who conducted practical flying tests on candidates wishing to gain a commercial pilot's licence (CPL), and/or to obtain an instrument rating (IR) in order to be able to fly in controlled airspace—such as airways or airfield control areas and zones—which could not be flown into unless under the specific instruction and guidance of air traffic control. At this time, all flying tests for the initial issue of the CPL and or IR were conducted by examiners from CAFU. Although the grade I pilots were employed in all the tasks of the unit, the grade II pilots were either new recruits, with the necessary qualifications but awaiting promotion, or they did not have instructing experience and were therefore employed on those tasks that did not involve training or testing of other pilots, such as communication flights, calibration of radio aids to navigation, photographic survey, and target flying for ATC radar controllers.

All grade I pilots were, therefore, required to be qualified on and maintain competency on all of the CAFU aircraft: Anson, Oxford,

Dove, Prince, and Chipmunk. Newly recruited pilots to CAFU were all experienced flying instructors with either a civil or military background, and quickly became qualified to undertake all the unit's many different tasks.

Duties as a whole were assigned on a weekly basis, usually alternating between a week of local flying followed by a week away from base (AFB); both examining and calibration duties could be either assigned as local or AFB for one week, such as to Scotland, or GCA target training conducted at the school of ATC at Bournemouth, (Hurn) airport. On fine weather days, mapping flights were made with the Anson for the conduct of aerial photography on behalf of Ordnance Survey.

It is also understood that some of the CAFU pilots were freelance flying as this was not frowned upon—at this time.

The Ministry structure for telecommunications at this time had a number of directorates whose functions were to see that an up-to-date and efficient system of radio navigational aids and communications was planned, provided, and maintained. The requirements that this system had to meet could come from the Directorate of Control and Navigation, from new ICAO standards, from the growth of traffic, or from engineering progress. It was composed of three deputy directorates. CAFU was mostly associated with the deputy directorate (DD) of Tels E (Engineering), although it was the Directorate of Aviation (Technical) 2 (DDAT2) that lay down policy to administer.

The deputy directorate of Telecommunications (Engineering) (DD of Tels E) was responsible for specifying, obtaining, and putting into service the electronic equipment needed at civil aviation ground stations and for laying down the standards to which this equipment must be maintained. It was also responsible for the approval of aircraft radio equipment and controlled the Radio Measuring Station (RMS) and the Installation Test and Repair Unit (ITRU), which, in addition to the duties indicated in its name, cooperated with the MCA Flying Unit in the calibration of radio navigational aids and manufactured special equipment on a small scale. The RMS monitored civil aviation radio stations and had general responsibility for the accuracy of all MCA radio test equipment.

One of the first tasks assigned to Charles Marchant as the deputy superintendent was to evaluate a system, proposed by his boss Mike Whitney that accurately measured the height of an aircraft when calibrating the ILS. It involved photographing markers on the ground and the use of mathematical equations, which, after successfully trialling a system on the ground, was then passed to the MCA Operational Research Branch (ORB), which required a satisfactory report before allowing them to continue.

The CAFU navigators were involved in organising markers on the ground at all of the necessary airports, which took some time to complete, as well as taking on the film readings and the calculations required for use in later ground analysis.

Flight inspection work during this period involved flight checking en route aids such as radio ranges at Watford, Epsom, Dunsfold, and Maidstone in the South and Burtonwood in the Manchester area and Prestwick in Scotland. Fan markers were also checked at this time, as they assisted both as positional markers for the en route aids and in conjunction with the landing aids such as SBA and the new instrument landing system. GCA, the radar ground controlled approach aid, was also checked, while MF direction finding was giving way to the more popular VHF direction-finding aid.

The Bishop's Stortford branch of the Royal Air Force Association held their second Air Display at Stansted Airport on September 26. There was a varied programme of static and display flying. Some seven thousand spectators enjoyed the Meteors from North Weald in formation, more formation flying by Sabres from North Luffenham, and by contrast, Chipmunks of the Cambridge Reserve School.

A red-trimmed Meteor gave an aerobatic display, and in the afternoon, visitors enjoyed four Canberra from Binbrook, while the USAF at Wethersfield sent F84 Thunderjets doing low-level passes across the airfield.

CAFU was involved both in the flying and static display, as G/C G. F. K. Donaldson did a purposely unpolished display of crazy flying in a Tiger Moth. However, this would not have been either of the CAFU Tigers as GRA and GRB had retired in August the previous year, and the group captain probably used a Tiger owned by Helliwell.

During the mid-afternoon interval, the static show proved a worthy visit. Among the MCA Telecommunications Unit's exhibits was a Prince, as well as an ingenious model showing SBA, ADF, and ILS operation. Most of this report was printed by *Flight* magazine, but what wasn't known is that the model was a cooperative effort by two of the CAFU Tels engineers, Freddie Constable and Iain Smith (Iain's electric train set being the motive power for the aircraft and Freddie's remarkable expertise in modelling making it such a success).

Helliwell Ltd., maintenance contractor for the MCA Flying Unit at Stansted, showed a Dove's retracting nose wheel.

Geoff Gurr reports that there was a steady, never-ending stream of candidates for the CPL and IR tests. The daytime CPL General Flying Test (GFT), no longer taken in the open cockpit of the Tiger Moth biplane, was now undertaken in the more comfortable DHC Chipmunk. Unlike the RAF service Chipmunks, CAFU did not use a parachute, but did have the parachute seating element to park one's bum.

The instrument rating test was still conducted using the Airspeed Consul, using the amber screens and blue-tinted goggles for another couple of years, a system unloved by "Bee" Marshall, the now deputy commander.

Around the middle of October, after eight years, the MCA was merged with the Ministry of Transport (MOT) to become the Ministry of Transport and Civil Aviation (MTCA). Following the formation of the MTCA, it was reorganised to form the Civil Aviation Safety and Licensing Directorate.

This was the first of a number of Ministry changes that CAFU "endured" perhaps a sign that government was already requiring costs to be cut, though civil aviation was still in a period of rapid advancement.

Each time there was a change of Ministry, CAFU not only had to change official headed paper, but it was also necessary to change the uniform buttons and badges of the aircrew! It was always interesting to see the variety of badges as most of the aircrew waited until they required new uniforms.

Mr. A. Lennox-Boyd was the MTCA minister.

MCA CAFU Aircraft at the end of 1953 Total = 20

Miles	01	Communication, Refresher
Anson	05	Tels, Comm, O/S, VIP
Consul	05	I/R, Comm, Refresher, VIP
Dove	05	4 Tels & 1 I/R, Comm, Ref
Prince	03	Tels Flight Inspection
Chipmunk	01	CPL, Instructor Ratings, Ref.

1954

Aircraft maintenance for CAFU aircraft at Stansted was still carried out under contract by Helliwell, who were carrying out the entire task of equipping the newest calibration aircraft, design of which was carried out at their company Walsall division, to Ministry specifications.

MTCA CAFU Aircraft:
REGISTERED

| Dove | G-ANOV | MTCA | Mar 1954 |

MTCA CAFU Aircraft:
DEREGISTERED

Anson	G-AGWA	MCA	Jan 1954
Anson	G-AGUD	MCA	July 1954
Anson	G-AGVA	MCA	July 1954
Anson	G-AHIC	MCA	Oct 1954
Anson	G-AHIH	MCA	Nov 1954

In January, the first of the remaining five Ansons, G-AGWA, followed by G-AGUD and G-AGVA in July, G-AHIC in October, and finally, G-AHIH in November, were all retired. G-AHIC went to the College of Aeronautics at Cranfield, and the other four to the Wiltshire School of Flying.

It was a long time coming, but the second instrument rating de Havilland Dove, G-ANOV, was registered to the MTCA. This now left CAFU crews with just three main aircraft to be cleared on, Consul, Dove, and Prince.

Lloyd's reported in April that Prince, G-AMKX, had the nose leg of the undercarriage collapse while being towed at Luton; the exact date was not stated nor the extent of the damage.

Bill Eames, later to become chief officer at Belfast, Nutts Corner, Northern Ireland, told me that Trader Horn was still with the unit this year. Bill was doing his GCA training for air traffic control officers at the School at Bournemouth (not yet a college). He was invited to fly in a Consul of which Trader was the pilot. "When I told him I was a pilot, he sat back, folded his arms, and said, 'You have control.'"

In July, John Boyd-Carpenter was appointed minister of Transport and Civil Aviation (MTCA) by Winston Churchill.

In a paper written by Charles Marchant circa 2000, he explains the development of Flight Inspection Techniques in this period:

FLIGHT INSPECTION TECHNIQUES
In the initial years of flight inspection the methods used were largely subjective and dependent on the judgement and skill of the experienced pilots and navigators. Notably there was a lack of recorded evidence to confirm the findings to be used for post flight enquiries and analysis. There being inadequate documentation to prescribe procedures to underpin the methods being used.
By 1950 two factors had emerged which clearly influenced subsequent developments:
Basically flight inspection should be the comparison of the actual position of an aircraft with the position being indicated by the navigational aid under test. This should be done using measurement systems which have an order of accuracy considerably better than the tolerances allowed for the aid under test. Additionally, field strength and coverage, the component parts of a received signal and the presence and nature of interference should be examined.

Although the VOR was not yet officially adopted, as the ICAO preferred short-range navigational aid, most airliners already had VOR receivers fitted.

CAFU was increasingly asked to calibrate the new aids; Captain Gurr recalls flying a Tels Dove to Germany, with Charles Marchant acting as the NAI in order to do commissioning work on newly installed VORs at Dusseldorf, Hannover, and Hamburg.

Charles Marchant recalled there were four NAIs in 1950, all volunteers and all hoping for a flying allowance, which the Ministry was reluctant to give: "a recipe for trouble," he tells.

VOR equipment was being installed increasingly throughout Europe, especially at the busy traffic points near airports. London Airport had the Marconi VOR installed and tested on an operational basis, and it was found to give satisfactory results. More of these navigational aids were expected to be installed at suitable places in the United Kingdom to provide guidance on the airways. It was expected that until all airline operators' aircraft were fitted with suitable receivers, the VOR would not displace the present MF ranges (although accepted as being very unsatisfactory) that formed the basis of the current UK airway system.

Finally, in Information Circular no. 154/1954, the MTCA stated that a detailed programme for phasing-in ground and airborne installations was to be drawn up, and it was hoped that the VOR would be available on all UK airways by 1958.

It was in 1954 when the Fifth Session of the ICAO Communications Division recommended states to develop a long-range navigational system. The division specifically mentioned four projects as warranting further development; these were the Decca Navigator Company's Decora and Delrac, and the US Navaho and Navaglobe.

The division also mentioned Loran and Consol as good interim systems.

A story that Charles Marchant later tells in his paper to the Royal Institute of Navigation in 2006 is one that emphasised the importance of the work that CAFU was trying to achieve in the improvement of calibration in this period.

The story he tells is of his involvement in a post-accident flight inspection where CAFU crew and aircraft were made available on weekends and public holidays. However, the four navaid inspectors, who were still hankering after a flying allowance, withdrew their goodwill over this Christmas period. In his role as manager and confident that an accident was unlikely to happen, he rashly agreed that over this Christmas period, he would assume the duties of the disgruntled NAIs.

But in the early hours of Christmas Day 1954, a BOAC Stratocruiser, guided by the GCA and possibly by ILS, touched down just short of runway threshold, bounced up, then down, breaking a wing and turning over. The passenger compartment became detached and caught fire, with the loss of twenty-four lives.

A post-accident flight inspection was required, and 7:00 a.m. on Christmas morning found Charles driving to Croydon, where, because Stansted was closed for the holiday, a Dove was parked in case of emergency. So with Pilot "Bee" Marshall and Navigator "Bunny" Austen, they set off for Prestwick. At Prestwick, it was found that the ILS was off, but repeated flights on the GCA using the altimeter method for judging glide path angle showed the glide path to be out of tolerance.

At the subsequent accident inquiry, the MCA chief engineer was given a hard time under cross-examination, but in the accident report by the commissioner, it was stated:

In our opinion the attacks made in the course of the Inquiry on the GCA system and. the staff engaged in operating it were wholly unjustified. Flight checking cannot always be relied upon to test the Glide Path with absolute accuracy. It is not possible accurately to test a machine of the utmost sensitivity by use of a testing apparatus which in its very nature is less sensitive. It is gratifying to learn that a new and improved system of flight checking by photography is being tried out and will, it is hoped, in due time be completed. This will eliminate the possible errors in the present system of flight checking.
At CAFU, said Charles, *we felt that, if belatedly, we were nevertheless following the right course.*

The Airspeed Consul aircraft were nearing the end of their time with CAFU in their IR testing role. They were developed from the RAF Oxford advanced training aircraft and fitted out, Geoff Gurr reports, with a "two-stage amber" system to simulate instrument flight conditions for candidates under test. Amber-coloured Perspex panels were attached to the cockpit windows, and the candidate under test wore goggles fitted with dark blue lenses, which had the effect of making the windows appear black, as in night conditions—except that the candidate had no external vision at all—while a cockpit floodlight illuminated the instruments. As far as CAFU was concerned, the system was never entirely satisfactory because, in spite of the application of antifogging treatment, as well as a tube to suck out any moisture, the goggles tended to steam up. Also, there were four different coloured blue lenses to be selected by the examiner to suit the lighting condition of the day. If the wrong coloured lenses were selected for the goggles, or the lighting conditions changed, then either partial vision was restored to the candidate or the lighting was too dark to see the cockpit instruments! Even the Perspex amber panels could become scratched, which then reduced the examiner's ability to see.

When the second IRT Dove, G-ANOV, was registered to CAFU in March 1954, and in preparation for the departure of the Consuls, Captain "Bee" Marshall, who was dissatisfied with the method of Amber Screening for the conduct of tests, devised a system of angled screens. Effectively, they were venetian blinds that could be used in natural lighting conditions in daylight. They were painted light grey to simulate cloudy conditions, with sprung-loaded mountings for quick installation and removal. They were successfully trialled in September with the new IR Dove and were to be fitted into three new IRT Doves expected the following year.

MTCA CAFU Aircraft at the end of 1954 Total = 16

Gemini	01	Communications, Ref flying
Consul	05	I/R, VIP, Comm, Ref flying
Dove	06	3 Tels & 3 I/R, Comm, Ref
Prince	03	Tels Flight Inspection
Chipmunk	01	CPL, Instructor Ratings, Ref

1955

The initial move from Gatwick to Stansted, made in 1950, was thought to be only temporary; even in the midfifties, rumour was still rife that CAFU would be moving again. However, towards the end of this decade, the move of CAFU to Stansted, wrote Geoff Gurr, was at long last believed to be permanent.

By now, the grade I pilots at CAFU were no longer known as "staff pilots" but flight examiners (FE).

In the fifties, CAFU aircraft were used for GCA target training of air traffic control officers (ATCOs) at the School of ATC at Bournemouth, Hurn Airport. In an article from the 2001 *Transmission Lines* ("Radio Trainers and ATC Memories") by Brian Pegden, he recalled CAFU using Consul, Dove, and Prince aircraft. As the aircraft were flown by a single pilot, air traffic staff were encouraged to act as observer or "safety pilot" in the right-hand seat operating the R/T (radio telephony), allowing the pilot to concentrate on flying instructions given by the student ATCOs.

Towards the end of the year, BEA announced their decision to adopt DECCA as their short-range navigational aid. It was hardly surprising as Europe was better covered by Decca at this time, and the United Kingdom appeared to be backing it in preference to the VOR. However, BEA also intended to fit VOR receiver equipment, though with the proviso that

> *DME would probably never be provided in Europe, particularly in the light of the recent TACAN developments and that VOR deployed in Europe would, in the main, provide only airway track guidance of less than optimum quality.*

This step was necessary in order to comply with ICAO's "by-either-of-two-means" requirement, since full Decca coverage would not be immediately available on all the BEA routes.

The instrument landing system (ILS), which was developed after experience supporting the RAF BABS system, was adopted by the Royal Air Force in 1946. Further development of the design followed, and in 1955, it was adopted by ICAO for use at civil airfields in the United Kingdom and overseas. It is believed that the first European Civil installation was at Geneva.

The equipment was primarily intended for use as an aid to the landing of aircraft under conditions of poor visibility, but it quickly became useful as a standard approach aid in all circumstances. The complete system comprised a "localiser" transmitter, providing guidance in azimuth along the extended centre line of the runway; a "glide-path" transmitter provided guidance in elevation along a sloping path, which intersected with the ground at the optimum point of contact; and three "marker beacons" transmitters spaced along the approach path, which provided an indication of distance from touchdown. The complete system was monitored from a separate "remote control console" located in the main airfield control building. ILS would subsequently be developed to enable fully automatic approach and landing. ICAO finally adopted ILS as the international *standard* landing aid.

The tenth anniversary general meeting by the Technical Committee of IATA in New York, provided to member airlines, stated that Air Navigation was not keeping up with Air Transport developments—ground facilities were lagging behind.

Criteria for IFR (instrument flight rules) had to be revised. The ultimate solution would be the full control of all air traffic.

In communication, the Morse key was fast becoming obsolete.

The controversy in the USA over short-range navigation, TACAN and VOR, had caused countries to hold back their VOR programme. TACAN was still not proven, and governments were urged to fulfil the ICAO regional plans for VOR networks at the earliest opportunity.

Harold Watkinson was now the minister of Transport and Civil Aviation (MTCA).

The new Heathrow ATC Tower was due to be in operation on April 17. Using full talk-downs, a three-minute landing rate could be achieved, using techniques such as radar-monitored ILS landings, however, this figure could be improved, and a peak movement rate (landings and take-offs) of fifty aircraft per hour was planned for the immediate future.

Meanwhile at Stansted, in spite of the construction work on the 05/23 runway during 1955, Stansted was still relatively busy with over fifty-two thousand passengers using the airport. Importantly, in spite of the increased volume of air traffic, CAFU was still able to function with little, if any, difficulty.

MTCA CAFU Aircraft:
REGISTERED

DHC1	G-ANWB	MTCA	Feb 1955
Dove	G-ANUT	MTCA	Feb 1955
Dove	G-ANUU	MTCA	Mar 1955
Dove	G-ANUW	MTCA	May 1955

February saw the registration to the MTCA of the second DHC1 Chipmunk, G-ANWB, which brought back the numbers to two single-engine aircraft after the retirement of the two Tiger Moths back in 1952. The Chipmunks were used to conduct daytime general flying tests (GFTs) on candidates attempting to gain their commercial pilot's licence, and the second aircraft would assist in the ever-growing demand for these tests. As well as being used for the day element of the CPL, the Chipmunk aircraft also provided refresher flying for internal staff, as well as enabling examiners to keep up to date and maintain their instructor rating.

Following the change from the old Air Ministry "B" licence to the new MTCA CPL, tests were now more comprehensive, including basic handling (day and night), instrument flying on both full and partial panel, cross-country flights (day and night), and some radio navigation using direction-finding (DF) bearings. The nighttime element of the GFT (known as a GFT4) was conducted on twin-engine aircraft. Up until this time, night tests were flown at Southend or Croydon, as Stansted had no night flying facilities.

In February came the third instrument rating DH104 Dove, G-ANUT, followed closely by the fourth, G-ANUU in March, followed by the fifth and final IR Dove G-ANUW in May, making its first flight with CAFU on July 1, 1955. This now allowed CAFU pilots time to familiarise themselves fully with the new aircraft before the retirement of the Consuls. These IR Doves could be easily converted from the IRT configuration to a six-seat executive layout, with toilet facilities, for VIP and communication flights when required.

The first of the Airspeed Consuls to leave was G-AJXF, which went to Skyways in September; and the second, G-AJXE, left for BKS Transport Ltd. around November.

Finally, in September, the third and last Gemini, G-AKDD, was deregistered going off to Air Charter. This aircraft was later to crash in the sea in March 1963, off Warden Point, Isle of Sheppey, the wreck later dragged ashore at Leigh-on-Sea and taken by road to Stapleford; Eric Thurston now being the owner.

MTCA CAFU Aircraft:
DEREGISTERED

Gemini	G-AKDD	MTCA	Sept 1955
Consul	G-AJXF	MTCA	Sept 1955
Consul	G-AJXE	MTCA	Nov 1955

CAFU Aircraft at the end of 1955. Total = 17

Consul	03	I/R, VIP, Comm, Ref flying
Dove	09	4 Tels & 5 I/R, Comm, Ref
Prince	03	Tels Flight Inspection
Chipmunk	02	CPL, Instructor Ratings, Ref

1956

On March 1, ICAO introduced a change to the phonetic alphabet, from the well-known and liked wartime phonetic alphabet to a modern, at the time, alien-sounding one. The Pilots Association were particularly aggrieved at not being consulted and mourned the loss, at least, of "Able Baker Charlie Dog." At CAFU, it now meant the IR Dove, "Uncle William" would now be called "Uniform Whisky," which seemed almost like losing a dear relative, while the Dove "Fox Tare," though now more of a mouthful, had a somewhat musical ring.

OLD	**NEW**
Able	Alpha
Baker	Bravo
Charlie	Charlie
Dog	Delta
Easy	Echo
Fox	Foxtrot
George	Golf
How	Hotel
Item	India
Jig	Juliet
King	Kilo
Love	Lima
Mike	Mike
Nan	November
Oboe	Oscar
Peter	Papa
Queen	Quebec
Roger	Romeo
Sugar	Sierra
Tare	Tango
Uncle	Uniform
Victor	Victor
William	Whiskey
X-ray	X-ray
Yoke	Yankee
Zebra	Zulu

The change was particularly noticeable when asking for the pressure settings or QNH, which the earlier radio operators had to tap in Morse, "Queen Nan How." But of course, with VHF, they would now be asking for the "Quebec November Hotel"—although it was not unheard of for a pilot to ask air traffic for the "November Handicap"—during the appropriate season.

MTCA CAFU Aircraft:
DEREGISTERED

Consul	G-AJXG	MTCA	Jan 1956
Consul	G-AJXH	MTCA	Jan 1956
Consul	G-AJXI	MTCA	Aug 1956

Right at the beginning of this year, the third and fourth Airspeed Consuls were retired; JXG going to BKS and JXH off to Eagle Air Services. It would not be until August that the last Consul would disappear when G-AJXI went to the brokers yard of W. S. Shackleton Ltd.

A letter in *Flight* for 1956 pondered on some of the anomalies of ICAO:

The convention is not a law unto itself, has no tribunal or penalizing authority. It does, however, succeed in unifying a large amount of aviation practice and, though it continues to win a measure of agreement, one is surprised to find such extraordinary anomalies as still exist. For example, a Belgian Commercial Pilot's Licence may not be exchanged for the French equivalent; the MTCA in this country will accept neither, and in many other countries there is no reciprocal arrangement for crew licensing either.

It was the United Kingdom's view that Decca was the finest available short-range aid and had placed on record that it was their official intention to designate Decca as the aid on which UK air traffic procedures would be based. At the same time, although refusing to provide 1,000 mc/s DME stations for BOAC use, they would retain the VOR. It was thought that VOR/DME was not sufficiently accurate in azimuth to permit lateral separation in air traffic, and neither was the comparable US system known as TACAN. This aid, which operated in the 1,000 mc/s band, was a bearing-distance system but, according to official US reports, would appear to do very little more than VOR/DME could do.

Decca, on the other hand, was entirely suitable for lateral separation procedures, while VOR alone was seen as a valuable secondary aid, especially as a single airborne receiver could be used to receive both VOR and ILS with very little extra weight.

Two British systems were selected by ICAO for development as long-range navigational aids. These were Dectra and Delrac, and discussions were already in progress with the Decca Navigator Company aimed at installing an experimental Dectra layout covering the Prestwick Gander route. Trials were expected to begin in the near future. Dectra was an adaptation of Decca to cover a specific route, whereas Decca covered an area.

A perceptive letter was written to *Flight* in June that perhaps indicated the frustration as aviation industry (internationally) awaited a single standard of short range navigation to be set.

> *I read with interest and sympathy the article "Spring Cleaning the Annex," by "Visor" (Flight, May 18).*
> *All his arguments are sound and valid, but I fear he will in time become tired and depressed battering his head against the MTCA. The Ministry follows slavishly, and even improves upon, the standards and recommended practices of ICAO, standards designed to cover pilots of the whole world, good, bad, and indifferent.*
> *There must be moderation and adaptation in all matters. As our manufacturers are finding, it is no use to have very high standards and price oneself out of the markets. The burden of Government regulation may yet prove a greater drain on the taxpayer than he will feel able to pay.*
> *Woking, Surrey. D. F. SATCHWELL.*

MTCA CAFU Aircraft at the end of 1956 Total = 14

Dove	09	4 Tels & 5 I/R, OS, Comm, Ref, GCA
Prince	03	Tels Flight Inspection
Chipmunk	02	CPL, Instructor Ratings, Ref flying

1957

The extension to the main runway, which the Americans had started in 1953, was completed in April. Runway 05/23 was now 10,065 feet by 200 feet wide. To taxi from the CAFU pans for take-off on runway 23, they only needed to travel down taxiway 2 to the second intersection for a six-thousand-foot runway length, more than enough distance for all their aircraft to take off. There was never any requirement for the CAFU aircraft to cross the runway and further taxi down taxiway 4 to use the full length of the main runway.

Now that the airport had the huge extension to the main runway, it was probably from this point that CAFU commenced nighttime tests (GFT4s) in the IR Doves at Stansted due to the installation of bidirectional runway lighting, as well as approach lighting at both ends of the new extended runway.

Group Captain Douglas Bader, of WWII fame, and now in charge of the Shell executive fleet, successfully passed his initial IRT with CAFU at Stansted.

There was an increasing number of aids to be flight inspected in this era as more airways were being defined. At long last, ICAO had specified that VOR (VHF omni-directional range) with DME (distance-measuring equipment) should be the international standard short-range navaid for ATC purposes. But most authorities, including those in certain aviation circles, even in the United States, considered that VOR/DME was insufficiently accurate to permit any relaxation of separation standards. No 1,000 mc/s DME was installed in the United Kingdom at this time.

As promised back in 1954, the installation of a number of VORs had taken place in the United Kingdom. The first UK VORs installed were probably American, either Wilcox or Collins. They were installed at the extremities, or conflux of an airway; such as Green One, Strumble in the West to Dover in the East; Amber One, Seaford to Daventry; Amber Two, Lydd and Daventry. On Green Two, there was Halifax and Wallasey; and Red Three had Wallasey and the Isle of Man. Other VORs at this time were Clacton, Dungeness (later Lydd), IoM, Speke, and Bristol (later Brecon).

There were still radio ranges in the London TMA (terminal area) at Watford, Epsom, and Dunsfold, and there were a score or more of non-directional beacons (NDBs) on the airways together with a dozen or more fan markers to provide positioning along them.

A new upper limit to the height of the airway, above the present level of eleven thousand feet, was expected to be brought into operation during this year—but probably only when inhabited by the big jets. This problem was being discussed with the NATO Committee on European Airspace Coordination, and next year, it would come under the province of ICAO's Europe-Mediterranean Regional Air Navigation Meeting.

In order to expedite the handling of the increasing traffic between Britain and the continent, a number of new airways was proposed for this year:

> Blue X, a new airway to Belgium
> Red One, to Holland, passing over the Clacton area
> Blue Three and Blue Y, new airways between Cap Gris Nez and the United Kingdom (Belgium via Dover had been realigned)

Easterly extensions from the London Control Zone would eventually replace the easterly legs of Red One and Green One on the old airway map. The airways to Belgium and Holland were expected to be in operation in April 1957, and airways Blue Three and Blue Y by the end of that year.

It is always sad to mention just a few names, or at least to forget to mention certain people. There were countless characters making a memorable contribution to CAFU. The late forties saw the arrival of Jock Hunter. Jock had been shot down during WWII in North Africa and had had a long desert walk, taking a fortnight to get back to his base, a fact not commonly known until his funeral in the late nineties. Jock became one of the most feared examining pilots at the unit, a reputation given by his insistence and adherence to the rules of the tests (as well as his seemingly fierce demeanour). Candidates either loved or hated him, according to their flying ability. What is absolutely certain is that he was one of the fairest pilots who examined candidates for commercial and instrument rating tests.

Geoff Gurr, who later became a deputy commander and was one of the first principal flight examiners (PFEs) to be integrated with the Flight Operations Inspectorate before being selected as the commander in the seventies. Bill Wooden, also a deputy commander, looked after aspects of airline inspection and later the HS125, also assisting in the development and acceptance of simulators in the quest for zero flight-time training and testing on type, eventually ending up as chief flight operations inspector (CFOI) in the seventies.

Jack Picken was another well-respected pilot. He later became a deputy commander looking after all flying aspects of the Telecommunications section, also flying trials of new ground proximity warning equipment being introduced in the late 1970s. He is particularly well remembered for his artistic skills, as most of the crew members had a caricature drawn by him and hung on the walls of the building in the 1950s and 1960s.

Don Hale, another pilot who joined in the 1950s, later worked in the All Weather Operations Department at HQ in London, as well as becoming flight service manager at CAAFU in the seventies. Capt. Hughie McDowall, a flight examiner in the fifties, was later associated with much of the microwave landing system testing in the seventies. Jimmy Joy, later to manage the HS125 operations in the seventies, was another hugely respected man.

Names remembered by Brian Pegden when acting as observer on the GCA target flights, from his days at the School of ATC, Hurn, were Captains Don Tucker, R. O. "Bob" Whitehead (both Battle of Britain pilots), Len Yard, J. A. "Tony" Reid, John Belson, Roy Westgate, Ian Selwyn, and a couple of operations officers, John Stead and (could it be Norman?) Hildyard.

Tony Reid was otherwise known as "Jammy" Reid, who was a particularly careful, or should I say cautious, pilot; he rarely spoke to me directly when I first started at CAFU. When I asked why he was nicknamed "Jammy," I was informed that during the war, he had worked for the ATA (Air Transport Auxiliary) and had been shot down twice—by his own side. Other aircrew remembered around this time were navigators: Jimmy "Taffy" Moore, Ian Murdoch, and Dick Whittaker.

Even at this early stage in the life of CAFU, Don King, who had a long association with the unit, was known to be the engineer liaison officer acting between the Ministry and the aircraft maintenance contractor.

1958

By spring, a control zone and associated airways radiating from Gatwick were to be established. When it officially reopened on June 9, Gatwick had been transformed into a modern facility with an eight-thousand-foot runway, a terminal incorporating a rail station and a covered pier linking terminal with aircraft, the first of its kind in the United Kingdom.

In August, the MTCA published an information circular relating to the United Kingdom's policy on short-range navigational aids and summarized air traffic control requirements as follows:

(1) The maximum utilization of controlled air space must be achieved.
(2) A high-capacity route structure must be provided.
(3) Aircraft must be given the greatest possible freedom in the vertical plane.

They stated that VOR, NDB, radio range, and similar systems could not provide the necessary facilities (though a limited number of VOR beacons were being installed along the airways). It also stated that

> *extensive flying experience over the past six years, in many types of aircraft, had clearly demonstrated that the Decca Navigator system best meets the [above] requirements. It provides vastly improved means for navigating all types of aircraft in the departure, en route, holding, descent and approach phases of flight.*

The circular implied that airliners would be much better equipped with Decca. The United Kingdom was slow installing VORs due to their belief in the Decca system. There was now a period of catching up. Gradually, wartime aids, such as SBA and radio ranges, were

Safety Was No Accident

phased out, and CAFU's routine work became the inspection of ILS, GCA, and VOR.

The original Avro 748 design started in 1958, after the Duncan Sandys 1957 Defence White Paper, which ended most military-manned aircraft development in the United Kingdom. Avro then decided to re-enter the civilian market. The Vickers Viscount had the large end of the short-haul market neatly wrapped up, so Avro decided to design a smaller regional airliner design to replace the many DC-3 Dakotas that were now reaching the end of their lifespan. Avro was not the only company to see the potential for a DC-3 replacement, and by this point, the Fokker F27 Friendship was well advanced, as was the Handley Page HPR-3 Herald, though this type had originally planned piston engines. Avro decided to compete by producing a design with turbo-prop engines and better short-field performance allowing it to operate from smaller airports.

MTCA CAFU Aircraft:
REGISTERED

| President | G-APMO | MTCA | April 1958 |

In April, after twelve months' use of the new extended runway at Stansted, CAFU had an additional telecommunications aircraft, the Percival President, G-APMO. The President was, externally, very similar to the three Princes that CAFU was already using for flight inspections. About the only external difference to be spotted, and then not easily, were the twin main wheels and the de-icer boots on wings and tail-plane.

The livery of the CAFU aircraft was not at this stage entirely fixed. On delivery, the Doves, Princes, and Chipmunk were all aluminium silvery grey. But after arrival, during the early fifties, for instance, the aircraft were given a white, heat-reflecting upper fuselage and fin, with a black cheat line running from nose to tail, leaving the lower fuselage, wings and tailplane, silver. Once the Princes and President had arrived, they looked most unlikely for the important role of flight inspection. A more distinctive colour was required, especially for the telecommunications aircraft. At first, the President had the same colour scheme as the Doves and Princes but was then tried with a day-glow paint scheme. The day-glow paintwork was applied to the rudder only of the fin, with another orange cheat line below the black, extending to just under the nose. Geoff Gurr says it was not a success because the orange day-glow faded, which rather negated the requirement for the flight inspection aircraft to be more visible. The next change for the President was to have the orange changed for a deeper red. This looked very businesslike, particularly against its dull-looking sister ships, the Princes.

The deputy commander B, Capt. Jack Picken, then entered the frame. He was an artist of some merit, says Geoff, whose caricatures of pilots and navigators adorned the walls of the crew rooms, and he was invited to present his suggestion for a new colour scheme. The upper fuselage was left white, but then he extended the latest colour scheme of the President to have the complete fin and rudder red, as well as the whole of the lower fuselage below the black cheat line. On the Princes and President, the black cheat line was just below the windows, whereas on the Doves, the cheat line went through the windows. This was the successful colour scheme that CAFU aircraft adopted and subsequently became associated with until the late seventies/early eighties when politics, rather than common sense, was to prevail.

At a technical conference in Tokyo, IATA (International Air Transport Association) was firmly endorsing the VOR on a building block basis, supplemented by DME, in their consideration of an en route and terminal navigational aid.

Meanwhile, in Montreal in October, ICAO's Air Navigation Commission were still making the point that "there must be a highly accurate navigation system," and that for Holding (pattern), there may be a need for a specially located radio-navigational aid, since those provided for en route and terminal navigation might be unsatisfactory. It gave the suggestion that the last word in short-range aids had yet to be made.

MTCA CAFU Aircraft at the end of 1958 Total = 15

Dove	09	4 Tels / 5 I/R, OS, Comm, Ref, GCA
Prince	03	Tels Flight Inspection
President	01	Tels Flight Inspection
Chipmunk	02	CPL, Instructor Ratings, Ref

These numbers remained until 1963.

1959

Late in the 1950s, Mr. M. Whitney was promoted to Headquarters. Mike, who had joined CAFU at Stansted in the early fifties, was instrumental in the improvements to calibration techniques. He was succeeded by his deputy, Charles Marchant.

Stansted Airport, which in the fifties had SBA (Standard Beam Approach) as an approach to landing, now had a CA1000 ILS, with marker beacons, installed. This would have enabled the testing of CAFU telecommunications aircraft equipment, as well as allowing candidates taking their instrument rating tests, to be conducted on an up-to-date approach aid.

By the late 1950s, the Ministry, as a regulatory body, were now responsible for ensuring proper standards were maintained by airline operators. For this reason, CAFU pilots, collectively, were required to be given "Type Conversion" courses on the aircraft type for which they had become responsible. This ensured that the airline training captains involved in conducting type conversion training, as well as the periodic testing of their company pilots, were doing so at not only an acceptable but also consistent standard.

A requirement to achieve "All Weather" operations caused the Telecommunications department to seek improved ways of calibrating ILS "Bends," caused by reflections of the ILS signals arriving from airport buildings, or the movement and or presence of vehicular traffic in the vicinity of the runway aid. It was thought that this problem would never allow the ILS to be flown down to the ground. At this time, aircraft commanders would only be allowed down to a certain height (a decision height or DH), according to aircraft type, pilot experience, and the height of obstacles in the vicinity of the airport. This height was normally around 250 feet when, if the runway could not be approached visually, then the landing would be aborted, and the aircraft would have to overshoot. This type of ILS operation became known as category I (CAT I). It was expected that the ILS would have to be replaced by a new system in order to achieve "blind landings," as they were otherwise known, with details yet to be advised by ICAO of the higher categories (CAT II and CAT III) later to be announced.

Within the sphere of influence of ICAO, navigation aids were, to some extent, internationally standardized, the present short-range system being the American VHF omni-directional Range (VOR). A very considerable number of VOR beacons were set up in the United States, but the number installed elsewhere was not large enough to be able to claim that the ICAO standardisation requirements were yet fully implemented. This could be ascribed, in part, to the fact that a very large number were required to provide the coverage envisaged.

VOR was still not exceptionally accurate, average estimates of total errors in the system being of the order of five degrees in bearing. Some estimates put the total VOR errors as high as ten degrees. Though this might be acceptable for purely navigational purposes at moderate altitudes, it would not suffice in dealing with high-density traffic on crowded airways. Even the addition of the distance measuring facility, now afforded by the VORTAC system (see appendix B), was not likely to improve the situation.

However, compared with other aids, VOR was very popular among pilots, particularly because it was relatively simple to use, but it was said to have certain fundamental limitations that had become apparent even before complete implementation was accomplished.

There was division between the rest of the world and America on the subject of what exactly the new navigational aid should be. Even ICAO was still debating in Montreal, and it was difficult to predict either a clear-cut solution or one based on technical merits.

From the technical point of view, it is worth summarizing the United Kingdom's view on the situation. Britain supported the Decca Mark 10 Navigator system, which was still the only area-coverage system used extensively in airline operations, and for which a considerable coverage of ground stations already existed.

The MTCA believed that navigation requirements should be dictated by traffic control requirements, inferring that they should not be dominated by military thinking, which was originally responsible for VOR and TACAN. Both the capital and maintenance costs of these systems were in any case unnecessarily high, and DME was more complex than an equivalent designed especially for civil use.

Vertical separation alone was unsuitable for jet airliners because of the severe economic penalties imposed by operating at other than the ideal altitude. The ability to enforce lateral separation therefore became an important requirement for air traffic control. The MTCA was convinced that the real requirement was for an aid that would

- *". . . reduce lateral as well as longitudinal separation minima;*
- *enable greater use to be made of lateral separation in order to provide the greatest possible freedom in the vertical plane;*
- *be capable of serving any air-route configuration without the costly, lengthy and difficult process of redeployment of ground facilities;*
- *give the required quality of short-distance navigational service over sea areas;*
- *permit flexibility in the siting of holding patterns and economy in their size;*
- *enable pilots to make smooth and accurate approaches to both instrument and non-instrument runways;*
- *provide accurate navigational information to helicopters as well as to high-flying turbojet aircraft;*
- *provide the pilot with a continuous and accurate presentation of his position in a manner which would enable him to follow the desired track during all stages of the flight;*
- *be capable of integration with long-distance navigation aids so as to accommodate additional equipment progressively as requirements developed;*
- *be easy to site and maintain;*
- *require no regular air calibration checks;*
- *provide a high coverage/cost ratio."*

In spite of the February article seen in *Flight*, it now reported that in March, ICAO had decided on the VOR as the *recommended* international short-range aid, in preference to the British Decca area-coverage system. BEA had installed Decca in their aircraft, believing that it would be adopted, at least for European operations.

It was thought, by some within the Ministry, the Americans had bought off many of the smaller countries in their attempt to have the VOR system chosen. The decision did, of course, have huge monetary implications for those companies selling the system. *Flight* went on to say:

> *"Only the wisdom of history could judge this controversial decision. At best, it would seem with disfavour, for the world's two leading air transport Powers clashed bitterly over their rival aids and reached a doubtfully honest and far from unanimous decision on which one to adopt."*

By October, *Flight* was particularly scathing of the whole process of selection.

> *"To put it bluntly, Montreal has become the annexe of Washington in the business of radio facility standardization. . . . It would be wrong to leave the conclusion that VOR has not been one of the valuable radio facilities in use in civil air transport today. It had served operations reasonably well, even in high density areas, for some years and would continue to do good service in the simpler traffic complexes for many more years to come.*
> *. . . But it is right to criticize the forces which made it the international standard and especially right to see whether there are any other ways by which the constraints imposed by the demands of the common system can be removed and the way opened to a fresh attack on the whole problem of facilities development."*

CAFU was never directly involved in this argument, though I know there are still varying opinions among senior ex-CAFU colleagues as to the correctness of the decision. Little did they realise a similar scenario would be in the offing twenty years later.

After six years with the MTCA, in October, civil aviation was passed to another newly created aviation ministry, the Ministry of Aviation (MoA). The MoA was established under the Minister of Aviation Order 1959 (SI 1959/1768), which transferred to the Ministry of Supply all functions in respect of civil aviation of the former minister of Transport and Civil Aviation and changed the style and title of the minister of Supply to the minister of Aviation. The MoA would embrace the functions of the old MTCA as well as those of the now defunct Ministry of Supply (MoS). Duncan Sandys was appointed as the new minister.

Following the creation of the MoA, a reorganisation resulted in the creation of the Aviation Safety Directorate and the Flight Safety Directorate. These directorates would have, in time, direct implications in the future of CAFU.

THE MINISTRY OF CIVIL AVIATION

offer the undermentioned

AVRO XIX AIRCRAFT

FOR SALE

G-AHIJ — Certificate of Airworthiness expiry date: 23.2.50

G-AGWF — Certificate of Airworthiness expiry date: 11.12.50

THESE AIRCRAFT ARE FROM THE M.C.A. CIVIL OPERATIONAL FLEET AND ARE IN GOOD ORDER.

The aircraft can be viewed at Stansted Aerodrome, Essex on Monday to Friday of each week. Offers for purchase should be made by September 21st, 1951, and should be submitted in writing to :—

THE MINISTRY OF CIVIL AVIATION,
FAB3 (Ap),
ARIEL HOUSE,
THEOBALDS ROAD,
LONDON, W.C.1.

MCA Anson for sale
Photo: The Aeroplane, 1952 via Tony Doyle

Aerial shot of Stansted—RW 05, Hammerhead and CAFU Nissen Huts
Photo: Eddy Harris/JF

CAFU Tels Dove
Photo: Stella Barlow/JF

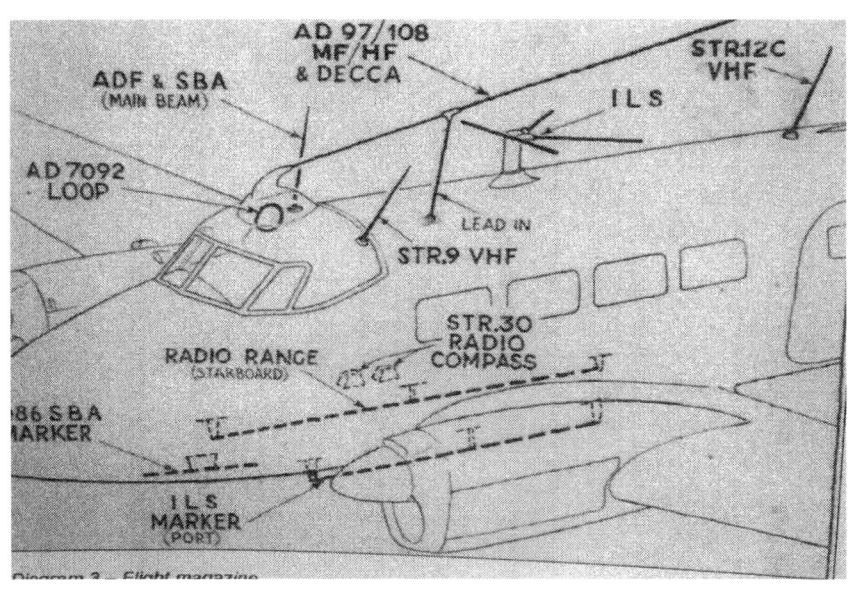

CAFU Tels Dove Aerials
Photo: Flight 3 October, 1952 p. 447

Safety Was No Accident 127

IR Dove, Registered Oct 1949
Photo: Eddy Harris/JF

IR Dove screens used after Consuls departed
Photo: Eddy Harris/JF

IR Dove cockpit
Photo: Eddy Harris/JF

MKY seen in the Cal Bay late 50's. All 3 Princes Registered Aug 1951
Photo: Eddy Harris/JF

DHC 1 Chipmunk, Registered Feb 1955, used for CPL Tests
Photo: Late Gerald Lawrence via Tony Clark/David Whitworth

Percival President, Registered April 1958, in early day-glow colours. NB. twin main wheels and de-icer boots
Photo: Eddy Harris/JF

Chapter Three
1960-1969

1960

In June, Captain A. D. L. Carroll, former CAFU commander, was awarded an OBE in the Queen's Birthday honours list.

The Directorate of Aviation Safety was formed in 1960. Though not directly affecting CAFU at this moment, it was to become the catalyst of change that enabled later changes to its structure.

It was the Air Navigation (Amendment) Order 1960 that put teeth into UK safety legislation. In it, the minister of Aviation was instructed to appoint a director of Aviation Safety, who would grant an air operator's certificate (AOC) once he was satisfied that an airline operator was competent to secure the safe operation of aircraft.

W. "Ted" E. B. Griffiths became the first director of Aviation Safety, and this was the year the Flight Operations Inspectorate (FOI) was formed, whose duty it would be to monitor all aspects of airline operating standards on all British-registered aircraft above a certain weight, which included any commercially used foreign aircraft type on the British Register, such as the Douglas DC3 or Boeing 707. All the British airlines covered by the Flight Operations Inspectorate were then required to obtain and maintain an air operator's certificate (AOC). FOI inspectors would then check the airline's base facilities, documentation, and records, while other Ministry departments would verify that finance and aircraft maintenance were satisfactory.

CAFU's involvement was checking the standard of airline crew training and testing. Reports from these various sources formed the basis of a final submission for approval of an Airlines AOC to the chief FOI (CFOI).

In this period, a number of people were involved in the setting up of the air operator's certificate (AOC): M. "Mike" A. H. Vivian, later to become a CAA board member; G. "Geoffrey" C. Chouffot, later to become CAA deputy chairman; Norman Hildyard, who became the first chief flight operations inspector (CFOI); and J. R. "Dick" Kilner, later to become CFOI.

When the Flight Operations Inspectorate came into being, it was established that what was required was a standardisation of training and testing across all the UK airlines. These standards would apply to all UK airlines with aircraft above a certain weight being flown commercially.

CAFU's involvement was the training and testing of company pilots for authority to conduct tests on the Ministry's behalf, and although seemingly unlikely at the time, the Flight Operations Inspectorate would be the house that would, eventually, swallow one-third of the Stansted operation.

One of the standards required was the company type rating examiner (TRE). A TRE would be an experienced company pilot qualified on a particular type of fleet aircraft, and it was left to the airline companies to nominate their proposed qualified pilots as a TRE. Once authorised, the company TRE could then sign a certificate of competency called a Certificate of Test (C of T), validating the companies own pilots as suitably experienced and qualified to fly that particular type of aircraft. In turn, a company TRE would require his/her authority renewed by a CAFU pilot, with the type on his licence, on an annual basis.

Aircraft training flights, by their very nature, could involve unusual or emergency manoeuvres and could not, therefore, be made part of a commercial flight. As flying-time costs soared, more companies began using simulators for training, as well as conducting tests such as Certificate of Tests, base and line checks, as well as the renewal of instrument ratings.

In the 1960s, simulators were introduced into airline flight-training syllabi. This resulted in CAFU's senior flight examiners (SFE) being involved in the initial and renewal certification of these machines for both training and testing of airline pilots. BOAC had their Comet simulator at Cranebank, Heston, close to Heathrow.

Geoff Gurr writes:

It was apparent to all, Industry, Airlines and the Ministry, the gains to be made using simulators with improvements in safety, training standards, and finance. The Ministry introduced a formal approval system whereby simulators were required to be inspected on an annual basis. Approval, when given, allowed for both Company Training and for the Renewal of crew Licence privileges.

In May, the MoA issued Civil Information Circulars 48 and 49/1960, which spelt out new rules for flying examination tests for the issue of a commercial pilot's licence (CPL) and instrument rating (IR) and renewal (IRR) tests.

For the CPL, the new rules prevented a pilot with only a single-engine endorsement from flying commercially at night. The effect would be that from July 1, he would have to take a night time test in a twin-engine aircraft—at CAFU Stansted, a Dove—if he wished to fly commercially at night.

For the CPL day test (in the single-engine Chipmunk at Stansted), the basic and cross-country tests were to be combined into one test, and spinning would no longer be required.

The IR and IRR tests were to be revised to bring them into line with "modern operational practices." The tests would be carried out over four alternative airway routings: Stansted to Birmingham, Birmingham to Stansted, Stansted to Gatwick, and Gatwick to Stansted.

When I went to CAFU in 1962, these routes were numbered respectively as IR1 to IR4. But by this time, there was also one of the most used and popular route, the IR5, which departed Stansted to join the R1 airway at Matching-Clacton-Matching, departing Matching (a fan marker) for the Stansted NDB beacon, before conducting the two required approaches, NDB and ILS into Stansted. The Asymmetric part, I believe, could be conducted between the two approaches.

Many, if not most, candidates who took their instrument rating at Stansted had probably trained mainly on the shortest local IR5 route and were subsequently dismayed if they were informed of any other route selection. On one occasion when I was in Ops, a candidate refused to fly any other route than the IR5. The commander's judgement was called for and, in one of his rare moments he smiled, told the candidate that of course he could take the test on the IR5 route. He warned him, however, that his licence would be endorsed for the IR5 route only!

Later, when candidates for test brought their own or school aircraft, one way to circumvent taking routes 1-4 would be to arrive singularly, rather than in twos, though it could be known for an examiner to choose a longer route for one individual. In this period, another two routes could be chosen by the examiner: Stansted to Cranfield and Cranfield to Stansted, routes 6 and 7.

For CPL candidates, when they arrived at CAFU's uncomfortable and dingy Nissen huts, they would be shown into the candidates' waiting room before awaiting their fate of a cross-country route, which was chosen by the examiner(s). One never knew which route might be given by any of the examiners. They were always of a triangular nature with any pinpointed mark on the half-million chart, to and from Stansted. Sometimes the candidate would return to Ops and say, "Where did you say?" or "I can't find those places!" Some of the routes, I recall, were Bury St. Edmunds, Ely, Oundle, Wisbeach, Saxmundham, etc. There was always a sting in the route, as it might take them through some Danger Area or Military Zone.

Charles Marchant reported that the size of the UK commitment to civil inspection had now risen per annum to

- 252 ILS per year
- 100 VOR per year
- 048 PAR per year
- 030 Decca 424
- 028 Fan Markers

- 042 VHF/DF
- 002 Radio Ranges

Occasionally, special inspections were carried out on VHF R/T, Surveillance Radar, and NDB coverage, all tasks met by the CAFU aircraft; four de Havilland Doves, three Percival Prince, and one Percival President. The flight inspection crew consisted of pilot, navigator, and a grade 1 telecommunications technical officer, i.e., a navigational aid inspector (NAI).

Field Aircraft Services Ltd. had a four-year contract for the maintenance of CAFU aircraft.

CAFU Staff at December 31, 1960:

COMPLEMENT		ACTUAL STRENGTH	
STAFF	EXMNRS	STAFF	EXMNRS
77	20	69	17

1961

In January, notification of the requirement for an air operator's certificate (AOC) was sent to all airline companies. Even CAFU was included; Capt. "Bee" Marshall, commander, was sent a letter by the director of Aviation Safety at this time, Mr. W. E. B. Griffiths, advising that the Air Navigation Order 1960 came into force on January 2, 1961, explaining that in Article 3A(2), aircraft registered in the United Kingdom and having a maximum total authorised weight of more than five thousand pounds are prohibited from flying on any flight after March 30, 1961, for the purpose of public transport otherwise than under and in accordance with the terms of an air operator's certificate.

The AOC came into being, I understand, largely at the urgent request of the operators of the day. The accident rate was bad; there was rapid growth in the volume of air transport, particularly in the case of charter operations; an increasing use of more sophisticated aircraft and operating procedures; and it presented a commercial incentive to the leading independent operators. This, it was said, provided the Flight Operations Inspectorate scope to use its expertise and knowledge to be of assistance to the industry.

An AOC was required to be held by all operators of UK registered aircraft engaged in the public transport of passengers or cargo or both. They were issued to virtually all the operators of the day covering the scope of their operations and to be effective from April 1, 1961. The holder of an AOC would be subject to continuing supervision by the Flight Operations Inspectorate and the Airworthiness Division. The supervision exercised by the inspectors was wide ranging, covering all aspects of an operator's organisation from the effectiveness of management, through to the training of crews and the acceptability of operating procedures, down to the adequacy of office accommodation.

The bible of the air operator's certificate would be a Civil Aviation Publication (CAP 360), information on requirements to be met by applicants and holders. In addition to CAP 360, inspectors were given guidance on the application of the requirements by means of the Inspecting Staff Manual and Inspecting Staff Instructions.

Initially, according to *Airway* March 1982, there were some seven inspectors and between twenty to thirty companies to supervise at the start of operations. The director of Aviation Safety laid great importance of the need for the flight operations inspectors (FOIs) to hold a current air transport pilot's licence (ATPL). Flight operations officers would be given several months' training on commercial operation legislation, aircraft loading, performance and airworthiness, etc., and the types of inspections, submissions, and recommendations they could make.

A piece in *Hansard* (March 23, 1970, vol. 798) titled "Flight Operations Staff," also advised of the size of the inspectorate, when the president of the Board of Trade was asked,

"What has been the target and the actual number of staff... for the Flight Operations Inspectorate?"

In reply, it was stated,

"The complement for 1961 (when the inspectorate had been formed) had been set at 18 and the actual strength was 14."

The Conservative Government, under Harold Macmillan, published a white paper on aerodromes showing that twenty-two airports were owned by the state. It envisaged the further sale of assets, apart from major international airports that would be managed by a British Airports Authority (BAA), which would also plan and oversee future development.

In August 1961, *Flight* magazine reported Lord Winster, the second minister of Civil Aviation from August 1945 to October 1946, died on June 7 at the age of seventy-six.

As minister responsible for building up British air transport in the difficult months immediately after the war, he was a firm believer in the extension of Commonwealth air services and cheaper air travel. He travelled widely abroad and, in 1946, attended the Pacific Civil Aviation Conference at Wellington, New Zealand. Lord Winster left the MCA before his work had had time to bear full fruit, but he was largely responsible for the Anglo-US Bermuda agreement of 1946 and for laying the foundations of the Civil Aviation Act. As Mr. Bulwer-Thomas, his parliamentary private secretary, wrote in the *Times:*

The independence of the airline corporations meant that he could not direct but had to persuade; and the personalities in civil aviation at that time were as prickly as could be found anywhere. Fortunately Winster was at his best in human relationships; his only failure was in handling the Civil Aviation Group of his own party—and not even the Archangel Gabriel could have succeeded there.

The two Airways Corporations, BOAC and BEA, set up a joint pilot training establishment at Hamble in Hampshire, called the College of Air Training (CAT). The first students were due to complete their course in June 1962 and used DHC1 Chipmunks for the day GFT test and PA23s for instrument ratings.

Britain's Visual Glide-Path Indicator (VGPI), the RAE/Calvert approach lighting system, was adopted by ICAO as a world standard. The system had been in use at Heathrow since June 1959.
The Ministry proposed VGPI as a world ICAO standard in 1959 and worked closely with the Federal Aviation Administration in helping the Americans to evaluate it. This led last year *(Flight,* November 11, 1962, p. 758) to a decision by the FAA—after extensive tests at the National Aviation Facilities Experimental Centre at Atlantic City—to recommend the system as a US standard. Once it had been accepted by the FAA, its adoption by ICAO was only a matter of time. The system became a world standard on October 1 unless, as seemed unlikely, a majority of the eighty-six member nations disapproved.
The patent is held by the UK National Research Development Corporation. Other manufacturers included GEC and Research Engineering.

TEE (the MoA Telecommunications Engineering Establishment) was located across the road from the famous old Beehive terminal at Gatwick—in fact the TEE MT garages were pre-war aircraft hangars. The unit was primarily responsible for carrying out major navigational installation work of all kinds across the country. They had teams who carried out in-depth maintenance on specialist items such as radar turning gear, aerial masts, and ILSs. Although involvement with TEE was not huge, CAFU was called upon to assist in site evaluations and commissioning flights of new installations.

All radio and radar aids used for the navigation of aircraft in the United Kingdom required continual flight inspection by CAFU. As a member state of ICAO, the United Kingdom undertook to ensure that all UK aids conformed to internationally agreed standards.

The Prince and Dove aircraft used for flight inspection were continually modified by the telecommunications staff of CAFU to accommodate new navigation equipment, or any changes to the method of calibration measurement.

Although the flight inspection of aids was routine at this time, the inspection of aids, particularly in Scotland and the North of England when crews were away from base (AFB), could be difficult. VORs and ILSs each had a periodicity when they were due to be flight checked, and the Doves, in the case of ILS and VOR, were only capable of checking either one or the other. For instance, Doves JLV and LFT only checked the ILS, while LFU only calibrated VORs. Further, the Tels Doves could only carry one set of calibration equipment. If, when AFB, they had any unserviceability, the aircraft would be grounded until spares could arrive. There rarely seemed to be enough time to conduct the necessary work of calibration, for if it wasn't serviceability that was a problem then there was always the weather to contend with. It was a constant battle for CAFU to ensure that en route and landing aids were inspected within their tolerance dates.

In 1961, the Air Registration Board (ARB) published Paper 367, "Airworthiness Requirements for Auto-flare and Automatic Landing," which admitted that at that time, it was not felt possible to write firm requirements. The British target was automatic landing, not merely automatic approach. Paper 367 started by laying down the overall level of safety required from an automatic landing system (a later paper, 423, dealt with category II operations); it outlined the prerequisites for ARB clearance of systems in visual and "blind" conditions, and listed the evidence, which the ARB required the manufacturers to provide, to substantiate their claims to meeting the overall safety requirement. It is from Paper 367 that the oft-quoted figure of 10^{-7} is derived. In the years previous to 1961 the worldwide average rate of fatal accidents "in the landing phase," was slightly less than one accident in one million landings, i.e., 10^{-6}. The ARB felt that in order to merit approval, an automatic landing system should be able to demonstrate a level of safety ten times higher, i.e., a risk of a fatal accident once in every ten million landings. This figure was to be taken as a maximum and included the risk attributable to failure in the ground-based part of the system.

More crew members remembered in the sixties were Trevor Green, Alan Marriott, Colin Mastin, Ron Crawford, John Timilty, John Winch, Dennis Marlow, Mike Tarrant. Oh! and Bill Topping, a charming man who lost his licence medically and moved to the Accident Investigation Branch (AIB). More navigators who may have started in the 1950s, or earlier, but were certainly around in the sixties were Eric Jenkins (senior navigator), Jimmy "Taffy" Moore (another senior nav), John Rathbone (later killed in a Trans Meridian flying accident), Dick Whittaker, Ian Murdoch, and Dick Hawkes who had joined in the 1950s and had flown in the Consuls.

Ian Murdoch, I particularly remember, because he attempted to show me how to use the sextant, which they held in the Navigation section. After several early lunchtimes using the sextant and Ian calculating my position, he reckoned I would have made an average bomber navigator—apparently, I was always about five miles out.

CAFU Staff at December 31, 1961

COMPLEMENT		ACTUAL STRENGTH	
STAFF	EXMNRS	STAFF	EXMNRS
81	20	77	20

1962

Peter Thorneycroft, now the minister of Aviation

In June, Captains Len Yard and Geoff Gurr were conducting CPL tests on twin-engine aircraft at the College of Air Training at Hamble. This was the first time a CPL was conducted on a twin. Later in the month, candidates were taking their IRT. Both examiners found the standard of candidates to be very high, a consequence of the selection process and high standard of training demanded by the corporations sponsoring them.

A Vickers VC10 had its maiden flight on Friday, June 29, 1962; destined for BOAC, it was the heaviest British-built aircraft yet.

For each new commercial aircraft type placed on the UK Register, a senior flight examiner from CAFU had to be "type rated" on it, and the type added to their licence. For instance, Captain Gurr had a Comet conversion course at Heston, while it was known that Capt. Bill Wooden was flying the B707 and Capt. Len Yard the DC8. It was also thought that Capt. "Bee" Marshall would be on the VC10 (later to be taken over by Capt. Don Tucker).

In the autumn, Julian Amery succeeded Peter Thorneycroft as the minister for Aviation.

Jock Keir, commander up until this point, eventually had to stand down with a medical problem. Although he lost his licence, he continued to work with Headquarters staff as an operations officer. On his retirement as commander, the post was filled by his deputy, B. E. E "Bee" Marshall. "Bee" Marshall, although not loved by all, I was informed, was probably one of the most successful pilots in this post, having assisted in the construction of tests for the new licences, as well as pioneering the development of screens to replace the old two-stage amber system, for the commercial and instrument rating tests.

By December, the deputy position was taken over by Captain G. B. Gurr.

The proportion of would-be professional pilots passing ministry examinations is very low; it was reported in *Flight* (April 26, p. 642), 30 percent for written and flying tests and about 10 percent for instrument ratings. Only AST Perth and the CAT had satisfied the Ministry's standards, and because of this, it was intended to raise fees for Ministry flying tests "substantially" very shortly.

For a number of years, a considerable amount of research and experimental effort was expended on the problem of approach and landing of aircraft in operational circumstances, where the visual references and the atmospheric conditions were below levels considered safe for the pilot, assisted only by conventional instrumentation.

However, the aircraft industry was now at a stage where a number of striking new advances were approaching practical reality; supersonic transport, vertical take-off and landing, and variable geometry were three developments that spring to mind. Less spectacular, but equally important, was the intensive development work in progress devoted to producing aircraft instrumentation—particularly in civil aircraft—capable of safe operations in all weather conditions.

CAFU Staff at December 31, 1962

COMPLEMENT		ACTUAL STRENGTH	
STAFF	EXMNRS	STAFF	EXMNRS
86	20	80	19

1963

As an intermediate step in the development of a true blind-landing system, ICAO introduced rigorous standards for the instrument landing system in use at UK and international airfields. The new standard would enable an aircraft to approach a runway down to one hundred feet. The current standard, CAT 1, allowed an approach down to a runway threshold height of two hundred feet, or higher, according to the country, airfield, pilot experience, and company instructions.

ICAO Instrument Landing Category Standards:

Category	DH (ft)	DH (mtrs)	RVR (ft)	R V R (mtrs)
CAT 1	200	60	2600	800
CAT 2	100	60-30 *	1200	400

* CAT 2 was 60 m or below but not less than 30 m.
DH = Decision Height at which a pilot could descend on approach to land before deciding to abort.
RVR = Runway Visual Range, the forward visibility at runway surface.

MTCA CAFU Aircraft:
DEREGISTERED

DHC1	G-AMMA	MCA	May 1963

It was probably due to the 1960 ruling on the requirement for the day CPL test that allowed the Ministry to reduce the number of CAFU Chipmunks from two to just one. Consequently in May, one of the DHC1 Chipmunks, G-AMMA, was no longer required. It was a sad departure after an eleven-year association with CAFU. A very well-maintained two-seat light aircraft, it was sold to the Luton Flying Club, who sold it on two years later to the College of Air Training at Hamble. I am reliably informed that Mike Alpha still flies today, even after a bad accident in Denmark.

The remaining Chipmunk, G-ANWB, was retained not just for day CPL tests but for the examiners to have instructor rating refresher training and testing.

In June, Captain A. D. L. "Dan" Carroll, OBE, the squadron leader who was seconded from the RAF in 1944 to command the Civil Operations Fleet, which later led to the formation of the Civil Aviation Flying Unit, retired after an almost twenty-year association with CAFU. At a special retirement evening held at the Longs Ballroom in Bishop's Stortford, one of the many tributes was a message, played on tape, from his old friend Group Captain Douglas Bader. Group Captain Bader later became a board member of the CAA.

In the United Kingdom at this time, helicopters were not equipped to fly IFR (instrument flight rules); consequently there was no requirement for a helicopter pilot to hold an instrument rating. Hence, there was no requirement for any legislation, wrote Geoff Gurr. This meant that helicopter companies had been virtually left to their own devises. But with the increased use of helicopters in the North Sea, due to the oil industry, as well as British European Airways Helicopters (BEAH) introducing scheduled services to the Scilly Isles and the suggestion of a possible shuttle between Gatwick and Heathrow, it was apparent that the Ministry needed to appraise the situation with tighter regulations. Because of this, CAFU was authorised to commence training with one of its senior examiners (Captain G. B. Gurr) as well as the recruitment of helicopter trained staff, both for CAFU and the Flight Operations Inspectorate.

One of the tasks CAFU was involved with was acting as a radar target for the air traffic control (ATC) school (later the ATC college) at Bournemouth, Hurn Airport, Dorset. This is where the ATC controllers attained their radar certificate rating by performing a number of "live" talk-downs—which is where CAFU came in.

Each week throughout the year, when the school was in session, an IR Dove would be sent to Bournemouth to act as a radar target. CAFU pilots, as well as Dove qualified operations officers from Headquarters, were used. Later, the CAFU navigators, who had by then gained their CPL licence, were also used. Around one thousand hours were flown by CAFU each year providing a good deal of flying hours.

The air traffic control officers (ATCOs), usually ex-aircrew, or young cadets, were often invited to fly as "lookout" in the right-hand seat and sometimes allowed a little "hands-on" while in this role. One ex-cadet, Doug Rough, recalled flying with a certain operations officer, who always wore his white leather gloves and seemed a tad pompous:

In the RHS seat I spotted something close coming out of Tarrant Rushton (a possible Charlie 119). I pointed it out to him. "I've seen it" he says in a snuffy manner. Next, flying over the sea just below the cliff at Bournemouth (to try and fool the trainee radar controller) when a Superfreighter passed over us. "I have it in sight," says he, even more snuffily! So, when we were on very short finals to land at Hurn with no "3 greens" showing (re the undercarriage not yet selected), as a young ATCO Cadet I was reluctant to say anything further but managed to get around it by coughing loudly and pointing at the offending panel. "Aaah," he says, "You spotted it . . . just wanted to see if you'd notice" as he quickly lowered the undercarriage not a nanosecond too soon and the wheels greased the runway. My first stop was the loo," said Doug . . . *"I learnt a lot about flying from that"* as Uncle Roger used to say in Flight.

Doug also remembered a number of other CAFU "Jockeys" he P3'd with at Hurn in the period December 1963 to Jan 1964; Captains Dan Thomas, ? Williams, Dennis Marlowe, and Jack Cook. The aircraft involved were G-ANAP, NUT, NUW, and NOV.

Listed here are some of the numerous tasks undertaken by CAFU and qualified operational staff from Headquarters:

- ordnance survey
- lighting inspections (approach and airfield)

- noise abatement procedure trials
- letdown procedures
- disability flying tests
- oil pollution at sea tests
- dinghy radio trials
- ATC procedures
- ab initio pilot training of certain civil servants

To these tasks could be added the regular training programme for both CAFU pilots and all those persons cleared to fly on CAFU aircraft, who themselves had to pass the tests required by law and the CAFU Operations Manual. Roughly they were

DOVES, PRINCE/PRESIDENT	
Base Check	Six Months
Line Check	13 Months
Instrument Rating	13 Months
Chipmunk CoT	13 Months
Instructor Rating	Three Years
Medicals	Every Six Months. Over 40s required an annual ECG

Additionally, the CAFU senior flight examiner company aircraft type records, for base and line checks, had to be maintained. All of these records were held in Operations by the ops officer as part of a long-term programme, which was then displayed showing the next six months' tasks. Included in the planning was the CAFU aircraft maintenance schedule, which provided information on availability (or perhaps unavailability).

As part of a short-term programme, the last four weeks would then be held by the briefing officer who had control of day-to-day events. These would include future local candidates requiring tests for the CPL and instrument ratings to be taken at Stansted by a CAFU examiner; companies requiring tests on their training captains; simulators requiring approval; telecommunications crew requirement; aircrew refresher and VIP flights—when they gave sufficient notice. Finally, there was a two-week plan that included the external candidates also requiring CPL and IR tests at nominated schools, as and when they were ready for an examiner. Aircrew leave (holiday) would be noted and approved by the deputy commander subject to the schedule that was shaping. Flight inspection aids were selected within their periodicity dates and selected for either an away from base (AFB) or local schedule. Crews would know by now whether they were planned to be local or AFB.

During any week of activity, weather, aircraft unserviceability, aircrew sickness, and/or unplanned last-minute tasks such as a VIP flight or an incident involving a navigational aid requiring unscheduled flight inspection, could all throw previous planning into disarray. Each day was taken as the situation unfolded. Priorities were then set and any cancellations rescheduled in the nearest timescale, which would also require the two-, three-, or four-week programmes to be adjusted. Finally, any local examining test candidate, given a partial pass that might require an immediate retake, could only be undertaken if an examiner could either "squeeze it in" with his own schedule or because there had been a cancellation.

CAFU Staff at December 31, 1963

COMPLEMENT		ACTUAL STRENGTH	
STAFF	EXMNRS	STAFF	EXMNRS
105	25	98	24

MTCA CAFU Aircraft at the end of 1963 Total = 14

Dove	05	I/R, OS, Comm, GCA, Ref
Dove	04	Tels flight Inspection, GCA, OS
Prince	03	Tels Flight Inspection
President	01	Tels Flight Inspection
Chipmunk	01	CPL, Instructor Ratings, Ref

1964

In February, a Certificate of Airworthiness was granted, after more than two years and 1,600 hours of flight testing, to the HS121 Trident, a three-engine airliner destined for the BEA fleet. CAFU Captain Jack Picken was type-rated on this aircraft.

The Vickers VC10, which had its maiden flight in June 1962, went into service with BOAC.

The BAC One-Eleven went into service with BEA. Captain C. M. "Jimmy" Joy of CAFU would be type-rated on this aircraft.

As an indication of the work that a pilot at CAFU could experience in the 1960s, in February of this year, the deputy commander, Captain G. B. Gurr, was sent on a helicopter course, to find himself refresher flying in a Bell 47 Helicopter, then refresher flying on the BEA Comet 4B aircraft, followed by refresher on the DHC1 Chipmunk, instrument flying practice in the S61N Helicopter, a Dove competency check, conduct an IRT on the Piper Apache, and then renew his own type rating on the Comet 4B!

During the months of March to October, the UK Ordnance Survey Department completed its largest ever flying programme, including major tasks in the Highlands and Islands of Scotland. In addition to Hunting Survey Princes, CAFU Doves were used flying North South operating from Blackpool. These aircraft obtained photography for mapping in various parts of Britain, but their main work was over Scotland. CAFU Dove G-ANUW was used on a full-time basis, and G-ANAP and G-ALFU on an opportunity basis.

At Stansted, there was a backlog of candidates for both the general flying test (GFT) for the commercial pilot's licence (CPL) and the instrument rating test (IRT). Candidates would usually have to wait six weeks for a test booking, turn up on the day hoping (praying) for good weather conditions, aircraft serviceability, and what they supposed, or hoped, to be a kindly examiner. The weather, especially in winter for the GFT test, and an icing level below five thousand feet (lowest available flight level on the airway for an IRT) could be unfavourable and require a cancellation of the test. This would then put the candidate at the back of the queue again. Most candidates were cash strapped, if not completely broke, and a cancellation, even a partial pass of a test, would mean more continuation training to keep them in readiness for when they were lucky enough to be given another booking.

The experience for the candidates was long lasting. In the nineties, my wife booked me a B747 simulator experience at Burgess Hill, and the captain, learning that I had worked at CAFU, asked, "Did you know John Belson?"

"Yes," I replied, "he was a short thickset man with a goatee beard."

"I hated the b*****d," he snorted, "he failed me on my initial instrument rating!"

Certainly there were many stories about CAFU examiners who were complete ogres, who would chop you for the slightest thing and were pedantic in the extreme. Yet on the other side of the coin, I also received stories from ex-IR candidates who were pleasantly surprised at the fair treatment they received. One candidate recalled having a partial retest of his instrument rating, expecting that he would have to do the "whole nine miles" of the pre-flight walk-around check, despite having just flown in from Booker. Only to find when the examiner asked for his licence and discovered he also had a flight nav. licence, being told to get aboard while the examiner completed the outside checks. This calmed him (the candidate) down sufficiently to achieve a pass.

The main schools for candidates wishing to obtain their CPL and/or IRT at this time were the College of Air Training (CAT) at Hamble, run by the two corporations, BEA and BOAC. Air Services Training (AST) school at Perth, Scotland, and the Oxford Air Training School (OATS), at Kidlington airport.

CAT, at Hamble, were using the DHC1 Chipmunk for the daytime CPL test and the Piper PA23 for the GFT4 (night test) and IRT. As might be expected at this corporation-sponsored school, the standard of candidates was very high with many first-time passes and few failures. Most candidates could expect to be drawn in to one or other of the corporations.

AST in Scotland used Cessna aircraft; the single-engine C150 for the CPL test and C310 twin for the IRTs. Many, if not most, candidates were students sponsored from overseas. One of the exasperations of the examiners with the overseas students was that they would invariably answer *"Yes"* to any or every question, making it difficult to know if they understood what had been said. Even so, AST were highly successful with their students.

OATS students could be privately financed or sponsored by other sources or airline companies. They used Piper aircraft; the PA28 single for the CPL test and the PA30 for the IRT. The school had a good reputation, and it may be remembered that the chief training captain, Colin Beckwith, later taught Sarah Ferguson to fly.

For examining purposes, CAFU had split the examiners between the two main types presented for tests, Piper and Cessna, so that AFB examining was either in Scotland or the South of England.

The question of choice of new aircraft for CAFU, particularly on the telecommunications side, was not straightforward. The requirement for a modern aircraft environment for CAFU flight crews lent itself towards the DH125, a small executive jet that could also be used for the carriage of government VIPs, as well as for high-level radar flights required by the Tels department. Even Tels headquarters in London seemed to be leaning towards the 125, but when Charles Marchant, CAFU's telecommunications superintendent, was asked to meet with the director of Safety specifically to discuss the subject, and asked what aircraft would be best suited to replace the ageing Tels Doves and Princes, he strongly voiced that he wanted the DC3 replacement, the HS748, eventually managing to convince the director of CAFU's flight inspection requirement.

Later in the year, Hawker Siddeley brought their HS748 demonstrator, a low-wing twin-turboprop aircraft, to Stansted for CAFU to assess as a replacement for the ageing Doves and Princes. It appeared eminently suitable, wrote Geoff Gurr, albeit somewhat slow—he had hoped for a jet.

In November, a visit was made to the Hawker Siddeley factory at Hawarden to see a series 1 DH125 that was nearing the end of the production line.

The BAC One-Eleven short-haul aircraft was now entering service. In October 1963, a One-Eleven was lost when it went into a deep stall. Captain C. M. "Jimmy" Joy was type-rated on the BAC1-11, Capt. Don Tucker on the Vickers VC10, and Capt. Jack Picken on the Trident. There was much discussion between the CAFU pilots who were type-rated on these new high "T-tail" aircraft as to the cause of the accident and the solutions employed.

CAFU (Captain Gurr) was asked to give an opinion of the RAF's Comet 4C simulator.

Field Aircraft Services Ltd. renewed their four-year contract for maintenance of CAFU aircraft. It meant a continuity of work for the engineers employed who had an excellent working relationship with CAFU. I remember George Harding was the hangar foreman in the sixties, with George Todd and Rodney Prior the licensed engineers.

CAFU Command:
- Commander, Captain B. E. E. Marshall
- Telecommunications Superintendent Charles Marchant
- Senior Navigator Eric Jenkins
- Senior Navaid Inspector Alec Barrett

CAFU Staff:
A second deputy commander was appointed in December, Captain W. A. "Bill" Wooden.

There were nine navigators, six navaid inspectors, and around forty ground telecommunications engineers.

CAFU Staff at December 31, 1964:

COMPLEMENT		ACTUAL STRENGTH	
STAFF	EXMNRS	STAFF	EXMNRS
110	25	103	22

1965

While working mainly on behalf of the Directorate of Safety, administratively CAFU was under the control of the director of Aerodromes (Technical). These were the areas of responsibility that CAFU worked:

- Directorate of Safety: flight examinations for pilot proficiency
- Directorate of Air Telecommunications: flight inspections of en route navaids, instrument landing installations, and radar.
- School of Air Traffic Control at Hurn: flying as radar targets for "talk-down" ATC trainees

The commander, Capt. "Bee" Marshall, now had two deputies: Deputy A, Captain G. B. Geoff "Gurr"; and Deputy B, Captain W. A. "Bill" Wooden. Deputy A was primarily responsible for the flying aspects of the unit's work and maintaining pilot competency. In addition, he had a special task—developing an instrument rating for helicopters. At the beginning of the year, Captain Gurr was in discussion with BEAH on how to clear the S61N helicopter, together with its pilots, for IFR flights in controlled airspace.

As Deputy Commander B, Captain Wooden had responsibility for the allocation and availability of aircrew for the various duties, as well as being a training inspector on B707 aircraft and overseeing the development of simulators for training purposes.

Operation personnel, under the watchful eye of the senior NAI, were responsible for the preparation of the telecommunications flight inspection programme, the booking of candidates for tests, and, under the direction of the deputy Commanders, the allocation of aircraft and aircrew.

The British Airports Authority (BAA) was set up as a government agency to assume responsibility for London Heathrow, Gatwick, and Stansted airports.

On June 10, a BEA Trident, G-ARPR, flew from Paris to Heathrow, achieving the world's first auto flare (autopilot retards the engines at fifty feet and initiates a pitch-up manoeuvre) on a commercial flight.

Also in June, CAFU was involved in extensive parallel runway trials at Heathrow. Thirty hours of actual monitored twin approaches had been performed, and the initial experience was believed to be encouraging.

Towards the end of this year, it was decided that the replacement for the ageing telecommunications Doves and Percival aircraft was to be the Hawker Siddeley HS748.

The Prince, G-AMKW, was fitted with a nose lamp by Field Aircraft Services, for trialling experiments with the telecroscope, a ground tracking devise that could follow the exact positioning of the lamp on the aircraft.

With a new Tels flight inspection aircraft to be received at Stansted in the near future, CAFU's Eddy Harris was appointed as project manager, with Eric Edmondson as his assistant, in the installation of new flight inspection equipment to be installed in the HS748.

The Handley Page HPR-7 Herald (now with RR Dart engines) was another possible replacement aircraft for the Doves and Princes, being about the same size as the HS748, but with its high wing and subsequent longer undercarriage, it seemed less suitable for the requirements of the lower approaches, and possible subsequent heavy landings, expected during future testing operations entailing the new ILS Category landings.

Unlike the smaller Doves and Princes, the HS748 would be roomy enough to carry both duplicated VOR and ILS calibration equipment, together with the Smiths SEP6 autopilot system capable of making approaches down to one hundred feet (CAT II).

As well as having had demonstrations of the latest Smiths Flight System, SFS6, with its associated SEP6 autopilot, which was about to be launched, CAFU was invited to witness demonstrations at Bedford by the blind-landing experimental unit (BLEU) with their Vickers Varsity.

Although CAFU had raised a couple of issues with the Smiths flight system, it was agreed to purchase it for the HS748. CAFU was assured that modifications could be made to the equipment, which was, so far, untried. Geoff Gurr later reported that eventually the whole system worked very well indeed.

The proposed autopilot installation was a concern to CAFU. Airlines had duplicate, even triplicate, systems on their aircraft, but CAFU's HS748 was to have only one, and any malfunction during a coupled approach could be disastrous. Geoff Gurr tells how CAFU asked if there could be a "fail-safe" characteristic in such an event. The airframe manufacturer jokingly said that the airframe had already proved "fail-safe" as in a recent heavy landing the aircraft had only lost a wing, the aircraft rolling over onto its back, with everyone on board hanging in their straps. There had been no fire, and everyone had escaped with minor injuries. Well, the CAFU navaid inspectors would not have been amused with that story—they were rarely strapped in on the approach as they sat sideways at their console, checking onboard equipment and instrumentation!

In early November, CAFU staff attended meetings in Manchester, endeavouring to resolve specification problems with the HS748. In particular, it was thought there might not be sufficient power supply for the lamp associated with the new flight inspection tracking device. Fortunately, it was later discovered that the lamp, trialled in the nose of the Percival Prince back at Stansted, only required one 1,000-watt lamp, rather than the expected cluster of five lamps. The lamp was to enable the ground-sited tracking device (telecroscope) to lock onto the lamp at five miles while on the approach.

CAFU pilots were organised into advisory groups covering air safety, examining, telecommunications, survey, emergency equipment, and air traffic control (ATC) liaison.

Between them, CAFU pilots were now type-rated on more than thirty different types of aircraft—all the different types on the British Register with a Public Transport Certificate of Airworthiness (C of A). CAFU pilot type ratings ranged from single-engine DHC1 Chipmunks to multiengine jet aircraft, such as the Boeing B707 and Vickers VC10.

The senior pilots were required to be qualified instructors, hold an airline transport pilot's licence (ATPL) with a minimum of two thousand hours as pilot with not less than five hundred hours in command, and to have recent experience on large multi-engine aircraft.

In this period, all the senior CAFU pilots were required to be type-rated on Chipmunk, Dove, Prince, President, and Cessna or Piper-type aircraft, as well as at least one large current transport aircraft. Generally, CAFU had two pilots qualified on each of the commercial aircraft types in current service.

It was the policy of the unit that every senior pilot should take his turn at every form of duty—alternately based at the home airfield and away from base (AFB). Thus, examining flights were alternated with radar target flying and with telecommunications flight checking or VIP communication flights.

It was found that the various duties were complementary; experience gained in precision flying for navaid inspection work being of value in examining pilots undertaking an instrument rating examination. Familiarity flying the larger commercial aircraft assisted assessing the "flyability" of navaids. There was no doubt that CAFU pilots were a unique link between the commercial operators, MoA Headquarters operational planning staff, and the training schools.

Norman Hildyard, the first chief flight operations inspector, retired.

It is believed that it was in late 1965 that CAFU pilot salaries were merged with the flight operations staff pilot salaries (see 1968 Edwards review), with the intention to form one group. It was a political move whereby two sets of Ministry pilots were renamed and given the same salaries. The grading were flight examiner (Stansted based) / flight operations inspector (London based), FE/FOI; principal flight examiner (Stansted based) / principal operations inspector (London based), PFE/PFOI; and Chief Flight Examiner (Stansted-based CAFU commander's position) / Chief Flight Operations Inspector (London based), CFE/CFOI. This now made the commander a CFE and his deputies PFE. Yet at Stansted, the titles of commander and deputy were retained as the nomenclature CFE and PFE were now their civil service grading. There were also two training grades; initial entrants were grade II, and once qualified became grade I before gaining sufficient qualification to become an FE (flight examiner). This particular change for CAFU pilots, though not liked at the time as I shall explain later, would allow further moves in the decade to come.

Details of the proposed issue of a Certificate of Test (C of T) to fly helicopters in controlled airspace in accordance with instrument flight rules (IFR) were completed. These tests would now be conducted on BEAH pilots. However, as appropriate legislation was not yet changed, there could still not be an official helicopter instrument rating. So although the standard of the proposed test was the same as for fixed wing aircraft, for the time being, only a C of T could be issued.

Capt. Geoff Gurr would be the first to take the helicopter IRT test. CAFU's Bill Wooden was asked to conduct the test as examiner sitting in the jump seat, and a BEAH training captain acting as co-pilot and safety lookout in the right-hand seat. It was a first, successfully completed on May 26, 1965.

In October, BEAH had to ask CAFU for help as their pilots were still not cleared for IFR flights, and the oil company they were dealing with wanted to be shown that night flights would be possible. Fortunately, Captain Gurr of CAFU and a BEAH training captain were able to demonstrate exactly what could be done.

CAFU Staff at December 31, 1965:

COMPLEMENT		ACTUAL STRENGTH	
STAFF	EXMNRS	STAFF	EXMNRS
125	25	110	21

There were nine navigators and six NAIs at this time.

1966

The MoA were carrying out extensive trials of Guernsey's Plessey AR-1 radar, the first to be installed in the world. It worked in conjunction with Plessey's 424 radar and was designed for short-range high-accuracy approach work. The equipment was also being fitted at Heathrow, the Isle of Man, and many other airports overseas.

The previous year, the deputy commander B, Captain Gurr, had voiced concerns with the commander over his difficulties with the burden of his tasks. By March of this year, he wrote a letter to him. He believed that the unit did not have the resources in either manpower or equipment to undertake the tasks expected of it, with a consequence of staff feeling a lack of morale, (five of seven examiners recruited to Stansted over the previous three years had left to go to commercial airlines because of CAFU conditions, changes, and workload imposed). His deep concern caused him to express that he was unwilling to continue in post unless steps were taken to remedy the situation.

In June, Captain Gurr was sent a letter "out of the blue," he said, informing him of a level transfer to the inspectorate in London as a principal flight operations inspector (PFOI), heading up a new section, Flt Ops 4. He took up this new appointment in July. The requirement for a new Flight Operations Department had come about because of the increased requests for AOCs and the necessary expansion of the Flight Operations Inspectorate, a situation that was also having an impact on CAFU training inspectors; more companies to be seen, more aircraft types to be covered, and more delegated examiners to be seen.

Geoff Gurr readily admitted that his transfer may have occurred because of his disquiet at his workload as deputy commander at CAFU. Worse, he was not exactly welcome in his new position in London, as Flight Operations staff believed they already had one of their own lined up for promotion. The move was made just one year after Geoffrey Chouffot was made chief of Flight Operations Inspectorate (CFOI), and Gurr's level transfer was probably a smart move on his part in the strengthening of the inspectorate. It should be pointed out that Geoff Gurr, a training inspector, was the first man from CAFU to join the Flight Operations Inspectorate.

Captain D. L. "Don" Hale was promoted to principal flight examiner, taking over Geoff Gurr's role as deputy commander B.

The British Airport Authority (BAA), which was set up as a self-financing body, took control of Heathrow—which had been substantially developed during the 1950s—Gatwick, Stansted, and Prestwick. The government's decision to develop London's third airport at Stansted was controversial, as there was strong local opposition with their "No" to Stansted campaign.

BOT CAFU Aircraft:
REGISTERED

| DH125 | G-ATPC | MoA | Feb 1966 |

Five years had gone by since the last addition to the CAFU fleet, but with a new requirement for a high-level radar target aircraft, to enable the development of new area radar equipment for air traffic control's upper air services, CAFU was brought up to date, in February, with its first jet aircraft, the DH125, G-ATPC. It was a series one aircraft—one of the first ten off the production line—with two Rolls-Royce Viper 520 engines, a lovely-looking aircraft used as a small, six-seater executive jet. In fact, it was to be used in this role when CAFU was asked to fly VIP flights carrying UK government ministers to cities anywhere in the United Kingdom and across Europe. CAFU senior pilots would be allocated a number of hours each to provide necessary modern jet operating experience.

The aircraft was originally destined for a washing machine magnate (John Bloom) who suddenly became broke and the aircraft became available. With the manufacturer keen to sell, the Ministry was eventually to purchase what must have been seen as a bargain.

As one of the first ten of the series, it had six passenger windows, the last one looking into the engine—probably why the next series only had five. As the other nine aircraft in this batch had all gone to American owners, it meant that was where most of the spares were held, causing a little problem when things like the brake linings were required, as they differed in requiring ten for each main wheel.

One problem that the DH125 experienced, according to Eddy Harris, was St. Elmo's Fire, a blue or violet light, discharging across the pilot's screen. Douglas Bader, who was working for Shell, complained to the manufacturer who asked CAFU for assistance, though it was thought they were not able to give any help. The resolution came when Hawker Siddeley installed earthing strips, which cured the problem.

One of the first VIP flights carried out by CAFU with the DH125 this year was when they carried the UK home secretary, Roy Jenkins.

Unlike the Doves and Princes, the HS748s would require to be operated with two pilots, although certain flight inspections would still necessitate the skills of a flight navigator. CAFU found an easy solution to this problem by training their navigators for "co-pilot" duties. They were sent to the Oxford Air Training School, which took place between 1966 and 1968, where they gained a commercial pilot's licence (CPL) and instrument rating (IR). Two of them, Captains Benn Gun and Ian Selwyn, went further, gaining instructor ratings and eventually becoming flight examiner II (FEII) grade. Dick Hawkes, as well as John Smith, I believe, went on to gain an ATPL, becoming Tels 748 captains. A small minority elected to remain as flight navigators; these were later involved in the development of providing position fixes during flight inspections via Decca and an onboard specially programmed computer.

On July 1, seven years after the creation of the MoA, civil aviation functions were transferred to another Ministry, the Board of Trade (BOT), in the belief that this was where civil aviation matters should abide. Roy Jenkins was the last minister of Aviation and was now appointed as the new home secretary.

Now that CAFU had a DH125, with one of its functions the carriage of UK government ministers, an air operator's certificate was issued in September for operations within Area C (covering most of Northern Europe, North Africa and the Middle East). It was sent to Capt. "Bee" Marshall by the director of Aviation Safety, certifying that:

"the Board of Trade are competent to secure the safe operation of the following types of aircraft: HS125."

The certificate was for one year until March 31, 1967, requiring an annual renewal (n.b., HS had taken over DH while the 125 was in development, but the DH was kept for this aircraft at registration).

By the end of the year, there were some forty British operating companies holding an air operator's certificate (AOC). Each company aircraft type had a CAFU inspector assigned to the training captains flying that type. There were approximately four hundred airline training captains at this time for which CAFU was required to keep records, including inspection of flight simulators and type trainers.

As soon as the airways came into existence in the early fifties, there were so many pilots requiring a renewal test for their annual instrument rating (IR) that it became necessary for CAFU examiners to train operators' pilots to conduct the IR renewal (IRR) tests, on behalf of the Directorate of Flight Crew Licensing, on their own company pilots. These company pilots became known as delegated examiners (DEs), later known as authorised examiners (AEs). Initially, their authority was granted for one year, later extended to three years, when a CAFU examiner would witness a delegated examiner examining one of his own company pilots attempting to renew their IR.

To become a DE, a company would submit a pilot, usually a company training pilot, for a two-week course at CAFU Stansted, which involved both classroom and flying training, ending with a final test known (locally) as an "Examinability," undertaken in one of the IR Doves. A CAFU pilot would act as a "guinea pig," taking his IR test in the left-hand seat. The company pilot under test, but undertaking this test as an examiner, sat in the right-hand seat. Behind, in the jump seat, sat the CAFU examiner witnessing the performance of the company pilot.

These courses were held at Stansted in CAFU's old Nissen huts. Often a company would send two pilots so the would-be DEs could practice on each other and share experiences in techniques of briefing and debriefing. The course would rarely run smoothly, as it could often be disrupted by weather or aircraft unserviceability.

Now that Captain Gurr was with the Flight Operations Inspectorate, the Ministry at long last engaged the services of a second helicopter pilot, Captain D. "Don" Sissons.

The telecommunications superintendent, responsible for the airborne technicians (NAIs), also controlled a staff of some forty Tels ground engineers—who installed and maintained the airborne equipment—photographers, draughtsmen, Storeman, and supporting executives.

The unit administrative officer, Mr. G. L. Russell, had a staff of around twenty whose duties included general administration, technical records, where the aircraft logs were kept, as well as staff in the Cost Accounts office, drivers, and cleaners.

Operations consisted of an operations officer, Mr. E. "Ted" Crisp, who had a separate office, and a briefing officer, Don McLaughlin, who controlled the operations area together with an air traffic control assistant (ATCA).

By the mid-1960s, the flight operations inspectors were known to be still engaged in ramp inspections, whereby they would fly an IR Dove at the weekend to the near continent, and inspect the operation of UK operators, inspecting aircraft documents and crew licences. I remember in particular Mr. R. "Dickie" Kilner and Geoffrey Chouffott on these trips. Mr. Chouffott later became a board member of the CAA.

Around this time, CAFU was flight testing a new Doppler VOR (DVOR—see appendix B), while still, on occasions, flight inspecting the Scillies VDF.

Due to new standards of flight inspection being asked by ICAO, CAFU sought new ways to flight-inspect the instrument landing aid and, for this reason, was engaged in developing a new system of calibration that could provide the required accuracy. The aim that the Telecommunications department was seeking was to find an accurate method of checking the "bends" in the ILS system such that, with other criteria, civil aircraft could achieve "All Weather Operations."

The solving of the problem of ILS "bends" was the attempt by the manufacturers to eliminate the reflections of the ILS beam signal, caused by nearby obstructions, such as buildings or vehicles. Once these problems could be overcome, then it was the turn of the calibrators to ensure that the beams, for both localiser and glide path, could be accurately measured to ensure that these new high standards were being maintained, thus enabling improved autopilot equipment to be capable of making lower and lower approaches to land.

Under the control of the superintendent, Mr. A. C. Marchant, CAFU finally adopted a ground-based optical and electrical equipment called telecroscope. Mr. Marchant remembered one of the CAFU NAIs, Iain Poulter, who brought to the attention of Dave Reiffer (who was then working at HQ) of the work being undertaken by the Ministry of Supply (MOS) on a powerful laser lamp, possibly for use as a landing aid or missile tracker.

The telecroscope was able to measure the deviation from a reference line of an airborne light to an accuracy of twenty seconds of arc (about six inches), at a range of one mile, and it could achieve this with the flight inspection aircraft up to five miles away. Air-to-ground radio links between the telecroscope and the aircraft permitted synchronisation of both air and ground measurements. It was really a precision infrared telescope sited at the extension of a runway for the localiser calibration and at the side of the landing end of the runway for glide-path calibration, using a laser to follow a lamp installed in the nose of the calibrating aircraft while conducting an ILS flight inspection. After much experimentation and evaluation, it finally became the UK instrument for measuring the accuracy of an ILS landing aid. Charles Marchant wrote later that

> *this method (of calibration) played a significant part in ICAO eventually being able to prescribe acceptable criteria for the measurement of ILS bend. (see appendix F). The development and implementation of this technique placed CAFU at the forefront of those ICAO member states endeavouring to achieve the same aim.*

In November, the importance of this work was demonstrated when a BEA Trident, G-ARPB, made a series of "blind auto landings" at Heathrow with a visibility of less than three hundred feet.

As a result of the 1963 All Weather Operations Panel (AWOP) study of the requirements for the three categories of ILS guidance, the ICAO COM/OPS meeting, in late 1966, defined the performance specification for category 3 (CAT 3).

Category	DH (ft)	DH (mtrs)	RVR (ft)	RVR (mtrs)
CAT 3	0	0	700	200

Obviously, one of the criteria required to achieve All Weather Operations was a high-quality ILS on the ground to match the automatic landing performance of the next generation of aircraft. At this time, only Tridents and Super VC-10s could land in category 2 conditions (400 m runway visibility and 100 ft decision height); but by 1975, it was expected there would be at least six more aircraft types in service with this capability and some, possibly, certificated for category 3b (50 m decision height and 0 ft forward visibility).

On the ground, the crucial elements of the system were the ILS system of glide path and localiser structures, runway and approach lighting, standby power supplies, as well as designated areas within the ILS equipment. All of these had to be certificated to at least the same category as the aircraft before operations in the appropriate weather conditions could be allowed.

The time interval between the calibrations of an aid varied with the type of aid being inspected. Routine flight inspections were carried out on

- 25 ILS installations every four months;
- 28 VOR en route aids and one TACAN, seen every three months;
- 14 Type 2000 radars, seen every two months;
- 4 Decca 424 radars and one Marconi radar, every three months;
- marker beacons every six months.

Any unscheduled tasks would be signalled to CAFU from Headquarters in London and would then be phased in with routine flight inspection tasks. Unscheduled tasks could be the flying of an initial inspection on a new, or proposed, site installation. Additionally, CAFU also assisted with new developments and special equipment. They would help in the siting of new VOR stations; transportable transmitters would be set up on possible sites, and CAFU would report on their suitability, which could take up to a week. CAFU could also be requested to investigate any aids reported as below standard—although the UK navaids at this time seldom gave any problems.

Any aircraft accident or incident in the United Kingdom could also be investigated, immediately if the aid was thought to be a contributing factor. This was a twenty-four-hour, seven-days-a-week service, including public holidays, provided by CAFU, which was covered by ground staff and aircrew alike.

Tasks would be grouped as being capable of being flown from Stansted on a daily basis throughout the week, and those tasks that could not be achieved in a single day would be grouped together and scheduled as "away from base" (AFB). Crews were normally sent AFB for a period of one week (Monday to Friday). The order of tasks would be allocated from a list of priorities; periodicity remaining for a particular aid before its next due inspection date, aircraft capability, weather—actual and forecast—ATC restrictions, ground aid maintenance times, equipment limitations, as well as transit economy.

For the flight checking of radar and certain other installations, the crew would consist of a pilot and navigator. For ILS, VOR, and TACAN installations, the crew would include an NAI in order to carry out the technical performance measurements for which the aircraft carried modified receivers, feeding information to a specially installed instrument panel and chart recorder.

In addition to the quantitative measurements made by the NAI, the pilot would also be required to make a qualitative assessment of the "flyability" of the aid. The navigator would assist with this, as well as act as camera operator, recording all the positional data. Other data would be recorded photographically: Decca information (forming the primary means of positioning the aircraft and installed in all of the Tels aircraft), heading, pitch roll, etc. An F24 vertical camera was also installed to record the ground track and, where necessary, the height of the aircraft. This tied in with the chart recorders by means of a pulsed signal that was operated every time the camera was fired. Test sets were also installed on the aircraft so that calibration of the onboard equipment could be checked when the aircraft was AFB.

CAFU Staff at December 31, 1966:

COMPLEMENT		ACTUAL STRENGTH	
STAFF	EXMNRS	STAFF	EXMNRS
138	29	123	20

As can be seen from the *Hansard* information (March 23, 1970, vol. 798), there was a shortage of overall CAFU staff, and examiners were 30 percent down on complement.

BOT CAFU Aircraft at the end of 1966 Total = 15

Dove	05	I/R, OS, Comm, GCA, Ref flying
Dove	04	Tels Flight Inspection, GCA, OS
Prince	03	Tels Flight Inspection
President	01	Tels Flight Inspection
Chipmunk	01	CPL, Instructor Ratings, Ref
HS125	01	Radar, Comms, VIP, Ref flying

1967

CAFU had flown 5,639 hours in the twelve months up to March 31, 1967. Hours flown by flight examiners in aircraft and simulators belonging to operators totalled 2,343. Around thirty company examiners (DEs) were authorised each year to conduct tests on behalf of the Ministry. To date, CAFU had conducted around twenty-seven thousand tests.

In June, two Douglas DC4s crashed, one at Perpignan on the third, and the second (actually an Argonaut—a DC4 with Rolls-Royce Merlin engines) the following day at Stockport. This prompted the president of the Board of Trade, Mr. Douglas Jay, to order a special review of the safety performance of UK operators. It was this review that would have a significant impact on CAFU.

In December, a BEA Argosy, G-ASXP, on crew training at Stansted airport, crashed from about one hundred feet after take-off on runway 23 and subsequently caught fire. The three crew members, the only occupants, escaped unhurt, but the Argosy was a total loss.

Due to the blocked runway, CAFU flights were cancelled for the rest of the day.

In July, the government set up a committee of inquiry under the chairmanship of Sir Ronald Edwards to inquire into Britain's Civil Air Transport. Part of its remit was to inquire into the

- economic and financial situation,
- method of regulating competition and licensing, and
- development of safety.

Standard Telephones and Cables Ltd. began a "private venture" development, in close liaison with the UK aviation authorities, of a new-generation ILS to meet the anticipated requirements of CAT 3 operations.

Prolonged recordings of the performance parameters of existing STC type STAN 7/8 ILS equipment in operation, one of these at London Airport, achieved the distinction of being the first promulgated as a CAT 2 facility, established that their stability was of an extremely high order. For example, over a period of a year, the standard deviation of shift of the STAN 7 localiser course line was less than the equivalent of one-foot displacement at the runway threshold. From this experience, it was clear that the envisaged requirements in accuracy and stability for CAT 3 could be readily achieved.

Additionally, it was recognised that CAT 3 demanded an extremely high order of equipment reliability and integrity performance monitoring, to achieve the overall system safety, i.e., the average accident rate in all landings should not exceed one in ten million. Since the risk was apportioned between the constituent elements of the overall landing system—the ground and airborne equipment—the accepted safety criterion demanded that the risk of an accident, attributable to a localiser or glide-path ground equipment failure, should be less than one in one hundred million.

The design philosophy, wrote *Flight*, for the STC CAT 3 ILS, known as STAN 37/38/39, was to retain the basic system concept of the CAT 2 equipment, but with the equipment design targeted to the highest order of reliability practically achievable. In many respects, its predicted performance was superior to the ICAO standard, and a long trial period would be necessary to substantiate these predictions before CAT 3 operations would be permitted. It was expected that a number of examples of this equipment would shortly be installed in the United Kingdom and Australia. All would then be subjected to continuous proving trials to establish their CAT 3 performance by accumulated statistical evidence related to their reliability and integrity.

The Board of Trade was assuming direct charge of testing instructors engaged on commercial pilot and instrument rating training. CAFU's Capt. Bob Whitehead, senior flight examiner, is the head of the BOT panel of instructors.

To obtain a CPL (or higher licence), it was necessary for the candidate, in addition to the written exams, to satisfy a Ministry CAFU examiner as to his proficiency in practical pilotage; furthermore, under certain circumstances, he could only exercise the unrestrictive privileges of his commercial licence if he also had an instrument rating; that is, he had demonstrated separately in an instrument rating test his knowledge of ATC procedures and his instrument flying ability. These were the tests carried out by CAFU examiners. The basic CPL comprised two flights: a day test, usually conducted in a single-engine aircraft; and a night test in a twin-engine aircraft. The daytime test consisted of a cross-country flight, basic aircraft handling, and instrument flying.

The instrument rating test was an addition to the CPL licence to allow a pilot to fly within controlled airspace, i.e., airways, etc., and was normally carried out in a twin-engine aircraft, though a private pilot (with no commercial licence) with a PPL (private pilot's licence), with sufficient experience, could bring a single or twin-engine aircraft for test.

The IR test had four main parts:

- Pre-flight, take-off, and climb
- Asymmetric power
- Airways flight
- Two letdown procedures: an instrument landing (ILS) with missed approach procedure plus another letdown procedure such as ADF or VOR.

Failure in two or more parts resulted in a complete retest. A failure in any one part would result in the requirement for a retake, i.e., Airways plus ILS or ILS and ADF letdown. If, after three attempts, a candidate failed, he would have to start a new series of three tests from the beginning. A test would have to be completed within six months of passing the written exams. If he failed a test nine times (three attempts of the full and partial tests), then he/she would be unable to go any further. In my time in Operations, 1962-1968 and 1974-1987, I never knew a nine-times failure by any candidate, though there was one known case of a pass on the ninth attempt. All initial tests for the IR were conducted by a CAFU examiner, including the PPL IR, which was slightly different from the professional test.

After passing the initial IR, a candidate would need to have it renewed on an annual basis. These were usually conducted by an authorised delegated examiner (DE) but were occasionally conducted at Stansted by a CAFU examiner, if so expressly requested, such as a private pilot who might not have easy access to a DE. A very well-known, at the time, TV games host, Hughie Green, used to fly a Cessna 310 and often came to Stansted to renew his IR. Yet he always elected to have the test using one of the CAFU Doves (the test then only cost ten pounds!), but this was before candidates were asked to provide their own aircraft for test.

I remember one year when Hughie failed one part of his IR renewal test and he had to do a re-take. The game he hosted, *Double Your Money*, consisted of contestants who were asked to choose a box to open. Each box might contain something inexpensive (like a cabbage) or something more exotic (such as a holiday). They would be given a key to open the box, but first offered money so that they could choose whether to open the box or take the money. Hughie offered me a ten-pound note to pay for his retake. Shamefully, I couldn't resist saying to him—"No, I want to open the box." Stone-faced, he put the money into my hand—but I had had my day.

There were now just under six thousand aircrew licences current.

The work of CAFU had been reported on by *Flight* magazine, first in the fifties and now again at a time of change in the sixties. The article from June 1967 is worth reproduction, as it describes the flight inspection role once the HS748s were to be operational. The writer was an A. C. Merchant, a corruption of his name, confirmed to me by Charles Marchant (when he phoned me one day at the age of ninety), made by one of the *Flight* assistant editors ("who *cocked* things up," he told me). It is most likely that the article would have provided the MCA with the explanation for the need to purchase updated aircraft in order to be able to flight-inspect modern improving aids, which were already in advance of the post-war aids that CAFU's current outdated aircraft were calibrating. It was titled "The Work of the Civil Aviation Flying Unit" by A. C. "Merchant," and explained how calibration of landing aids needed to be changed in order to meet the requirements of ICAO, how ILS was only, in its CAT 1 state, an approach to landing, and that CAFU had had to develop new devises and methods of calibration. He explained how CAFU's current aircraft were not up to the job and required an aircraft type with sophisticated equipment to enable automatic approaches, perhaps down to ground level, which he perceived for the future. It is too long, detailed, and technical here for me to intrude in this excellent description of events in 1967, so I will ask the reader to find the work in appendix F.

CATEGORY 1-3 Minima:

Category	DH (ft)	DH (mtrs)	RVR (ft)	RVR (mtrs)
CAT I	200	60	2600	800
CAT 2	100	30	1200	400
CAT 3A	0	0	700	200
CAT 3B	0	0	150	50
CAT 3C	0	0	0	0

The above table, shown in *Flight*, requires a little more explanation as my searches have shown various figures that, at times, do not appear to tie up or agree. Below is a further explanation of the figures in the boxes above:

CAT 1:
An approach to land operation down to a minima of 60 m (200 ft) DH and RVR 800 m or 2,600 ft with a high probability of approach success. When RVR is not available, 800 m (2,600 ft) visibility is intended.

CAT 2:
Operation down to a minima below 60 m (200 ft) DH and RVR 800 m (2,600 ft), and to as low as 30 m (100 ft) DH and RVR 400 m (1,200 ft), with a high probability of approach success.

CAT 3a:
Operation to and along the surface of the runway, with external visual reference during the final phase of the landing down to RVR minima of 200 m (700 ft).

CAT 3b:
Operation to and along the surface of the runway and taxiways with visibility sufficient only for visual taxiing comparable to RVR value in the order of 50 m (150 ft).

CAT 3c:
Operation to and along the surface of the runway and taxiways without external visual reference.

Up until now, seven British types had performed automatic landings: Argosy, Belfast, Comet, Canberra, Varsity, Trident, and VC10. The Trident 1 flight trials, which had finished in January, 1967, provided data for triplex autopilot operation down to category 3a weather conditions.

In 1967, the commander had three deputies:

1. Deputy A, Captain W. A. Wooden
2. Deputy B, Captain D. Hale
3. Deputy C, Captain S. Spence

The third deputy commander position, Deputy Commander C, filled by Capt. Stuart Spence, was responsible for the arrangement of testing candidates for the commercial pilot's licence flying test and the instrument rating test that involved close liaison with the director of Flight Crew Licensing at Headquarters in London. This post also included the inspection and approval of flying training establishments throughout the United Kingdom, as well as the training and provision of flight examiners to conduct the various tests at these establishments. Captain Spence, I believe, was in position much earlier than I have shown here.

The superintendent, Mr. Charles Marchant, was promoted to Headquarters, and Mr. W. "Bill" Aitkin took up the new position. Charles had joined the MCA in 1953, becoming superintendent in 1959.

CAFU Aircraft at the end of 1967. Total = 15 (though 17 registered—the two HS748s didn't arrive until 1969).

BOT CAFU Aircraft:
REGISTERED

| Hs748 | G-AVXI | BOT | Nov 1967 |
| Hs748 | G-AVXJ | BOT | Nov 1967 |

BOT CAFU Aircraft at the end of 1967 Total = 17

Dove	05	I/R, OS, Comm, GCA, Ref flying
Dove	04	Tels Flight Inspection, GCA, OS
Prince	03	Tels Flight Inspection
President	01	Tels Flight Inspection
Chipmunk	01	CPL, Instr. Ratings, Refresher
HS125	01	Radar, Comms, VIP, Ref flying
HS748	02	Tels Flight Inspection

CAFU Staff at December 31, 1967:

COMPLEMENT		ACTUAL STRENGTH	
STAFF	EXMNRS	STAFF	EXMNRS
144	29	137	23

There were still nine navigators and seven NAIs at this time.

1968

Ramp inspections were still undertaken using the CAFU IR Dove. Geoff Gurr, currently a PFE/PFOI, remembers trips to Venice and Innsbruck this year as well as Hannover and Hamburg.

President of the Board of Trade (BOT) is Anthony Crosland.

In the BOT Special Review—Safety Performance of UK Operators (see June 1967), set up by the former president of the Board of Trade, Mr. Douglas Jay, many suggestions and recommendations were made that were put forward to the Edwards Review. There was comment made of both the Flight Operations Inspectorate and CAFU, and it was suggested that staffing levels and pay should be addressed.

The findings of the Edwards Committee were made known in May. In its report, "British Air Transport in the Seventies," one of its principal recommendations was the establishment of a Civil Aviation Authority (CAA), to be established as a statutory corporation.

But for CAFU, there were more significant findings. Within the BOT, there was to be a new aviation structure. The recommendations were that the Directorate of Aviation Safety should be split between two directors:

- Director of Flight Operations Safety
- Director of Training and Licensing (both new posts).

The BOT went further than the Edwards Review by recommending the director general also be in command of five other directorates, giving him unified control. His task would be to reorganise the work to provide simplified lines of command.

Because of the new structure, CAFU aircrew would now work, in the interim period, for three separate directorates: flight inspection, under the director of Flight Safety; examining CPL candidates under the new post of director of Training and Licensing; conducting airline training inspections for another new post, the director of Flight Operations Safety. This had the total effect of splitting CAFU's tasks into three separately headed directorates.

It takes time to take in exactly what was going on. But if you look at the diagram at the end of this chapter, you can see that the commander would, in time, no longer be responsible for CPL and IR tests, or flight inspection calibration work.

This ties in with Geoff Gurr's story in his biography, *A Testing Time,* where he writes that in the mid-1960s, the Establishment Branch in London decided it was nonsense for the Ministry to employ two separate groups of professional pilots, the flying examiners (FEs) at CAFU Stansted Airport and flight operations inspectors (FOIs) who worked from the London Office. *"The intention,"* he writes, *"was to form one Group with titles merged at the same level with the same pay scales."*

It is probable these happenings came about after the Edwards Review. This would explain the later merging of the Stansted CAFU training inspectors and the London flight operations inspectors into one group, and the decision to pay both sets the same salary. It had been difficult, from both groups' perspective, to comprehend the rationale behind the decision because they both had separate responsibilities, one flying and the other on the ground, yet with similar objectives—the operational safety of UK Civil Aviation. London-based staff were inspectors of commercial airline companies checking pilots' licences, aircraft documentation, etc., and issuing air operator's certificates to companies where standards of competency were satisfactory. While at CAFU, the flight examiners were testing "pre-airline" pilots for commercial licences and testing "post-airline" training captains for the delegation of authority to flight-check their own company pilots. Both the London and Stansted staff were required to be the holder of an airline transport pilot's licence. The difference was that the Stansted CAFU training inspectors were required to hold a "type rating" of the aircraft flown by the pilots whose company they were inspecting. It meant that an FOI could be medically unfit and still continue working, whereas a CAFU pilot who lost his licence would be unable to continue as a training inspector. It was hardly surprising that both sides were reported as being suspicious of the other and opposed to any merger.

This review, which came into force later in the 1970s, was probably the most influential instrument of change to affect CAFU.

It scrutinized the organisation and responsibilities of the Aviation Safety Division of the Board of Trade and of the Air Registration Board. It recognised that the Directorate of Aviation Safety had suffered many staffing difficulties and, in particular, until recent months, the Flight Operations Inspectorate was at no more than half the complement that was accepted as necessary.

CAFU was no better placed. The organisation and complement of the sections that dealt with pilot licensing and training matters had become increasingly inadequate for their task and, for those reasons, had already been reorganised.

The review also made note that the United Kingdom safety record was up to the level of most ICAO countries, but it needed improvement, and further attention had to be given both by the department and the industry to the overall raising of standards.

The special study made of the accident records of all United Kingdom operators had shown that timely information, not only on notifiable accidents but also on all occurrences that could endanger aircraft, would be a valuable means of preventing accidents.

Some of the recommendations made were the following:

- The director of Aviation Safety, Board of Trade, should have none other than his statutory role, and his title should be changed to director of Flight Operations.
- A director of Training and Licensing should be appointed whose duties would include those other functions at present carried out by the director of Aviation Safety.
- The director of Flight Operations Safety should have direct control of all matters in the Civil Aviation Flying Unit connected with the air operator's certificate. Appropriate arrangements should be made to ensure that all pilots were kept in flying practice.
- In order to fulfil his statutory duties, the director of Flight Operations should have, directly responsible to him, an adequate and properly trained staff.
- Rates of pay for the Board of Trade flying staff should be realistic in the light of salaries paid in the aviation industry generally.

- Board of Trade flight examiners should move away from observing single pilot competency checks and, from time to time, concentrate on observing a series of tests in each company.
- As soon as the CAFU examining unit is fully staffed, it should become a condition of appointment of all check captains, type rating examiners, and instrument rating examiners that they should have successfully completed a course in examining techniques conducted by that unit.
- That the director of Flight Operations should be enabled to take account of an operator's financial status and resources when considering the grant of an AOC.

These careful words show that under section 2. Flight crew licensing work conducted by CAFU would now come under the director of Training and Licensing, while under section 4, any CAFU work that would affect an airline companies AOC would now be controlled by the newly created director of Flight Operations Safety.

In April, the College of Air Training at Hamble had delivery of the first of eleven new aircraft, Beech Barons, a twin aircraft type not often seen by CAFU examiners, who would now require another type on their licence, as CAT had previously used Piper PA23 and DHC1 Chipmunk aircraft.

There was a policy change this year, when candidates for the CPL were asked to provide their own aircraft for test. This was an advantage to the Ministry as they were no longer able to charge an economic rate. Candidates, it was thought, were better positioned as they were now able to be tested on the aircraft with which they were familiar and on which they had conducted their training. But to the examiners, as they were always the official "pilot in command," it meant that they would have to be rated on each of the types they flew.

Geoff Gurr recalls that he already had nine types to be qualified on, with all the frequent subsequent renewals to be achieved, and remembers the London School of Flying from Elstree requiring an

Anson to be given approval for IR tests, which meant he now had to renew his rating on this aircraft type.

The policy changed the way tests were conducted, when candidates were advised they would have to present their own (or a school's) approved aircraft. Approved mainly because of the necessary screening each type required, as well as checking documentation to ensure the aircraft was properly maintained. However, CAFU was not too strict, and if a one-off PPL IR was required, and the owner/candidate wanted to use his own private aircraft, the examiner would provide sufficient advice to the candidate/owner on how to make his own cardboard set of blanking screens, just for the one-off test, until a pass was successfully achieved.

At the same time, the ten-pound fee for taking a test on a CAFU aircraft was stopped and an increasing levy made. It was hardly surprising there was an endeavour to claw back money as the annual cost of CAFU had now risen to about £1 million. This major change resulted in the slow release of CAFU's fleet of aircraft, the remaining single-engine Chipmunk and twin-engine Doves. Most candidates would now present themselves with a school aircraft, which required annual renewal approval, and these records were kept within Operations.

There were many small schools at the time. I recall Gordon King with his Apache, G-ARJV, out of Biggin Hill; and Len Richards, who had a small office at Stansted and used a PA30, G-ASSB, for his candidates. Len's PA30 was always easy to hire for any Stansted examiner requiring training or refresher on the type. One occasion, I recall, was a new examiner, ex-RAF Vulcan captain, who required the PA30 to be on his licence, and Len Richards being called to supply both the aircraft and his presence. On the first circuit, with the new examiner thinking that Len was in command and Len, somewhat overawed by the Vulcan captain, thinking the examiner was in command, the aircraft embarrassingly landed wheels up. No damage to occupants or aircraft, just red faces all around.

Eric Thurston's PA23, G-ASMY, from Stapleford Tawney, was probably the most frequent aircraft using the services of CAFU, seen almost weekly, if not daily, at times with two candidates ready for test. One of his candidates, "Deli" Grayfisk, became an instructor for him, and I remember him praising her skills when she encountered a double-engine failure on approach and having the presence of mind to ensure the "props" were horizontal before belly-landing. Ms. Grayfisk became, I believe, part of an all-female crew with Dan-Air.

From my nineteen years with CAFU, I cannot remember an examiner or candidate having any major flying incident while under test. Though come to think of it, I do recall in the 1960s when a senior examiner, Capt. Bob Whitehead, was conducting a night test (GFT4) in one of the Dove aircraft at Stansted; all the approach and runway lights failed. All that Bob could do was remain in the area while a solution was found. I phoned his wife to let her know Bob would be later than normal. Twenty minutes later, his wife appeared in Ops with a pack of sandwiches! After about an hour, the runway lights were restored, and Bob was able to land with his candidate—who passed after having gained welcome additional dual instruction. Not entirely a walk in the park for the candidate, I suppose, but a bit of a picnic for me.

Capt. Don Hale, who was promoted to principal grade in 1965, was now transferred to the All Weather Operations Directorate. Captain J. "Jack" Picken replaced him as the PFE in the deputy commander B position.

Simulator inspections were carried out by a Ministry team comprising an Airworthiness Test Pilot from their Flight department, who assessed handling characteristics of the simulator relating to the envelope of the aircraft, with a senior flight examiner from CAFU, in his role as training inspector, together with a representative from the Directorate of Training and Licensing (DTL), in order to assess the simulator's records. It was the man from DTL who was responsible for making the recommendation with regard to the approval of the simulator.

CAFU aircraft maintenance was now contracted to Short Brothers and Harland.

It was towards the end of 1968 Capt. John Oliver was informed by the deputy commander A, Capt. Bill Wooden, that he was to be put forward as the CAFU training inspector for Concorde. It was a great surprise, said John, because he had only joined the MoA three years previously and was still one of the junior flight examiners at CAFU. On December 31, Captain Oliver attended the first Concorde Introductory Course.

CAFU Staff at December 31, 1968:

COMPLEMENT		ACTUAL STRENGTH	
STAFF	EXMNRS	STAFF	EXMNRS
146	29	144	31

The two HS748 aircraft, purchased and registered to the Board of Trade in November 1967, were expected to be delivered sometime in 1969. These would eventually replace the four calibration Doves, three Princes, and one President, currently used for flight inspection operations since the 1950s.

1969

CAFU commander, Captain B. E. E. Marshall, was awarded an OBE in the New Year's honours list.

The importance of the HS125 was not only felt by CAFU aircrew, who required flying hours in a modern sophisticated environment, but also UK government cabinet ministers were increasingly able to take advantage of this small executive aeroplane.

In May, Captains W. Wooden and John Oliver flew from Stansted to Heathrow to pick up the minister for Technology, Mr. Anthony Wedgwood Benn. He was flown to Moscow, via Helsinki, not only to refuel but also to pick up a Russian courtesy crew member, an Aeroflot pilot, Capt. Alexi Zouroff. When discussing diversionary airfields, Zouroff was told that the choice was Leningrad, as it had one of the only two American VORs in Russia. "Leningrad!" exclaimed Alexi. "Who would want to go to Leningrad?" It later transpired that the small airfield he would have chosen was close to the town where his girlfriend lived. Moscow's Sheremetyevo airfield had severe security, and the 125 was sealed with wire and old-fashioned wax, which was stamped whenever left unattended.

They returned the same day flying to Stansted via Helsinki to drop off Captain Zouroff. Six days later, they flew the same route again to bring Mr. Benn back into Heathrow.

The 125 had a small galley where hot water could provide the usual cup (plastic) of tea or coffee. Two cups were always given because the water was so hot. Coffee was the choice of most 125 pilots, but of the VIPs carried whenever Mr. Benn was asked if he would like a cup of coffee, he would dig into his case and provide his tin mug. No one was sure if he simply disliked plastic or wished to show his proletariat leanings.

In February 1969, BEA was authorised to operate the HS121 Trident aircraft to mid-CAT 2 limits (60-30 metres decision height [DH] and 600-400 metres runway visual range [RVR]), with full CAT 2 clearance, depending on a history of successful operations at the interim limits and improvements to ground facilities at a number of airfields. Initially, only automatic landings were allowed, but manual landings in CAT 2 conditions—30 metres DH and 400 metres RVR—were now permitted.

Hawker Siddeley handed over the two aircraft to the commander "Bee" Marshall at a presentation to staff at Stansted (see photo); the other two gentlemen were believed to be a man from Hawker Siddeley and possibly the minister from the BoT.

G-AVXI and G-AVXJ first flew on February 14 and June 4, 1969, respectively, says Richard J. Church, and additionally underwent modifications at Hawarden after their initial first flights from Woodford. They were delivered in July and September. This gave time for the flight inspection equipment, already prepared by CAFU, to be installed at pace for each of the aircraft. CAFU worked closely with the ARB Surveyor, who had a regional office in Southend, in the installation of equipment.

The equipment was completely new, either built by CAFU staff or new and modified to CAFU requirements. Internally, the racks and consoles, designed by Eddy Harris and turned into workable drawings by the design and draughtsmen team of Ron Turner and Ray Monk at Stansted, were to be located on the seat tracks of the standard cabin. Forward was an extra navigator's desk, installed behind the flight deck where the normal forward baggage compartment was normally situated. Between the navigator seat and the main equipment area was a passenger compartment with eight seats in facing pairs across fixed tables. Behind the main cabin was a small galley, toilet, and baggage compartment as on standard HS748 aircraft.

The onboard equipment was all of modular design for easy removal and replacement and was a great improvement on the smaller Prince aircraft, where everything was built in, and any changes of equipment meant a lengthy grounding. Metre panels were installed, and the newly designed racks and consoles prefabricated for quick installation.

In numerous ways, CAFU Tels staff were able to incorporate ideas evolved during the development of the HS121 Trident aircraft for All Weather Operations. The flight inspection aerials and the ILS receivers in particular were beneficiaries, being suitably modified to the exacting standard required by CAFU for the work of flight inspection.

One of the many modifications was the 1,000-watt high-intensity narrow beam tungsten nose lamp. It was noise free and adequate power supplies specified. The lamp, specially developed to work in conjunction with telecroscope ground equipment, could usually be detected at a range of seven miles and known to track from as far as eleven miles. In addition to the lamp, externally there were over thirty aerials attached for flight inspection work.

In the 1960s, it can proudly be said that CAFU played a significant part in the adoption of a method of calibration that achieved not only CAT 2 (down to about 30 m DH) but also CAT 3, which, in its various naming of A, B, and C, would eventually enable approach landings, using ILS, down to zero feet decision height (DH) and zero forward visibility.

It was only after a great deal of work by CAFU Tels engineers that these two aircraft now became operational. The two HS748 aircraft, G-AVXI and VXJ, were, by the end of the year, flying with the latest calibration equipment available anywhere in the world, capable of operations above ten thousand feet, as well as having the ability to fly auto-coupled approaches; the Smiths SFS6 flight control system gave the HS748 the technical capability of making a coupled approach down to seventy-five feet in category 2 conditions, and down to fifty feet in fair weather.

Aircraft instruments included Marconi Landing System (ILS) receiving equipment (AD260), specially modified by the manufacturer for CAFU. This was the same basic equipment as used by the BEA Trident for all-weather landings, but since CAFU had to use the equipment for checking the instrument landing systems that were used by the Trident, it was necessary to take measures to extract greater accuracy from the equipment than that which was needed for that aircraft.

The comprehensive aerial system included localiser and glide-slope aerials, developed by ITT (*STC*) for CAFU's special purposes. The installation also contained a Cosser 555 Field Test set, modified by the manufacturer to CAFU requirements, used as a transfer standard for checking the airborne equipment stability; or it enabled the ILS receivers to be referenced to the Wayne Kerr Precision Calibrator (see letter below) also carried in the aircraft. A Decca Doppler 72 was fitted, with its associated computer, developed by the manufacturer for flight inspection purposes.

The telescroscope system and associated telemetry equipment were made by Milligan Electronics, and the servo controlled target lamp manufactured by Plessey.

Both aircraft were equipped with a modern Smiths Flight System (SFS6) and Sperry Roll Stabilized CL11 Compass System, eventually cleared by the CAA Airworthiness Department (AWD) for automatic flight under CAT 2 approach conditions.

A second phase, to be introduced in the near future, would include the provision of a digital tape recording system, which could produce tapes for playing directly into the computer in the CAFU Analysis Section.

It was reported in the Bishop's Stortford local weekly, *Herts and Essex Observer*, that the unit ". . . had received two flying laboratories which, with instruments, cost a total of £2 million and with an annual budget of £1 million represented one of the world's most vigorous air safety and navigational accuracy organisations."

There was worldwide interest in the Stansted-developed telescroscope system. Complete systems were bought by Brazil, South Africa, East Africa, Germany, Switzerland, and Australia. Other countries to have shown an interest included Canada, New Zealand, and Yugoslavia.

When the two HS748s became operational, which was not before time as the Princes were soon to be grounded with main spar failure, CAFU had an Open Day on October 29 at which the press were invited, and the minister, Mr, Fred Mulley, attended.

An interesting letter passed to me from Eddy Harris was a press information letter from Wayne Kerr, titled "ILS Calibration," providing a brief explanation of Difference in Depth of Modulation (DDM):

> WAYNE KERR
> The Wayne Kerr Company Limited, New Malden, Surrey, England
> Telephone 01-942 2202 Telegraph Wayne Kerr, Maiden Telex 262333
> PRESS INFORMATION
> For Immediate Release 27th October, 1969.
> CAFU Open Day (29th Oct. 1969)
> ILS CALIBRATION
>
> The accurate determination of zero DDM was of critical importance in the calibration of the Instrument Landing System (ILS). This vital measurement was entrusted to a Precision Calibrator type N100, developed by Wayne Kerr, engineers for the Royal Aircraft Establishment (RAE). It was used by CAFU for the calibration of their flight inspection aircraft and by airport and airline authorities throughout the world.
>
> *The N100 was portable equipment which measured not only DDM, but absolute depth of modulation for the Localiser and Glide Slope signals. In addition, it could be operated directly from the audio tones used to modulate the two carrier signals, and also measured the relative phase of the tones. Sensitivity of the ILS Precision Calibrator when reading zero DDM is 0.01%. This corresponds to an azimuth error which, at the threshold of a runway, is equivalent to a displacement of only 7 cm.*
>
> *This instrument has made a major contribution—as a master calibrator for the alignment of transmitters, monitors and aircraft receivers—in the progress towards the use of ILS for all-weather landings. Recent studies had shown that it was possible to make the measurements automatically and extend the use of these new techniques to in-flight calibration of ground transmissions.*

Notably in 1969, ICAO produced DOC 8071 (Manual on Testing of Radio Navigational Aids), the first edition of which was based a great deal upon advice provided by CAFU.

The CAFU commander, Capt. "Bee" Marshall, recent recipient of the OBE in the New Year's honours list, who had joined in the late forties, instrumental in the setting up of flying tests for the issue of instrument ratings and oversaw the design and implementation of the angled screens in the Doves, resigned over the issue of the use of visors being used by candidates under test. The new director of Flight Crew Licensing, under pressure from the private pilot sector, was going to allow private candidates to use a visor rather than a screen. The reason for visors was said to be cost, yet CAFU, who did not believe visors gave satisfactory conditions under test (examination), had already compromised by allowing the use of stiff card and sticky tape to be used in certain cases. If Captain Marshall's resignation was a (serious) loss, then it was the Church of England's gain when he joined the cloth.

One can only ask if this was the only issue that caused the resignation. As commander, he would have been aware more than most of the consequence of the recommendations of change to the structure and terms of conditions, which Captain Gurr already noted, which may well have assisted in his decision to terminate his civil aviation career.

April 9 saw Concorde 002's maiden flight from Bristol Filton, piloted by Capt. Brian Trubshaw.

You may remember that at the end of 1961, the number of flight operations inspectors was fourteen; but by the end of 1969, the complement was thirty-four, and the actual strength was now up to thirty-one. The FOI complement had increased by 100 percent since 1961.

One of the criticisms of the structure of the Flight Operations Inspectorate and CAFU, recognised by the BOT special review in 1968, was the insufficient numbers of staff in both departments.

Although the Princes were not to be deregistered until 1971, David Lacey (ex-CAFU engineer, using the Mitchell Library, Glasgow [File TD578/4]), tells me that the last flights of the Princes were in November 1969. Geoff Gurr's biography, *A Testing Time,* says that they suffered from main-spar corrosion, and Charles Marchant, in his paper to the Institute of Navigation, tells how the 748s came into service just in time.

It is known that the Airworthiness Division had declared, after a review of the life of the Princes' main spars that their life had already been reached, and promptly grounded all three aircraft. The story is worth relating, as the Princes were flying until the last. G-AMKX was on a week's AFB calibration work in Scotland, based at Prestwick. On Wednesday, November 12, it had set out for Edinburgh just before 0930 and, for whatever reason, returned before 1030 the same morning. The crew had probably then phoned back to base at Stansted to report a problem. CAFU may then have asked the KX crew to do an air test, as they did a local forty-nine-minute flight at about 1330. At 1605 the same day, G-AMKW, a second CAFU Prince, flew into Prestwick, perhaps with the intention to assist the grounded crew with the problem. These were the last flights made by these two aircraft, as they never left Prestwick—by air. Possibly, MKW was sent to assist in some way, and it was probably determined over the next two days exactly what the problem was, and both aircraft were grounded, as was G-AMKY back at Stansted.

Two days later on Friday, the HS748, GAVXJ, now operational, was despatched to Prestwick, landing at 1052. This was possibly to finish any flight inspection work and pick up the two stricken crews to take them back to Stansted (to be continued).

CAFU Staff at December 31, 1969:

COMPLEMENT		ACTUAL STRENGTH	
STAFF	EXMNRS	STAFF	EXMNRS
158	29	145	29

Since 1960, the examiner complement had grown by 45 percent, and the total staff complement by just over 100 percent.

BOT CAFU Aircraft at the end of 1969 Total = 17

Dove	05	I/R, OS, Comm, GCA, Ref flying
Dove	04	Tels Flight Inspection, GCA, OS

Prince	03	Tels Flight Inspection—actually grounded in November
President	01	Tels Flight Inspection
Chipmunk	01	CPL, Instr. Ratings, Ref flying
HS125	01	Radar, Comms, VIP, Ref flying
HS748	02	Tels Flight Inspection

Safety Was No Accident 187

Prince MKW with nose lamp
Photo: Eddy Harris/JF

Testing an early Telecroscope
Photo: Eddy Harris/JF

First CAFU HS125, G-ATPC at Stansted. Registered Feb 1966
Photo: Peter Moon/JF

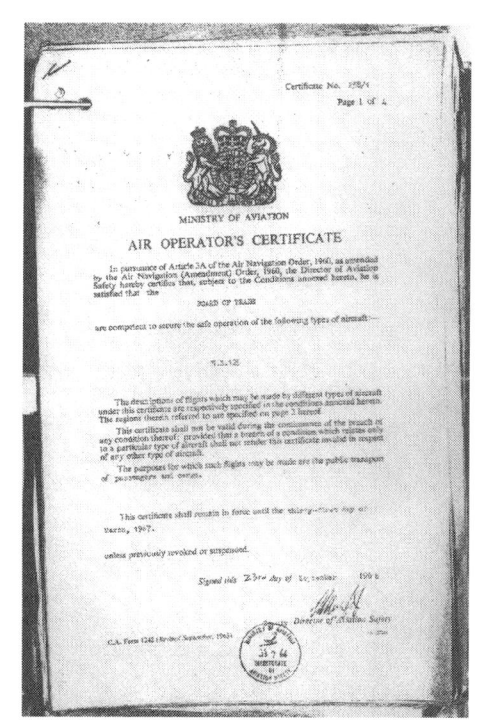

Caption: CAFU AOC for HS125
Photo: Steve Dench, via National Archives (BT267/24)

Safety Was No Accident 189

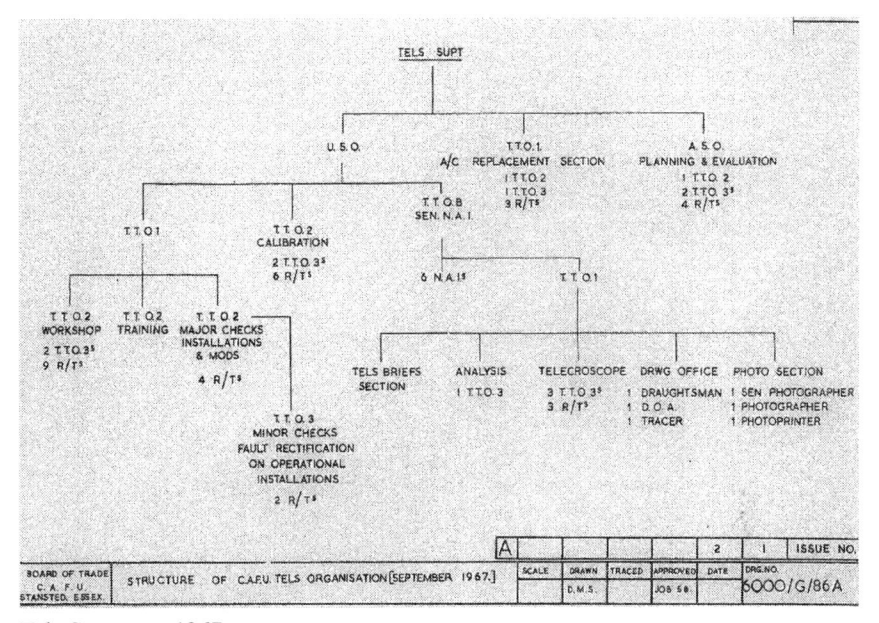

Tels Structure 1967
Photo: Eddy Harris/JF

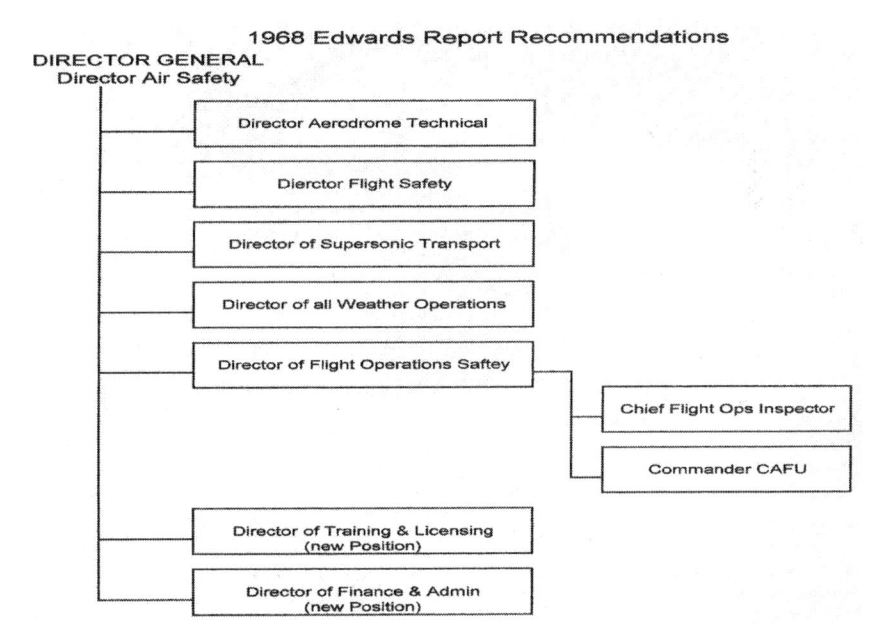

1968 Edwards Recommendations
Photo: JF

1968 Captain Marshall, CAFU Commander, at HS748 Handover 1969
Photo: Eddy Harris/JF

VXI at work calibrating landing aid
Photo: Eddy Harris/JF

Chapter Four
1970-1974

1970

After twenty years in the old wartime Nissen huts at Stansted, work commenced on a new building to house all of the CAFU staff of which there were now around 160, which included the technical staff under the Tels superintendent. Had the new build anything to do with CAFU receiving an AOC back in 1966, I wonder, when one of the requirements was "adequacy of accommodation."

BOT CAFU Aircraft:
REGISTERED

| HS125 | G-AVDX | BOT | June 1970 |

DEREGISTERED

| DH125 | G-ATPC | MTCA | Dec 1970 |

CAFU's first jet aircraft the DH125, G-ATPC, was about to be replaced by a later version. In June, an upgraded HS125, (de Havilland now part of the Hawker Siddeley group), G-AVDX, a Series 3B aircraft was registered to the Department of Trade and Industry. VDX was previously with Air Hanson, but was acquired through Hawker Siddeley.

Powered by two Bristol Siddeley 522 Viper engines, each of 3,360 lb thrust, the maximum payload was increased by 400 lb to 2,000 lb, and this could be carried, with reserve fuel, over stage lengths of 1,278 nm. Zero fuel weight was increased from 13,000 lb to 13,500 lb, and the maximum landing weight was 20,000 lb.

Although only built a year later than TPC, it had a greater maximum take-off weight (MTOW) due to the slightly improved engines of the Viper 522. One important difference was its capability for CAT 2 operations, i.e., land in lower weather minima conditions, and was frequently used for VIP flights; carrying UK government ministers around the United Kingdom and Europe. The two 125 aircraft were used in tandem for a short time while the crews were rated on the new type and then G-ATPC was deregistered on December 7.

After the resignation of Captain Marshall, over the issue of the use of visors, his post was filled, in February, by Captain G. "Geoffrey" B. Gurr.

CAFU was also now responsible for the standard of training and testing of commercial flying instructors. At approved flying training schools, this responsibility was delegated to pilots approved by CAFU examiners, and their continuing standard had to be monitored in the same way as delegated type and instrument rating examiners. Captain R. O. (Bob) Whitehead, one of CAFU's senior flight examiners, was engaged in this period producing a manual of flying instruction.

Geoffrey Chouffot, who in 1966 was made chief flight operations inspector, was now made director of Flight Operations with responsibility for the Stansted-based CAFU as well as the Flight Operations Inspectorate. This was the new post created after the Edwards Review of 1968. Mr. Kilner now became CFOI.

It was during the latter part of the sixties that a computer was installed in the CAFU Tels Analysis section, by John Cook, it was believed. (John, it was said, was used as a photographer at the unit in the fifties and may be the source of many of the earlier aircraft photographs.)

This was one of the early computers (Apollo) that was first installed in the Scottish Oceanic Centre and given a new lease of life at CAFU. Four people from administration were trained to work in this section, according to Sheila Vincent, who later helped run the outfit. The work required a great deal of concentration as figures were closely taken from the pen-recorder readings from the aircraft and passed to an assistant who input the data to the computer.

The number of ILS installations in the United Kingdom now numbered about forty and were increasing in number. These required a flight inspection every four months. It was expected that by 1975, there would be up to sixty ILS installations.

At ICAO, the technique-assessment team of the Radio Technical Commission for Aeronautics (RTCA) studies Standing Committee 117 (SC117), which was studying the requirement for a new landing aid, released its recommendations for signal-format development. The committee concluded that the wavelengths most resistant to interference and reflection problems lay in the aeronautical mobile portion of C-band (5,000-5,250 MHz). But the degree of accuracy for flare guidance dictated that Ku-band frequencies would also be required (15,400-15,700 MHz). The need for two frequency bands—and hence two receivers on each aircraft—was challenged, but the SC117 report is generally recognised as the beginning of the microwave landing system (MLS) story.

CAFU's HS125, G-AVDX, was now regularly used by numerous government departments on VIP flights. The pick-up point for senior government cabinet ministers would usually be Heathrow, Stansted, or Northolt, but could be any suitable airport. Destinations were sometimes in the United Kingdom but also to any airport in Europe, even the Middle East, though many flights were to Brussels and Luxembourg.

Roy Mason, president of the Board of Trade, plus an entourage of four, was flown by Captain Oliver to Vienna and on to Bucharest on March 9, returning on the eleventh from Vienna to Heathrow. On the twenty-third, Captain Oliver flew the minister for Technology, Mr. Anthony Wedgwood Benn, from Heathrow to East Midlands and return.

On May 21, Mr. Roy Mason, with four passengers, was taken from Heathrow to Munich and on to Budapest, returning to Heathrow.

Then in June, after the general election on the eighteenth, which the Conservatives won, John Oliver carried the new minister for Education, Mrs. Margaret Thatcher, to Tel Aviv Lod.

In October, Capt. Dan Thomas and Capt. Brian Morgan flew the 125, carrying the minister of Housing from Heathrow to Blackpool. In the same month, Captain Morgan flew with Ron Crawford from Heathrow to Leconfield and return with the minister for Education, Mrs. Margaret Thatcher. The return was memorable in that the minister showed a keen interest in the approach back into London Heathrow.

The minister for Technology was flown Heathrow to Manchester with his son, returning back into Heathrow.

Finally, in October, Captain Morgan flew with Dan Thomas, bringing back the minister for Transport, Mr. Peyton, from Paris Le Bourget to Heathrow. Quite often these journeys would be split between two separate crews because of length of day and the "duty times" to which the crews were limited.

After criticism in the BOT special review on safety in 1968, the UK aviation accident figures were now below the ICAO member state average. In fact, British standards of airline safety were now thought to be comparative with the leaders, America and Australia, who were at the forefront.

The July 1970 edition of the *Scottish Air News* reported:

At Prestwick are the two BoT Prince 6B's, G-AMKW and G-AMKX, which were discovered last November to have exceeded their spar life by several hundred hours. On discovery they were immediately grounded, one of the replacement HS748's collecting much of their equipment. It is assumed they will be scrapped eventually, unless an aircraft preservation body can step in in time.

BOT CAFU Aircraft at the end of 1970 Total = 17

Dove	05	I/R, OS, Comm, GCA, Ref flying
Dove	04	Tels Flight Inspection, GCA, OS
Prince	03	Tels Flight Inspection (grounded)

President	01	Tels Flight Inspection
Chipmunk	01	CPL, Instr. Ratings, Refresher flying
HS125	01	Radar, Comms, VIP, Ref flying
HS748	02	Telecommunications

CAFU aircraft at the end of 1970. Total = 17

1971

Another change affecting CAFU happened in January when the Board of Trade merged with the Ministry of Technology to form the Department of Trade and Industry (DTI), which had come into being on October 20, 1970, now becoming responsible for civil aviation matters.

After the Edwards Committee's recommendations on the administration of civil aviation were published, Ted Heath, Conservative prime minister, asked John Boyd-Carpenter to be chairman of a proposed Civil Aviation Authority. It will be remembered that Boyd-Carpenter was previously appointed as the MTCA minister back in 1954. The Civil Aviation Authority would be given a broad remit to ensure that services met demand cheaply and profitably.

The Civil Aviation Act of 1971 created the Civil Aviation Authority and the British Airways Board, the latter to function as a holding company for BOAC and BEA.

CAFU's telecommunications superintendent was now assisted at this time by Gerry Wilcox, a man highly rated by Charles Marchant. The telecommunications staff at CAFU had responsibility for the maintenance of all CAFU ground and airborne radio and electronic equipment, as well as operating the calibration laboratory in which the measuring equipment, used for flight inspections, was itself periodically calibrated and checked for continued accuracy.

Alec Barrett, the senior navaid inspector (SNAI), was promoted and went to the London Air Traffic Control Centre at West Drayton (just north of Heathrow) to become a Tels system controller on one of the ATC/Tels watches. The position of SNAI at Stansted was taken over by Mr. J. (John) Bennett, who had joined CAFU in 1966.

There were six navaid inspectors (NAIs). Each flight inspection normally carried one NAI per flight together with an assistant. The NAI made the assessments regarding the navaid being checked, liaising with the airfield chief telecommunications officer as to the aid's serviceability and certification.

Airworthiness Division had approved two more departments within Tels: one on the inspection side, headed by Mr. A. J. Cook; and the other on the design aspects of new and modified aircraft equipment, headed by Mr. J. "Jimmy" Weekes, the chief design engineer.

At long last, CAFU was able to work in some comparative comfort when they moved into their newly completed building on March 26. It was two-storey in the shape of an *H* (minus the bottom right-hand leg). The front ground floor contained a reception area where visitors could report to Operations. Management was on the first floor on the right-hand wing, while Administration had the front first floor, immediately above Operations and Reception.

The other wing upstairs held rooms for examiners, inspectors, and navaid inspectors, where they could be suitably adjoined.

The bottom half of the left-hand wing belonged entirely to the Telecommunications section. It lay near to CAFU's WWII T2 hangar but, more importantly, had a bay for the HS748 where it could be attached to the new telecommunications laboratory or CAL Bay. It was a most satisfactory relief for staff to be housed decently after twenty years in the primitive conditions of the deteriorating WWII Nissen huts.

In addition to the commander and his two deputies, *Flight* reported there were now twenty-eight flight examiners, twelve navigators, and some thirty administrative staff.

The reporter of this article, himself a pilot, probably spoke on behalf of hundreds of candidates when he recalled "'the old days' when candidates had to present themselves in the grim surroundings of the Nissen Hut at Stansted—an unnerving experience."

The network of en route navigation aids operational within the United Kingdom had grown over the years. By the end of 1971, there were

- 59 NDBs (20 en route),
- 42 VORs (including one DVOR),
- 25 DME (including some TACAN ranging elements)

Navigational aids such as the NDB, VOR, and DVOR were serviced, in the South of England, by SAMU, the Southern Area Maintenance Unit at Heston, and there was a southwestern outpost at Davidstow Moor for the facilities in that part of the country. SAMU shared the role with NAMU (Northern Area Maintenance Unit) at Runcorn, and the Scottish Maintenance Centre (SMC) at Barnsford near Glasgow. CAFU had a minor interface with these ground maintenance units.

The Telecommunications Engineering Establishment (TEE), based at Gatwick, was involved in the commissioning of new aids like the DVOR. CAFU was sometimes asked for airborne help with site selection, and, after satisfactory installation, engineers from TEE were involved with CAFU in the commissioning flight, which was a lengthy process.

In 1971, the Foreign Office, through the Directorate of Operational Services Overseas (DOSO), sought the help of CAFU to commission a VOR in the Seychelles. Eddy Harris and Eric Edmondson were at least two of the CAFU staff flown out via Bahrain in an RAF Britannia aircraft (XM491).

After completion of this task, a letter was later sent by Government House, Seychelles, to DOSO, thanking those (RAF and CAFU) who had worked to achieve the successful landing of the first VC10 aircraft of BOAC to land at Victoria airport in the Seychelles on July 4.

Plessey acquired Standard Telephones and Cables (STC) and with it the expertise of its landing guidance system, which eventually led to the company being selected by the CAA for development of a new landing system.

The navigators were crewed for VOR/DME flight inspections, providing positional information of range and bearing from the facility as the orbits and radials were flown. The information was taken from Decca and used by the NAI in real time in order to compare with the received signal information, thereby deriving any errors.

Navigators were not normally required, in flight, for ILS inspections. Their involvement with ILS was ground navigational support in terms of map preparation and ground analysis of photographic positional data, etc.

Although the majority of the navigators had trained as pilots, they still remained in the Navigation section, and in addition to their "co-pilot" duties, they also did the work referred to above. It is believed that the last two navigators to train as pilots were Ben Gunn and John Smith, which left Peter Kenworthy and John Kime as pure CAFU navigators.

BOT CAFU Aircraft:
DEREGISTERED

DHC1	G-ANWB	MCA	Apr 1971
Prince	G-AMKY	MCA	May 1971
President	G-APMO	MTCA	June 1971
Prince	G-AMKX	MCA	July 1971
Prince	G-AMKW	MCA	July 1971

This was a period when CAFU was able to relinquish many of the older aircraft; the remaining single-engine Chipmunk, NWB, with CAFU for eighteen years, was sold, and instructor rating refresher and training would now be taken, when required, on a hired aircraft. Even up until 2010, it is believed that NWB had virtually operated with the same owner at Blackpool since it left CAFU, still flying in almost the same colour scheme.

PRINCE SAGA (part two). I was told by my aircraft guru, David Lacey, through ex-ATCO, Dave Moffat, that the two Princes eventually ended their days abandoned at Prestwick. The story that Dave Moffat tells is that the two Princes, MKW and MKX, languished at Prestwick airport, unloved and forgotten in the central area near a Scottish aviation hangar. Although this had happened in November 1969, they were still awaiting their fate in 1971. But by August of that year, they were partially dismantled—inexpertly on-site—and taken to Jackson's (obviously dabbling in scrap metal) timber yard in Lochwinnoch, where they lingered for some time. Curiously, they then disappeared, replaced by two mounds of fresh topsoil where it was eventually discovered their remains lay!

The third Prince, MKY, also immediately grounded in 1969, had been taxied to the other side of the airport to the Fire Service Training School (FSTS) at Stansted where it lay for some while.

G-APMO, the President, had an inglorious end when, after a major overhaul, it had a fatal accident; a set of ground maintenance steps was blown in to it during a gale at Stansted, and the aircraft was declared beyond repair. This aircraft was rested at first with FSTS at Stansted and then presented to 1163 Squadron of the Air Training Corps cadets at Earls Colne, Essex. David Lacey tells me that it was seen at the FSTS in May '72 and believes the shell was moved to Colne Valley by the USAF at Wethersfield in February 1973. Tom Singfield, another aircraft enthusiast, said he believed that another ATC squadron, at Saffron Walden, may also have been involved, however, the 1974 edition of *Wrecks and Relics* says that it was stored off-site at Hay House Farm, Earles Colne, and reported as being scrapped c. 1976.

Captains John Oliver and Brian Morgan flew Mr. Peyton in G-AVDX back from Liverpool to Heathrow in March, and the minister of Housing, Mr. Julian Amery, was flown from Heathrow-Leconfield-Binbrook-Manchester. Later in the same month saw Oliver and Morgan flying from Heathrow to Linton-on-Ouse, with Mr. Jim Prior, minister for Agriculture. Jim Prior was also carried to Lyneham the following month by Captains Dan Thomas and Brian Morgan.

In May, Jim Prior was flown again, this time by Captain C. M. "Jimmy" Joy and Capt. Brian Morgan, from Norwich to Bournemouth, Hurn Airport.

May was a busy month for the 125 pilots as they flew the chancellor of the Duchy of Lancaster from Brussels to Prestwick; Mr. Davies, minister for Trade and Industry, from Reykjavik, Iceland, to Aberdeen, and then onto Glasgow. The month ended with Joy and Morgan carrying the Foreign secretary, Sir Alex Douglas-Hume, from Heathrow to Le Bourget.

Safety Was No Accident

In June, Captains Oliver and Morgan flew Heathrow to Belfast with Mr. Davies, secretary of state for Trade and Industry, and Capt. W. Wooden and Capt. Brian Morgan flew Heathrow to Edinburgh with the Right Honourable G. Campbell, secretary of state for Scotland.

July saw the CAFU 125 carrying the minister for Environment, Mr. Peter Walker, to Carlisle; and in August, Mr. Davies, secretary for Trade and Industry, and Lord Cromer, HM ambassador to the USA, were flown from Heathrow to Nice.

September saw three more VIP flights; one was from Paris Orly to Heathrow with the chancellor of the Exchequer and HM ambassador to France, and the second when Capt. Brian Morgan and Capt. Ron Crawford flew from Aberdeen to Heathrow with the Right Honourable Edward Heath, prime minister.

Between those last two flights, G-AVDX was being serviced. Certainly it must have been unavailable, and CAFU, rather than turn down an important task, borrowed a 125; and Captains Wooden and Morgan flew G-AYOJ, a series 400B 125 belonging to Hawker Siddeley, to Madrid to bring back Mr. Geoffrey Jackson, HM ambassador to Uruguay, following his release by Tupumaro guerrillas, landing back in the United Kingdom at Gatwick.

Mrs. Thatcher, then minister for Education, was flown from Heathrow to Tel Aviv, via Brindisi, on November 14, with the return flight on the sixteenth.

Finally, for Brian Morgan this year, in December, he flew with Bill Wooden from Paris Orly to Thorney Island with the minister for Aerospace, then Heathrow to Brussels with Sir Alec and Lady Douglas Home.

BOT CAFU Aircraft at the end of 1971 Total = 12

Dove	05	I/R, Comm, GCA, Refresher flying
Dove	04	Telecommunications, GCA
HS125	01	Radar, Communications, VIP, Refresher flying
HS748	02	Tels Flight Inspection

1972

In January, it was announced that John Boyd-Carpenter would be the chairman of the Civil Aviation Authority (CAA). Among the board members were Mr. R. R. Goodison, deputy secretary in the Department of Trade and Industry; Mr. G. W. Stallibrass, mentioned earlier in chapter 2 and now the controller of the National Air Traffic Services; and Professor D. Keith Lucas, professor of aircraft design at the Cranfield Institute of Technology and chairman designate of the Air Registration Board. Mr. Goodison would be acting chairman until Mr. Boyd-Carpenter took office on April 1.

The CAA owed its existence to the recommendations of the 1968 Edwards Report (Prof. Sir Ronald Edwards). He recommended that the widely dispersed and varied activities of government, in connection with civil aviation, should be brought together under one organisation and should be set up outside the machine of central government. This was accepted by Harold Wilson's Labour government and set out in a white paper. The legislation was carried out by Edward Heath's Conservative government in the shape of the Civil Aviation Act 1971. Before this, civil aviation was, as Geoff Gurr wrote, "nobody's baby" for a long time and passed from one government department to another. It was written in Boyd-Carpenter's biography that "the CAA had a general duty to be the champion and supporter of British Aviation."

Although not directly a government department, the CAA would still, for the time being, be financed by the Treasury. Staff, still civil servants, retained all their old rights, and it would take some prising to relinquish them from these privileges. In many respects, this was the turning point, an establishment to enable change that direct government ministerial departments could not, or were unable to, provide or execute. It was the intention, of course, that no longer being civil service, but now a public corporation, it would recover all costs from its customers.

An immediate effect at CAFU, said Geoff Gurr, is that local management were now to be budget holders, providing them with the ability to control more directly all of their finances.

On May 1, John Boyd-Carpenter was made a baron of the Crux of Easton (in the ancient county of Southampton).

Formal CAA approval clearing the HS121 Trident aircraft for use in CAT 3a conditions was granted on May 22, 1972, and an HS121 Trident of BEA was the first scheduled aircraft to achieve a CAT 3 landing at Heathrow, an event in which CAFU had played no small part with its more precise calibration techniques of the instrument landing aid.

The Airworthiness Requirements Board (ARB) had earlier expressed concern at the continuing high proportion of fatal accidents resulting from collisions with high ground, which moved the CAA to acquire a Sundstrand Dash 060 ground proximity warning system (GPWS) and have it fitted into one of the CAFU aircraft, hoping thereby to gain direct experience. Sundstrand, an American company, was developing the system in the 1960s for Scandinavian Airlines (SAS).

CAFU NAI staff were involved, being asked to log "fault balls" while the aircraft flew profiles, requested by an Operations department in Kingsway (home of the CAA). "Fault balls" was a Sundstrand term for a method of recording the type of warning mode that had triggered the "pull-up." It was mildly descriptive, tells Tony Bird, in that through an aperture (one for each mode), a ball would appear. During the trial, each mode was recorded then cancelled, ready for the next profile. When the gear was in operational service, however, the warning would latch (with no one to cancel it) and so be available for any postflight analysis of what had caused it.

At first, there were concerns the GPWS equipment would only give the "pull-up" command under genuine terrain closure conditions, as false warnings would lead to crews not trusting it. Accordingly, says Tony Bird, the CAFU 748 flew up and down Wales on different profiles designed to give the alarm. However, there was concern by crews with these trials, and the pilots' Union, the Institute of Professional Civil Servants (IPCS), insisted that the CAA insure all crew members.

By 1972, there were installed at UK airports

- 15 CAT 1 ILS
- 07 CAT 2 ILS
- 01 CAT 3 ILS

It was reported in the July *Airway* (the CAA's own staff paper) that the development work on the telescroscope, undertaken by Bob Phillips and Pat Moylette at CAFU, had earned them each a £100 prize under the CAA Suggestion Scheme. Their contribution had earned valuable sales in various overseas countries.

In January, Eddy Harris made a second visit to the Seychelles in conjunction with the installation of a VOR/DME at Victoria Airport. This time, the visit was courtesy of the DTI as a "tourist" passenger on a BOAC aircraft.

As well as the major Scottish airports, Edinburgh, Glasgow, and Prestwick, that CAFU was concerned with, there were other highland and island airports also visited, all of which required flight inspection of their navigational and landing aids: Aberdeen (Dyce), Benbecula, Inverness (Dalcross), Islay (Port Ellen), Kirkwall, Stornoway, Sumburgh (Scotland's most northerly airport), Tiree, and Wick. These airfields were also visited, from time to time—normally annually—by senior CAA management, flown by CAFU/FOI crews in the HS125.

Sometime in the early 1970s, CAFU was again approached through DOSO, the Directorate of Operational Services Overseas of the DTI, to conduct flight inspections for a number of Middle Eastern countries for both en route and landing aids.

CAFU management must have felt great confidence with the aircraft's serviceability record and workload capacity to allow one of the two HS748 Tels aircraft to be away from base for ten days (possibly even up to three weeks), allowing the rest of the country to be serviced with just one aircraft. Alan Richardson, ex-CAFU navaid inspector, explained to me the big problem was what would happen in the event of a UK accident requiring instant flight inspection? He believed that in the event of such a situation, there was an understanding between CAFU and the RAF to help each other.

One reason for the greater work capability was the 748's ability to flight-check as many as four VOR systems simultaneously; whereas on the smaller aircraft, it was only possible to flight inspect one at a time.

Middle East aids calibrated during this period:

Abu Dhabi ILS/VOR, Bahrain ILS, Doha VOR, Dubai ILS/VOR, Kuwait ILS, Malta ILS/VOR (Gozo), Nicosia ILS, Muscat, Oman VOR, Ras al Khaimah, UAE (RAK) ILS/VOR, and Sharjah ILS. CAFU commissioned both the ILS and VOR at RAK, a relatively quiet airport in the United Arab Emirates at that time, and the Gulf of Oman was the furthest they were asked to flight inspect.

The very first flight inspection of Middle East navigational aids did not go entirely without incident, as Tony Bird recalled a story that a fellow NAI, Colin Sheppard, related to him:

The flight was somewhere over the Gulf, Capt. Hugh McDowall was the pilot, Derek Caruthers P2 and it is believed that John Kime was navigator. Colin Sheppard was the NAI and John Bennett the Senior NAI was also aboard to check the whole feasibility of the task. It being the first trip to the Middle East, CAFU had also organised Mr. Ken Camp, hangar foreman, as Chief Ground Engineer.

The 748 was not equipped with HF equipment for its normal operations in the UK. However, there was a need to fit it for work in the Gulf because, on transiting, it was necessary to talk to the ATCC in Baghdad (or Damascus, I can't remember) on HF as there was no VHF coverage over the desert at that time!

Hugh was trying to make the call without much success and suspecting an equipment problem he asked Colin to do what he could to resolve it. In the event there wasn't a lot that Colin could do apart from checking the fuses and making sure the Collins Transceiver was housed correctly in its mounting tray. It was located in the Starboard side radio crate, roughly

where the jump seat was stowed, so Colin took off his headset to give himself some freedom from headset leads etc.
Finding the fuses OK, he decided to check the mounting and gave the equipment a good pull to re-seat it. As he did that, both engines ran down!
His immediate thought was "Oh! ****t," what have I done? He was shocked to the core, to say the least!
It transpired that at the exact moment that Colin pulled the transceiver, the flight crew, after noticing some build up on the engine intakes, had "upped" the engine deice, and the ice then having melted, had been ingested and put the fires out in both engines.
Impeccably performed relight drills restored normality, but all was quiet for a short time!

It is believed that because of this incident, Hawker Siddeley took the view that the section of the operating manual that dealt with engine deicing was misleading, and they did a rewrite.

There was no fault with the HF; it was just poor propagation on the radio path, and Hugh did eventually get the calls through.

One other flight inspection was vaguely recalled by Alan Richardson, who told me that Nick Cowan, NAI, and his assistant, Eric Edmondson, went out to Liberia, or at least one of those countries on the west coast of Africa, to commission an ILS and VOR.

This year, there were 488 flight checks made of navigational aids at both home and abroad.

Other departmental heads at the time were

- operations officer: Mr. George Craig
- ops supervisor: Mr. Don McLaughlin
- unit engineer: Mr. Don King
- unit administration officer: Mr. George Bartle.

CAFU Aircraft Maintenance was now with Aviation Traders Ltd., and the hangar foreman was Mr. Ken Camp.

As an indication of the workload that examiners had faced, CAFU had conducted some thirty thousand tests up to this period, and the number of tests conducted during the 1971/72 period was 1,800. The number of professional pilots had doubled from four thousand to eight thousand between the period 1962 and 1972.

Flight tests were also being conducted on behalf of the CAA Medical Branch in London to determine whether pilots with a physical disability were able to safely fly. These tests were usually conducted by the senior examiner, Capt. Mike Edwards.

In order to give the reader an idea of the training that was given to a would-be examiner, I include details from Capt. Dai Rees's flying logbook when he joined CAFU in September of this year. Dai Rees was flying Piper Aztecs and an Aero Commander aircraft in 1971 and in December renewed his instructor rating with Duff-Mitchell, an instructor from Hamble. Dai would have required this if he was seeking employment with the flying unit.

It was not until May 2, 1972, that he had an interview in the morning at CAFU Stansted and a flight test with the CAFU commander, Captain G. B. "Geoff" Gurr, and Captain C. S. "Spence" Spence, the deputy commander C, who looked after all aspects of examining. He flew for just under two hours as P1 under supervision in one of the IR Doves.

The following day, he was back at his regular job flying out of Rochester. His interview was obviously successful, as four months later, in September, he joined CAFU at Stansted. An ex-navy pilot, Dai had flown Gannets and Sea Hawks off the Ark Royal, and up to joining CAFU, he had amassed almost 4,500 hours flying time.

His examiner training started almost immediately when he was given "general handling" in the Dove with Jock Hunter. The following day, he did an 1179 (a CAA form required to place an aircraft type on his licence), continuing with instrument flying. The following day, he flew the IR routes 1 and 2 to Birmingham and back with Captain Hunter in the Dove, doing IR training on the airway, followed by NDB and ILS letdown procedures.

The next week, in the Dove again, he did instrument flying with Captain R. (Ron) Shilcock, another ex-navy pilot, as well as asymmetric, limited panel, and letdown approaches of ADF and ILS.

IR training continued all week with an IR 5 and the usual letdowns and asymmetric procedures.

Over the next two days, he completed base check training on the Dove with Capt. John Belson as well as completing the 1179. From here on, he flew the Dove as P1 (pilot in command). By the end of the week, he had a route check and IR test with Capt. John Harris, completed on the IR routes 6 and 7, Stansted to Cranfield and return. It must be remembered that for each airborne training session, there would be classroom briefing/debriefings before and after each flight.

After these first two busy weeks, he was sent in the Dove to Bournemouth Hurn airport, with Capt. Brian Morgan to show him the ropes, flying GCA target practise for the ATC officers at the College of Air Traffic Control. By the afternoon, he was on his own for the rest of the week.

It is curious that the training had commenced with what was required of an examiner testing candidates for the instrument rating, rather than first training for the CPL test on the single-engine aircraft. But on his fourth week, he started his GFT training with Captain (Bernie) Sercombe, completing a Certificate of Test to fly the Cessna 150 that was specially hired for this session. However, the following day, he was introduced to the Delegated Examiner training course, which was conducted at Stansted in the CAFU briefing rooms, with flights using the IR Dove. The senior examiner conducting the course, Capt. Bob Whitehead, had two students, one from BEA and the other from BMI. Captain Rees acted as the "guinea pig" candidate under test for his IR while being observed by the would-be company delegated examiner (DE) pilots, with Bob Whitehead watching the "watchers." The DE (or AE) course was a two-week course, and the second week ended with what was called an "Examinability" when the company pilots had their final test. This was usually completed on a Thursday, which left time for any bad weather or aircraft unserviceability to be carried over to the Friday—if necessary, which it often was. So for Dai, the course he had witnessed was probably in its second week, ending on the Thursday, as on Friday he did some dummy GFT training with Captain W. "Bill" Aust in the single-engine Cessna.

Safety Was No Accident

The next week, he was let off again with GCA target training at Bournemouth Hurn airport.

During the sixth week of training, deputy commander C, Capt. Stuart Spence, cleared him to conduct the daytime general flying test for candidates requiring the issue of a commercial pilot's licence.

In week seven, he was back on the Delegated Examiner training course. Capt. Ron Crawford had two candidates from Bristow's, and Captain Rees was playing the part of the "guinea pig" again. Later on the same day, Captain Aust gave him a Certificate of Test (C of T) on the Piper PA28 Cherokee, another single-engine aircraft on which some of the schools did their GFT training. This was a little unusual, as most of the CAFU examiners either flew just the Cessna 150 (at Perth and/or Stansted) or the Piper PA28 (Carlisle, Hamble, Oxford, and Stansted). Dai was one of the few who, probably because of his previous experience on Cessna aircraft, was given the chance to go to any of the schools with either Piper or Cessna aircraft.

Finally in this week, he flew his first communication flight to Luton in one of the IR Doves carrying the commander, Captain Gurr; and deputy commander B, Captain Picken; together with Mr. Don King, the CAA Engineering liaison officer; and his assistant, Mr. Ken Rogers, to Luton.

By the end of October, he was conducting GFTs on foreign students at Carlisle on the PA28. GFT examining continued at Hamble during November where he also did some refresher and a competency check on the twin-engine Beech Baron—probably in readiness for conducting IRs there.

By the last week of November, he was back doing IR examiner training. In a period of just four days, he flew with Captain (Bernie) Mitchell, Capt. Stuart Spence, Capt. Jimmy Joy, and Capt. Ron Crawford on IR training, interspersed with acting as "guinea pig" on a DE course run by Capt. John Barbour, as well as squeezing in some GFT4 (Dove night test) training with Captain Spence.

Apart from another communications flight, this time with navigator/co-pilot Dick Whittaker to Heathrow, his IR training continued with Capt. Hugh McDowall, before finally having his own final Examinability test, witnessing Captain Spence, the deputy commander C, and the commander, Captain Gurr, acting, respectively, as the candidate under test and examiner. Even here, there was no easy way through, and he was asked to witness two one-hour-thirty-minute IR flights. This would appear to be his final acceptance as an examiner on December 11, 1972, concluding three months' training.

Dai then had a couple of weeks conducting GFT tests at Hamble before being cleared to fly the twin-engine Piper PA23 Apache aircraft by Capt. John Oliver before conducting, on the same day, his first ever IR test, a partial, on the Apache at Stansted.

The number of fatal accidents to UK scheduled flights between 1962 and 1972 almost halved.

Although Capt. John Oliver had attended the first Concorde introductory course during January 1969, it was not until this year that he attended the second course at Bristol Filton.

If I have given the impression that Capt. Brian Morgan did all the VIP flying, then I apologise; the flights mentioned so far are only from his logbook and that of John Oliver, which should give an indication of how busy the HS125 was and how useful government ministers found the services of CAFU. From this point, I will only describe the destinations flown to and from, and the VIP concerned, unless there is a new CAFU pilot name that I can bring in.

The Lord Privy Seal was flown from Heathrow to Copenhagen and return in January. In March, Lord Widgery was taken to Belfast, and later in the month, the minister for Trade, Mr. Noble, was flown to Budapest.

In April, Captains John Sweet and Brian Morgan brought back the minister for Aerospace, Mr. Michael Heseltine, from Hannover to Heathrow and, in the same month, brought back the then Chancellor, Duchy of Lancaster, Mr. Geoffrey Rippon, from Luxembourg.

In May, Mr. Heseltine flew from Heathrow to Toulouse. In July, Mr. Rippon was brought back from Luxembourg and Mr. Heseltine from Heathrow to Paris Orly, then on to Toulouse.

The Isle of Man figured in the next two flights, the first in July when Lord Colville, secretary of state at the Home Office, was flown from Stansted to the IoM and back again, and in August, Mr. Carr, the home secretary was flown from Heathrow to the IoM and returned to Heathrow.

Captain Morgan then didn't fly any further VIP flights until October, when he and Capt. Dan Thomas flew from Heathrow to Warsaw and Gdansk, back to Warsaw and then back to Manchester airport with Mr. J. Davies, minister for Trade and Industry.

There were two further flights in November, the first to bring back Mr. Peter Walker from Brussels to Manchester, and the second when Captain Morgan and Captain (Bernie) Mitchell flew the CAA chairman and group captain, Douglas Bader, from Stansted to Manchester and Heathrow.

The unit's aircraft were now logging over six thousand hours flying time a year, while the aircrew flying time was almost nine thousand annually. This included approximately seven hundred hours in flight simulators. CAFU examiners conducted 2,100 pilot flying tests and observed a further 320. Intensive training was also given to sixty-six airline pilot examiners (the Authorised Examiner course). Eighteen flight simulators were inspected and assessed.

Individual flying time for the unit's twenty-nine pilots varied from five hundred hours a year down to the commanders' forty-two hours. Although the five hundred hours compared favourably with the annual flying time of a commercial airline captain, the workload was believed to be heavier at CAFU; flights involving the testing of a pilot included a pre-flight briefing on the nature of the test, followed by a series of ground checks before the flight. The flight itself only constituted one-third of the total time spent with an individual candidate, as after the flight, there would be documentation to be completed and finally the debriefing.

The unit operations officer at this time was George Craig, ably assisted by the supervisor, Don McLaughlin, performing the trick of making the diverse operations of CAFU work—where crews and available aircraft were matched with the demands of the customers; schools, students, airlines, government departments, and various airport authorities, with all tasks on the day at risk of crew sickness, unsuitable weather, and aircraft unserviceability.

In July 1972, the CAA paper *Airway* recorded the functions of CAFU:

- *Calibration and testing of radio/radar navigational aids provided and operated by NATS (National Air Traffic Services).*
- *Flight-testing of candidates for the initial issue of professional pilot's licences, instrument ratings and instructor ratings.*
- *Training and testing of candidates for appointment as CAA Authorised Instrument and Type Rating Examiners.*
- *Observing and reporting on the conduct of pilot competency tests (including type and instrument rating renewals) by CAA Authorised Examiners, making recommendations as to continued authorisation. Observing and reporting on airline standards of pilot training and testing.*
- *Examining and reporting on the standard of flying instruction at schools approved for the initial training of professional pilots.*
- *Testing and appraisal of flight Simulators approved or to be approved by the Authority.*
- *Flight checking of ATC and Instrument Approach procedures.*

To interrupt here, it should be noted that *Airway* had forgotten to note the calibration and testing of radio/radar navigational aids provided and operated by non-state airfields and overseas countries requesting these services.

Airway then gave a list of secondary functions, writing:

Within the productive capacity surplus to essential CAA requirements, and for approved fees:
- *Flights for the carriage of Government Ministers and officials.*
- *Radar flying for the College of Air Traffic Control.*

- *Airport lighting checks or any trial or procedural experiments that may be authorised.*

Airway also noted:

that much time and effort is spent on future planning, seen as the maintenance of high standards set in flight training and navigational aid inspection, especially during a period which will see the introduction of civil supersonic travel and the increased use of automatic landing systems. However, CAFU will not lose sight of the basic task of ensuring that the people who fly aircraft and the systems which guide them perform to the highest standards of safety.

CAA CAFU Aircraft:
DEREGISTERED

Dove	G-ALFU	MCA	Nov 1972
Dove	G-ALVS	MCA	Nov 1972
Dove	G-AJLV	MCA	Nov 1972

REGISTERED

HS748	G-ATMJ	CAA	Dec 1972

During November, two telecommunications Doves, G-ALFU and G-AJLV, were no longer registered as being with the CAA. LFU had served twenty-three years, and JLV, the first-ever Dove registered to the MCA, twenty-five years. As flight inspection aircraft, both had calibrated landing and en route navigational aids between the Channel Isles and Northern Scotland. Both were "permanently withdrawn from use" (PWFU). Dove G-ALFU can still be seen, resplendent in its old colours of white, red, and black cheat line, hanging, as if in flight, in one of the hangars at the Aviation Museum at Duxford, a fitting tribute to the calibration unit. G-AJLV was to become a star in a film, which entailed being pushed into a quarry. It has not been on the scene since.

Also in November of '72, the first instrument rating Dove registered to CAFU, G-ALVS, was taken off the register (PWFU). It was, unkindly or no, taxied to the Fire Service Training School on the other side of the airport and burnt. This IR Dove had served for twenty-three years.

Eight months after the creation of the CAA, the Flight Operations Directorate, under which CAFU was controlled, recognised the need to provide examiner/inspectors, as well as flight operations inspectors, the necessary experience of operating an aircraft in an airline environment, particularly in light of the burden of ever more air operator's certificates (AOCs) being issued. With this in mind, the CAA purchased another HS748, this time a forty-four-seater G-ATMJ. It was delivered to Stansted as VP-LAJ on October 20; its Antiguan registration was cancelled on November 22, and it was registered to the CAA as G-ATMJ on December 28. It had previously been registered to Autair/Court Line in Pink livery, named as "Halcyon Beach," and operating in Jamaica and Antigua on charter work. It was expected that this aircraft would at least provide crews familiarity with modern airline practices.

When the CAFU 125 started VIP work in the late sixties, it was seen necessary to employ a hostess. Stephanie Flanders, who ran her own business, Orientair Cabin Services, offered to provide CAFU with a hostess on a freelance basis. Only one hostess was required for the maximum of just six passengers on the 125, however, with the advent of a new forty-four-seat HS748 aircraft to be used by CAFU, two hostesses were now required. After the collapse of Channel Airways in February, Kim Newton, who had been working with Channel, was offered employment with Orientair and started to fly with CAFU.

BOT CAFU Aircraft at the end of 1972 Total = 10

Dove	04	AE Course, Refresher flying, Comm
Dove	02	Tels Flight Inspection, GCA
HS125	01	Radar, VIP, Comm, Ref flying
HS748	02	Tels Flight Inspection
HS748	01	VIP, Communications, Ref

1973

The HS748 G-ATMJ, which had arrived at the end of the previous year, was delivered in its pink livery and required refurbishment both inside and out. Aviation Traders did the work, and it was given the CAFU colours of white upper fuselage, red lower fuselage and fin with a black cheat line through the windows. Its first flight after conversion was on January 29.

Since 1970, teams in five countries had worked on the best way of satisfying the ICAO AWOP (All Weather Operational Panel) requirement. Though this requirement made no specific reference to microwave frequencies, most of the development teams chose to use this band. But as far as ICAO was concerned, the new landing system could have been based on "foghorns and ear-trumpets," wrote *Flight* magazine, just so long as the requirements were met.

Britain and the United States launched the two most significant national programmes. Eight-month phase 1 development contracts were awarded by the FAA to six US companies. Four were instructed to study frequency-referenced scanning beam techniques (FRSB) (Texas Instruments considered mechanically scanned systems, with Bendix and Raytheon working on electronically scanned alternatives), and two concentrated on commutated Doppler (Hazeltine and ITT Gilfillan).

Phase 2, which did not begin until much later, called for the demonstration of hardware representative of future landing-guidance systems. Four companies won phase 2 contracts; Texas Instruments and Bendix were asked to build FRSB systems, with Hazeltine and ITT Gilfillan working on commutated Doppler equipment. Hardware was called for by the end of 1973, in readiness for flight evaluation in January 1974.

The British followed a similar two-phase timescale. The initial phase involved theoretical studies and simulation of the three preferred techniques—frequency-referenced and time-referenced scanning beam (FRSB and TRSB) and commutated Doppler. Much of this work was carried out by the RAE (Royal Aircraft Establishment) Farnborough, and it was when the RAE comparisons of predicted performance showed up in its favour that UK interest shifted, finally, to the commutated Doppler system.

A report in *Airway,* November 1977, indicated some of the key features where the United Kingdom believed Doppler MLS (DMLS) scored outright:

- Highly stable and accurate coding in space is achieved with a simple method of signal generation requiring no adjustments.
- Long-duration angle guidance signals aid accurate processing.
- Immunity to interference and simplicity of monitoring.
- No routine flight checks required.
- Ample development potential.

British phase 2 work began with the award of a £1 million contract to Plessey in June 1973. Under the terms of the contract, Plessey— to which STL's experience had passed with the acquisition of its landing-guidance interests in 1971—continued to share UK MLS funding with the Civil Aviation Authority, the Ministry of Defence, and the Department of Industry. By November, trials were completed at Manchester, and further trials were planned in Switzerland. Other British MLS research had concentrated on a ground-derived interferometer system, and Marconi carried out studies of ground-derived Doppler and hybrid scanning-beam MLS.

Internationally, five states made initial submissions to ICAO in 1973. These, with the techniques proposed, were

1. Australia (TRSB)
2. France (FRSB)
3. West Germany (DME-based landing system, DLS)
4. United Kingdom (commutated Doppler)
5. USA (FRSB and commutated Doppler).

The Australian TRSB "InterScan" was radically different from the other submissions. Germany's DLS was a DME based ground-derived system that remained virtually unchanged; it is not strictly an MLS at all, demonstrating that the ICAO requirements did not specify microwave guidance.

ICAO planned to select the winning system for worldwide adoption in April 1978.

CAA CAFU Aircraft:
DEREGISTERED
Dove   G-ANAP   MTCA   Aug 1973

G-ANAP, the Dove used in the fifties and sixties for Ordnance Survey and GCA Target work was taken off the register in August as PWFU. David Lacey, ex-CAFU Tels, advised me that it was a longtime resident of the fire dump at Bristol before disappearing altogether. NAP had been with CAFU for twenty years.

April 10, Invicta Airways Vanguard VC9, G-AXOP, crashed on approach to Basle, killing 104 passengers and four crew out of 145 people on board. Invicta had three Vanguards (one a freighter) and a DC4.

Flight magazine asked the question:
Has the creation of the CAA cured any deficiencies in liaison between the sections of the organisation that existed before? A multitude of fresh and complex tasks confront the Authority and we all rely upon it to secure a sharp and continuous improvement in safety standards.

A few more of the aircrew flying in the seventies: John Murphy, Maurice Knowles. Helicopter pilots, Tony Lister, Don Sissons, and Capt. Charles Walden.

It was a feature of the unit that managers never seemed to mind when an excellent senior flight examiner moved to, or back to, the airlines. It was seen as a positive step in sending a probable training captain, with the standards that CAFU was gradually endeavouring to establish in all the companies.

Following a request from the Italian government, the country's domestic airline, Aero Transporti Italiani, set up a national navigation aid inspection unit based on CAFU's operating techniques. A twelve-man team from the airline visited Stansted for a four-week course. The decision to follow CAFU's lead was taken following the team's visit to other European authorities and companies. CAFU was chosen because of its unparalleled knowledge and experience in this field. The Italians had selected the Fokker F27 aircraft for flight inspection.

After a midair collision between an Iberia DC-9 and a Spantax Coronado near Nantes on March 5, probably due to the French civil Air Traffic Controller strike that had started on February 20, CAFU temporarily stopped flying over French airspace, using a more westerly Atlantic route when required.

Only five VIP flights were flown by Captain Morgan this year, two of them with Captain W. "Bill" Aust. Destinations were variously Brussels, Cologne, Pershore, Newcastle and East Midlands. Those carried were HM ambassador to Belgium; then the minister for Industrial Development, Mr. Christopher Chataway (later to become CAA chairman); Peter Walker, minister for Trade and Industry; Mr. Godber, the minister for Agriculture; and finally, with Capt. Bill Aust again, Mr. Peyton, minister for Transport.

As well as government ministers using the CAFU HS125, the forty-four-seat 748 was also, around this time, carrying Members of the European Parliament (MEPs) to Strasbourg, Luxembourg, and sometimes Brussels. CAFU was first asked to cover this requirement of the MEPs because there were no scheduled flights from Heathrow at the time, and all flights were undertaken at commercial rates.

During this year, sixteen flight simulators were inspected in the United Kingdom and seven abroad.

Capt. John Oliver, the CAFU flight examiner chosen to be the Concorde training inspector, had several visits to Toulouse during this period for demonstrations, of various sorts, on the Flight Test Development Simulator, originally designed for work in relation to the flight testing programme and for the instrument rating renewal (IRR) testing of the BAC pilots who were undertaking flight test work on the aircraft. These included some BALPA (British Airline Pilots Association) Technical Group handling exercises provided by BAC.

For the first time, a flight simulator for a light aircraft was approved for the conduct of instrument rating renewal (IRR) tests for a restricted category of professional pilots. This was the Piper PA31 Navajo flight simulator, designed, constructed, and operated by Simulated Flight Ltd. at Booker.

The number of commercial pilot's licences (CPL) issued by the end of this year was 465, and the number of CPLs current, 2,860. For the airline transport pilot's licence (ATPL), 328 were issued, and currently held were 4,703. The numbers for helicopters: CPLs issued 17, and current 84; ATPLs issued 41, and the number current 343.

CAA CAFU Aircraft at the end of 1973 Total = 09

Dove	04	AE Course, Refresher flying, Comm
Dove	01	Tels Flight Inspection, GCA
HS125	01	Radar, VIP, Comm, Ref flying
HS748	02	Tels Flight Inspection
HS748	01	VIP, Communications, Ref

These numbers remain the same until 1977.

1974

The overall number of staff employed by the CAA was 8,496, almost 19 percent of which were employed in London.

In 1974, both British European Airways (BEA) and British Overseas Airways Corporation (BOAC) were dissolved and merged into British Airways (BA).

CAFU Tels were still headed overall by a superintendent, Joe Gidman, who had taken over from the retiring Bill Aitkin. The navaid inspectors who did all the flying were headed by the manager flight inspector, John Bennett, a senior NAI who no longer flew, or only when a situation dictated. He had nine staff, NAIs and assistant NAIs, on flying duties.

The ground staff engineers each had their own sections and section heads. There were four main functions for the Tels organisation, and listed below are the Tels sections with each of their functions:

WORKSHOP AND CALIBRATION
The normal repair and replacement of the airborne radio, radar, and avionics necessary to keep CAFU aircraft and flight inspection systems running.
CALIBRATION (CAL)
To provide calibration of the flight inspection equipment and support to the NAIs (the NAIs were, of course, Tels engineers as well who enabled both sides, flying and ground, to work closely together).
PLANNING AND EVALUATION (P & E)
Development of flight inspection equipment and other experimental work for the CAA involving airborne installations.
TELECROSCOPE
The tracking of the aircraft from the ground whilst testing ILS.

At one time, there had been an Installation Workshop, which was soon disbanded (in 1975). Its responsibilities of installing flight inspection systems in aircraft became less and less as the 748s settled down, and the work was split between Calibration and P & E.

There was also a technical library used for holding aircraft manuals, as well as the Tels department documentation. This section was run by Jack Straw, the father of the politician. At this time, Jack Jr. was a student agitator (allegedly) and labour party researcher. Jack Sr., I'm told, often opined that Jack Jr. was a fool! I guess that fathers are sometimes dissatisfied with their prodigies—junior has, after all, done his father proud.

The previous year, in January, a BEA Viscount aircraft had had an accident on a flight out of Glasgow, coming to grief on Ben More, a hill to the north of the airport. It was a post-maintenance test flight, and both crew and two engineer passengers were killed. As this flight was seen as a classic "terrain-related" accident, CAFU, who was testing the Sundstrand GPWS system, was asked to fly the Viscount track profile. CAFU NAI staff became involved because each profile required recordings of radio-altimeter height during each run, a parameter readily available at the 748 ILS console desk.

Tony Bird remembered standing, with Capt. Bill Topping in the jump seat, watching the "fault balls" whilst the terrain closed. Of course, they were flying in VMC (visual meteorological conditions)' even so, Tony recalled Captain Picken voicing it was his opinion that it was an effective warning in time to avoid the hill.

As part of its evaluation of both the requirement for and the operation of ground proximity warning systems in aircraft, the CAA invited four airline pilots to test-fly the GPWS, the Sundstrand Dash 060 system in the CAFU HS.748 test aircraft. As well as a senior CAFU pilot (Capt. Jack Picken), there were two senior operations officers, a further CAA pilot, who acted as co-pilot, and a flight-test technician. All of the modes were flown that warned against

    Mode 1, high sink rate
    Mode 2, high terrain-closure rates
    Mode 3, sink rate after take-off

Mode 4, ground proximity with the aircraft not in the landing configuration

Mode 5, flight below the ILS glide slope, at less than 650 ft AGL (which was optional under the present FAA ruling).

After take-off, the invited pilots were given the chance to fly some of the modes, including Llanbedr on the Welsh coast and flying inland over Snowdonia at 2,500-3,000 feet, the aircraft heading towards some very solid-looking hillsides.

Flight reported the CAA was expecting to consult the industry as a whole on the development of requirements, and by April, the CAA had decided to make GPWS mandatory "as soon as possible."

The trials on the Civil Aviation Flying Unit's 748 were not quite complete, and an interim report was issued recommending the fitting of GPWS. The CAA was still consulting industry on the operational and technical requirements and said the ruling would be flexible enough to allow both available designs and future developments to be used.

The British CAA expected to have four Doppler VORs (DVORs) in service by the end of April. In 1972, the CAA had ordered fifteen DVORs, having decided that solid-state double-sideband DVOR would be the standard ground-based navigation facility in the United Kingdom. The order, including aerials and new buildings, was worth just over £1 million. Five sets of equipment were ordered from Standard Electric Lorenz for sites where early replacement was necessary. The order for another ten, an all-British DVOR, went to Plessey Radar, which had privately developed a DVOR to meet the CAA's specification.

The first four operational DVORs—at Ongar, Clacton, Daventry, and Biggin Hill—were all supplied by Standard Electric Lorenz. The sets were in fairly advanced stages of commissioning and flight-test calibration.

In order to make maintenance easier, it seemed likely that the remaining SEL-supplied set would be installed by the CAA's Southern

Maintenance division. The first Plessey set would be installed at Berry Head and the second at Ibsley.

According to its annual report, the CAA expected to replace all forty-one "conventional" VORs installed in the United Kingdom with Doppler equipment. It was already evaluating tenders for the next batch to be ordered from Decca, for the supply of a second batch of DVORs (see *Flight* for March 7, p. 307).

It was an extremely busy period with a new DVOR eventually being commissioned every month until completion. At first, they were to prove difficult to maintain but, when established, would only require to be seen every five years.

The initial ICAO Working Group meeting, set up to evaluate the technical submissions of a new proposed landing aid, was held at The Hague in March 1974, followed by a second meeting in September. The Working Group comprised ten members, eight of whom were considered to have sufficient expertise to judge the proposed techniques. They came from Australia, Canada, France, West Germany, Netherlands, United Kingdom, USA, and USSR and were joined by two delegates nominated by the International Air Transport Association (IATA) and the International Federation of Airline Pilots' Association (IFALPA).

In December 1974, there was a sudden announcement by the American MLS Executive Committee that it would not develop commutated-Doppler MLS further, concentrating instead on scanning beams. Furthermore, although all American scanning beam research up to this time was concerned with FRSB, the system now chosen was TRSB. This decision was complicated by reports that the committee had not appeared to be impartial. The committee's final vote saw two abstentions out of seventeen members. Nine votes were cast in favour of scanning beams, and six in favour of commutated Doppler. The required two-thirds majority was only achieved when the two abstaining voters came down on the scanning-beam side. Amongst the repercussions was a decision by the Hazeltine Corporation, one of the two losing commutated-Doppler development teams, to take court action against the FAA. However, the case was dropped three months later!

Flight inspection work away from base particularly for any period would produce a great deal of analysis for both the NAI and the Navigation section to be completed back on the ground at Stansted. Because of this, the navaid inspectors' time, when returning to base on a "dead leg," as they called any non calibrating leg of the journey, would be taken up by the NAI catching up with some of the analyses to lessen the load when he arrived back at the office.

One flight, Tony Bird recalled for me, was when they had a lightning strike somewhere over Lancashire. Tony had settled down to some analysis work at the ILS console and, by agreement, removed his headset to avoid any distractions, when suddenly

I heard a VERY loud bang and a blue glow which came and went down between my feet. My first thought was that an inverter, of which there were several under the floor, had had a problem and I thought I should tell someone!
However, when I got my headset back on everybody was saying it was a lightning strike and all the crew had experienced the same blue glow. The weather radar was out, as was the Decca, and the CL11k compass. However, the aeroplane still flew and we made it back to Stansted.
Trevor Green was the captain and I remember him saying that he had been flying since he was a lad and that was his first experience of a lightning strike.
Shortly after we got to our individual offices, George Todd, one of the senior engineers, came from the hangar to round us up and suggested we should go across and have a look at the fin and listen to the rudder!
When he moved the rudder it sounded like a creaking barn door because all the bearings were shot, and the fin had a small hole at the top where the strike had either entered or left the airframe! It had obviously been a cloud to cloud strike—in one end and out of the other.

The United Kingdom had used one TACAN in the fifties, Wallasey TACAN. It was installed in support of TSR2 test flying undertaken by English Electric at Warton. When TRS2 died, mid sixties, so did Wallasey, later becoming a VOR/DME. Set on a peninsular just northeast of Liverpool, it cut through several airways: Amber 25, Blue 1, Red 3 and White 37, proving itself a useful intersection between Northern Ireland to the London area, Dublin to Holland, as well as Scotland to the Channel Isles and France.

There was a small drop in the number of flight inspections carried out for NATS this year, but this was more than made up when CAFU had a contract with the Belgium authorities to calibrate seven or eight TACANS, a military version of VOR with DME. The Belgium Air Force, which used a DC3 aircraft to check their navigation installations, found main spar corrosion, which grounded the plane, and they were left bereft. CAFU was asked if they could take over, and the senior NAI, John Bennett, and Tony Bird went over to discuss the situation. TACAN was a Rho/Theta aid (like a VOR/DME but with subtle differences) designed for and used by the military; it was even used on aircraft carriers. CAFU Tels section installed a TACAN airborne kit (left over from Wallasey calibration days) into one of the 748s, having to carry out some modifications to the inspection metre panel in order to be able to look at additional parameters the Belgians required, while the Navigation section did some work on the appropriate European Decca chain, and the profiles were then flown as for CAFU's own domestic VOR/DME inspections.

In 1974, CAFU flew to Esbjerg, where a number of countries, Denmark, Switzerland, Sweden, and the United Kingdom, were participating to compare flight inspection methods, together with a great deal of discussion on how to interpret ICAO's annexe 10. Kjell Haug, in charge of the Norwegian Flight Inspection Unit, remembered Tony Bird and Dave Reiffer in attendance. Some of the Norwegians were invited aboard to witness a CAFU flight inspection.

Also at this time, a removable navaid flight inspection kit was being developed to allow CAFU's HS125 aircraft to add VOR checking to its current VIP/Communications/high-level radar target role.

This year, the BBC TV *Horizon* produced a documentary programme explaining the work of CAFU.

Although there were few opportunities in this period, Captain Oliver was able to get a few exercises in the Toulouse Concorde simulator.

When British airways started using the Lockheed L1011 Tristar wide-bodied aircraft, Capt. Ron Crawford was selected to be type-rated as their training inspector. I overheard his conversation in ops about his first day in the classroom when on the conversion course. The instructor had continually referred to one piece of equipment as "PFM," and by the end of the day, one of the candidates dared to show his lack of knowledge and ask exactly what "PFM" meant. The short reply was "It's Pure 'F****ing' Magic!"

In September, CAFU was represented at the Farnborough air show. Not because they particularly wanted to but because Hawker Siddeley required an aircraft to use as a demonstrator. Unfortunately for them, or perhaps CAFU, their own demonstrator had been sold, so Hawker Siddeley leased CAFU's flight inspection HS748, G-AVXJ, for the period.

It was flown by Hawker Siddeley pilots, Charles Masefield and Bob Dixon-Stubbs. I recall seeing it on one of the "Trade" days being demonstrated as if it was one of their own aircraft with its full range of STOL capabilities—thrashed to the limit, it seemed. It was impressive but painful to think our own little calibrator was being pushed so hard.

The HS125 VIP flights using Northolt figured more this year. Ministers found it attractive, as it was close to Heathrow with far less problems in boarding and disembarkation due to this now less busy RAF station.

Flights were going to Brussels, Glasgow, Luxembourg, and Paris Le Bourget. Ministers flown were Mr. Peter Shore (twice), minister for Trade; Mr. Tony Benn, minister for Industry; Mr. Peart (twice), minister for Agriculture; and Mr. Peter Shore again when he later became secretary for Industry. Last, Mr. Roy Hattersley, secretary of Foreign and Commonwealth Affairs, was also flown with CAFU.

What CAFU called Educational Flights started in 1974. They were pioneered by Capt. Geoff Gurr and operated on a once-a-week basis. CAFU had a contract with the Essex County Council Education Department who organised schools within the area, to send a class of school children to CAFU at Stansted where they would board the forty-four-seat HS748, TMJ. The flights, lasting about one and a half hours, were used as a form of incidental teaching and used as the basis of projects from the experience gained, the flight being charged at cost with a group of forty-four people being accommodated.

The route could vary according to the school and weather. One route would take the children over Bishop's Stortford and Epping, continuing northwards, then down the Thames estuary flying over the Tower Bridge, the London and Tilbury Docks, Foulness and Maplin Sands, the Atomic Power station at Bradwell, as well as Chelmsford and the Sugar Beet factory at Felsted, before returning to Stansted.

They would be given a running commentary, very often by the co-pilot Derek Carruthers, and the children were given the chance to take turns in visiting the flight deck. Two hostesses were in charge of each group, and plenty of sick bags were provided by the hangar.

Schools would phone the day before and be given a brief on the weather forecast. If there was any doubt about the weather, they would phone early the next day to be given the latest update and chances of the flight taking place. Once the children arrived at Stansted, the building would be awash with excitement; it was contagious. There were very few days when a school arrived but didn't fly, and those were disappointing times for all concerned, children, crew, and ops.

The scheme was popular enough for other authorities from as far as North London to be interested.

Geoffrey Chouffot, who had joined the newly formed Flight Operations Inspectorate in 1961, promoted as CFOI the following year, and as director of Flight Operations in 1970, was further promoted to the position of director general, Operations Division, dealing with flight crew licensing, aerodrome licensing, airline certification, as well as operation of the CAA's aircraft.

Practical flying tests of candidates for professional pilot licences fell by 9 percent this year, partly due to the introduction of the combined instrument rating/general flying test, which simplified and updated the examining process.

CAFU Dove & Chipmunk used for CPL and IR tests
Photo: Eddy Harris/JF

Calibration Visitors from Brazil
Photo: Eddy Harris/JF

Caption: Italian Calibration team at Stansted
Photo: Eddie Harris/JF

RAF Argosy in CAFU Cal Bay at Stansted
Photo: Eddy Harris/JF

HS748s in new CAFU Calibration Bay at Stansted
Photo: Eddy Harris/JF

Telecroscope at the Glide Path locked onto 748 lamp
Photo: Eddy Harris/JF

Chapter Five
1975-1979

1975

Up until December of the previous year the Training and Licensing branch (TL4) was responsible for the receipt of applicants for the Delegated (now called "Authorised") Examiner course held at Stansted and the issue of certificates and administration, but from this year, that work was now conducted directly by CAFU.

In the CAA's Annual Report for this year, it announced that "an organisational improvement had made the Flying Unit responsible for the appointment of all Authorised Examiners (AEs) and this, together with its long established responsibility for assessing examining ability, makes the Flying Unit a complete organisation for regulating this activity."

Since CAFU's inception, Operations was traditionally headed by an operations officer (OO), but, perhaps because of savings that the CAA were now endeavouring to make, when Bernard Fitch, the unit ops officer retired, one of the senior navigators, Sidney Pritchard, was asked to take control. Sid, who had joined the Ministry of Civil Aviation back in 1947, first as a navigator through the fifties, gaining his CPL and IR in the sixties and becoming a co-pilot on the 748, was now asked to become operations manager. It was one of the smarter moves at CAFU as Sid, a quiet undemonstrative and unflappable man, was not only able to use his man management skills but also transfer some of his operational skills, sometimes lacking in Operations.

Around this time, CAFU operations, under the control of the new ops manager, were given responsibility for the records of all authorised instrument rating and type rating (IR and TRE) examiners in the United Kingdom. An additional senior ATCA was employed, Mr. Peter Bond, with an administrative assistant, Mrs. Eileen Van Drees, to run the office. Many retiring service candidates found the service useful when looking for either an authorised IR or TRE examiner on a particular aircraft type in their location. In addition, these authorised examiners were also advised of the requirement for the renewal of their authority.

In addition to the IRE/TRE office, simulator approval records, previously kept at Aviation House, London, were also now kept at CAFU Stansted, the office run by an operations officer, Mr. Cyril Hannigan.

Most CAFU staff, who had been badgered for sometime by the CAA with payment incentives, eventually terminated their contract with the Civil Service at the end of February 1975. The new CAA terms and conditions were said to be similar, or as good as, the Civil Service, but only time would tell of the changes to be implemented.

In May, the HS748, G-ATMJ, was being leased to Dan-Air. It was picked up by *Flight* and reported, in their July 17 magazine, that an HS748 of the Civil Aviation Flying Unit was operating weekend charters for Dan-Air:

The aircraft, complete with Dan-Air livery stickers, is positioned to Lydd each Friday and operates some of the airline's cross-Channel routes. Crewing was shared between Dan-Air and Flying Unit Flight Examiners, an arrangement enjoyed by the examiners as it gave them current route operating experience. The aircraft, one of three HS748s operated by the Civil Aviation Authority, would normally be idle at weekends.

In fact, the only 748 leased to Dan-Air was the forty-four-seat G-ATMJ, and the lease, during May-October, provided CAFU crews the opportunity to gain flying hours and experience of airline operations. Crews, including the contracted stewardesses, would assemble at Stansted on a Friday evening and fly to one of Dan-Air's operating airports, usually Bournemouth, where they would fly Dan-Air passengers for the whole weekend, not returning until the Sunday evening. Sometimes this would entail flying twice to Jersey and return on a Saturday, and twice to Paris and return to the Channel Isles on the Sunday.

For the relatively inexperienced CAFU Operations room staff, it was somewhat daunting to be finding themselves using not the CAFU trim wheel or load sheet but the Dan-Air load sheet. This was because CAFU used pounds to calculate aircraft weight and fuel, whereas Dan-Air used kilograms for aircraft weight and litres for fuel, the fuel weight adjusted for temperature. Perhaps because it required much concentration, nothing ever went awry.

Crews would often tell stories when they returned on the Sunday. The last entailed picking up the passengers, usually at one of the Channel Island airports and flying them to Bournemouth, the final destination. On these last flights, stewardesses would tell of passengers enquiring what time they would arrive at Swansea or Cardiff, not realising that Dan-Air would be "bussing" them to their respective airports on the mainland. There was always a good tale to be told.

The British Aircraft Corporation (BAC) flight simulator at Bristol was approved for certain compulsory flight tests.

Both Captains John Oliver and Geoffrey Packham, CAA FOI, attended the first British Airways Conversion Course at Bristol Filton on what was BA's "nucleus course."

Training inspections began later in the year using the Filton Simulator with BAC test pilots, Brian Trubshaw, John Cochrane, Johnny Walker, and Eddie McNamara as the instructors.

In December, the CAA certified Concorde, the Anglo-French supersonic airliner, was to enter commercial service after twelve years of development and testing.

There were thought to be around sixty ILS installations in the United Kingdom that CAFU was currently flight-checking.

According to the CAA 1975/6 Report, there was a decline in flying sold to overseas authorities for navaid calibration, which was offset by the lease of a calibration aircraft to Hawker Siddeley Aviation Ltd. for training purposes.

By the early 1970s, CAFU had stopped checking radio ranges.

Within the United Kingdom, the calibration of aids was shared by the RAF (115 squadron) for military installations and by CAFU for all civil aids. But as early as 1975, there was a proposal to transfer the work of calibration from the RAF to CAFU. A National Archives record (BT384/22-1975 AP 21/082) stated that Mr. Tebbitt, in the House of Commons, had been querying the decision not to proceed.

Numerous countries abroad were influenced by the decision of CAFU to use the HS748 aircraft as an instrument for the aerial inspection of navigational aids. The West German equivalent, the Bundesanstalt Fur Flugicherung (BFS), also ordered two 748s from Hawker Siddeley (fitted with the Rolls-Royce Dart R Da.8 power plants) to enable high-altitude sorties, as well as normal flight inspection duties. Norway and India also bought the HS748 for calibration work. In addition, personnel from various countries, Denmark, Italy, Austria, Brazil, Japan, and also the Royal Air Force, were all helped or trained by the CAFU Telecommunications section.

The Norwegian Civil Aviation Authority (NCAA) had previously used a Convair CV-340, a twin-piston-engine aircraft rather like a DC3 but with a nose wheel. These aircraft were operated by the Fred Olsen Airline (FOF) and used for flight inspection.

It had become necessary for the Norwegians to upgrade their aircraft because in 1968, Norway had begun construction of a number of short eight-hundred-metre runways in the west and north of the country, which were being used by STOL turboprop aircraft. These airfields were difficult for the CV-340 to operate into, and in any case, they did not provide 100 octane fuel. A number of replacement aircraft were considered, and in early 1975, NCAA staff attended an

HS748 factory course at Woodford to prepare for the installation of calibration equipment.

Although not scheduled, two of the Norwegians, plus wives, took the opportunity to spend one weekend with CAFU staff where they were able to *"talk shop and be given generous hospitality by the hosts (served tea in bed by the lady of the house),"* said Per Aakvik.

Capt. Don Hale returned from his detachment with the All Weather Operations Directorate, taking up his old position of deputy commander at CAFU.

Instrument Landing Category Standards

Category	DH (ft)	DH (mtrs)	RVR (ft)	RVR (mtrs)
CAT 1	200	60	2600	800
CAT 2	100	30	1200	400
CAT 3A	100	30	700	200
CAT 3B	12	3	330	50
CAT 3C	0	0	0	0

Clearance for category 3B operations came in 1975, allowing ILS landings to be made with the visibility down to 330 feet (RVR) and a twelve-foot decision height.

During the year, many airlines were able to land at UK airports in visibility as low as four hundred metres runway visual range (RVR). For British Airways (BA) Trident aircraft, this was two hundred metres RVR, due to the very foggy periods that had occurred in the last months of 1975.

There were now twelve runways in the United Kingdom, which were equipped for operations down to four hundred metres RVR: three at Heathrow now conforming to ICAO CAT 3 requirements; the remainder, all category 2. Progress was being made to bring Heathrow's fourth runway, together with Belfast and Glasgow, to CAT 3 standards.

When the CAA was created in 1972, government was releasing itself from the difficulty of directly overseeing UK civil aviation. There was, of course, a subsidy that needed to be paid in order to keep the CAA running. It was clear that the government's brief to the CAA was—you need to recover costs.

In 1975, inflation was so high that the CAA difference between income and expenditure had expanded to £43 million. It was a dilemma that the chairman, Lord Boyd-Carpenter, endeavoured to redress. The CAA pushed out a paper to industry proposing how costs ought to be applied.

Some of the suggestions that CAFU might have to apply annually were

- Simulator approvals, £6,500
- School approvals, £6,500

Charges for authorised examiners (senior flight examiner hourly charges were £365)

Additionally, Training and Licensing Department was going to charge for the renewal of a licence. Later, some of these proposals were reduced, such as the annual simulator inspection, which was settled at around £3,000, I believe.

A *Flight* magazine leader called the proposed simulator charges "grotesque" and the annual School Approval Inspection "exorbitant." It likened the CAA role to a government agency, which should, they believed, be "a highly professional inspectorate carrying out 'snap checks.' Safety would not be served by keeping pieces of paper. Who would be 'Checking the Checkers'?"

The industry as a whole suddenly seemed awake to the problems of the new regulator and wished to express their own ideas on what ought to change. There was an immediate response from both the public and industry:

Mr. G. D. Peacock, Berkhamsted, called the CAA "top heavy, with no manufacturing industry to lean on except Concorde, . . . they would then have to climb on the back of British Airways who had more depth and expertise than the regulator (CAA)."

Harold Best-Deveraux, Welwyn Garden City, agreed with Lord Boyd-Carpenter that "a 50 percent reduction in CAA staff would be political suicide."

Rex Smith, managing director of CSE Aviation, said, "All in the industry receive with trepidation the CAA yearly accounts and the size of the 'grant in aid' it has to receive to balance its books."

The CAA had already stated that in its opinion, "The civil aviation industry had reached a point where it does not need and ought not to be subsidised. The CAA must be self supporting by 1977/8."

Rex Smith believed "this date to be completely unrealistic, and success remote."

He wanted the industry to demand that the 1971 Civil Aviation Act be re-examined and that the government should develop a more practical understanding of the industry.

J. Nichol, a principal at the Oxford Air Training School, argued that the annual school and simulator inspection renewals were not necessary, as CAFU and the flight operations inspectors could do the job during their frequent visits of testing, inspecting, and maintaining their own proficiencies. Renewals, he suggested, should be a function of ongoing activities.

Geoff Gurr, in his book *A Testing Time*, tells how CAFU brought in revenue making tasks, such as the Middle East flight inspections, educational flights, the carrying of ministers to the European Parliament, and the leasing of an aircraft and crew to Dan-Air. Not only did these tasks bring in revenue but also provided crews the hours and flying time, which were required anyway. At the time, senior CAA managers were delighted with the efforts CAFU made. But clearly the writing was on the wall; times were changing for all concerned.

In June, the CAA chairman, Lord Boyd-Carpenter, wrote in *Flight* that civil aviation should not be subsidised by those who never fly:

"Why should the tax-payer pay for CAA surveillance?" he asked.

In September, *Flight* was reporting:

Progress of CAA self sufficiency was undermined by inflation which had caused the gap between income and expenditure to rise to £43 million.

The CAA was denied effective control of charges for en-route navigational services, which were half the total expenditure, as these were determined by Ministerial agreement within Eurocontrol.

The largest component of CAA costs was staff, also under Government control, which represented 55% of CAA operating costs.

It can be seen that the CAA were in a tough situation, endeavouring to establish realistic charges on an industry that was positively hostile to any increases.

The third ICAO Group Meeting of AWOP was held at Melbourne, Australia, in February 1975. It decided a method of assessing the system proposals, which were due in by December 1, 1975. The Working Group should have met once more before the end of the year, but delays in the collection of flight-test information caused postponement of this deadline.

By late 1975, the British phase 2 Doppler MLS was working satisfactorily, and the United Kingdom, through the CAA, lodged their proposal with ICAO for the adoption of the Doppler microwave landing system.

In America, phase 3 development contracts were being awarded by the FAA, going to Bendix ($6.75 million) and Texas Instruments ($7.45 million). The Australian TRSB proposal had not been developed as much as its US counterpart since the beginning of the year.

However, West Germany had continued to refine DLS. Although it was a ground-derived system, and for that reason unlikely to be favoured by ICAO, there was no denying that it was cheap and cleverly conceived, if slightly less accurate than the competition. DLS was widely admired, and even its most ardent detractors could find little wrong with it (see appendix B).

In an effort to release the use of its Dove aircraft and cut the cost of the two-week Authorised Examiner course run at Stansted, the CAA awarded a three-year training contract to Simulated Flight (Training) (SFT) Ltd. of Wycombe Air Park—their headquarters—for an HS125 simulator to be installed at Stansted for CAFU use. Installation began in late December, and operations started on February 9, 1976. This would release the use of the Doves for the AE course, which could often be interrupted due to weather or aircraft unserviceability.

There were now over seven hundred UK AEs, most of who were trained on the CAFU Dove, though all future courses would now be trained using the simulator.

The simulator was installed in the old Stansted Airport Fire Station, close to the new CAFU building. SFT, who also operated a small simulator at Bournemouth, would own and run the 125 simulator with Tony Angel, a director of SFT, being the simulator operator acting out the part of ATC, air and other traffic, a much-appreciated assistant to CAFU examiners running the course. The first week was run at CAFU, and later the second week with the company's own equipment. The 125 simulator also fitted in very nicely with the training of new FE/FOIs requiring HS125 flying experience, making further savings.

The simulator resembled almost exactly the flight deck of the 125 and, in addition to the two pilot seats, it accommodated two observers (for the purpose of the course), plus the simulator operators panel. It had motion in pitch and roll controlled by a Flytsim computer incorporating a new digital and analogue technique.

Just as throughout the forties, fifties, and sixties, CAFU aircraft were still being used as a live target for ATCO trainees at the now College of ATC at Bournemouth, Hurn airport. Dave Moffat, who late in 1973 had just started his ATCO training, looked forward to his approach radar course and the chance to fly with CAFU. The Doves were operated as single crew, and spare student ATCOs were encouraged to go along for the trip; the lucky ones sitting in the right-hand seat, and a few were even allowed to log the time as "P2 U/T" (right-hand seat under training). Some of the flying, he recalled, involved disappearing below radar cover for the enlightenment of the trainee radar controllers, which necessitated quite low flying and hiding behind terrain in the local area—so nothing much had changed over the years.

However, much to Dave's disgust, "live" training was abandoned before he was due to start the radar course, which had its last flight on behalf of the college on February 28, 1975. Capt. Dick Hawkes flew the last flight in Dove G-ANUT, and ATC Cadet Richard Taylor, attending 194 Approach Radar course, was the observer.

The college had moved from Aldermaston to Hurn in 1948, and CAFU had continuously supplied aircraft for the radar training of air traffic control officers and cadets since then. Airspeed Consuls were mainly used at first with the occasional Anson and Gemini. But by 1953, these were being replaced with CAFU's DH104 Dove and the occasional visit of the Prince aircraft.

Over the period, CAFU had clocked up twenty-five thousand flying hours and covered nearly four million miles, with many hundreds of controllers gaining experience of directing them. Altogether there were twenty-seven years of accident-free flying, a credit goes to the standards set and crews that flew from CAFU.

CAFU guests attending the last flight ceremony were Capt. "Bee" Marshall, ex-commander; and Capt. Jock Hunter, one of the first radar target pilots in the early days. "Bee" Marshall was now a parson at Edenbridge in Kent.

Simulator training for ATC radar controllers would now take the place of the CAFU Dove.

VIP destinations were still Brussels, then Warsaw, Jersey, Luxembourg, Rome, Biarritz, and Venice.

VIPs were Mr. Peart, minister for Agriculture (four flights); Mr. Peter Shore, the secretary for Industry (twice); Lord and Lady Boyd-Carpenter, who travelled to Jersey; Mrs. Barbara Castle, minister for Social Security; Mr. Jim Callaghan, Foreign secretary (twice) who went out to Rome and returned via Venice; finally, Mr. Roy Jenkins, Home secretary, who was brought back from Biarritz.

At a meeting in October, delays were announced in the implementation of ground proximity warning systems (GPWS). The CAA had said they wanted GPWS to be mandatory on UK registered commercial jet aircraft by mid-1976 and on commercial turbine aircraft six months later. However, with development and evaluation still in progress, it looked as if there would be a delay. British Airways was seen as the key to progress as they operated 210 of the 400 UK registered commercial aircraft and were expected to choose the American Bendix system. But there was pressure on them to choose a British system, Plessey, the only UK company involved with GPWS. Unfortunately, the Plessey system was neither in production or flight-tested. However, they had told *Flight* they would soon have a GPWS in the Royal Aircraft Establishment's One-Eleven as well as the CAFU HS748, which still gave little time for fitment before the deadline of mid '76.

As well as trying to be European leader in air safety, the CAA had chosen to further refine GPWS warning profiles and technical integrity. Both attempts were quite valid, said *Flight* (October 16, 1975, p. 582) as GPWS was a vital flight-safety aid, and it must be of the highest integrity. But the CAA had left itself an impossible task, having called for profile definition, some technical redesign and certification inside fifteen months, which proved too short a period for such an important system. So at a meeting called on October 3, with operators and the pilots themselves represented, it was decided to postpone the proposed dates while maintaining the CAA's stricter specifications. The alternative was to relax the rules to the American "FAA standard" and to maintain the in-service dates. The CAA had therefore defined modes 1-4 and decided to leave the definition of mode 5 until later. The whole concept of mode 5 was being vigorously debated both in the United Kingdom and the USA. So the in-service dates were put back six months to January 1, 1977, for jet aircraft, and July 1, 1977, for turbine aircraft. GPWS would be applicable to aircraft over fifteen thousand kilograms or those capable of carrying thirty passengers or more.

From this point, I have started to use information from the CAA annual reports, found for me by Tony Doyle in the CAA Safety Regulation Group (SRG) Library at Gatwick. Unfortunately, the year runs from April 1 to March 31, which means one can never be exactly sure when an event took place, however, the statistics can be seen to be growing or shrinking.

Inspections of airline training captains exercising their examining authority increased by 12 percent, while the amount of helicopter pilot examining more than doubled. Flight examining of helicopter pilot instructors was introduced in 1974/5.

1976

While Concorde would have its inaugural flight with British Airways and Air France, CAFU's Capt. John Oliver started his conversion to type on March 3 at Heathrow. Training was with BA's reserve aircraft for the Bahrain service, which could only be used once the primary aircraft had departed in a fully serviceable state. Departing from Heathrow meant that the full noise abatement procedure was used on the trip down to Fairford for the training exercise. Captain Oliver would remain the Concorde type-rated training inspector until 1993.

Refinement of the landing ground-roll phase for BEA's Trident aircraft was now completed (see *Flight* for June 8, 1972), and the system ready for CAT 3b operations (under which the pilot did not have to see the runway lights for any great distance ahead until the landing roll was almost complete). In practice, zero visibility meant anything up to twenty-five metres—the first figure beyond zero on the RVR scale.

Captain Ormonroyd of BEA had said that the programme had been "a national effort and might have faltered but for the patient guidance of the CAA's All-Weather Operations Group."

It was they who ultimately approved regular airline operations in low visibility. Several other government agencies were involved, and recently it was the airfield operators and air traffic control services that had also contributed to the success of the latest series of CAT 3 landings.

By 1973, with the categorisation system fully approved and aircrew training well under way, the British Airports Authority found itself under increasing pressure from British Airways to provide the necessary ground installations; airfield clearance for CAT 2 and above involved not only the quality of the ILS equipment but also lighting standards, topographical layout in the final approach zone, and such support facilities as RVR measurement.

An illustration of the way in which the various agencies worked together is shown by British Airways use of Heathrow's runway 28R for automatic landings. The Smiths Industries Autoland equipment fitted to the Trident did not require glide path guidance below 133 feet; a CAT 2 ILS glide path is therefore sufficient, although a CAT 3 localiser is required. When it was realised that the 28R glide path would not be upgraded to category 3 for the coming winter, steps were taken to amend the flight-manual clearance wording to allow for use of a CAT 2 glide path and for the CAA to promulgate separately—both by NOTAM and on ATIS (Air Traffic Information Service, broadcast via the VOR)—the category of ILS glide path and localiser so that the Tridents could operate on that runway.

A comprehensive Mandatory Occurrence Reporting (MOR) system is introduced by the CAA covering both aircraft incidents and defects. This was probably the result of the Edwards Report in 1968.

In 1976, TRSB and Doppler MLS performance was simulated by computers at Lincoln Laboratories in the United States under contract to the FAA, and results of these assessments (first seen in late 1976) suggested that Doppler MLS had "some shabby performance characteristics." These results were not only refuted by the British but also later were demonstrated to be inaccurate.

The ICAO fourth All Weather Operations (AWOP) Working Group meeting on the provision of MLS took place at Brunswick, West Germany, in February 1976, to be closely followed by an April meeting in Washington. It was thought the ultimate objective was in sight, and not a "sweepstake," as had been reported in America. It was the group's intention to work as a purely technical forum, to provide technical assessment, carried out by responsible experts, following the Working Group's agreed procedures and be free of national policies and prejudices.

In July, the AWOP meeting was held at The Hague; the US member presented the results of simulation studies carried out by Lincoln Laboratories. This work suggested that multipath propagation effects would affect the British Doppler MLS proposal. The British development team refuted the study's conclusions and set up Doppler MLS demonstrations for the next AWOP meeting, to be held in London in three months time.

Mike Whitney, the CAFU superintendent in the 1950s, and now holding the post of deputy director, Telecommunications (Navigation) of NATS, was the British member of the Working Group. At a press conference held afterwards, Mr. Whitney indicated that about 50 percent of the outstanding work was complete. The group was reasonably confident that the one remaining meeting—set for London—would provide enough evidence for preparation of the final report. This would be the group's last word to AWOP on the best future international landing aid and would eventually be presented to ICAO.

On November 1, the ICAO All-Weather Operating Panel Working Group started its penultimate microwave landing system meeting at the World Trade Centre in London, which was expected to last until the twelfth. Then in London, another Lincoln Laboratory report further criticised Doppler MLS performance in severe multipath conditions. The British team worked vigorously to counter the accusations and began flight trials to provide practical evidence of what Doppler MLS could do. Meanwhile, throughout the ensuing debate, senior British officials made it known that they distrusted the American simulations.

The British commutated-Doppler MLS, installed at RAE Bedford, was to be inspected, and approaches with MLS guidance were demonstrated in an effort to answer criticisms of the Plessey system's performance made at the previous meeting in the Hague in July.

By the end of the month, it remained only for the All-Weather Operations Panel (AWOP) to make its recommendations on the next generation of civil landing aid. However, the group did not come out in favour of any of the three main contenders—Germany's DLS, the British Doppler, or the American time-referenced scanning beam.

According to Mike Whitney, the UK's group representative, the demonstration proved that the simulation techniques used in the report produced exaggerated results. He also suggested that Doppler MLS could be readily modified to overcome the reflection effects mentioned in the report. The group also saw Doppler MLS signals received by a portable set while the elevation antenna was close to a hangar wall. With raw Doppler transmissions, the receiver recorded errors of ±0.3 degree, but using "lateral diversity" transmission techniques—instead of scanning left and right alternately, the commutated signal was scanned left six times, then right six times, and so on—the recorded error falling 90 percent.

The Working Group's seven subdivisions judged the competitors on performance, reliability, comparative costs, monitoring, interference, power requirements, and multipath performance.

They presented seventy-three working papers and sixty-eight background information papers in the course of the fortnight long London meeting, and it was the final reports, delivered on the last day of the meeting, that would be taken to AWOP when it would meet in Montréal on March 1 the following year.

Mike Whitney confirmed reports that the German DME-based MLS was found to suffer serious and probably incurable problems when operating close to reflecting surfaces. For this reason, AWOP was almost certain to recommend either time-referenced scanning beam (TRSB) or Doppler MLS to ICAO after next year's Air Navigation Conference in Montréal. New York's Kennedy airport was nominated for the MLS comparative trials.

There were more questions asked in the House about ministerial flights on May 1, when *Hansard* reported the prime minister being asked what rules applied to the use by ministers of military or other aircraft in the course of their duties, and what rules for repayment were applied in cases when such planes were used for unofficial purposes.

The prime minister replied:

Whenever possible, Ministers use civil scheduled services. Official transport by air is only provided free in special circumstances in connection with official business, and there is no provision for its use for unofficial purposes at public expense. Where civil scheduled services are not available, or consideration of urgency or security make their use inappropriate, members of the Cabinet and certain other senior Ministers may use aircraft of the Civil Aviation Flying Unit or Ministry of Defence aircraft. If aircraft are not available from either of these sources private chartering may be used.

Ministers, other than those travelling on defence business, who are not covered by these arrangements, must obtain the prior approval of the Prime Minister. Those Ministers for whom the appropriate authorities consider it essential for security reasons are able to use official transport on a repayment basis for journeys of a private or party political nature. All these arrangements have applied under successive Governments.

Within the last 12 months I have made 11 flights on a repayment basis on the equivalent first-class scheduled air fare.

Later in the month, *Hansard* reported the prime minister being asked if flights by ministers included flights in Civil Aviation Authority aircraft.

Mr. Harold Wilson, PM, replied,

There had been three flights in the period 1st April to the 3rd May when Ministers had flown in CAFU aircraft. These were flights on 17th April, the Secretary of State for Employment, together with the Secretary of State for Scotland and his Under-Secretary had travelled from Northolt to Aberdeen to attend the Scottish Trades Union Congress Conference.

25th April the Secretary of State for Industry had travelled to Blackpool to address the Amalgamated Union of Engineering Workers and then gone on to Newcastle on the 30th April, to address the Boilermakers' Union.

Northolt featured more often this year for the VIP flights conducted by CAFU. In the eight flights up until May that Capt. Brian Morgan flew on VIP flights, five were either to or from Northolt. It would not remain so, as later the RAF seemed to make it clear that they would prefer not to have what could be quite late flights returning to them. They may also have felt that their own Royal Flight squadron had the spare capacity to take on government ministerial flights (which they later did).

Flights this year had gone to Grenoble, Paris Le Bourget, Brussels, and Luxembourg. While in April, Mr. Benn, secretary of state for Energy, was taken around Scotland by Captains Brian Morgan and Dan Thomas, visiting Prestwick, Wick, Inverness, Aberdeen, and Edinburgh.

In 1976, a panel was set up, headed by Sir Henry Phillips, to review the work of CAFU at Stansted. They would investigate the structure of the Directorate of Flight Operations (which controlled CAFU), as well as the work undertaken for the directorates of Telecommunications and Flight Crew Licensing (FCL). All three strands of work at CAFU, seemingly inextricably intertwined as one, were somehow to be unravelled.

The panel would consider the desirable and practicable changes necessary to benefit the authority and the industry, both by way of economies in expenditure and improved utilisation of resources, while paying due regard to the need for securing continuing improvements in air safety. Sir Henry, a part-time member of the authority, would be joined by Professor J. B. Heath, economic advisor to the authority; Dai Morris, chief scientist; and Dick Kilner, chief flight operations inspector. The proposal of Mr. Kilner on the panel should not have been a total surprise. As one of the cofounders of the Flight Operations Inspectorate, he would have been the man with the knowledge to assist the panel in the future, existence even, of CAFU. The man from whom he had taken over as CFOI around 1966, Mr. Geoffrey Chouffot, was now director general of Operations and doubtless looking for the best way to deal with the conundrum of CAFU. Yet no one from CAFU was asked to assist. It is interesting to note at this point that the Flight Operations Inspectorate, headed by Dick Kilner, had had an OSAP (Operating Standards and Appraisal) on CAFU in May of this same year lasting just over a week. It was the first OSAP on CAFU. Undertaken by Mike Lewis, head of Flt Ops 1, it was not signed off by the CFOI until October of this year. All most fortuitist, it might be thought, but probably the reason why the CFOI was selected as a member of the panel. He, more than anyone else, would have all the understanding of the structural work, providing knowledge of current set-up, practices, and standards employed at CAFU.

The resultant review panel decisions had the most fundamental effect on the structure and working of the flying unit. Previous attempts at commercial flying by CAFU, in order to minimise costs, were now deemed inappropriate, and all such activities were to be stopped. The CAFU air operator's certificate, gained for these commercial activities, would subsequently be withdrawn. The various tasks performed by CAFU would be divided between a new command structure:

> National Air Traffic Services (NATS), Tels flight inspection (calibration)
> Directorate of Training and Licensing (DTL), all tests concerning the initial issue of a pilot's licence (CPL and IRs)
> Flight Operations Inspectorate, training inspections.

The post of commander would become redundant, and staff, in particular the aircrew, would now be reporting up to three separate command posts so that they would initially be working for these three separate directorates.

Captain G. B. Gurr, commander at the time, was offered a position as a director in London but, due to his previous experience of working closely with the FOI section, declined the offer.

With no commander, no effective overall head at CAFU, this would leave the three deputy commander positions as principals, each reporting to their own directorate:

- Flight examiners to Training and Licensing,
- Senior flight examiner/FOI to the Flight Ops Inspectorate, and
- Telecommunications crews to NATS.

Perhaps at this point, it is time to explain that NATS was a joint CAA/Ministry of Defence service and a division of the CAA.

One senior manager from Stansted gave his explanation, saying that the CAA had had to make cuts; CAFU was one of the most expensive departments because of the aeroplanes and were therefore targeted. CAFU aircrew, he believed, were to be downgraded while the headquarter staff pilots upgraded.

As Captain G. B. Gurr wrote in his biography,

It was, effectively, the end of CAFU as it had been structured for the past thirty years.

Additionally, CAFU, a name which had lasted for around twenty-five years, would now be known as the Civil Aviation Authority Flying Unit (CAAFU), to reflect to whom it belonged. It was not a change taken easily by Stansted staff who felt it was neither required nor necessary, particularly to many of the older members. However, although it looked a mouthful, the pronunciation remained the same, "CAF U"; it was only the written word that had to be digested.

The Phillips Review was an extension of the 1968 BOT Special Review, which assisted and made additional recommendations to the Edwards Review conducted at that time, which had looked at the financial situation as well as the development of safety. This latest panel, with experienced, carefully chosen people on board, were now able to finely formulate the requirement.

The 1968 Edwards Review had created the three directorates that CAFU should work to, but the practicalities of prising tasks from an individual pilot had not happened. Certain individual pilots were still examining for DFCL and conducting training inspections, where qualified. In addition, training inspectors that flew the 748 all still flew the telecommunications aircraft. These changes could hardly happen overnight, and for the immediate future, each directorate would have to take steps to ensure they had sufficient qualified staff for either just the flight crew licensing or training inspection side. And for the moment, NATS would have to share pilots from both the other two sides. So for the present, operations would still remain the same.

The few remaining aircraft did continue to be operated and administered much as they had previously; the Tels HS748s still on calibration work; the HS125 continued to give training and refresher to CAFU and staff from Headquarters, as well as fly initial radar site trials for NATS. Surprisingly, at first, CAFU appeared to be operating in much the same way, but these policy changes were to allow long-term consequences; new homes for each of the split structure, and even eventual sale of flight inspection services, though few ordinary staff realised or suspected it at the time.

In October, Capt. Dick Kilner retired as CFOI. Captain Kilner had already celebrated over forty years as a pilot and was in at the birth of the Flight Operations Inspectorate together with Geoffrey Chouffot, the now director general of Operations.

Captain Kilner was replaced by ex-CAFU training inspector, Captain W. "Bill" Wooden. Captain Wooden had joined CAFU in 1953 as a staff pilot, becoming a deputy commander in 1963, responsible for the training of Authorised Examiner courses at Stansted and introducing the HS125 aircraft later in the decade. He transferred to the Flight Ops Inspectorate in 1974 as a principal flight examiner/principal flight ops inspector (PFE/PFOI), and was currently qualified on the HS125, Boeing 707, and 747 aircraft, and was one of the first British pilots to qualify on the B747 and held a GAPAN Master Pilots Certificate.

During the first full year of use with the HS125 simulator, seventy-five pilots attended the CAFU AE course to obtain approval as instrument rating renewal examiners.

1977

April saw the end of the five-year term of the first chairman of the CAA, Lord Boyd-Carpenter. His replacement was Mr. Nigel Foulkes, who promptly declared:

"Our job is to pay the way—the Government thinks so and I heartily agree."

CAA CAFU Aircraft:
DEREGISTERED

Dove	G-ALFT	MCA	Feb 1977
Dove	G-ANUT	MCA	Feb 1997
Dove	G-ANUU	MCA	Feb 1977

The 1975/6 CAA Annual Report stated that only one Dove remained, yet these Doves were not deregistered until February of this year. In addition, two other instrument rating Doves, G-ANOV and NUW, would not be taken off the register until 1981.

In February, the final Flight Inspection Dove, G-ALFT, one of four Dove calibration aircraft used by CAFU, was retired after just over twenty-eight years' service. It was the longest-serving Dove aircraft with CAFU. The registration document showed it being permanently withdrawn from use (PWFU). It is not entirely clear why the final calibration Dove was retained this long; maybe it had to do with the fact that when CAFU started using the HS748 for calibration work, the non-state airfields, such as the Channel Island airfields and Luton, etc., would specifically ask for a Dove to be used, as the costs were considerably lower. Although LFT's deregistration date was February '77, it was, I am told, in Devon sometime before that date; and after initial preservation at the Torbay Museum, it was known to have moved on to a museum at Caernarvon where she was sadly scrapped around 2004. Also in February, two more of the IR Doves, NUT and NUU, were permanently withdrawn from use; both last seen at Biggin Hill, initially used for spares, and later seen as scrap between 1978 and 1983, although NUU was known to have been burnt. These stories are sometimes quite painful to relate, as I know it will be for all those who knew and worked with them. This left CAFU with just two of the initial five IR Doves, G-ANOV and NUW. These two aircraft remained for FE/FOI refresher flying, or any other staff from CAFU or HQ in London, who did not require turbine experience.

On April 1, Hawker Siddeley Aviation became part of the new British Aerospace Group (BAe) when united with the British Aircraft Corporation, Scottish Aviation, and Hawker Siddeley Dynamics.

The final ICAO AWOP meeting at Montréal, held in March 1977, had to look at a further simulation study that concluded that Doppler MLS would not operate satisfactorily on Runway 07L at Brussels Airport. The meeting finally concluded, with a controversial vote, which was widely interpreted as a sign of confidence in the American TRSB system. The details of the vote are recorded in the meeting's conclusions and recommendations, which were printed by *Flight:*

> *A proposal was put forward to proceed with system selection whereby the following questions would be decided by a simple majority vote:*
> 1. *In view of the benefits of the new guidance system for civil aviation, balanced against the cost, and. given the development status of the contenders, can the AWOP recommend the selection of one or more systems at this time?*
> 2. *Is the choice TRSB, Doppler MLS or DLS?*

Of the ten members, seven panel members answered yes to the first question, one no, and two abstained. The two abstentions were West Germany and the United Kingdom.

In the second vote, the United States, Australia, the Netherlands, the International Federation of Air Transport Pilots' Associations (IFATA), the USSR, and Canada voted for TRSB; the International Federation of Airline Pilots' Associations (IFALPA), supported Doppler MLS; and the German DLS had no votes. Germany, France, and the United Kingdom abstained.

There were other hidden stories, but it was put to me there were those on the committee who believed it would be quite improper, indeed prejudicial to the AWOP Final Assessment Report to render ineffective by a simple yes/no vote the massive and detailed assessment activity undertaken by the panel. They believed events at AWOP/6 had proven there were important areas where responsible technical assessment was impossible because of the lack of validation of claims made relating to the Lincoln laboratory simulation results, made during the course of the meeting. It was, therefore, impossible to render reasoned engineering judgements without intensive and time-consuming study. If a simple majority voting procedure was adopted, they would have no alternative than to withdraw from the proceedings. The conclusion, I was told by members at this meeting, could only be that the UK and others abstained because they did not agree with the procedure.

It may now all seem innocuous stuff, but with the Lincoln Laboratory false results it caused a bitter rivalry that produced deals, counter deals, reneging on deals and even incentives made to less technically voting members, reaching an intensity that was much to the distaste of the British team leader, abstaining must have appeared the only course to steer.

However, despite the voting, the countries were asked to collaborate and bring in a joint TRSB/Doppler proposal in not later than a year's time. It was significant that while Doppler MLS was even now showing up well in flight trials, the American-developed TRSB was still physically incomplete.

What most concerned the British team at the Working Group meeting was the fact that neither system had accumulated experience at a variety of sites. It was thought that, ideally, TRSB and Doppler-MLS should be tested under identical circumstances. This, it was thought, would show the relative performance of the two systems in the presence of reflecting objects such as terminal buildings, terrain, and moving aircraft, and would probably draw attention to the phenomenon of "shadowing" (an effect whereby aircraft near an aerial cause disturbance of the TRSB beam), which was still a source of concern. The British offered to demonstrate Doppler MLS at those airports that the Lincoln Laboratory described as incompatible with the UK system. The UK proposal was, said the British, in a more advanced state of development than its US counterpart, and they were satisfied with the present minima (runway visual range down to 150 m), having already performed over 1,300 category 3a landings.

British Airways' Concorde received the CAA's agreement to operate in CAT 2 conditions (100 feet DH and 400 metres RVR) at London Heathrow and Washington (Dulles) airports, while Trident aircraft were cleared to CAT 3B (12 feet DH and 100 metres RVR) where facilities permitted.

In spite of the Phillips Review recommendation that CAFU should lose its AOC, in July, the first of the CAA staff Flying Association's day trips was undertaken using CAFU's forty-four-seat HS748, G-ATMJ. Staff, mainly from London, took a day's leave to fly to St. Peter Port, Jersey. The captain was Capt. Dai Rees and co-pilot Dennis Mobberley, accompanied by hostesses Kim Newton and Stella Wallman.

The pressure of air traffic growth was restricting the accessibility of some airports. At Heathrow, for instance, it was expected that it might soon be necessary to perform ILS calibration at night.

In an article by *Flight* (1977, September 27), they reported the world's-first MLS-guided automatic landing at an international airport, flown at Gatwick by a CAFU HS748 aircraft on August 31. It was the first time that MLS guided landings were flown under operational conditions, alongside the traditional instrument landing system beams, which continued to operate without interference from the microwave system. Plessey and CAA engineers were using Doppler MLS, which was co-located with the airport's category 2 ILS.

This was a prototype MLS installation, and both the azimuth and elevation were not as large as the ILS installation (and were expected to be even smaller in production). A piece of neat engineering on the elevation antenna was the PTFE (polytetrafluoroethylene) waveguide cover, which replaced the pulsating rubber boot used initially to prevent ice formation. The PTFE panel was a non-stick surface that never gives ice the chance to accumulate—it would just slide off.

Tests were flown using either all or only half of the ninety-six waveguides in each antenna. Halving the number of waveguides increases the guidance beam width from one degree to two degrees, and trials in each configuration were equivalent to the American "International" and "Small Community" systems. Plessey was confident that the full array would be able to provide CAT 3 guidance (zero feet DH and zero feet RVR) and that the reduced system would allow CAT 2 approaches (down to 100 feet DH and 1200 feet RVR), thereby abolishing the distinction between non-CAT 3 systems.

The flight was made in CAFU's HS748 aircraft equipped with a Smiths SEP6 flight-control system and a simplex automatic-landing device. The latter equipment, also built by Smiths, was cleared for visual flight demonstrations, but with a monitoring device to be added. In the coming winter, it was expected to be cleared for use in low weather minima conditions. Modifications introduced to link MLS into the aircraft flight-control system were limited to sensor components. Autopilot control laws were therefore unaffected by the change from ILS guidance, so either input could be selected by the crew.

On the following day, *Flight* was given a demonstration. Three approaches were flown under MLS control, glide-acquire was indistinguishable from the traditional ILS-guided manoeuvre. The ride was reported as comfortable, although turbulence was much fiercer than one would expect when flying a low weather-minima approach, due to the fact that the runway in use was 26 and the MLS was on 08. Each flare was smooth but prolonged by the tailwind. Contact with the runway usually occurred about five seconds after passing the elevation antenna, and the scatter of touchdown points was not large. Azimuth guidance kept the aircraft pointing towards the wind, and none of the MLS-guided landings was more than ten feet from the runway centreline. The only potential embarrassment was a flight-control system disconnect on one approach at only 1.2 nm range. This was due to some heavy turbulence that fired a safety disconnect. The control system was reengaged less than one mile out, and it immediately re-established the MLS centreline to fly an automatic landing without difficulty. Normally, of course, an automatic landing would not be flown under such severe conditions. *Flight* were shown the airborne recorder graphs after landing and the smooth plots of MLS-guidance signals contrasted sharply with the equivalent "noisy" ILS signals. The plots, thought the *Flight* reporter, were tabletop proof that MLS had the quality and capability sought by using high-frequency approach guidance systems.

In October, G-AVXI the CAFU HS748 aircraft flown by Captain B. (Bernie) Sercombe, co-pilot John Smith, navigator John Kime, navaid inspector Gilbert Harding, and Tony Bird, his assistant, flew the Plessey Doppler MLS trials at Kjevik Airport, Kristiansand in Norway, where the British Doppler MLS antenna was offset from the runway. Although navigators were not usually flown on ILS flight inspections, they were used on the MLS trials.

On the first occasion that CAFU flew at Kjevik, the weather was good with pleasant temperatures, recalled Kjell Haug, Norway's flight inspection chief; there was little air traffic, and ATC was very cooperative.

Kjevik had been chosen for these trials by both the Americans and the British because of the topography. There was an ILS on the southwest runway but only a back beam on the northeast approach, as it was believed, by the Norwegians, the terrain would be hopeless for ILS. Kjell told me that they found the MLS approaches very interesting.

The Americans were there at the same time as CAFU, using a Boeing B727 (which was very noisy). The Norwegians noted intense competition between the teams; some of the Americans appeared somewhat arrogant (noted by both the Norwegians and the British), and when they saw the British 748 taxi out, they switched their system off. The Americans were not without problems, and they had to send for spares (though unknown if they were for the MLS or the aircraft) from Germany, which were brought in with a C130 Hercules aircraft.

During this period, two of the CAFU teams were flown as guests on the Norwegian HS748. Kjell said CAFU was amazed at the operations that were performed on their short eight-hundred-metre airfields, as it was not always easy with the 748, but the pilots managed very well.

In September, *Flight* reported that the CAA chairman, Nigel Foulkes, was giving CAA staff the impression of a chairman with direct commercial views:

> *He is cutting out interdepartmental committees, unnecessary travel, and other bureaucratic growths, and showing scant regard for anyone in industry with the "boosey-lunch" approach to business.*

Around 1977, the air traffic control assistants (ATCAs) went on strike. It was over the senior ATCA negotiating a pay settlement to be in line with senior administrative staff. Management had agreed in principle with the union, the Civil and Public Services Association (CPSA), but it came to a halt when payment was refused. At LATCC, a few members were suspended over the issue, and the situation escalated. As senior ATCAs at Stansted, the CAFU operations staff supported their colleagues at LATCC, at least until the suspensions were lifted. Unfortunately, it took six weeks to resolve. One of the consequences was that when the chairman, Mr. Foulkes, visited staff at Stansted, the ATCAs were not around to hear him speak about the future. As to how CAFU coped, I realise it must have been inconvenient for all concerned, especially the supervisor, Ron Golds, and the operations manager, Sid Pritchard, but what actually happened, I am unsure—I wasn't there!

Airway reported Sir Nigel Foulkes, CAA chairman, saying he was glad the ATCAs were bringing their strike to an end and believed that the travelling public could look forward to a return to normal service.

"Slim Line CAFU Proposed." This was the headline reported by the CAA paper, *Airway,* in November, when the changes proposed by the Phillips Review were announced. As part of the reorganisation plans for the Operations Division, it was proposed that CAFU should be streamlined and many of its functions integrated into the mainstream of the authority's safety activities. These proposals were still being discussed with the staff side because, in addition to the transfer of functions and duties between various directorates, these changes would lead to some staff moving to Aviation House, London. It was expected there would be the achievement of saving thirty positions.

The core of the changes would mean that training inspectors, concerned with testing airline examiners, would move to the Flight Ops Inspectorate in Aviation House, as would the examiners (to flight crew licensing) conducting tests on "pre-airline" candidates wishing to gain a commercial pilot's licence. Those staff remaining at Stansted would continue to serve the director general of Telecommunications in carrying out commissioning, calibration, and periodic checking of navigational aids.

Commercial flying was to end. The CAA Board had decided "the Authority should not compete with the industry it regulates."

The director general, Operations, Mr. Chouffot, told *Airway*: "There is at present a split between the policy makers, based at Aviation House in London, and the workforce at CAFU which has to implement the decisions."

However, he believed, "Ex-CAFU staff would be more closely involved in matters of policy."

He also stressed, "Over the years CAFU had undertaken a great deal of responsibility and earned a great deal of respect throughout the aviation industry."

The overall effect of the changes would be to reduce the current CAFU staff to thirty-eight (presumably those belonging to the Telecommunications section), and the cessation of commercial flying would enable the authority to sell one of the HS748s—the other two would remain as Tels "Flying Laboratories" used for calibrating navigational aids. There was a question mark over the HS125 jet aircraft. It could either be retained to enable pilots to continue practical flying, or, alternatively, it could be sold and "time" on outside aircraft bought when necessary. Either way, FOIs and FEs would be given the flying practice required. Certainly up to this point, individual pilot hours on aircraft were slowly being reduced.

It was thought that the plan could take up to two years to be put fully into effect. The reason, it was explained, was that the CAA must ensure that the people involved be given the maximum amount of consideration.

"We must aim for efficiency and economy, but we shall not overlook the importance of people," concluded Mr. Chouffot.

The CAA Annual Report for 1977 reported changes to the Air Navigation Order. The first amendment required the carriage of a ground proximity warning system in all public transport aeroplanes exceeding fifteen thousand kilograms (maximum authorised weight) or which are authorised to carry thirty or more passengers. The second was an amendment requiring operators of all public transport aircraft to hold an air operator's certificate (AOC).

Additionally, the CAA introduced a "non-expiring" AOC to reduce administrative costs without, the CAA said, reduction in supervision standards.

During the year, ninety pilots (including twelve from overseas companies) attended the CAFU AE course to obtain approval as instrument rating renewal examiners.

Nearly one hundred new AOCs were issued to the operators of small public transport aircraft bringing the total to 143.

CAA CAFU Aircraft at the end of 1977 Total = 06

Dove	02	Communication & Refresher flying
HS125	01	Radar, VIP, Comm, Refresher flying
HS748	02	Tels Flight Inspection
HS748	01	VIP, Communications, Ref flying

1978

In January, CAFU again visited Kristiansand, this time to also observe the American TRSB system. Both systems were installed (an American B727 was seen flying the TRSB system). This time the 748 aircraft, flown by Capt. Hugh McDowall, co-pilot Dick Hawkes, navigator John Kime, NAI Gil Harding, and Tony Bird, his assistant, found the airport in real winter conditions. To make matters even more difficult, the port-wing de-icer boot on the aircraft "ballooned," requiring a spare to be sent to them. CAFU sent Capt. Peter Franklin in the forty-four seat 748, TMJ, to the rescue. All he could do was drop off the spare parts and return as quickly as possible due to the commencement of a heavy snow fall. Then, in blizzard conditions, Captain McDowall and the rest of the crew all worked into the early hours of the morning under the direction of the chief engineer, Ken Camp, to repair the grounded Tels aircraft on the hardstand in freezing cold conditions!

But the de-icer problem was not the only incident that CAFU experienced at Kristiansand. Kjell Haug, the Norwegian flight inspection boss, was one of the many international observers carried during this set of trials, and told me of his alarm when the 748 suffered a decompression failure during one of the MLS demonstration flights.

Tony Bird, assistant NAI at the time, filled me in with the details, saying that it happened in the same week as the de-icer boot incident, and although Kjell had attempted to get the Norwegian engineers to provide a spare from their own HS748 aircraft, it was not possible. So CAFU at Stansted had to arrange a second support flight, this time to bring a replacement hatch. Tony Bird continues:

> *Our 748's had a small compartment between the Navigator and Flight Inspection stations that would allow eight people to sit at a couple of tables. (four on each side). So it was, during the MLS trials at Kristiansand, that we found ourselves flying observers from all over the world to see what we were up to and not cooking the books!*

The crew were—Hugh McDowell, Dick Hawkes, I think John Kime, Gilbert Harding, and myself. Ken Camp was with us to give engineering support. (See the de-icer story).

On this particular flight, we had additional recording equipment installed to obtain data for RAE Farnborough. Gilbert and I, only had four hands between us so we roped in one of the Telecroscope crew, Brian Cone (who was doing nothing else at the time and who loved flying) to switch on, at our bidding, these additional recorders.

We took off, with sundry Japanese, Germans, Poles etc. aboard and as we started to climb away (at I guess about 1200 ft) there was a loud bang and the cabin filled with dust and loose papers etc. I was sitting at the MLS inspection station adjacent to the F24 terrain camera hatch which rose into the air and then went down again with another loud bang. My immediate thought was that the glass optical flap on the bottom fuselage skin had fractured and that was why we had lost cabin pressure.

However, the culprit was the Starboard over wing escape hatch which had decided to launch itself on to the bit of Norway below. It was a bit of a mystery. I remember the hatch being checked before take-off, as was usual, but the thought did occur to us that with all the strangers on board, inquisitive fingers may have been to blame. The hatch was quite a heavy substantial item and the mind boggles to think about the consequences of it hitting the tail-plane. It was after all only meant to be pushed out with the aircraft on the ground.

My overwhelming memory is the look on Brian Cone's face who was at the rear with the recorders!

Dick Hawkes remembered being ten days at Kristiansand before moving down to Brussels airport to prove to the ICAO AWOP team that the Doppler MLS could be flown on runway 07L, despite American claims to the contrary. Reaching Brussels, Captain McDowall and Dick Hawkes then returned to Stansted and were replaced by Capt.

Peter Franklin and Ben Gunn, co-pilot, who with the rest of the crew continuing, as Tony Bird recalled, "to the bitter end."

Flight wrote that

"in practical demonstrations and with flight-trial measurements the British team quashed all the simulation-based criticisms. US integrity," it was written, "took a severe blow."

After successfully completing the MLS trial at Brussels, the 748 crew then took the aircraft down to Berne (Belp), Switzerland, where an RAE Andover was seen on a similar MLS task. The reason the RAE was also doing trials was because CAFU was flying approaches down to CAT 2, while the RAE, with additional aircraft instrumentation, was flying to CAT 3 standards.

Berne was not suitable for ILS installation because of the mountainous terrain and considered the most challenging location for the MLS equipment to be evaluated. Additionally, it had a narrow runway of only thirty metres wide and 1,200 metres long (Stansted for instance was forty-six by three thousand metres). Together with the RAE Andover, over fifty completely automatic landings were made, many in difficult conditions with crosswinds up to 30 knots. Fifty precisely tracked flights were made to confirm the accuracy of the DMLS guidance signal and further flights were along a narrow valley at a thirty-degree offset to the final approach course. All the results showed that DMLS provided safe, accurate guidance, unaffected by the mountainous region of Berne Airport.

The comprehensive trials programme was witnessed by a number of independent ICAO observers, including the USA, and, *Airway* reported, that the Swiss authorities were prepared to offer equal opportunities to the US FAA of their TRSB MLS.

Airfields were categorised as either A, B, or C. Category A had no significant approach or departure problems, while category B airfields had situations in which the crew should be briefed before the flight. Category C airfields were considered the most difficult, usually with high surrounding terrain and/or many procedures. The crew were not only briefed beforehand but also one of the crew members had to have flown into the C airfield within the last six months.

After an accident at Tenerife North, where a UK B707 aircraft turned the wrong way in the holding pattern and crashed into high ground, CAFU inspectors flew the 125 into a number of C airports: Lisbon, Tenerife North, Tenerife South (not a category C airfield but there to refuel), Madeira, Gibraltar, and Tarbes (Ossun Lourdes). Not only were they able to check the pattern at Tenerife North, as well as the English spoken by ATC, but also took the opportunity to visit the other category C airports on that route. The flight was accomplished using the 125 hours allocated to each inspector. These flights also enabled the inspectors to compare the written briefings of individual companies against the carefully prepared CAFU briefings.

It was around this time that certain company pilots were directly soliciting the CAA chairman about the "Jollies" undertaken by CAFU.

CAA CAFU Aircraft:
DEREGISTERED

| HS748 | G-ATMJ | CAA | July 1978 |

Capt. John Robinson, who retired later in the year to take up an appointment as chief training officer with McAlpine at Luton, reported that he flew his last UK MEP flight in G-ATMJ to Strasbourg this year.

In the CAA staff paper *Airway* for July 7, they reported the sale of G-ATMJ, with a picture of George Bartle, CAFU administration officer, receiving a cheque from Capt. John Ryder of Dan-Air (see photo). G-ATMJ had been chartered on weekends to Dan-Air between the months of May and October each year. It was delivered to Dan-Air on the thirtieth of the same month and in use with them the following day. Later, TMJ was taken on by British Airways and operated from Glasgow, Renfrew Airport. Eventually, she ended her days with Emerald Airways at Blackpool where she continued until around 2006. CAFU had made great use of this aircraft, and *Airway* reported that TMJ had flown 5,200 hours, made nearly six thousand landings, carried forty-two thousand passengers with four thousand of them children from Essex schools.

In January, representatives from the United States and Britain were testified before the US House of Representatives' transportation subcommittee, investigating accusations that the Federal Aviation Administration (FAA) deliberately misled the ICAO All Weather Operations Panel about microwave landing system performance.

The claim was made by Britain following the discovery of errors in computer simulations of Doppler MLS performance, and taken up by subcommittee chairman John Burton. US witnesses on the first day included Barry Goldwater Junior and FAA and Lincoln Laboratory representatives.

On the British side were witnesses from Plessey and the Civil Aviation Authority (CAA). Bendix, manufacturer of the US MLS time-referenced scanning beam, also had a representative at the inquiry. Burton insisted that the subcommittee should not judge the technical merits of the British and US systems.

When UK and US representatives gave evidence to the US government transportation subcommittee, both sides were in conflict. Countering the British allegation, representatives of the FAA opened the meeting with strong criticism of Britain's anti-US attitudes, but found themselves at loggerheads with some US observers who contended that the United Kingdom had not been treated fairly.

Committee chairman, John Burton, said at the meeting,

"Exaggeration should give way to the plain truth."

His impartiality contrasted with the attitude of most of the witnesses who testified in Washington. Republican Barry Goldwater said,

"I'm totally convinced that our allies, the UK, have not been treated fairly and equitably in this MLS business."

He claimed that the subcommittee

"did not conduct a thorough investigation of this controversy. If we had, we would not be sitting here today."

FAA administrator, Langhorne Bond, was not, however, sympathetic towards the United Kingdom.

"Why wasn't the chairman of Britain's Civil Aviation Authority at the meeting?" he demanded. Bond had not spoken to Nigel Foulkes in London, but the CAA had believed it more appropriate that the United Kingdom should be represented by technical experts and had sent Michael Whitney, deputy director in Telecommunications, the UK's representative on ICAO AWOP.

Bond said that

"by 1981 the US would have 740 instrument landing systems in use, while the UK would have only 43, so the US was more interested in getting the right choice."

He also accused Britain of failing to produce unprocessed flight trials data and quoted date changes that affect the arrival of a US team to view MLS data in Britain, as evidence that Britain was trying to reduce American chances of seeing more raw data. The CAA claimed, however, that the dates suggested by the United States were inconvenient.

Dr. James E. Evans of Lincoln Laboratories and Geoffrey Bailey of the UK CAA clashed over the availability of Lincoln Laboratories simulation results. The British engineer claimed that on several occasions, he was denied access to MLS computer programs, but Evans said, "We find his statement just incredible . . ." Adding that several of Bailey's requests were for programs that did not exist or were being modified.

Republican Robert Walker commented that the relationship between the FAA and Lincoln Laboratories, whereby the latter was under contract to the FAA to complete simulation studies on US and British MLS proposals, was not specifically wrong,

"But anyone looking at it from the outside can take this relationship . . . and run off with it. You left yourself open for criticism."

Burton admitted also that he was disturbed to find that the FAA was about to award a $2 million contract for a preproduction US MLS and that he did not regard this as timely.

On the last day of the inquiry, the FAA admitted that problems with their laser tracking equipment had invalidated much of the data obtained at Kennedy in December and that they were hoping to repeat trials before the end of the month. The schedule would be very tight and might even cause the American team to relinquish trials in Iran and would certainly depend on how the weather affected Kennedy in the next few weeks. Trials were due to be completed before the British team arrived at the airport—they had to give the FAA three weeks' notice and had not notified the FAA so far. Mr. Whitney admitted during cross-examination that the United Kingdom too had experienced its share of optical-tracker problems and that not all data collected during trials with Doppler MLS would be suitable for analysis.

It was generally understood that the subcommittee expected its inquiry to serve as a clearinghouse for conflicting US and UK opinions. But with both teams now in the mood to find fault with the other's technique, as confidence grew out of demonstrations, the exchanges at Washington had been more heated than expected.

During January, the Americans had trialled three TRSB MLS sites in Europe; Kristiansand, Norway, a "small Community" and "Basic" systems, later moving the "small Community" to Belgium's Charleroi airport, where they also installed their biggest "Expanded" MLS on runway 07.

New York Kennedy airport was nominated as the MLS test site by the Americans and was one of the airports at which comparative trials were to be flown with both TRSB and the British commutated-Doppler MLS. An evaluation flight was carried out by an FAA test crew to check system integrity and operation. Present aboard the second flight were several non-US observers, including Les Hardwick, a UK CAA engineer. According to *Aviation Daily,* the UK CAA observer said afterwards:

> *The TRSB receiver acquired a firm elevation signal at approximately 12 n.m. While the pilot was manoeuvring the aircraft to try to locate the 38° right radial, the ground tracker reported the aircraft was 50° to the right of centreline. By this time the range had decreased considerably. At a range of about 5 n.m. the TRSB receiver acquired an azimuth signal that indicated the aircraft was 20° to the right of centreline. The flight-test engineer, Mr. C. Mackin, said the 20° indication was the result of a side lobe and demonstrated this on an oscilloscope.*

Why the airborne equipment could lock on to a side lobe remained unexplained, and a report that the ground equipment was only producing guidance in a plus thirty-degree arc, because setting-up checks were still in progress, astonished British engineers who believed that such a fault should have been recognised by the ground monitor. Furthermore, it should not be possible to attempt an approach outside the available guidance arc if the outside-coverage indicators (OCIs) were operating. Proponents of the UK developed Doppler MLS saw these problems as fundamental difficulties that could not be disregarded as easily as were the erroneous Lincoln Laboratories simulation reports, which had embarrassed FAA officials the previous year.

It was becoming clear that the incident was no anomaly. Another UK observer, John Benjamin of the Ministry of Defence, witnessed a fifty to sixty degrees transient heading error during TRSB demonstrations at Buenos Aires in a US Air Force T-39 Sabre-liner. Flight trials at Kristiansand in Norway had also taken longer than expected, allegedly because of further operating difficulties. If the earlier House of Representatives hearing in Washington—which was primarily concerned with the Lincoln Laboratories simulations—generated more scepticism about FAA procedure, it was likely that the administration would come under increased pressure to be more open about TRSB trial results.

The Americans, according to British sources, had to extend their trials because of receiver problems. The receiver was said to overload when it was close to the runway and to give failure indications. John Benjamin said that an attenuator had had to be included in the receiver circuit. The FAA admitted that one receiver had caused problems "because it had insufficient dynamic range." It likened introduction of the attenuator to the way that autopilot gains are reduced during approaches. Several receivers had operated free of problems, and the American team believed that only one receiver was a rogue unit. But it had insufficient time to solve the problem completely before finishing the New York trials. Even so, said the British team, in its retrial at New York, the FAA had installed larger antennas than those used previously, and the glide slope aerial had been moved to the opposite side of the runway. The FAA was also having to face further challenges from the British MLS development team, which maintained that Doppler MLS had fully lived up to expectations in the demonstrations and trials that had been completed since last June. When Doppler MLS was taken to Brussels, the team was happy to get the equipment operational within a few days. Now, after working at several more test sites, they could install complete azimuth and elevation aerials and a monitor set in less than forty-eight hours. Power-supply quality was the biggest unknown facing the team, though careful planning usually ensured that most details were in order before equipment was delivered to a new test site.

The British would soon be demonstrating Doppler MLS at Kennedy and were confident that they would be able to add yet another faultless set of trials and demonstrations to the list. Meanwhile, the American TRSB system had reached the controversial test site at Brussels and would be on view to observers in Europe for the first time.

Over the weekend of March 11/12, however, the FAA was installing a new MLS at Atlantic City, New Jersey, which was developed by the Hazeltine Corporation. The set used compact antennas and was designed to US small-community standards—it produced only a ±10 degrees azimuth guidance arc, and elevation guidance up to 10 degrees—but could be expanded to full ICAO (±60 degrees azimuth and up to 20 degrees elevation) specification, according to a Hazeltine spokesman. The new system had been produced under a privately funded programme within Hazeltine. It was bought by the FAA a few days before installation at Atlantic City. Hazeltine reported that performance was good on the bench at its New York factory, and the company expected good results in flight trials. It was understood that the FAA might show the new system at the Montréal demonstration during the next month.

If the Hazeltine-developed system did live up to expectations, the new development diluted many of Britain's criticisms of the American TRSB concept. The FAA said that it could monitor TRSB performance just as well as the United Kingdom could monitor Doppler MLS, but there was certainly a large difference of opinion between the two teams on this subject.

Criticism was not being confined to a one-way street, and the FAA was still determined to draw attention to what it regarded as deficiencies in Doppler MLS. Mike Nelson, an FAA engineer, said that Britain had never demonstrated an out-of-cover (OC) antenna and that several time-division multiplex signal features were still unexplored. He cited the "jitter" technique that the United Kingdom had proposed as a propeller-modulation countermeasure, the lack of flare and back-azimuth elements, and reduced "guard time" between signals as typical of the aspects that Britain had not explored during recent tests.

The next meeting was to be held in Washington when it was thought that at least two extra meetings might have to be held.

In March, Nigel Foulkes, chairman of the UK Civil Aviation Authority, had told FAA Chief Langhorne Bond and John L. Burton, chairman of the US government's activities and transportation committee, that the UK CAA would be supplying data on Doppler microwave landing system trials to the United States as quickly as possible. According to Mr. Foulkes, the FAA now had copies of or direct access to information on all British trials except the recent tests at Berne and Tehran (CAFU had been to Berne while the RAF Andover had visited both airfields). Foulkes said,

The CAA would appreciate information on the trials and demonstrations of the American time referenced scanning beam (TRSB) MLS at Buenos Aires, Honduras, Cape May (particularly Twin Otter trials), New York, Kristiansand and Brussels, and on the helicopter trials at Fort Monmouth.

At the Sixty-Sixth IATA Technical Committee meeting, all members agreed that there was no early requirement for the operational use of MLS. The majority of members felt that it would be ten years before commercial airlines would be using MLS on a significant scale. Nevertheless, the need for an early decision by ICAO, in respect of the MLS technique to be adopted, was strongly supported solely on the basis that the current requirement for MLS at small airports was already leading to a proliferation of nonstandard systems. No evidence as to the scale of implementation or locations where this was occurring was offered, nor was it explained how this would affect international aviation.

In March, British engineers installed Doppler MLS at Kennedy, New York, virtually beside the American TRSB system, which had

had to be reinstalled after data from previous trials were "lost"! British engineers also claimed that TRSB could not be developed to meet ICAO specifications. Existing hardware was not representative of the equipment that was described in proposals to the ICAO All-Weather Operations Panel, according to Plessey's Roy Lawson. He claimed that the Hazeltine compact antenna was the key to successful TRSB development but that it was abandoned after only sixty minutes of flight tests during early 1977. Jim Lawson, CAA DD Tels N, believed that "the TRSB proposal made by the US to ICAO did not exist."

Capt. Hugh McDowall and co-pilot Dick Hawkes, NAI Gil Harding, and his assistant, Laurie Park, flew the HS748, G-AVXI, over the Atlantic via Keflavik in Iceland, Narsassawak in Greenland, and Goose Bay, Canada, where they had to stay awhile due to a heavy snowstorm. Only then did they fly on to Bangor, Main, and finally New York. Because the navigator was not on board this trip, assistant NAIs Laurie Park and Eric Edmondson did a short course on LORAN C to give positional information over the water—if needed.

At Kennedy, they flew the Doppler MLS installed by the British engineers. Although the Americans were not flying their system at the time, Captain McDowall flew the British Plessey Doppler MLS, both during daylight hours and night. This came about because the RAE Andover, which had been due to fly in from Farnborough, was stuck at Accra.

As each team readied to show off its brainchild at Montréal in April—where both sides would install equipment for ICAO representatives to be given demonstrations to decide which system should be adopted as the international standard—it appeared that neither was likely to concede any points to the other.

After completion of the flights at Kennedy, Captain McDowall flew VXI on to Dorval, Montréal's airport, meeting up with the takeover crew of Captain Franklin, co-pilot Benn Gunn, and NAI Alan Richardson with Eric Edmondson, his assistant, who had travelled on commercial services. Alan told of his experience on arrival in Canada and of his difficulties in explaining to the immigration authorities the reason why he did not have a return-trip ticket. The second crew would be required to provide the demonstration flights to be given to the many ICAO representatives.

Gilbert Harding, NAI, flying back to the United Kingdom, remembered the "luxury of flying back from Canada" to allow the second crew to take over with the demonstrations.

Capt. Don Hale, who had joined CAFU in 1953, becoming flight service manager at Stansted in the eighties and had worked with the All Weather Operations group in Headquarters, London, was in New York as one of the UK representatives. He is reputed to have said that he was "positively jostled" by the Americans. An indication, perhaps, that the Americans were uncomfortable with another British system vying strongly with a lucrative business at stake.

ICAO was to deliberate on their findings on the MLS contenders between April 4 and 21. Two working groups operated throughout the meeting. Group A concerned itself with technical matters, and Group B, with operational data and costs. The basis of the discussions was the all-weather operations panel (AWOP) report produced the previous month.

To this, each proposing state added papers describing their own systems and spelling out the deficiencies of the opposition. It was estimated that each delegate had to digest two thousand pages of technical data. British observers were concerned that many delegates would not be able to cope with this mass of information, a view supported by the fact that it was typical for 50 percent of those present to abstain at early votes.

By the nineteenth, the ICAO panel had decided to adopt the American time-reference scanning beam. The voting had gone thirty-nine for TRSB and twenty-four for Doppler MLS, with eight abstentions. The division had 133 members, plus nonvoting representatives of four international organisations. Although the last-mentioned could not vote, they played a big part in the meeting.

The Americans were jubilant.

The British gave an official statement that congratulated the United States and Australia (their TRSB systems to be combined) on their success and wished them well with continuing development of TRSB and expressed their natural disappointment that the meeting had not selected commutated-Doppler MLS. The statement went on to say that those members participating in the meeting had faced the impossible task of studying and acting upon a great deal of material and complex operational and technical issues, and the time allocated had not permitted adequate study by those states that had not previously participated in the many years of preparatory work.

Most observers expected that TRSB, given sufficient development, would meet all the claims made in the US presentation to ICAO. Their only reservation was that at the time, TRSB was not as well proven as commutated-Doppler MLS. This did not mean that Doppler was better, but there were many engineers who still believed that it was the case and would continue to criticise TRSB if its future development ran into any trouble.

Plessey and the CAA had prepared and shown well the Doppler system. Yet the Americans, embarrassed until the last, still in the process of producing a viable TRSB system, had won the day.

At this stage, I simply cannot help myself but show the reader an article from *Flight* magazine:

> *The basic reason, Flight considers, is that decisions about radio systems requiring air and ground counterparts are in the end made internationally, and it can happen that an important development on which great resources and money have been spent over years is killed by a simple democratic vote. On the evidence of the last ten years or more of ICAO facilities standardization, the risks involved in this sort of endeavour are far too great; and the mood is growing that the chances of success are too slender to warrant the committal of large-scale development funds to products on which an international decision will finally be made.*

Words never truer, you might think—even though they were written in October 1959!

Geoffrey Chouffot, the former operations officer who, in 1960, had helped set up the Flight Operations Inspectorate to which part of CAFU now belonged and one of the instigators of the air operator's certificate, was awarded the position of group director of Aviation Safety.

In the CAA Annual Report for this year, it was noted that CAFU had conducted 1,200 flight tests for the issue of a professional pilot's licence or rating.

The report also announced that some 250 pilots were tested and appointed as CAA authorised examiners, and over two hundred existing authorisations were renewed (the previous year there had been ninety AE candidates on the courses at Stansted). The figure of 250 on the course at Stansted does not seem to me to be accurate. Even if the HS125 simulator at Stansted had operated with two people on the course each week for fifty-two weeks of the year, that would only have amounted to 104. I had either missed something here, or the figure is wildly inaccurate. Perhaps the courses were also conducted on company simulators at the same time, which is something I was never aware of.

The report also announced that the Civil Aviation Authority's Flying Unit (the first time I had seen the change from CAFU to CAAFU) should no longer undertake public transport flights and that all such flying be ceased by March 31, 1978. The function of the flying unit would now be confined in future to the operation of two aircraft (HS 748) for navaid inspection and calibration work, and one aircraft (HS 125) for training of CAA staff.

The 748 MEP flights were taken over by Dan-Air, while the ministerial 125 VIP flights, started over ten years previously, were taken over by the RAF Royal Flight at Northolt. Capt. John Oliver remembered flying with four separate prime ministers: Mr. Harold Wilson, Mr. Jim Callaghan, Sir Alec Douglas Hume, Mrs. Margaret Thatcher, as well as Jim Prior, Lord Widgery, Shirley Williams, and many others.

CAA CAFU Aircraft at the end of 1978 Total = 05

Dove	02	Communication & Refresher flying
HS125	01	Radar, Comm, Refresher flying
HS748	02	Tels Flight Inspection

1979

Although the telecommunications side was already using computers, this year, the administrative side was also supplied with an ICL CPM system. It was a large desk-sized server with the ability to serve several offices and be connected, if ever required, to the mainframe in London. The main server was held in the IRE/TRE office under the control of Sid Pritchard, manager of operations, who oversaw the introduction of word processing in several offices. The power of the ICL machine was used by the ops manager to computerise the IRE/TRE renewal advice to authorised examiners.

This arrangement also led to the introduction of a computerised flight planning system used by Operations for the HS125 flights. The IT department in London hired a contractor, Mr. Nigel Smith, to write the program in ICL Basic language. The ops manager explained what was needed and provided several algorithms. The system held about three hundred files. The several old filing cabinets that held master paper copies of old flight plans, which required each one to be checked, updated, and photocopied each time they were used, were now made redundant. Changes to a route or an individual waypoint could be input at any time and held good for any route that used those waypoints. Still-air plans could be printed beforehand, and a wind adjusted plan made on the day with clean printouts for the crew.

Telecommunications engineering staff were recruited from many sources, including the armed services. There were two classes of entry: direct entrants, with previous experience in engineering, and cadets who were school leavers. Cadet places were much sought after with sixteen in a class and two classes starting each year at the CAA Bletchley Park College. (Apparently, if you ask a Tels man the question, "Why Bletchley?" he will probably ask another question—"Why did the ATCOs have Bournemouth while Tels had Bletchley?" The answer—because Tels had the first choice!) In truth, Bletchley had, in its wartime, "spook" role, radio facilities on site—the aerials were still there in the seventies. After the war, civil service departments were clamouring for "technical" accommodation, and the MCA was offered Bletchley. In its early incarnation, it was very busy with Tels personnel spending weeks and weeks there. The 1950s, 1960s, and early 1970s were certainly the high points.

New recruits did not normally go direct to CAAFU at Stansted, as the work there was probably not considered core business, but one who did was David Lacey. His first choice of posting was to Heathrow, the second to Stansted, as he had heard of CAAFU and was an aircraft enthusiast, so he plumped for Stansted and was surprised to get a direct posting.

The college also ran specific courses for engineers already working in the field. For example, an engineer at an airport would go to Bletchley to be trained on ILS and/or radar. The facilities at Bletchley were certainly impressive: a full kit of navigational aids, DME, DVOR, DRDF, DME, fully functioning primary and secondary radars, labs full of communications kit and computers, residential and office blocks, etc. (DRDF was Digitally Resolved Direction Finding; its predecessor, the AD210, used at airports.)

All engineers could expect to spend a few weeks a year at Bletchley becoming fully trained on the equipment they would be expected to work on. It was unusual for CAAFU engineers to find themselves back at Bletchley, though they would do the first two weeks of ILS and VOR, which were both four-week courses, as these were deemed relevant to flight checking work. Another that was taken was the Microprocessor Technique course.

When British Airways began operating the Lockheed L1011 Tristar, the third wide-bodied aircraft to enter commercial service, Capt. Don Hale and Capt. Ron Crawford were selected to be type-rated on this new type on the British Aircraft Register.

On July 1, the CAA became the first European Civil Aviation Authority to adopt the Joint Airworthiness Requirements, JAR 25, as the national airworthiness code for large transport aircraft.

Around this time, three German SEL DVORs were installed in the southeast of England. However, these suffered incompatibilities with some aircraft designs, and because two of the DVORs were at each end of the airway Red One (R1, Clacton-Ongar [or Ockham]), this manifested in radial bends. With R1 East having parallel airways, one north and south of each other, it was not the best of situations. It was a catalyst for change of equipment. CAAFU were busily employed in the measurement of these bends using their 748 flight inspection aircraft.

When Peter Kenworthy, one of the two remaining navigators retired, CAAFU knew they would have to do something about the VOR/DME requirement for in-flight positional data. The solution was to install a PC in each aircraft (VXI and VXJ) and use software to process the Decca information into range and bearing. Prior to the PC installation, Tony Bird said he could not remember a co-pilot (ex-nav) sitting in the navigator position for VOR flight inspections; only navigators Peter Kenworthy or John Kime were used. John, it was said, did magic things with Decca, utilising two chains at a time in order to improve fixing accuracy and that he discovered that the Isle of Wight was not where people thought it was!

Ernie Jay, ground Tels engineer, wrote the software for the aircraft PC, working very closely with John Kime (the last navigator). It was John Kime who oversaw and approved the system before he retired. The NAIs then took over the task, deriving their own data, one driving the computer, and the other at the flight inspection console.

Essex schoolchildren boarding an Educational Flight
Photo: Eddy Harris/JF

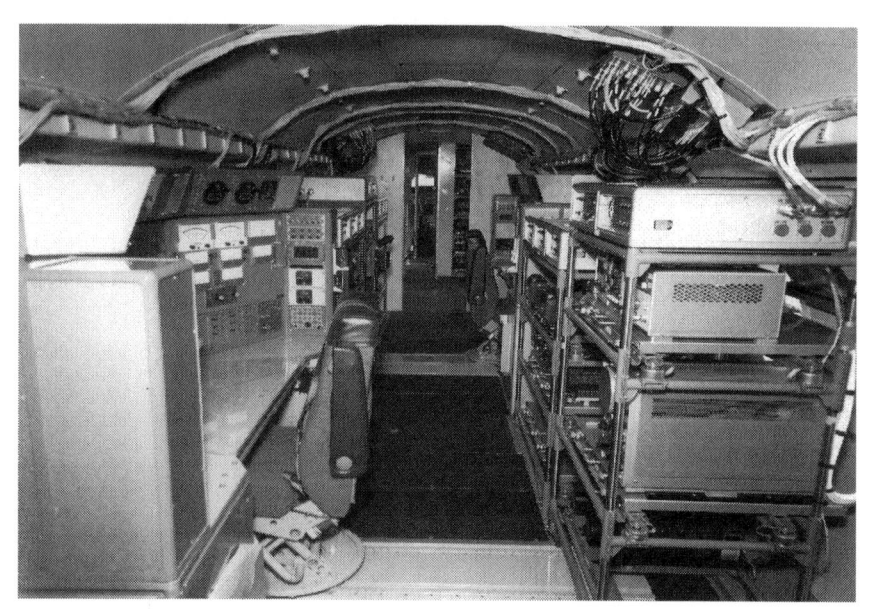

HS748 ILS Flight Inspection Consul on the left & VOR Consul top right.
Photo: Eddy Harris/JF

Searle Baker with improved Telecroscope at ILS Localiser end
Photo: Eddy Harris/JF

CAFU's second HS125 G-AVDX, departing Greenham Common
Photo: Copyright Steve Williams (Airliners.net) 0291111[1]

CAA Chairman with Eddy Harris & Joe Gidman, Superintendents—and Tels managers, extreme left Alec Brock, Eddy Dovey & Pat Moylette
Photo: Eddy Harris/JF

TMJ sold to Dan-Air, July 1978>>
Photo: Eddy Harris/JF

Chapter Six
1980-1989

1980

Airway announced an advanced calibration and display system for the inspection of instrument landing aids. The USA, Britain, and other countries were working out proposals for microwave landing systems for adoption by ICAO, and while working on a quick way to provide results of these trials, it was seen that there was a possible way to provide quicker routine calibration results.

Called Skycal, it was a move from the analogue system—used in the early CAFU HS748s—to a digital system that was thought to be a breakthrough by enabling the NAI on the aircraft to dispense with paper printouts, recording digitally calibration measurements that could then be displayed on a visual display unit (VDU).

The strength of the system, it was said, was that there was no limit to the amount of data it could store and provide; three runs were required to check an ILS glide path and/or localiser in the air, and a single disk could store the processed details of up to seventy runs. The whole system could provide results in near real time rather than a matter of days.

Mr. Geoff Bailey, Tels. N3, CAA House, London, was instrumental in the design, using a Hewlett Packard 9825 computer, and, working closely with CAFU engineers and technicians at Stansted, it was fitted into one of CAFU's 748 aircraft for trials. The staff involved at CAFU were Bob Phillips, manager, Tels Design Service; Jim Reynolds, head of the Avionics Development Laboratory; and Colin Sheppard, navigational aid inspector providing flight inspection liaison. Among the tasks CAFU was concerned with was the construction of the interface printed circuit boards from Geoff Bailey's design. Skycal had been on operational trials with CAAFU for the previous six months and used at several UK airports.

A perceived difficulty was the size of the equipment that used up the left-hand four passenger seats in the 748. And while it was found that Skycal could comfortably handle VOR inspections, it struggled with the more critical work of ILS flight inspection.

The Navigation Directorate and CAAFU P & E (Planning and Development) investigated the digital encoding of the flight inspection signal, and in spite of all the praise and hopes for this equipment, it faded into the background, mainly because the Hewlett Packard computer employed in Skycal at this time was just not capable of running the software at anywhere near the speed required to encode the variations in the flight inspection signals, even if it coded only one channel at a time. Geoff Bailey was, perhaps, a little ahead of his time. I was informed it would have required a mainframe computer to fit in the 748! Consequently, it was not put into operational use.

While digital systems were replacing the original 748 aircraft flight inspection equipment required for the calibration of aids, "mobile" phones, with huge heavy batteries, were now also carried on the flight inspection aircraft. This enabled the NAI crew member to speak direct to the ground station chief telecommunications officer about the serviceability of the ILS and likelihood of a positive report. In the past, the airport telecommunications officer would have had to wait until the aircraft had returned to base before the NAI could pass any results.

In July, Tony Lister, an FOI who had passed his helicopter instrument rating with Geoff Gurr, gained his type rating on the Bell 222 when he was checked out at the Bell plant, Fort Worth, Texas.

It was from this time that most of the 1976 Phillips Committee recommendations came into operation, and the three main tasks of

CAAFU, flight inspection, pre-airline examining, and post-airline inspection, were slowly separated. Capt. Don Hale now headed the flight inspection side as flight service manager; pre-airline examining, headed by Capt. Stuart Spence, now came directly under the Directorate of Flight Crew Licensing, and post-airline inspectors at Stansted became part of the Flight Operations Inspectorate with a new department, still based at Stansted, known as Flight Ops 6 (F Ops 6), headed by Capt. Jimmy Joy.

It was a long slow process for the CAA, but it now seemed that they knew exactly what was needed to accomplish the task of collecting staff from many separate areas and putting them together under one roof.

To me, within Operations at CAAFU, the movement was so slow that I had hardly noticed the incoming trickle of new pilots required for just the examining side. Nor did I notice the absence of training inspectors who were either moved to the inspectorate at Aviation House in London, or those who were now retiring from the scene. Although CAAFU Operations sat between all the tasks, it was not noticed the training inspection side was now directly part of the inspectorate and known, in London at least, as F Ops 6.

Directly within Operations at CAAFU, there were now only four senior ATC assistant/briefing officers—one supervisor and three within the Operations room. Each of them shared, rotating on a weekly basis, the tasks of booking tests, aircrew rostering, flight planning, and telecommunications planning. Work carried on as normal, it seemed, with the threat of pending change looming only in the midst of a distant future.

Capt. Tony Lister, later to become CFOI, together with his fellow FOI, Spencer Lewis, arranged from around the mid-seventies an annual cricket match between Operations staff in London and CAFU staff at Stansted, cementing relationships. These light-hearted yet sometimes intense games were, at first, played on the local Stansted village pitch on the edge of Tony's house, a most beautiful spot. When short of players, Tony's daughter, then a student at Loughborough College, joined in as an accomplished spinner for the opposition.

One year I was allowed to captain the CAFU team, and standing with Bill Wooden, who was introducing one of the CAFU pilots to a new FOI, he said, "This is Capt. Dan Thomas." My young daughter immediately piped up with, in derisory tones, "He's not the captain—my dad is!"

The British Airports Authority that ran Stansted Airport asked the CAA to find a new home for the Fire Service Training School, due to future plans held for the airport.

The CAFU, or rather CAAFU name, was seldom mentioned now in CAA Annual Reports, even though the following services were mostly carried out by staff from CAAFU at Stansted. The report for 1979/80 showed that there was little change in the amount of hours flown by CAA aircraft, 2,500 hours; 245 (?) pilots were tested and authorised to become authorised examiners on behalf of the CAA, and 192 existing authorisations were renewed. Just over two thousand flying tests were conducted by examiners. These were either for the initial issue of a professional pilot's licence or the initial or renewal of an instrument rating.

1981

On the last day of March, Capt. Stuart Spence, principal flight examiner on the Flight Crew Licensing side, together with one of the newer flight test examiners, Capt. Peter Fish, flew the IR Dove G-ANUW on its last test flight.

CAAFU Aircraft:
DEREGISTERED

| Dove | G-ANUW | MCA | July 1981 |
| Dove | G-ANOV | MCA | July 1981 |

The last two Doves, G-ANUW and G-ANOV, previously used for IR tests, were struck off as PWFU (permanently withdrawn from use) in July of this year. Though both were retained, it is likely that only one of them was used, the other being held back for spares. These IR Dove aircraft were, at first, retained for use with the Authorised Examiner course as well as enabling the provision of refresher flying for operations officers, which is why, now that they were withdrawn, there was a need for another light twin aircraft, a Piper PA23 Apache or PA 34 Seneca, it was thought—though a replacement would not appear until the following year. NUW had been with the flying unit for twenty-six years accumulating over twelve thousand hours. Although still resting at Stansted in 1982, by 1993, it was photographed at North Weald aerodrome in a state of neglect. It was later known to be at Long Marston, Warwickshire, from 2001 until 2011 when it was passed to, or retrieved by, East Midlands Aero Park. There it will be restored, perhaps in previous CAFU colours. As most of the CAFU restored Doves were given the best known livery of white, black, and red, East Midland Aero Park are proposing to give it a less-known livery.

G-ANOV, the longest serving of the IR Doves, in service with the unit for twenty-seven years, is probably the best preserved of all the Doves; having spent all her ex-CAFU life under cover in Scotland when she went to the Royal Scottish Museum of Flight at East Fortune where, apparently, it is still (2011) in good condition. It is interesting to note that NOV had actually retired well before deregistration in July 1981, as it was not remembered at Stansted in early 1979.

At this time, the structure and staff of the Telecommunications section was overall headed by the superintendent, Mr. Eddie Harris, who had taken over from Mr. Joe Gidman in 1979. The principal air traffic engineer (PATE), which explains the association with the National Air Traffic Services (NATS), still held the title of superintendent. Mr. Harris had had a long association with CAFU, having joined in 1947. During WWII in the RAF, he had worked on Supermarine Walrus and Short Sunderland aircraft.

The manager of Flight Inspection (MFI) or senior navaid inspector was still John Bennett. Under him were five navaid inspectors, Colin Sheppard, Alan Richardson, Nick Cowen (a previous submariner), John Williams, and Harry Culley. Harry later went to the ATC Tower at Stansted as the chief telecommunications officer. There were also four assistant NAIs, Pat Moylette, Eric Edmondson, Laurie Park (later to be an aircraft surveyor in the Bahamas), plus one other. The ground-telescroscope team, who occasionally flew with the aircraft and sometimes travelled by road, were Norman Allan, George Rogers, Clifford Searle-Baker, and Brian Cone.

The manager of Quality Assurance (MQA) was Alec Brock; he had responsibility for the Avionics Workshop section where they repaired and maintained both operational and flight inspection avionics (while airframe, engine, and electrical engineering and maintenance were contracted out to Aviation Traders Engineering Ltd. [ATEL]).

AVIONICS WORKSHOP

Staff, remembered in this period by David Lacey, were Graham Rough, who had worked on Sunderland's in the RAF and then gone on to the RAE at Farnborough in its glory days; new starts around this time were Ted Pillinger, fresh from the army; John Watson, from the RAF; and Clyde Best from Cable and Wireless.

CALIBRATION LABORATORY

The work of the Calibration Laboratory, headed by Alec Brock, set the critical standards to be met by the aircraft equipment and the airport's ground facility, which was adjusted in the light of the results obtained by the CAAFU 748 aircraft—a vital responsibility shouldered by ground staff.

In addition to its "headline" task, it also provided "line engineering" and installation resource for avionics and stores, where "Dick and Mick" (sorry, surnames elude me) worked. "The best organised and managed stores that I came across in the CAA," said David Lacey.

In the Calibration Lab were Ken Chappell, Eddie Dovey, Eddie Stockton, Bill Gourlay, John Walford, Bernie Pallet, and Noel O'Brian who all worked shifts.

AVIONICS DESIGN LABORATORY

Manager of Design Services (MDS) was Bob Phillips; under him were the Avionics Design Laboratory (ADL, once described by one of the engineers as "Hobby Electronics Unlimited"!). ADL was run by Jim Reynolds, ex-Marconi, staffed by Bob Flanagan, another from Marconi, and Colin Howland, ex-RAF. When Colin moved over to the ATC Tower at Stansted, his replacement was David Lacey. Later to arrive were Bill Oscroft and Ian Miles. The Design Lab had a drawing office, with Ray Monk, Ron Turner, and Rose Wheatman, later replaced by Nicola Jackson (when Rose went to ATEL), and finally, a software engineer, Ernie Jay.

One story, believed to be attributed to Bob Flanagan (maybe even Joe Gidman), involved the name of Norman Allen in the ground telecroscope team and told of when Bob Flanagan joined the unit, he asked about his likely deployment; the response was "I don't know where you are going but it won't be telecroscope—we have already had 'Rogers and Hart,' and there is no way I am going to allow 'Flanagan and Allen'!"

There was always plenty going on in the Avionics Design Laboratory. ADSEL (Address Selective Secondary Surveillance Radar) was one, a radar project sponsored by Tels C (Communications) in London, and the precursor of much of the air-ground data-link technology being deployed at this time. The Headquarters engineer who worked on this with CAFU was Phil Platt. The work largely carried out by Bob Flanagan, involved interfacing the avionics with ADSEL transponders. This would allow an aircraft to be interrogated from the ground with all sorts of information being passed. The work eventually featured on a television programme looking at whether it might be found possible to dispense with the pilot. The work also involved working with Cossor. CAAFU's 125 also had a minor role in this work for high-altitude evaluation. On one occasion, when the CAAFU 125 was not available, a French Caravelle was used.

David Lacey later moved to the Scottish ATC Centre and was shocked to discover that ADSEL had not been implemented, nor was it planned to be. He recalled that before he left CAFU in 1982, a group from British Airways visiting the ADL section indicated that they were not going to carry any more experimental boxes on behalf of the CAA/NATS, as nothing ever came of it! In the USA, their ADSEL programme was known as DABS (Discrete Address Beacon System). It went on to become the basis for the universally adopted TCAS (Terrain Collision Avoidance System). ADSEL morphed into Mode S (Secondary Surveillance Radar) and is now used in Swanwick (the UK Air Traffic Control Centre in the South of England) for highlighting potential collision avoidance situations.

Sometime during the early eighties, Canadair sent a Challenger aircraft to Stansted. Perhaps the 125 was about to be replaced, and it was thought that CAAFU, as a whole, might be better served by a single aircraft that could be used in all the roles: flight inspection, training in a modern cockpit, VIP area with large enough space for flight inspection equipment, and the capability of flying the Atlantic— as was previously required during the MLS trials. Needless to say, the whole concept seemed to die a quiet death. Curiously, John Oliver told me that his brother had flown a Canadair aircraft from Canada to Stansted around this time, for display purposes, and it may well have been him.

The Fire Service Training School (FSTS), which had lived at Stansted for many years enduring changes of ownership just as CAFU had, was moved by the CAA to Tees Valley aerodrome, Durham. The premises were formally opened on September 3, 1981. The ex-CAFU Prince, G-AMKY, was left behind by FSTS in its old non-destructive compound on the other side of the airport. Its friend, a camouflaged Whirlwind helicopter XP330 that used to lie on its side beside MKY, was taken by the FSTS to their new northerly home.

The CAA Annual Report 1980/1981 showed that the CAA's aircraft for the inspection of navigational aids and the training and practice of the authority's flying staff had amounted to 2,500 hours this year; 295 pilots were tested and appointed as CAA authorised examiners (AEs), and 255 existing authorisations were renewed.

It was also reported that the number of aircraft capable of landing in very low visibilities at suitable aerodromes in the United Kingdom continued to increase. A total of thirty-six UK and foreign airlines were now authorised for operations in CAT 2 and CAT 3 conditions. The CAA had cleared British Airways Tristar (Lockheed 1011) aircraft to operate in CAT 3b conditions with no decision height specified.

CAAFU Aircraft at the end of 1981. Total = 03

| HS125 | 01 | Radar, Comm, Refresher flying |
| HS748 | 02 | Tels Flight Inspection |

1982

Mr. John Dent, CBE, previously managing director of the Dunlop Rubber Company, was appointed as the new chairman of the CAA, replacing Mr. Nigel Foulkes whose tenure had seen the CAA become self-financing. Mr. Dent's aviation background included employment as chief engineer in the Guided Weapons Division of Short Brothers and Harland in the 1950s and chief engineer at Hawker Siddeley in the 1960s.

The UK Civil Aviation Authority and its activities were defined by the Civil Aviation Act 1982. The act, which had been in existence since at least 1923, contained provisions that would enable further legislation to be made regarding specific procedures. Section 60 of the act permitted an Air Navigation Order (ANO) to be made. The ANO is the principal legislation governing all aspects of air navigation within the United Kingdom. It is authorised by Act of Parliament and the Queen's signature. Any changes to this legislation would require the consent of Parliament.

Captain W. Wooden, previously a deputy commander at CAFU and now CFOI, chaired a session of the Royal Aeronautical Society's (RAeS) Flight Simulation Group symposium. The theme was "Experiences of Civil and Military Flight Simulator Users."

CAAFU Aircraft:
REGISTERED

| PA31 | G-BFBH | CAA | April 1982 |
| HS125 | G-CCAA | CAA | Dec 1982 |

In April, CAAFU had its first and only foreign aircraft, an American Piper PA31 Navajo,

G-BFBH came from Jersey-based Aviation Beaumont Ltd., and was flown from St. Peter Port to Stansted by Capt. Don Hale, flight service manager, and Capt. Eric Markwell, one of the unit's newer flight examiners. FBH had reputedly suffered a wheels-up landing on one of the beaches in Jersey. A small twin-engine American aircraft, it was an excellent replacement for the Dove allowing CAAFU and operations staff from London to maintain flying proficiency. Captain Hale told the staff paper *Airway*:

> *It will provide cheaper flying than CAA pilots are currently able to obtain outside for the same or equivalent type of aircraft, and the radio and navigation equipment will be superior to that found in most hire aircraft of the type.*

This aircraft was to remain in the livery it came in, a subdued (beach) beige with a light-brown cheat line flowing from nose to the top of the fin, leaving it "incognito" when it flew to the near continent.

At the end of the year, in December, the CAA had their last HS125 registered to them. Previously registered as G-DBBI, it now became G-CCAA, a series 700B. Built the previous year, it had an increased MTOW of 11,567 kg. The twin engines were the very economical Garrett Air Research TFE 731-3R. These Fan engines were not only quieter but also about 30 percent more economical than the older Rolls-Royce Viper engines, offering 65 percent greater range than G-AVDX. In addition, it was equipped with up-to-date Collins radio and navigational equipment. It also had a low-frequency area navigation and inertial navigation system (INS) interfaced with each other and the autopilot, providing a modern sophisticated training tool for CAA pilots. It also had an enlarged galley area providing space should a small flight inspection station be required.

Under an existing training maintenance agreement, McAlpine would be providing conversion flying for the authority's pilots, and the chief flight operations inspector, Capt. Bill Wooden, was the first to receive the training.

Now that G-AVDX was about to depart, the CAA must have decided it was opportune to change the livery of the CAAFU aircraft. Although at Stansted myself, I was never aware that the 125, G-AVDX, was ever painted in the CAA Corporate livery. However, much to my surprise, David Lacey was able to present me with a photograph of the aircraft painted in new CAA Corporate colours. The red under fuselage was changed to blue, and the red fin and rudder painted blue under the cruciform tail-plane, with white above. It looked quietly nice, though somewhat old fashioned. The other minor change is the ownership; "civil aviation authority" was now painted in black above the windows, and the words "Flying Unit" in white on the black cheat line. It still leaves a conundrum, why would the CAA have VDX painted in new corporate colours when it knew it was about to be replaced, which leaves me concluding that the new paint job was completed just before its departure—perhaps as a trial.

Although the CAA Chairman Nigel Foulkes was due to hand over to Mr. Dent, the decision to put flight inspection aircraft into corporate colours was probably made during his tenure. These were the only aircraft left that required colour change—if any were needed—as the two flight inspection 748s, VXI and VXJ, required the highest possible visibility because of the nature of their work. With only two aircraft left, it would, at least, be at moderate expense. But it was thought, by most staff at Stansted, a misjudgement by a CAA management that clearly showed they had little idea of the nature of the task of flight inspection. So surprisingly, shockingly some thought, the aircraft were painted in the CAA's own logo colour of cyan blue. The top half of the fuselage was white, including the fin and rudder, and the bottom half in light blue with a black cheat line running through the windows from the nose to the base of the tail, and a thin white line underneath the cheat line. The tail, though white, had a thick blue band running through it that displayed the registration. The black de-icer boots on fin and wings seemed to complement the quiet arrangement. But there was one other important change; a Union flag was placed centrally at the top of the white fin and rudder, small, not too obtrusive, but setting out the important change made; for the first time since the inception of the Civil Operations Fleet in 1944, an aircraft flown by CAAFU and all its predecessors no longer displayed the Civil Air Ensign. Not displaying it somehow symbolised the CAA as wanting to be seen, perhaps, as distancing itself from immediate public or state department, merely displaying that is was British. It set out the intent of change. The new colour scheme for the calibration aircraft was not seen, particularly by those from the telecommunications side at CAAFU, as a sensible one; these aircraft continually flew unusual navigational procedures, often in poor weather conditions, and required distinct colours in order to be seen by other air, and ground, traffic. The ground telescroscope team was particularly dismayed when trying to view the aircraft against a pale sky with mist and low cloud. Apparently, although CAAFU challenged the decision, almost impossibly they were told that the new colour scheme was reflective and should therefore be no problem!

For the new HS125, G-CCAA, I am not sure that it required any change, as it arrived in a quiet livery of overall white with three smart blue cheat lines running from the point of the nose, under the windows, through the fan engines, and swept up two-thirds of the fin and rudder. It was beautiful. Steve Dench from Flight Ops at SRG told me the colour scheme was that of Barclay's Bank who used it under the registration G-DBBI. It was quietly inconspicuous, which is probably what the new owner required. Only the name running on the top half of the fuselage, just above the windows, gave the game away. This aircraft had no flags on display at all. Perhaps the late trial colours on VDX had convinced the CAA that G-CCAA required no corporate livery.

With UK VORs steadily replaced by the DVOR, the bread-and-butter work of the unit was ILS flight inspection. A flight remembered by David Lacey, Tels engineer, was one where he had worked on triple DME fixing for John Kime, navigator:

He had given me some navigational algorithms which I turned into programmes to run on the Skycal HP9825 (I'm not sure that Ernie Jay, Software engineer, was too pleased about this). The intent was to investigate alternatives to the Decca Navigator based referencing for VOR checking. To assess the merit of this, a flight was arranged with VXI, the 748 going all the way up to 25,000 feet. We operated in the vicinity of Clee Hill and used DME's at Wallasey, Pole Hill and one other. I believe it turned out OK.

Up until this time, charges for the flight inspection of instrument landing aids at non-state airfields were made on a flying hour basis.

But over the last three years, the CAA had been in negotiation with the UK Airport Consortium Group, made up from the Aerodrome Owners Association together with the Joint Airports Committee of Local Authorities, to change the previous scheme to one that would be more advantageous to the customer and one that enabled CAAFU to budget more effectively, reported *Airway*. Both flight service manager, Captain Hale, and the superintendent, Mr. Eddie Harris from CAAFU, were involved in these negotiations.

Since the inception of the air operator's certificate, it had been considerably expanded in size. There were now a total of 186 (reported in *Airway*, but 183 in the CAA Annual Report) AOC holders, which included 142 minor operators. Largely due to the Phillips Committee recommendations in the midseventies, air-taxi operators were absorbed together with twelve air-taxi operation inspectors, followed shortly after by the training inspection element with ten CAAFU training inspectors—which had now become F Ops 6—located for the time being at CAAFU, Stansted.

The Flight Ops Inspectorate consisted of seven sections, mostly in London, all headed by a principal training inspector, five of whom were all previously training inspectors with CAAFU at Stansted; F Ops 2, Helicopters, Capt. Tony Lister; F Ops 3, Capt. John Harris; F Ops 5, Capt. Ron Crawford; F Ops 6, (Stansted) Capt. Jimmy Joy. Captain Joy dealt with a wide range of activities including policy and standards for the inspection and supervision of airline and air-taxi pilot training and testing procedures, CAA pilot training, and approval of authorised instrument rating and type rating examiners. F Ops 6 also looked after the supervision and scheduling of the HS125 operations for the TI/FOI refresher flying programme. Plus, he had the important task of the inspection and approval of airline flight simulators. Last, there was F Ops 7, which looked after the Operating Standards Appraisal Programme (OSAP), recently reformed under the direction of Captain A. J. "Jack" Cook.

Captain Crawford had previously been the L1011 Tristar training inspector, and his place was now taken up by Capt. Hector Skinner. The Tristar was operated by British Airways.

Recruitment of flight operations inspectors was usually from the ranks of experienced airline pilots and required to maintain their licence qualifications on a modern airline type and on one of the CAFU fleet aircraft types, HS125 or 748. These were the changes being slowly introduced by the CAA, ensuring that senior pilots from CAFU were being assimilated into the Flight Ops Inspectorate, even though there were still a few years left before the final split of the unit.

Two other London sections covered Administration, F Ops 1, and the Dangerous Goods section, F Ops 4b, headed by Kaye Warner. The wide range of air-taxi operations also called for supervision by experienced pilots and the inspectorates' air-taxi operator inspectors (ATOIs) who were required to hold a minimum qualification of CPL/IR.

The CAA training inspectors were sometimes invited by the company, whose training captains they were visiting, to fly on line as co-pilot. This was in the P2 position, nevertheless enabling the company to have access to an additional pilot and provided the CAAFU training inspector additional hours on type, as well as maintain current operating practices. For instance, Capt. John Oliver, who was still the Concorde training inspector, had a conversion course in Dallas with BCAL to obtain the DC10 type on his licence. Subsequently BCAL invited him to fly the line with them.

These figures were in the 1982/3 CAA Annual Report: Flying by the CAA's aircraft (again no mention of CAAFU) for the inspection of navigational aids and the training and practice of the authority's flying staff had amounted to 2,800 hours; 258 pilots were tested and appointed as CAA authorised examiners, and 237 existing authorisations were renewed. Nearly 1,342 flight tests were conducted by CAA examiners for issue of the professional pilot's licence and instrument rating. Income from flight inspections was £413,000.

There were 192 air operator's certificates current at the end of the year 1982.

Particularly persistent low visibility had occurred on December 10, 1981, and January 26, 1982, when some 170 landings were made by British Airways aircraft at Heathrow in reported runway visual ranges (RVRs) of between one hundred and two hundred metres, and many costly delays and diversions were avoided by the use of CAT 2/3 landings.

CAAFU Aircraft at the end of 1982 Total = 05

HS125	02	Radar, Communications, Refresher
HS748	02	Tels Flight Inspection
PA31	01	Communications, Refresher

1983

CAAFU Aircraft:
DEREGISTERED

| HS125 | G-AVDX | CAA | Jan 1983 |

G-AVDX was sold to MAM Aviation and departed Stansted on January 28 for Southampton, Eastleigh Airport. A former Hawker Siddeley demonstration aircraft, it had acquired over 8,300 hours.

In January, *Flight* reported that Britain's Civil Aviation Authority was to begin microwave landing system (MLS) trials this year. The tests were intended to aid CAA evaluation of MLS equipment, said to replace ILS worldwide by 1985.

A single Bendix-built MLS was to be installed at a UK airport, probably Stansted, by the CAA. Stansted, the base of the CAA flying unit, had comparatively little traffic and could, therefore, expect little interference. Trials were expected to last a year. Racal-Decca was to act as the Bendix agent for the ground based MLS. One of the CAA's 748s would be fitted with a Bendix-built MLS receiver, and the second aircraft would receive one at a later date.

Installation of MLS was already underway in the USA, where more than 1,200 units were, reportedly, to be installed over the next ten years or so. ICAO expected to coordinate and finalise its plans in the next two years.

Back at home, the UK CAA planned to buy twenty-eight new instrument landing systems (ILSs) as replacement for ageing equipment at about ten airports, including Heathrow and Gatwick. Twenty or so municipal airports would have to replace their ILS for similar reasons. ILS replacement was advocated by the CAA, despite plans to introduce MLS in the late 1970s. This was because there had to be a transition phase during which both ILS and MLS were available (each system demanding a different airborne receiver). ICAO had agreed that ILS would be available internationally until 1995, hence Britain's need for another generation.

Safety Was No Accident

The CAA requested industry bids in the middle of this year. Plessey, Wilcox (via Racal), Thomson-CSF, and SEL were expected to bid for the provision of these ILS installations, which would be worth around £10-£15 million. A single supplier was preferred, and an announcement expected by the end of the year. Five or six sets would be purchased initially; the rest to be bought after the first batch had been proven in service. ILS deliveries were expected to begin in 1984 and extend over six years. Nearly all Britain's existing ILSs were Stan 37/38, supplied by STC, now part of Plessey.

Because all records for IR/TRE examiners were now kept at Stansted, CAAFU was approached by Ken Crisp of the Flight Operations Inspectorate, based in London, to create a database on the ICL equipment at CAAFU, which could then be used via a data-link modem to the ICL mainframe at Aviation House, London.

London IT staff, together with Nigel Smith who had created the flight planning system, demonstrated at Stansted what was possible to John Allinson, deputy director FCL, Ken Crisp from Flight Ops, and Jim Fuller, CAFU Ops.

Later in the year, Flight Ops at Aviation House was given demonstrations and training in the use of this IRE/TRE database created by CAFU operations staff at Stansted.

In May 1983, Capt. Don Hale, who had joined CAFU in 1953, retired, his place taken over by the principal training inspector of Flight Ops 6, Jimmy Joy, who now took on the additional responsibility as CAAFU flight services manager.

John Bennett, manager of Flight Inspection since the mid-1970s, retired in August; his position taken by Tony Bird.

In October, Capt. Bill Wooden, who had also joined CAFU in 1953, ending his career as chief flight operations inspector, responsible for all aspects of planning, supervision, and training of flight operations for the CAA, and influential in introducing zero flight training on simulators, also retired. Bill was the first training inspector from CAAFU to become CFOI, embracing it with his well-known, noisy, enthusiastic style.

Capt. Tony Lister, his deputy, would now take over the position of CFOI, the first helicopter pilot to do so. He had joined Stansted in 1972 on secondment from the navy, promoted to PFE/PFOI in 1976, transferring to F OPS 1 in 1982 as deputy CFOI. I believe Captain Lister did much, in his quiet way, to bring the two sides, CAFU and HQ flying staff, together.

In December, Geoffrey Chouffot, now deputy CAA chairman, previously involved with all aspects of flight operations since its inception, and perhaps with the foresight of merging CAAFU training inspectors with the Flight Operations Inspectorate, retired after a career spanning over forty years.

CAFU Aircraft at the end of 1983 Total = 04

HS125	01	Radar, Communications, Refresher flying
HS748	02	Tels Flight Inspection
PA31	01	Communications, Refresher

(These numbers remained the same until 1987.)

1984

The relocation of CAA Headquarters had been discussed by the CAA Board. The locations were Milton Keynes, Swindon, and Farnborough. This was reported by the staff paper, *Airway*, and I wonder if CAAFU staff had noticed that it probably meant the selection of a site for the new Safety Regulation Group (SRG) building, which would also house both the Stansted FCL and F OPS 6 staff. Apparently, there were still a number of operational obstacles preventing a final decision as to whether or not a move could be taken.

In February, *Flight International* was reporting on the final draft of CAP453, the document set to provide the guidelines for simulator training standards for both commercial fixed and rotary wing pilots. The document, sent out to industry for comment the previous summer, had just returned, with feedback. The CAA said the replies showed that it is "not at odds" with the simulator operators, although there were several minor differences to sort out. Talks with industry were set for later this year. Sometime after that, CAP453 would become official.

The authority's view on simulation training and flight crew testing today realised in the contents of CAP453 had been recently explained to *Flight*.

> *One of the questions often asked of the CAA, especially in the light of the US Federal Aviation Administration's plunge into zero flight time training, concerns its own attitude to total simulator training. The answer will not be found in the pages of CAP453. But for airlines wanting to go the total simulation route, CAP453 will provide the basis upon which the approach to type-to-type training without the aircraft should be made.*
> *The CAA's (and, indeed, the FAA's) philosophy on simulation is that, from an operational point of view, the machine must reproduce the aircraft it copies as exactly as possible. But despite the technical advances that have been made during*

the last five or six years, the CAA still needs to be convinced about certain aspects of simulation. It is interested in particular about the reproduction of the right "atmosphere" on the flight deck.

"It's no good if outside telephones ring when you're supposed to be in mid-Atlantic," says Capt. Jimmy Joy, the CAA's Principal Fight Operations Inspector (from F Ops 6 at Stansted). The problem lies in bringing pilots up to the same state of awareness that they should have when flying an airliner-load of passengers. Small details like creating genuine-sounding radio traffic are all important. Jimmy Joy says, "if only we could plug into Heathrow Airport for a while to pressurise them a bit."

The need to create the right atmosphere on the simulator flight deck is considered just as important as matching the machine's characteristics to those of the aircraft it will copy. The CAA's judge of both these qualities are its test pilots, who must always have flown the real aircraft before flying the simulator, and the flight operations team. Most of its approval of a simulator is therefore subjective, but based on objective guidelines. These will be set out for the first time in CAP453. The CAA wants top-level simulators to have a high degree of self-test capability, so that digital software remains glitch-free during training flights. CAP453 will not lay down exactly how this should be done, as the CAA, in keeping with its general attitude to simulation, is only interested in the end product. The problem it faces at the moment, however, is how to test a self-test system. A standardised plug-in terminal, for example, is out of the question, since each manufacturer can use unique self-test methods, and software.

The increased sophistication of simulators means more approval work for the CAA, which says that despite this its charge for initial approval has fallen from £6,500 five years ago, plus £6,500 for each successive annual renewal, to £8,000, plus £4,000 for annual renewal. It notes that after inflation is taken into account, this means that its charges have dropped considerably in real terms. Approval for pilot

Safety Was No Accident

> *testing on simulators is granted by way of the CAA's form 1179 (form 1180 for flight engineers). The recipient knows at a glance how his simulator has fared at the hands of the test pilot and flight operations team, for items passing inspection are ruled over with a green felt tip pen. An operator receiving a largely white 1179 will not therefore be able to use his machine for very much. With a properly maintained and operated full-flight machine, the maximum amount of colour will usually be seen. This currently leaves the operator with about an hour's flying time in a real aircraft.*
>
> *After CAP453 becomes official, he will have the option to try and reduce this. The increasing electronic sophistication of simulators means that many of the checks now necessary deal exclusively with software. So, one of the demands of CAP453 is that a software expert is included in the flight operations team. His responsibilities would, for example, cover the self-test capability of the simulator, and programme loading techniques. This latter has arisen because the CAA is aware of the possibility of changing the flight plan, or aircraft characteristics, by a slipup in the computer room.*

A Cessna Citation was flown in to Stansted. Capt. Jimmy Joy, principal flight inspector, was asked to look at it as a possible 125 replacement. Although the idea was never taken up, Steve Dench at SRG Gatwick did tell me he had wondered why his department had a miniature model of a Citation curiously registered as G-CAFU!

CAAFU was busy evaluating the Bendix microwave landing system (MLS) installed at Stansted Airport. The CAA needed to build up as much technical and operational experience as possible before contributing to the May 1985 ICAO meeting on the introduction of MLS. The principal CAA aim was to show that MLS would be a simple effective substitute for the ILS systems now deployed in the sixty or so UK civil airfields. It was particularly interested in an improved solution for category 2 and 3 automatic landings, and wanted to be certain that there were good reasons to support the introduction of the system to the United Kingdom. The CAA would then look more closely at some of the other capabilities unique to MLS.

As part of the need to verify that ICAO Standards and Recommended Practices for MLS could be achieved, the French Civil Aviation department, STNA (Service Technique de la Navigation Aérienne, the French Air Traffic Services Authority), and the UK CAA, with Tels N (Navigation services), agreed to participate in exchange trials.

In September, CAAFU flew G-AVXJ to Brive in the Dordogne to evaluate the Thomson-CSF MLS equipment. Brive had a short runway of about one thousand metres and no refuelling facilities for turbine engine aircraft, so the 748 base was at Periquex, some thirty miles away. Over a three-day period CAAFU flew ten hours. On the last of the three days, Tels N staff were invited to Brive, courtesy STNA, where they were shown over the MLS by Thomson-CSF and STNA engineers. The UK CAA contingent also spent some time studying the French Minilir infrared tracker system. It was an upgraded form of telecroscope used by the French for the calibration of instrument landing systems, primarily carried out by tracking an infrared lamp on the nose of the aircraft using a ground tracking device (Minilir) with a data link to the onboard computer. Position fixing was by computer optimised twin Decca (SkyNAV) backed up by visual and photographic fixes. The results could be processed on board, which enabled immediate assessments to be given in most cases.

In return during October, the French were invited to Stansted to fly their Nord 260 aircraft with receivers designed and built by STNA engineers. An evaluation report was to be prepared by both French and UK authorities for completion by the end of the year.

The 748 used by CAAFU for calibration was too aerodynamically clean to behave like a short take-off and landing (STOL) aircraft and had to be flown at a greater pitch angle. The technique was developed in association with BAe, to extend the capability of CAAFU's 748 without airframe modifications, and was now able to fly MLS glide slope approaches of up to nine degrees using this specially developed technique; with undercarriage down and flaps lowered to 22½ degrees the aircraft was flown to 10 knots above normal speed down the glide slope, pitch being controlled manually and roll by the autopilot.

MLS guidance in the approach sector was available to ±18 degrees from the centreline of the Stansted runway. In addition, it could provide for missed approach/departure operations using a back azimuth transmitter. It was also intended that segmented approaches in azimuth would be made when an area navigation computer, capable of taking MLS input and managing the segmented approach calculations, was available.

It was first thought that MLS would supplement then replace ILS as a primary landing aid. In November of this year, *Flight* reported on developments with MLS in America. It was believed that, in the following year, MLS would get off to a flying start when it was believed the FAA would purchase over one hundred units as replacements for ILS, which were expected to be replaced by 1995.

With MLS effective at airports with terrain difficulties, it would offer greater flexibility than the older ILS system, which was mostly restricted to a three-degree glide path approach, and could only be received within a narrow band width each side of the runway centreline. In addition, ILS demanded a flat area in front of its transmitters and was sensitive to reflections. MLS, however, would allow a wide approach path of up to fifteen degrees and provide bearing information in an approach sector covering forty degrees either side of the centreline. These wider levels would be useful to short take-off and landing (STOL) aircraft in particular and might eventually allow curved approaches.

Already there was worldwide agreement, including the Soviet Union, on MLS standards; and with America closely involved, geographically speaking, in the formulation of ICAO policy, it was thought vital there should be international agreement if airborne equipment was to work at global airports.

There were general assumptions that airborne receivers would eventually be replaced by MLS types, although it was thought possible that an ILS/MLS receiver would be developed. On the ground, MLS could operate alongside an ILS setup. The FAA planned to introduce MLS in hub-and-feeder networks across the USA. This, it was hoped, would encourage the airlines to invest in airborne MLS equipment, since it would be useable at several airports in a particular region. The first three networks were to be in New England, Colorado, and Alaska.

The UK requirement for MLS was significantly different from that of the USA. The United Kingdom had maintained its lead in the use of ILS under category 2 and 3 conditions, and because there was less volume of regional commuter traffic for which MLS would provide enormous air traffic control benefits, the CAA was running its test programme more or less independently of the FAA. The UK CAA maintained that changes caused by the introduction of MLS would be evolutionary and would happen in tandem with the introduction of new aircraft and new procedures to land them. It noted, however, that changing approach patterns was not always easy because of existing noise regulations.

It was proposed that CAAFU would cut the time and costs of its MLS test programme by using computer simulation, made available through Tels N3. The idea was to try and predict anomalies in the MLS beam so that the number of 748 flights necessary could be reduced. The programme was being carried out in conjunction with the USA and West Germany. Mathematical models of various airfields were being created to which MLS transmitter and receiver characteristics were added. The predicted anomalies could then be compared with the real thing in flight trials.

The CAA was just completing acceptance of the Bendix ground and flight MLS equipment at Stansted, which had been hired for twelve months through Racal Avionics. The Bendix MLS would be replaced at the end of the one-year hire period with Plessey equipment. Plessey's MLS would first be installed at RAE Bedford, where a series of trials were to be carried out, followed by a second installation at Stansted.

The Bedford site had special advantages for MLS-testers, including the first Precision Distance Measuring Equipment (DMEP) installation in the UK. Bedford's HS748 was also DMEP and Autoland equipped, so the CAA would be able to evaluate MLS Autoland ability along with DMEP. Another advantage of the location, it was equipped with a three-dimension optical tracker, called a Kinetheodolite, which enabled the positional accuracy of the test aircraft to be determined more precisely than before. Bedford airfield also boasted a runway hump. This would help the CAA check the tolerance to such land features claimed for MLS, an advantage that could be of considerable benefit, since ILS systems depend on completely flat ground to form the beam. In the past, this had meant a costly earthmoving operation and disruption of the airport when installing ILS.

The MLS at Stansted was co-sited with the existing ILS equipment. Ground-based installations had been in place since November 1983. Azimuth and elevation transmitters were situated in front of the corresponding ILS devices. But the extreme sensitivity of ILS to movement near the transmitters had meant operational problems when adjustments to the MLS were needed.

The position of the unit operations officer was left vacant when Sid Pritchard retired. Surprisingly, to some, the position was not filled, and Ron Golds, operations supervisor, took responsibility for staffing.

Capt. C. M. Jimmy Joy, who had joined CAFU in 1954, becoming principal training inspector of Flight Ops 6 at Stansted, retired. Always active, Jimmy Joy went on to fly a Cessna belonging to the Essex Flying Ambulance at North Weald.

His place at Stansted was taken by Capt. Dai Rees, who also appears to have taken over responsibility for the pre-airline examiners and the position of flight service manager in a somewhat lengthy interim period. This meant that CAAFU almost had a single position of leadership again, but not at the commander level, that would have equalled the position of CFOI. Most probably it was not a situation the CAA had envisaged or wanted but a short-term interim measure to take them to the split of the unit.

The introduction of a computer for flight planning at CAAFU had proved highly successful, allowing crews more time in preparation and providing quick access to a wind-adjusted printed plan, particularly when a change of venue was necessary, due to late cancellation of task or weather deterioration at an intended destination. Due to the nature of the work, CAAFU could be asked to fly almost anywhere in Europe and had soon amassed routes and diversionary airfields on the system. Unfortunately, it was discovered that when the system held about 350 plans, each new route input to the computer cancelled, randomly, a previously stored plan.

The IT department in London suggested that a new personal computer (PC) could store twice as many routes, and a new contractor, Doug Kershaw, was hired to move the CPM Basic programme to a small Apricot computer with a 3086 processor using Microsoft DOS (Disk Operating System) and a Basic programme named GWIZ. Unlike the ICL machine, which was huge, the much smaller PC sat neatly within Operations, allowing easier access and local experimentation with other programs, in particular spreadsheets (Supercalc). Another programme, locally produced, used Great Circle calculations for flights that were not compatible with the computerised flight planning system, such as the flights to Berlin, where the aircraft was expected to descend to ten thousand feet when crossing the border to East Germany. Don Gannon, the CAA chief navigator, had already written an Applesoft Basic program on his home Mac computer and kindly presented a copy to Jim Fuller, who now looked after the CAAFU computers since Mr. Pritchard had retired. The programme was converted to GWIZ Basic, which enabled any radar flight plans to determine waypoints from any given latitude and longitude, either by selecting two known positions, to give a true track and distance between the waypoints or, given a true track and distance from one known position, could now determine the new waypoint lat and long. This was especially useful when the 125 was used for checking the new radar sites such as Pease Pottage and Ventnor. These flights usually involved flying over the facility and continuing on track for a couple of hundred miles before returning at the same level.

Also converted was the previous ops manager's HS748 (unused) loading programme on the ICL mainframe, which was turned into a loading programme on the PC for the PA31. Crews were now able to self-use the programme to quickly print a load sheet in duplicate, one to take with them and the other left at base.

In 1984, ICAO was considering the introduction of new extended range twin (engine) operation standards to be known as ETOPS. With twin-engine aircraft such as the new Boeing 757 and 767 and the Airbus A310, operators were looking to use them to cross the Atlantic using great circle routes.

To that end, the CAAFU HS125 did a tour of the North Atlantic aerodromes that could possibly be used as alternate or diversionary airfields. CAAFU Operations were able to use their PC computer flight planning system, but because their assigned area (C) only covered Northern Europe and the Middle East, they first had to obtain the magnetic variation tables for the North Atlantic routes, which were obtainable from Edinburgh. After installation on the computer at Stansted, CAAFU was able to provide accurate flight plans for Iceland, Greenland, Canada, and the United States. Although because of the lack of designated waypoints across the Atlantic, it was decided to invent them every two hundred miles because of the large changes of magnetic variation that occurred the further north the aircraft flew. It was also necessary to gain approval for flights into the American airfields in both Iceland and Greenland—which was not too forthcoming. The closer the timing of the flight, the more signals were sent until, eventually, Washington had to be signalled before permission was finally granted.

Airfields flown to were Reykjavik in Iceland, Sondre Stromfjord on the west coast of Greenland, and Narsarsuaq in the south. Sondre Stromfjord, an American base with a long runway, was just about to have a heavy snowstorm when the 125 arrived. Although the crew landed just in time, they were delayed the following day due to the conditions. One of the diversions for this airfield was Frobisher, Canada. It had also been the intention to fly into the northerly Icelandic airfield Akureyri, another American base, but that was also abandoned due to weather conditions.

The crew flying G-CCAA were the chief flight operations inspector, Tony Lister, together with Captains Brian Morgan, Flight Ops 5, and Dave Quilley, Flight Ops 4. They were accompanied by navigation specialist Ron Plater and Paul Mahoney of the Chief Scientists Division. Chief 125 engineer from Stansted was Rodney Prior.

In the annual report by the CAA, it showed there were now 197 air operator's certificates current at the end of the year, and the number of operators authorised to conduct category (CAT) 2/3 operations in the United Kingdom increased from forty-one to forty-six. Guidance on CAT 2 operations was given to an increasing number of business jet operators.

There were 273 pilots tested and appointed as CAA authorised examiners, and 274 existing authorisations were renewed.

There were 1,097 flight tests conducted by CAAFU examiners for the issue of a professional pilot's licence and instrument rating.

1985

CAAFU Tels were in a continuing era of change as solid state devices made for greater stability both in the air and on the ground. This slowly led to the reduced frequency of flight inspections. Digital systems were replacing and augmenting the original aircraft installations, and onboard computer equipment speeded up the time taken for analysis and the production of results.

Engineering staff at CAAFU, remembered by Ian Miles, were Geoff Burt, Duncan Petrie, Mike Spanner, John Bugg, and Mark Taylor. While on the administrative side, he recalled Valerie Bartle, Jean Miller, and Geraldine Loddy. Ian had joined the CAA in 1980 as an engineer cadet and studied for two years at Bletchley. He was then "posted" to CAAFU where he was immediately persuaded to embark on further education at Cambridge.

In March, Capt. John Robinson, McAlpine, flew an HS125, G-FIVE, a series 1 aircraft from Southend to Luton airport. This aircraft was broken up and the cockpit sold to simulated flight training to be used as part of a new simulator. This would eventually be installed in British Caledonian's simulator building at Gatwick, to be ready for the CAA Authorised Examiner course after the breakup of CAFU at Stansted.

It was reported that when NAVSTAR (eighteen operational satellites) came in to operation, GPS (global positional satellite system) could conceivably be used for instrument landings, a receiver at the airport providing position corrections to incoming aircraft.

Training flights by CAAFU involving the 125 could be anywhere in Europe but often used the same airfields due to stage length and convenience in timing. If a flight was delayed, for whatever reason, a short flight could be set up quite quickly with a wind-adjusted flight plan using the computerised flight planning system. Rennes was an often chosen destination; just over one and a half hours from Stansted, it was a flight that could be accomplished in a morning, allowing plenty of time for a second training flight in the afternoon.

In December, Capt. Dennis Mobberly and Capt. John Eastwood were able to use their 125 training-hours allocation as part of a charity exercise to raise money for the RAF Museum's Bomber Wing Appeal. CAAFU was approached by the vice chairman of the Royal Aero Club, David Hamilton, to carry commemorative covers to Rennes for stamping in recognition of the Sherbourne Line, one of the French Resistance's escape routes for moving aircrew and escapees during World War II. As it turned out, the flight also qualified for three jet-class world point-to-point speed records: London/Rennes, Rennes/London, and London/Rennes/London, taking the GPO Tower in central London as the start and finish point. It should be pointed out that the records were achieved with a great deal of help and cooperation from NATS staff at Heathrow.

By the mid eighties, together with the changes that were going to apply when the split of pre-airline examining and post-airline inspection was going to take place, the CAA brought in Human Resources to take stock of the situation. All CAAFU staff were interviewed, establishing those staff who could, or could not, or even would not, move. The location of a new establishment was not known to ordinary staff at Stansted. Rumours were numerous; one day it would be Teesside, the next it might be Milton Keynes or Swindon, and the effects that any transfer would have on housing costs and ease of travel were uppermost in people's mind.

The slow changes taking place were hardly noticed by most ground staff, particularly in Admin, though they would be the most affected in the longer scheme of things. In the Tels section, there was the threat of losing their assistant to the NAIs on flight inspection work. One NAI resigned over the issue, choosing to work at Headquarters.

One problem on the FCL side would be that after the split, there might not immediately be enough examiners to accommodate the amount of examining (testing) that was required. However, the consequence of having three separate directorates to be reported to at CAAFU meant that FCL were now able to recruit examiners purely for examining, and this was slowly introduced until the split. It should be noted, however, that pilots wanting to be examiners were required to have a CPL and an instructor qualification to apply as a permanent FE2 grade, but perhaps with little or no prospect of being upgraded. On the Flight Operations Inspectorate side, they too were going to lose staff through retirement alone, though this could only have a beneficial effect on the lower-grade pilots who were looking for promotion, yet at the same time might be a further loss for FCL. Many of the senior pilots, who currently lived in the Stansted area, were not keen to go to another base, be it a regional office or elsewhere, but the latter were few and far between, so for them, early retirement was an option. Flight Ops would hardly be left with a surplus of FE/FOI and SFE/SFOI training inspectors, yet there was a possibility that they might still have to help out both FCL and the telecommunications side who would be left at Stansted. At least on the FCL side, there was a possibility that some pilots wanting the opportunity for advancement from FCL could be used after a certain amount of training. It was not going to be an easy task for the CAA.

Stansted Airport had a Thomson-CSF 381T instrument landing system installed, commissioned by CAAFU and operational on runway 23 by the end of October. Four more installations, Heathrow, Dunsfold, CTE Bletchley, and TEE, at Gatwick were to be added to help confirm the system's suitability, with particular emphasis on the need to support CAT 3 operations. A number of improvements had been made, aiming at providing a high level of service availability, minimising the cost of maintenance. It also had a telesurveillance (TSV) facility, manufactured in the United Kingdom by DB Instrumentation of Aldershot that could provide remote maintenance capabilities to enable routine checking and basic fault diagnosis to be carried out from a remote control point.

1986

To the surprise of most staff, the move of the flight crew licensing examiners and the flight operations staff was announced as a new Safety Regulation Group (SRG) building on land near to the Telecommunications Engineering Establishment (TEE) at Gatwick. In fact, it was close to the beehive structure (the original ATC tower at Gatwick) at the site of the old Gatwick airport, once the home of CATFU and then CAFU immediately after WWII. This would be the new SRG home, an imposing sight from outside of glass and dull grey panels. The structure cleverly housed two buildings of three floors, each building connected with a covered atrium. It would not only house staff from Stansted but also most of the CAA offices from Aviation House, London, as well as the ARB who would vacate their two buildings of Knowles House and Brabazon House at Redhill. It would accommodate around seven hundred staff in all.

CAAFU Telecommunications staff would remain at Stansted until a new home could be found, though the talk now was of Teesside, home of the already transferred ex-Stansted CAA Fire Training School.

Although trials of MLS were taking place in the USA for some time, the only UK example of the system, other than at Stansted and Gatwick, was at Yeovil, home base of Westland helicopters and used for research only. The UK CAA had already endorsed the ICAO policy of introducing MLS into member countries by the 1990s.

McAlpine Aviation won its first order, from Hazeltine in the USA, for its tracking lamp for use in calibration of microwave landing systems. Currently trialled in an HS125-1B, it was claimed to be compact for use in small aircraft and automated, requiring no engineer.

In February 1979, a non-rigid airship of Aerospace Developments, Cardington, had made its maiden flight. Named the AD-500, it was intended for aerial advertising and transport in undeveloped countries, had long endurance and the ability to hover, which gave it the potential for offshore surveillance. It was designed with the intention of gaining a full transport category Certificate of Airworthiness (C of A) and was equipped for IFR operations.

In September 1982, it received a Special Category approval from the CAA. And in 1983, it won an Aerial Work Certificate of Airworthiness. However, the C of A fell short of the CAA Public Transport Certification.

CAFU had assigned Capt. John Sweet as the training inspector who, in the early eighties, flew numerous cross-countries and further flights with them. By 1985, Airship Industries were advertising for co-pilots with the minimum requirement of a commercial pilot's licence (CPL) and instrument rating (IR).

London City Airport was expected to be the first airfield to provide for the concurrent use of MLS with ILS. ATC would be run by the UK National Air Traffic Services (NATS), subject to proposals being accepted. The airfield controllers would have radar displays with a data link from Heathrow to keep them in the overall picture of London air traffic. The peak daily traffic capacity target was set at 120 movements.

Over the years that CAFU had used the 748, there were few tasks in flight inspection it was unable to perform. For example, the 748 aircraft operating envelope was flexible enough to allow steep angle approaches of up to nine degrees, which enabled CAFU to calibrate the ILS at London City Airport, first in its 7.5-degree glide-path configuration and later with a six-degree glide path. ILS glide paths in the United Kingdom were normally set at around three degrees, but Capt. Dick Hawkes, telecommunications pilot, was always up for the challenge. However, the navaid inspectors, sitting in the back monitoring the telecommunications equipment, were not so comfortably enamoured, not usually strapped in and sitting sideways at the ILS console during the approach phase.

1987

Sir John Dent (Knighted in 1986) was replaced by Christopher Tugendhat as the new CAA chairman.

In April, NATS was allocated £46 million to update their systems. The money would pay for

- modernised approach control room at London Heathrow,
- new navigation beacons for en route traffic,
- instrument landing systems at ten UK airports, and
- a new building at London Gatwick for collocating the CAA's safety services.

The last item was the new SRG building.

The CAA received a £23 million loan from the European Investment Bank (EIB) to help finance the updating of the nation's air traffic control facilities. They provided 50 percent of the £46 million needed, with the remainder coming from the UK government's National Loan Fund. The initial loan received by the CAA was £5 million from the EIB, and the rest to be taken up in stages until December 1990. Each loan, treated separately for repayment purposes, was to be taken up at the CAA's discretion and be repaid in instalments over a maximum of twelve years.

The CAA chairman, Christopher Tugendhat, said the money was required to meet the future expansion of the UK's air traffic. He said it was particularly relevant that the EIB was providing the loan because of the pivotal role the United Kingdom played in handling European traffic.

By 1987, the US Federal Aviation Administration had already planned for hundreds of airport MLS installations, arguing that it was the way to increase airport capacity. But major US airlines were now opposing these plans citing cost and benefits. Even the US Congress, which had been advised there would be a need for a thousand installations, had recently refused to approve funding for the equipment.

Even if MLS could increase capacity, it was thought that the FAA was not as far forward as they were saying; their MLS was only CAT 1, and not even upgradeable to CAT 2. Although the FAA talked of curved approaches, no civil aircraft had flown one using MLS.

Opponents were also pointing out that airframe manufacturers were saying that installation of both MLS and ILS in aircraft, thought necessary perhaps for the next ten years, would cause degradation in both sets of equipment.

While airport capacity was a top subject, it was being asked if MLS was really one of the solutions. The USA and Europe were at variance over the subject; Keith Mack, controller of NATS, stated that it was his impression that MLS had been oversold by the engineering fraternity, and it was dubious it would enhance airport capacity.

The US FAA thought that the difference between themselves and the UK CAA was that the CAA had only concentrated on the benefits of MLS in CAT 3 operations, while the FAA had in mind the wider benefits of accurate navigation.

Operations at London City Airport began in May 1987. It was equipped with two ILS, one DME and one NDB, plus a discrete airfield control frequency. ILS had been chosen in preference to MLS because it was familiar and compatible with receivers already fitted in aircraft to be used and immediately available. A steep ILS glide slope was possible with a direct approach, and its quality was expected to be enhanced due to its steepness, distancing the beam from obstructions.

Brymon Airways, one of its first operators, had already demonstrated 7.5-degree approaches at Stansted to the CAA, with a 5.5-degree glide path currently in operation. In fact, Brymon was already practising steep approaches with operational training at Plymouth, which now had dual 3.5-degree and 7.5-degree precision approach-path (lighting) indicators (PAPI). This installation was part of the airport's coordinated development with Brymon. On January 30, it opened up stage 2 of the development. Runway 13, 1,190 m long, would have a twin-slope ILS, due to be commissioned in the near future. It would be unique, with 7.5 degrees for training and 3 degrees for services. Visual steep approaches were being practised, and steep instrument approach training was to start the following month.

David Lacy, with CAAFU at Stansted in the late seventies and early eighties, passed to me a few of his memories:

> *During my five years at Barnsford, (Scottish Maintenance Centre) I managed to do a degree but had little contact with CAAFU. I did spend one wet afternoon out on the Fenwick Moor at the site of the old Glasgow VOR (and now the site of Whitelees, Europe's largest on-shore wind farm), speaking on the radio as the CAAFU 748 droned over. But conventional VOR's with their 6 month flight check cycle were a dying breed, even then—we had three in Scotland but they were soon all gone. The Doppler variant with a 5 year check cycle consigned that side of flight inspection largely to history. One day, though, the boss did call me in while perusing a flight check report. It said "Calibrated by Skycal," and he asked me what it was. It made me feel really proud.*

It was the oddest of times for most staff at CAAFU, a time when the establishment was about to break up. Even at this moment, the split still did not seem possible. Staff knew the plan; some would lose their job completely, particularly administrative staff, some were offered relocation or redundancy. Some accepted early retirement with a frozen pension.

At the same time, incredibly, new flying staff were appearing, already primed for a move to regional centres, while others were to see their world expand as their experience and usefulness was at last acknowledged with promotion. There were staff retiring after many years service, and there were those who were near to retirement who would be too expensive to move and would be offered early retirement. Even the engineers within the telecommunications side were subject to these events.

Both sides, FCL and Flight Ops, would require new staff, not just because of retirement or early retirement, but through an endeavour to sustain each separate directorate within the difficulties they now found themselves. New FCL examiners brought in to address these difficulties, who had joined around this period, were Dick Snell, Don Henderson, Wendy Crick (first lady CAAFU examiner), Mike Tinson, Geoff Baron, David Simmons, and Tony Kember.

CAAFU Aircraft:
DEREGISTERED

| PA31 | G-BFBH | CAA | May 1987 |
| HS125 | G-CCAA | CAA | Sept 1987 |

The PA31 FBH, which had replaced the Dove for training and refresher flying since 1982, was deregistered in May. It then became G-OMEG with AEW Engineering, Norwich before it was transferred to South Africa.

After just over twenty years, in September, the CAA no longer owned an HS125, now leasing aircraft from McAlpine (later to become Magec Aviation Ltd.—so named, as it was part of the GEC group). After five years service with CAAFU, the HS125, G-CCAA, was deregistered on September 4, 1987, and almost immediately reregistered as G-BNVU and transferred to America. G-CCAA was one of the early production 700 series aircraft, and cockpit equipment had changed significantly since its acquisition, no longer representing "state of the art." Tony Lister, chief flight operations inspector, told *Airway* that what was required was an EFIS (Electronic Flight Instrument System) display that was needed to keep CAA pilots up to date.

CAA personnel who required hours on the HS125 would now go to McAlpine, who now leased the aircraft to the CAA, at Luton Airport, where Capt. John Robinson, chief training captain, would be in charge of training. Captain Robinson remembered flying with Capt. Dennis Mobberley, a senior CAA flight operations inspector, in the HS125 700B, G-UKCA, the last 700B off the production line.

With just months to go to the separation, the CAA now only owned the two telecommunications aircraft. Even in August 1944, there were three aircraft, the two Austers and the Proctor. It truly was the beginning of the end.

CAFU Aircraft at the end of 1987 Total =02

| HS748 | 02 | Tels Flight Inspection |

In December 1987, *Airway* was reporting the involvement of the flying unit in the calibration of aids at the new airport of Mount Pleasant in the Falklands.

As the Falklands was geographically remote and subject to adverse weather conditions, it was essential to provide the airport with both a landing aid (ILS) and navigational aid (DVOR), which both the RAF and CAAFU could calibrate. However, the distances involved were too great for either the CAAFU 748 or the RAF Andover aircraft. As the RAF had a regular service to the Falklands with its C130 Hercules, CAAFU designed and built a portable flight inspection system (FIS) at its base at Stansted with the intention of allowing the RAF to calibrate civil equipment in the Falklands. Although the previous year (October 1986) a permanent package was placed on order, initially, a temporary set had been delivered to meet the tight schedule.

Airway said that the project was very much a team effort by CAAFU. "After a feasibility study by the RAF," explained Laurie Park, manager of Quality Assurance, "our Drawing Office designed the equipment and produced a full set of engineering drawings. All the metal was cut in our workshops and the equipment assembled onto the Hercules standard freight pallet. This was the first time that we had provided a major piece of equipment for the RAF 115 squadron calibration unit."

The equipment was delivered in the summer of 1987, and Tony Bird, the senior navaid inspector, flew with the RAF team, checking out the system and ensuring that civil operational techniques were understood. This was particularly important in the case of the DVOR (Doppler VOR), which was not in common use by the RAF. The new palletised FIS now allowed the RAF calibration cell to prepare the aircraft for the flight inspection task in approximately three hours, which was much quicker than the temporary equipment. The RAF at Lyneham had modified one Hercules transport aircraft to take the calibration equipment and planned to bring the number up to three.

Diversion Airfields being few and far between in the South Atlantic, it was essential that Mount Pleasant's navigational aids were working reliably and accurately. CAAFU's portable equipment provided for regular checks, and as an added bonus, 115 Squadron would also be able to use it to check the RAF TACAN navigational aids at Belize in British Honduras—a long way from their home base.

1988

This was to be the final year of CAAFU staff operating together under one roof at Stansted. Aircraft had gone, and some staff already dispersed. Most of the aircrew would be going to the new CAA Safety Regulation Group (SRG) building, still to be completed at Gatwick, and then to be split between the two separate departments of Flight Crew Licensing (FCL) and the Flight Operations Inspectorate (FOI).

By the end of this year, it was decided that the CAAFU flight calibration task at Stansted was inappropriate to the Safety Regulation Group. It would henceforth be called the flight calibration unit (FCU) as part of NATS and continue to operate the two 748s out of Stansted.

Only the telecommunications flight inspection side staff would remain at Stansted, albeit temporarily, in the Stansted House building. It was understood that the British Airports Authority wanted Stansted House for new tenants; the rent had increased significantly, and a move was only dependent on FCU management finding a new home for aircraft and staff to continue with flight inspection work. For Tels, their new name seemed more relevant than CAAFU. Now, under NATS, the name Flight Calibration Unit (FCU) was exactly all that was left of the old CAFU/CAAFU.

Staff simply accepted the new courses of action required by higher management. CAAFU staff—certainly some within Operations—still could not understand the need to break up flight inspection, examining, and post-airline inspection, where aircrew shared tasks, which together provided common sense planning, financial sense, diversity of tasks, interest, and a greater understanding and awareness of overall requirements. But all the talking was over; it was now a *fait accompli* that changes had now to be accepted, if somewhat resignedly.

After thirty-eight years, probably one of the last flying tests to be conducted by CAFU at Stansted Airport was undertaken by Capt. David Gray on March 31.

Safety Was No Accident

On April 1, flight test examining now came directly under the control of Flight Crew Licensing (FCL) at the new SRG building close to Gatwick airport, on land, ironically, belonging to the Telecommunications Engineering Establishment (TEE), a part of the National Air Traffic Services (NATS).

Flight examiners, now directly working for FCL at Gatwick, were slowly dispersed to Approved Regional Test Centres: Bournemouth Hurn, Oxford Kidlington, Perth, Leeds/Bradford, as well as sub-test centres at Coventry, Cranfield and Bristol/Exeter.

The solution worked well for some, particularly the newer recruits; David Heather-Hayes, an even later addition to the team, went to Perth; Wendy Crick went to Cranfield. Even some of the more senior examiners found it acceptable, as they were never locally based at Stansted; Peter Fish went to Leeds/Bradford airport; Mike Edwards, it is thought, to Bournemouth and or Hamble; and David Gray, occasionally, went to Bournemouth Hurn airport; while Dave Stuart probably went to CSE at Oxford.

Occasionally these examiners were recalled back to base, the SRG building at Gatwick (commonly known as the "Belgrano" because of its resemblance [in colour] to an unloved and dangerous grey battleship). Here they could conduct business within the FCL environment, meeting management, ensuring paperwork was up to date, etc.

It is doubtful if the split, when it came, was ever going to be smooth, with the change from a working system to a new untried one. Unfortunately, 1988/9 had become a period when the industry was short of pilots, and there was a rush to gain a CPL/IR. The delay now for a flying test by FCL staff, I was told, shot through the roof with a wait sometimes taking several months! One case I heard of took six months for a retest of a partial pass of an instrument rating!

It also seemed, by outsiders I was told, that staff, with barely the qualifications to be examiners, were now taken on within the Flight Operations Inspectorate, in positions that normally required an airline background. Certainly it was true that some of the longer-serving senior examiners were released by FCL to take promotion to flight operations who then provided the necessary training. Previously, this would have happened within what was known as CAAFU—but now, with the split, it just seemed a less natural process, as both sides were completely separate, both managerially and physically. (Flight Ops, for instance, was situated on the third floor on the west building, and FCL was situated on the first floor of the east wing).

For the first time, the ex-Stansted FOPS 6 department now resided in the new building at Gatwick together with all the other Flight Operations Inspectorate sections, with staff previously resident at the CAA building at Aviation House, London, who were also required to relocate.

Refresher training on the 125, previously organised by FOPS 6 when at Stansted, was now organised at SRG by Flight Operations (FOD 4) staff headed by Capt. Chris Eddy. At first, the CAA leased a series 700 HS125, reregistered as G-UKCA. The 125 was used principally for FOI jet conversion and continuation flying among other tasks, such as staff transport for CAA and NATS and Highland and Island Aerodromes Ltd., target flying for NATS radar trials, aerodrome categorisation, inspection and mock flight inspection for FOI training.

The AE course was still organised by FOPS 6. Simulated Flight Training, who had owned and ran the HS125 simulator at Stansted for CAAFU to conduct the AE course, now had their new 125 simulator, still run by Tony Angel of SFT, at the Caledonian Training Centre at Crawley, close to the SRG building.

The Telecommunications element, under the control of NATS, remained at Stansted for the time being, with both HS748 aircraft, G-AVXI and VXJ, with a reduced staff of about seventy. Renamed the Flight Calibration Unit (FCU), the superintendent was also given the title of general manager. Now that the flight examiners and training inspectors were at, or controlled by, SRG at Gatwick, the FCU now called their pilots "staff pilots," just as they had in the 1950s.

Having lost most of the aircrew and operations staff, NATS advertised for a staff navigator for the FCU still billeted at Stansted House. The post holder would be responsible for the combined Operations and Navigation room facilities, and duties would include the provision of navigational expertise to the senior staff pilot, operational management and support for flight calibration tasks, and provision of computer-aided navigation type data. The salary offered was in the range of £15,158-£17,732 with a performance range up to £20,744, depending upon qualifications.

Only two operations staff remained, temporarily; Ron Golds, supervisor, was near to retirement, and it was not practicable to move him. Keith Davies, also near to retirement, now worked solely on behalf of Tels, and his position was renamed as operations co-ordinator.

Even the telecommunications side were short of aircrew. One outside pilot told me of applying for a right-hand seat position, which he didn't get. But he considered this to be just as well because of the eventual "farming off," as he put it, of flight inspection work.

Although CAAFU had felt it was being torn apart, they were not the only ones. The ARB was in a similar position; they had had buildings at Redhill, and staff simply transferred to the new SRG building nearby; it barely seemed explicable. They were so close to the new building that they were able to negotiate with the CAA that they be bussed to the new building.

Almost from its inception, the CAA had been criticised by the industry for the charges it was imposing. The new SRG building was an opportunity to bring the main elements of the CAA into what would be the home of the regulator, an opportunity to share resources, to bring together ARB officers in closer alliance with London based operational departments. The medical department would share London computers with Flight Crew Licensing. Redhill ARB sections were also able to share computing facilities. Flight Ops were now close to ARB departments such as Flight who had the CAA's chief test pilot, the Safety Data Analysis Unit (SDAU), flight manuals, power plant, etc. The CAA's long-term plan was to draw in these separate elements of power, bring them all together in a much closer alliance, a single strategy to allow many new paths.

The calibration of aids at Gatwick, and particularly at Heathrow, had become stressful for some years due to the heavy amount of air traffic experienced at these airports. Heathrow controllers, when told that a calibration of one of their runways required flight inspection, were always asking, "Why on my watch?" and "Why could it not be performed in the middle of the night?" One reason at the time, flying was not allowed after 2300 until 0600 the following morning, which were not rules imposed by CAAFU. More practically, of course, flight inspection still required ground position fixing that involved the use of a camera. By the mid-1980s, CAFU was accommodating Heathrow Air Traffic Control, as best they could, at least during the summer months, by starting an ILS flight inspection exactly at 0600. This required CAFU Tels engineers, hangar, operations, and aircrew staff at Stansted, starting out as early as 0300 to accommodate air traffic controllers who were, not surprisingly, unhappy mixing their early morning traffic with a calibration aircraft. It should be pointed out that many trans-Atlantic flights into Heathrow specifically timed their arrival at 0600, the earliest they would be allowed to land, which was a serious problem for Heathrow air traffic controllers.

But by 1988, the FCU, providing the weather was good, was pioneering night flight inspections using a new ground tracking device called Minilir, a French tracking device first seen when CAFU went to Brive, which replaced the old telecroscope tracker devised by CAFU in the 1960s, but becoming more and more difficult to keep going in terms of replacement parts. Minilir, an infrared tracking system similar to the telecroscope, had a singular advantage in that it was an absolute angular measuring system, both in azimuth and elevation. The French had used it for flight inspection for several years, and subsequently two systems were purchased by the CAA. Apparently, says Peter Burrows from Tels, there were "fun and games" installing it as most of the instructions/drawings were in French and Tels had to use Vivienne flack from Administration to assist with translation because of the technical French used could not be found in standard dictionaries.

With the increase in air traffic, it had become more difficult for Heathrow and Gatwick ATC controllers to provide the separation required on approaches that were required during the day, which is why the night-time flight inspections were proposed (and became the norm), and Minilir was seen as a solution to position fixing in the dark. The telecroscope was only of use to give positional information during the measurement of bends on the approach profile, whereas

Minilir could be used for all the profiles that had to be flown as part of the inspection. For instance, at night, the usual photographic technique for measurement of the localiser alignment and glide-path angle could not be used—Minilir could do that. I understand that there is more to the Minilir story, both technical and political. Unfortunately, I have to stop at this point.

Peter Ray recalled some of his most memorable moments:

Flight inspecting Heathrow (& Gatwick) ILS in the middle of the night—what a privilege. The weather had to be CAVOK (aircraft clear of cloud and the visibility OK) *and it was magical—legalised night flying over London. Another was during dusk in Scotland as the light was fading but managing to finish the task."* It gave him great pleasure, he wrote, *"in the feeling that all the visual pinpoints you were going to give the engineers were on the button—like a premonition; this was in the days when we defined the position of the aircraft by mark one eyeball and one inch to the mile mosaic OS* (Ordnance Survey) *maps; only possible because of the very accurate OS mapping of the UK; and by the experience of the engineers to know when to disregard a questionable call.*

Because we were limited to good weather for most tasks the sheer pleasure of seeing our majestic scenery from the air in all seasons; skimming across the high ground at the start of the 1,000 ft slice to Manchester 24 ILS and popping over the escarpment; winding through the lumps and bumps on the semi-orbit for Glasgow 26, or lining up for the 1000 ft slice for Edinburgh 26—I have a photo of the hills to the right (sorry starboard) with sheep at our level.

While night-time calibration of the ILS must have pleased and relieved ATC, having the noise of twin-Dart engines flying low over highly populated areas must have caused some disquiet among the locals, not forgetting any castle residents who were known not to be averse to complain. One pilot recalled his experience at Heathrow one night when Air Traffic asked the captain to phone on landing. He did and was advised *that HRH had rung asking, "What the **** was an aircraft doing flying low-level near his residence (Windsor Castle) at 0200 in the morning?" You may recall the semi-orbits on the Easterlies took us, one more than the other, quite close to the Castle, which being about 200 ft higher than the runway thresholds meant we were only 800 ft above and not too far East of the Castle; and those Darts (Rolls-Royce engines) were noisy!! I often wondered if we should have looked out for the flag flying!*

He also remembered that flying into London City airport with its 7.5-degree glide slope was like

being on a lift, even more so when doing the "fly above" profile, and seeing the buildings at the western end rise up to meet you on the "go around."
We also had to do a special LCY (London City) instrument base check twice a year, in addition to the normal two on the 748. One year I had to do six; the normal two, two for LCY and two more as cannon fodder for the candidates on the approved examiner course to practice on (and I was failed on one of them!).

In July, *Flight* reported that the USAF was purchasing a BAe 125-800 for flight inspection, replacing C140 and T38 aircraft.

CAA FCU Aircraft at the end of 1988. Total = 2

HS 748	2	Tels flight Inspection

(remains this number until 1996)

1989

It might be thought that I could have stopped at this point, as most ex-CAAFU staff had departed from Stansted. But the CAA still owned the two HS 748 aircraft, and flight inspections continued—work undertaken since 1945/6. So it is with no apology, albeit surprise, that I continued my research.

In 1989, the CAA Board made a decision to identify more clearly the regulation of UK Air Traffic Services (ATS). NATS were not the only provider of Air Traffic aerodrome services, and the CAA was required to be seen as regulating all UK Air Traffic Services (state and non-state aerodromes), including personal licensing of state and non-state controllers and engineers. In practice, it meant certain Air Traffic personnel from NATS were transferred to SRG Gatwick, within a new Air Traffic Standards department, in order that NATS (on the state side) could not be seen (directly) as regulating itself.

Within ATS Standards Department (ATSSD) at SRG was an Engineering Regulation (ER) department that provided regulation of the operation of all ground equipment associated with air navigation. The ER section did this by setting standards for both equipment and organisations. One of the functions of ATSSD was to give approvals under the Air Navigation Order (ANO). Under article 79 of the ANO, ER could approve other organisations to carry out flight inspection of UK navigational aids. Any such approval was based solely on technical requirements. Economic factors were not a consideration in the approval, i.e., that another organisation would be competing with the existing CAA Flight Inspection Unit.

Shortly after the formation of the ER section, they received, apparently, queries regarding flight inspection. Some were from airports asking if the CAA had a monopoly on flight inspection or if other organisations could do this work. Other queries were from organisations seeking information concerning approval for navaid flight inspection work in the United Kingdom. But Engineering Regulation could only give approvals against specific requirements, and as, at the time of the enquiries, there was no suitable specification or requirement in existence, it became necessary to produce a "flight calibration requirements" document before any approval process could begin. The document was to be developed on the premise that all flight inspection records would be examined by the ER department, and a flight inspection organisation would be approved on its ability to make accurate repeated measurements.

The CAA, on behalf of the FCU, was now advertising for staff pilots. IRE/TRE would be acceptable and could expect to fly five hundred hours. Salary was £23k-£27k.

Due to the crewing situation at the FCU, one of the stipulations imposed on all the new FCU pilots was that they act in a dual role of pilot/co-pilot, which some of those previously with CAAFU accepted, such as John Smith, Ben Gunn, Paddy Carver, Peter Ray, and Ray Watson.

In the late eighties and early nineties, the original Plessey DVORs were being replaced. The new equipment was still a classic DVOR but a much improved design and very maintenance friendly. It was based on an original Amalgamated Wireless Australasia design adapted, with NATS help, by the then Racal Decca.

In 1989, G-AVXI was seen at Stornoway by photographer Peter Moore, in a new, or rather an additional, colour scheme. Obviously the Flight Calibration Unit management and NATS recognised immediately, after the split, the necessity of making the aircraft properly visible and, perhaps as an interim measure, had four wide orange bands painted right round the fuselage in addition to the fin, wing, and tail tips. The first band went just behind the nose cone; the second just aft of the cockpit, and the third and fourth band covered the last two windows that led into the fin, which was now orange with the rudder still white (see photo end of chapter 6). Though never intended to be pretty, it was at least functional. Unfortunately, it looked rather like a dog with a muzzle to which the owner had also added a scarf to keep its ears warm. Another slight change to the livery was the addition of the words NATS flight calibration unit under the black cheat line of the nose of the aircraft.

Although the Tels department was expecting to be moved away from Stansted, the destination was still not announced; rumours as to destination were still ongoing, and Castle Donington was apparently added to the list of possibilities. Some Tels engineers thought it would be best to depart the unit altogether while the decision had not been announced, as they felt certain the "portcullis" would descend once it was, there being little chance then of escape. There was also disincentive when overtime was stopped, which caused a drop in salary.

Source of much of the material, Eddy Harris, Superintendent, retired 1982
Photo: Eddy Harris/JF

Stansted ATEL hangar staff working on the PA31
Photo: Jan Jenkins/JF

Safety Was No Accident 333

John Bennett & NAIs
Photo: Eddy Harris/JF

HS748 CAAFU new blue livery, seen at Glasgow, 1988
Photo: Copyright Derek. Fergusonwww.abpic.co.uk & (Airliners.net) 0600444[1]

CAFU PA31 Registered Apr 1982-May 1987
Photo: Jan Jenkins/JF

Captain Rees & Examiners CAAFU March 1988
Photo: David Gray

Safety Was No Accident

Captain Joy & CAAFU Inspectors 1988
Photo: Jan Jenkins/JF

CAA HS125 at Jersey
Photo: Copyright Peter Moor/www.abpic.co.uk 1317297[2]

VXI seen bandaged at Stornoway 1989
Photo: Copyright R. B. Johnston/www.abpic.co.uk & (Airliners.net) ID: 174408. 12006-2012

Chapter Seven
1990-1996

1990

The Monopolies and Mergers Commission Report on the CAA was published, focusing on the supply of navigation and air traffic control services.

Another advert seen in Flight was directly from the FCU (rather than the CAA) for pilots in dual pilot/co-pilot role. Salary was £23-£27—under review.

The calibration frequency of aids was set to be reduced. The ILS, of which there were now around seventy in the United Kingdom, was due to be re-inspected every 180 days—up from 120—and the DVOR only required to be inspected every five years.

1991

Mr. Christopher Chataway was appointed as the new chairman, Mr. Tugendhat standing down.

UK legislation, apparently, did not give the CAA any right to exercise a monopoly in the provision of flight inspection, but up until this time, UK civil airports were obliged to use the CAA's calibration unit if only because there were no commercial operators willing to enter the market. However, Hunting Aviation Services (HAS) was studying the market in 1991 after taking over the nucleus of a new calibration system from a sister company, Hunting Communication Technology of the Hunting Defence Division. Because of this, HAS designed its own NAVCAL system for ILS calibration, which was compact enough to be used in a Piper Chieftain aircraft while the CAA's present usage of the 748 had, it was believed, higher operating costs. Hunting made a presentation to the CAA and reportedly received an unexpectedly warm response. HAS was essentially aiming to wrest market share from the CAA's own calibration unit through lower pricing and required CAA approval of the scheme as a precondition of whether it could, or should, progress. Even though the CAA was pursuing its own cost-efficiency drive, it was obliged to open up calibration to a technically competent operator, no matter if it eroded the CAA's own monopoly.

In April, Ms. J. A. Jenkins, manager of Finance and administration officer at the FCU, wrote a paper included in a document: "Current and Future Trends in Flight Calibration of Radio Navigational Aids." As part of the same topic on "Future Trends in Flight Calibration," Mr. J.G. Beddows of the CAA Safety Regulation Group Air Traffic Standards examined the problem involved in the formal approval of a flight inspection organisation. Both of these papers were later presented to the International Flight Inspection Symposium to be held in London sometime in 1992. Documentation for the formal approval of a flight inspection organisation was not yet complete and only in draft form. It was expected, when finally issued, it would form part of the Air Traffic Services Engineering Manual CAP 581.

Dave Reiffer was due to retire, and his position as general manager was taken over by Mr. Chris Tyler. Although Dave Reiffer was set to retire, there were still a couple of projects in which he was engaged. It's believed Mr. Tyler came from a helicopter company, possibly Westlands.

Two of the most senior ex-CAAFU calibration pilots, Capt. Trevor Green and Peter Franklin (both senior flight examiners and training inspectors), were soon to retire, and Capt. Peter Ray was left to take charge as the senior/management/line-training captain operating in the P1/P2 role. The FCU was desperately short of experienced calibration and training pilots; Peter Ray remembered being away from base for eleven consecutive weeks and had to call for assistance from Paddy Carver, Ben Gunn, John Smith, and Dick Hawkes to help at odd times during this period, as well as asking for help from the retirees Peter Franklin and Trevor Green.

If there was ever a thought that technical ground staff were not wanted, it was to become clear that those people, with certain qualifications, would indeed be required, especially aircraft maintenance engineers (AME), if later moves or paths were to be enabled. It was also pointed out to me that later on, with the possible advent of a NATS PLC, junior staff who were on basic grades for many years were becoming disenchanted and thinking of early retirement (it must be remembered that both air traffic controllers and ATC engineers belonged to NATS).

The FCU, still part of NATS, was highly engaged in making their flight inspection systems competitive. A new Digital Flight Inspection and Calibration System (DFICS), developed by the FCU, was introduced at a symposium held at the Harlequin Hotel, Stansted, on November 9. There were representatives from over twenty-five UK airports as well as airlines, electronic companies, and overseas authorities.

Delegates were allowed to see a mock-up of the new DFICS in the FCU hangar at Stansted as well as the current Analogue

Flight Inspection System (AFIS) equipment on board one of the 748 calibration aircraft.

It was expected that MLS, initially running alongside ILS, would increase inspection workload. AFIS was designed in the 1960s, and the new DFICS was required to cope with the expected increased workload, new systems, and working practices, according to Dave Reiffer. Steps taken to reduce the workload were the introduction of the new ground tracking system, Minilir. Minilir could be carried on board the aircraft that saved ground staff driving to distant airfields with a telecroscope and other associated ground equipment. Importantly, Minilir enabled night inspections at places such as Heathrow and Gatwick—the FCU aircraft using the call sign "Calibrator"—where there was a high density of traffic during the day, thus relieving air traffic controllers and airlines of much stress and delay. The next step was the development of the DFICS built by FCU staff at Stansted. Pete Burrows, avionics engineer at the FCU, outlined the new system in *Airway* that was to "create a good working environment using modern computer technology. Up-to-date low maintenance systems would replace the existing consoles and avionics."

The existing side-facing ILS and VOR console units were to be combined into one forward-facing console. A colour monitor, keyboard, switches, and metre panels were all designed with the requirements of the navaid inspector in mind.

Software engineer, Ian Miles, said there was a simple menu at the bottom of the screen guiding users through the calibration sequence. To test the software, a simulated flight calibration programme was written by the unit using data from actual calibrations. After testing the new system, it could be used as a ground-based training aid for inspectors, significantly reducing the number of training flights.

Dave Reiffer (still not fully retired) said the new system would be more efficient at gathering data, "There would be fewer approaches made during an inspection as both glide and localiser structures could be measured simultaneously." Less time in the air would save customers money.

1992

Already, other countries were thinking of releasing flight inspection into the private sector. In 1992, *Flight* magazine published an advert from the Australian CAA seeking a subsidiary company to conduct flight inspections.

The UK MOD issued an Invitation to Tender (ITT) to "contractorise" its UK military flight inspection work. The amount of work available was thought to be comparable (in flying hours) to the civil flight inspection task, though the military navigational side used TACAN rather than DVOR as the navigational aid, and PAR (Precision Approach Radar) rather than ILS as the approach to landing aid. Nineteen companies had been invited to tender, and the RAF would be "lending" their aircraft. The CAA was in the process of producing a tender, which could have potentially doubled their workload.

In May, the Calibration Flight of Field Aircraft Services (Heathrow) Ltd. based at Shoreham was advertising for an NAI.

Although the CAA (NATS) was saying since the previous year that formal approval of a flight inspection organisation was not yet complete and only in draft form, in January, Hunting Aviation services (HAS) conducted its first UK airport ILS checks in Scotland at Sumburgh and Stornoway airports. Commissioning of new ILSs at Humberside and Southampton Airports soon followed. Since then, HAS claimed it had won the calibration of half of the ILS-equipped UK airports. Altogether there were twenty-one airports, all for category 1 or 2 ILSs for which HAS was originally approved. By October, it received approval to conduct category 3 ILS calibration. Prior to the approval, discussions were held with the British Airports Authority (BAA), which ran most of the UK's major international airports.

HAS planned, they said, to keep the operation simple and cheap. The Piper Navajo Chieftain aircraft operated from Shoreham Airport in the South of England and employed six full-time staff and three part time. A calibration crew consisted of two pilots and an NAI in the aircraft and a systems engineer who operated the ground equipment.

The United Kingdom was one of the first countries to allow independent operators to conduct calibration—up until now most aviation authorities performed the task themselves. However, the increasing cost of running a calibration unit was leading several countries to examine the use of private operators; for example, the Australian CAA was now about to decide on three bids for calibration of its entire civil and military navigation network, which included a subcontract for New Zealand and Papua New Guinea.

Mr. Tony Dart was appointed general manager of the CAA's Strategic Business Group (SBG) in April 1992. There would be five strategic business units (SBUs), (other units were: Cheltenham printing works, Test & Measurement Centre at Pailton near Rugby, Keynsham, a huge NATS/MOD store near Bristol—all eventually sold off) a unique operation that could be run almost independently with limited support from other CAA areas. Almost immediately, the Fire Service Training School (FSTS), which had moved from Stansted to Teesside in September 1981, was nominated as the first SBU in the spring.

International flight inspection symposia had started in 1980 and held biannually since 1984. It was used by flight inspection teams from around the world as a forum to exchange information and ideas. In the past, it had been hosted by Italy, France, and the USA. This year it was the turn of the United Kingdom, and the venue was to be at the Royal Aeronautical Society's (RAeS) headquarters in Hamilton Place, London, hosted by the CAA Flight Calibration Unit (FCU), whose staff had spent the last eighteen months preparing for this four-day symposium to be held June 23-26. Two hundred and twenty delegates from forty-four countries were scheduled to attend.

The first day was opened by the UK National Air Traffic Services (NATS) chief executive, Derek McLauchlan. Papers were presented by Ray Favre, NATS general manager, Technical Services; and Martin Wills, FCU navaid inspector. Subjects covered included the current UK flight inspection scene, ILS flight inspection (FI) at night, and digital FI and evaluation facilities. Numerous other subjects were presented by visiting delegates including cost-effective flight inspection in Korea and a curiously titled paper on something called Minifis!

The second full day of the symposium took in a visit to BAe's manufacturing site at Hatfield aerodrome, Hertfordshire, where delegates were able to see FI aircraft and equipment. Six aircraft were on display; two HS 748s, one from the United Kingdom and the other from Germany, an Andover from the RAF, a Cessna Citation from Holland, a French Aerospatiale ATR42, and an HS125 800 operated by America's FAA. Publicity was provided by Anglia Television and BBC East, who interviewed the FCU manager, Chris Tyler.

On the third day, further papers were presented at the RAeS headquarters by Jim Lawson, NATS deputy director, Engineering Navigational Aids (an ex-CAFU employee at Stansted in the sixties and a UK AWOP member in the seventies); Geoff Howell, CAA chief scientist; and Gary Colledge, system engineer in CAA House-based Comms 3a department.

At an evening banquet arranged at the Shuttleworth Exhibition at Old Warden airfield, Bedfordshire, CAA Board member Brian Trubshaw, former chief test pilot of Concorde, gave a speech of thanks to delegates.

The final morning saw a presentation from Jan Jenkins. The paper was interesting in that she wrote on the advantages and other effects of competition in flight inspection; the symposium drew together countries that were able to exchange and pass on ideas for the betterment of calibration techniques.

If there was competition, would those conducting flight inspections be willing to continue with this sharing of experience, or would Governments, as regulators issuing approvals, be the only way of sharing knowledge? The increase in the navaid population and the need for diversification had encouraged commerce to offer to supply flight inspection services, but the long term effect of commercialisation of these services was not yet clear. The increase in air traffic density had resulted in the UK introducing night-time flight inspections. It was the open discussions at the Rome Symposium in 1986, that had assisted the UK in making night inspections possible. In a more competitive environment would open discussion still be possible?

To improve efficiency and reduce the levels of disruption at airports, flight inspections were reviewed regularly to ensure only the minimum number of procedures was flown. With commercialisation any requirement to reduce the number of hours should only be taken for their technical merits, rather than for profitability.

Ms. Jenkins also pointed out that in the United Kingdom, post-accident flight inspections were a standing requirement, its funding paid for by the organisation requesting the special flight. It had to be conducted in a timely and thorough manner, and she asked the question, "Could commerce respond in this fashion? Was the government body required to provide this service, and if so was there a possible conflict—could the potential for litigation represent a difficulty between two groups who were potential competitors for the provision of the service?"

In conclusion, she asked ". . . if the relationship, between providers of the flight inspection services, inhibit the free exchange of information on methods and procedures?"

Ray Favre then gave a synopsis of the current flight inspection in the United Kingdom. In his closing remarks, he said that several countries had expressed an interest in expanding the work of the symposium to include more basic material to help those starting out in flight calibration.

In September, the HS125 G-UKCA that was leased by the CAA to provide Flight Ops personnel with their flying needs was deregistered. The CAA then began using an HS125, previously registered to Magec Aviation as G-BHLF, but now registered to Lynton Aviation as G-OCAA. Both G-UKCA and G-OCAA, with registrations denoting association with the CAA, had the ensign placed on the fin. It is almost certain that Magec did not order this, but was probably, thought Steve Dench from Flight Ops, at the request of Capt. Chris Eddy from FOD 4.

Capt. John Oliver, type-rated on both Concorde and the DC10 on which he had flown with BCAL since 1982, was now invited by British Airways to line-fly Concorde. His BCAL Line-Flying ceased. Capt. Hector Skinner replaced Captain Oliver as training inspector on the Douglas DC10.

Most, if not all, training inspectors were associated with more than one UK operator and on more than one type of aircraft. For instance, Captain Skinner had previously held an RAF instrument rating on Hercules, HS125, and Lockheed L1011 Tristar aircraft before joining the CAA as a training inspector. Now he worked with Air UK and Logainair on Fokker F27, F28, and HS146 aircraft; British Airways on the HS748, L1011, and DC10; British Airtours L1011; Caledonian DC10 and L1011; BMI on the F27 and HS146 aircraft. While these aircraft were on the British Register, he would have to maintain each type rating on his licence with base and line checks; base checks were conducted every six months, and line checks yearly (or two in thirteen months), which could include his instrument rating renewal, if due.

As if this was not enough, he had also been an examiner on the school types at AST, Perth, CSE, Oxford, and Carlisle. Just like most of the senior flight examiners who were both training inspectors and examiners at CAFU in the sixties, seventies, and eighties, they were very busy people indeed.

Around September/October, the Flight Calibration Unit (FCU) was renamed as the Flight Calibration Service (FCS). A decision no doubt made by Tony Dart, the new Strategic Business Group (SBG) manager, who in an attempt to make the FCS more competitive, also made them a strategic business unit (SBU) as part of the change. The FCS was now to be run on commercial principles whilst retaining the previous high levels of expertise and experience (ran the blurb).

Tony Dart said that calibration was removed from the regulatory body, as "it puts some distance between the provider and the regulator." Prior to the restructure, the CAA had approved a refit of the calibration equipment in the 748 at a cost of £1 million. One aircraft had already received the new equipment, and the second would be refitted after April 1993. These moves were designed to boost the competiveness of the CAA's calibration service to secure its future. Even if it wanted to, he said, "The CAA could not just walk away from calibration, for it is legally required to be responsible for the service. If a commercial operator felt it no longer wanted to be in the business the CAA would be obliged to offer the service."

Dart said he was adopting commercial pricing strategies to offer airports a more flexible service and had endeavoured to keep the CAA charge at a steady rate, although he had not matched the lower HAS level. Dart was bullish about the CAA's prospects. He believed

> *there would be room in the UK market for both services, and that being the CAA "brand" would give advantages. Competition was good for UK airports, it would provide the chance to achieve further calibration savings, which had been reduced two years previously when calibration frequency had been lowered.*

Although I have not found an official announcement, all of this probably occurred at the same time as confirmatory news came of the move of the newly named FCS away from Stansted to a new home based in Teesside, County Durham. Teesside was, as you may remember, one of the original rumoured sites, so it would not have been too much of a surprise. Although it might appear strange they should move to the north of England, as a body only conducting flight inspection, it does seem a more sensible central location. After all, they were not required to give training and refresher flying to CAA staff based mainly in the south. The main questions now to be asked were, exactly where at Teesside, and when?

With the 748s in a temporary colour scheme, the FCU/FCS was already planning to have the aircraft in a new livery that would stand out during flight inspection. Unlike the 1950s when one man, Capt. Jack Picken, was invited to design the colour scheme for the CAFU Doves and Princes, this time it was a local joint vote on which scheme to adopt. I was told by one of the FFU/FCS pilots, Capt. Scott Anderson, that another of the flight inspection pilots, John Dunn, had taken on the project of designing an appropriate livery in liaison with the navaid inspectors (NAIs). All concerned were cognizant with the need to come up with a highly visible scheme for the type of flying that was required; usually going the wrong way in a traffic flow within a congested area and behaving in a nonprocedural way, something commercial pilots would not normally expect, making the flight inspection aircraft a hazard to all other air traffic, a nightmare to all concerned: air traffic controllers, other commercial flyers, and to the flight inspection team. One must not forget, of course, the requirement to be visible and identifiable by the ground trackers who would be in the hazardous position of the localiser and/or glide path ILS equipment, close to the runway.

Many 748 photos of proposed livery were photocopied and hung on the walls of the offices and corridors at Stansted and votes taken. A red-and-white scheme, rather like Jack Pickens's early design, was a clear winner, but it was thought that a dark blue top would give a better chance of being seen from above, with a white cheat line through the windows and the red on the lower fuselage, just as originally designed, to provide the best contrast from below. "flight calibration service" in white was printed over the dark blue above the windows. Importantly, the fin and rudder were also dark blue with the white CAA crescent logo running almost the full length of the fin, and the large letters "CAA" nestled just below printed in white. It was impressively smart and sensible. Quietly, though, something was missing—the union flag on the fin. It said nothing, yet to me, in retrospect, spoke volumes about any further possible intention.

1993

At long last, at the end of January, news filtered through to staff at Stansted about a twelve-month restructuring plan that had already been instigated. FCS would be moving into accommodation at Teesside, which already housed the former Fire Service Training School, now called the International Fire Training School (IFTC)—first of five SBUs (though not all based at Teesside). FCS too would now become an SBU and not only be in the same building as the IFTC but also share common management. It is not exactly clear when Chris Tyler, the FCU/FCS general manager, retired, but it was probably at the time of the move when new management would take command. Mr. Tyler is believed to have moved to somewhere within NATS. It is only now that one realises the scale and depth of planning that had brought the FCS to this point.

The move came on March 26, when it was relocated from its second home of forty-three years, to this third home at Teesside, Co. Durham. It was believed that this move would result in substantial cost and manpower reduction, to operate now with less than half of its former FCU staff.

The two SBUs were to be marketed under the banner of "Teesside Services" and headed by the new general manger, Colin Chitty, who was already based at Teesside with the IFTC. His deputy on the Flight Calibration side would be Capt. Ray Watson, AFC, with the CAA since 1983, FCU since 1988, and now chief pilot. There were three other pilots, Capt. Tom Gilmore (training captain) and Captains Scott Anderson and John Dunn.

A previous Telecommunications superintendent from CAFU, Charles Marchant, had, in 1967, written,

Its staff of specialist pilots is entrusted with the flight testing of initial entrants to commercial aviation, with the training and periodic inspection of authorised renewal test-examiners and with the inspection of approved pilot training schools. The combination of a pilot whose instrument flying ability has been passed by CAFU, and a radio navigation aid inspected by the same unit yields the highest standard of safety in this field to be found anywhere in the world.

Which is probably why a 1993 CAA Document made the point: *The three (other) pilots of the FCS all hold an ATPL and have a minimum of 5,000 hours flying experience ranging in roles from a light aircraft examiner to an airline jet training captain and embracing such qualifications as test pilot and aeronautics graduate. The range of skills available is such that all pilots are eminently qualified to make operational assessments of navigation aids.*

Around this time, the CAA had asked for an independent report that advised that the HS748s could be retained for up to ten years; the aircraft were fully amortized and, for this reason, could continue to provide a cost-effective service.

The FCS, the CAA was saying, was now actively studying new developments in modern flight inspection systems, with a view to upgrading its capabilities. Foremost among the identified benefits were dispensing with the need for a ground tracker, improved night calibration capability, improved MLS and GPS capability.

G-AVXI had been fitted with the digital flight inspection system (DFIS) to replace the old analogue system used since the early 1970s. The digital system was a computer-based data-gathering and processing package designed to accept a wide range of inputs from both flight inspection receivers and position fixing equipment. Perceived benefits were weight saving, as the new system was around 1,300 pounds lighter than the old one, with a more effective working environment for the NAI. The inspection reports, after any flight inspection, could be produced very rapidly, with all the resultant cost savings and enable immediate assessments.

The old analogue system had consisted effectively of two consoles, the forward one being the ILS/MLS console with the navaid inspector sitting sideways looking at the instruments, and the other being the en route VOR/TACAN console. The equipment racks were mounted opposite the relevant consoles that took up a great deal of space. There was also another work station at the front of the aircraft used for position fixing equipment along with the receiving devices and the computing that went with it. Effectively, there were three main operating stations, and this old system in G-AVXI was now replaced with two DFIS consoles. The main flight inspection console integrated the terminal and navaid flight checking, en route flight checking and position fixing instrumentation. Essentially, all the flight inspection work could now be carried out on the front console that effectively integrated the three old stations into one.

There was another console at the back of the aircraft purely for evaluation work, which was another aspect of the FCS tasks. This console was used for equipment such as the Cossor GPS set-up. This was being examined in terms of comparison with the current position fixing devices. Finally, there was a Mode S-SSR (Secondary Surveillance Radar) system fitted in this console.

The new forward console was a much neater installation than the previous one. Both digital and analogue flight inspection receivers were used in order for the NAI to have direct access to what was going on in both forms.

On the Tels side, certain ex-CAAFU staff had been retained; Martin Wills was the senior navaid inspector, Mike Humphries and Brian Buddery, navaid inspectors. Eddy Stockton, Bill Gourlay, Adrian Maude, and Mike Spanner, all ex-CAAFU, were the three flight inspection engineers responsible for the technical aspects of the flight inspection systems. One of the ground Tels engineers, Ken Chappell, who had not wanted to move to Teesside, was allowed early retirement. Even so, although he was not formally posted to Teesside, he was still asked to go for two to three months to assist in setting up the calibration laboratory.

Another smart move the CAA made was to employ the previously contracted ATEL hangar foreman, Ken Camp, from Stansted as their HS748 aircraft engineering manager, also now working at Teesside, to ensure that the high standard of maintenance continued. Line maintenance was now provided by British Midland at Teesside, and other maintenance would be carried out by Jersey European Airways at its Exeter base.

Safety Was No Accident 351

As the microwave landing system (MLS) was now believed to be destined to be the designated replacement for ILS, the FCS was heavily involved in MLS installations and trials.

Of all the aircraft that were with CATFU/CAFU/CAAFU and the FCU, none of them were ever given an official name. But when Eddy Stockton, one of the Telecommunications ground engineers, died at a very young age, his name was placed on the nose of the 748, G-AVXI. It was a wonderful gesture to a fine young man. Eddie had been involved installing the new flight inspection console into the 748, VXI. No sooner had he moved to Teesside than he became ill. It was the wish of the FCS staff that his wife should be asked to perform the unveiling ceremony in the hangar at Teesside.

In December, *Airway* announced that FCS at Teesside had won a contract to carry out flight safety checks on instrument landing systems and navigational aids in the Republic of Ireland, signed on November 26 at Dublin airport by CAA managing director, Tom Murphy, and Brian McDonnell, chief executive officer of the Air Navigation Service Office, Ireland. The service would begin in April 1994, when regular ILS checks would be made at Cork, Dublin, and Shannon, as well as other aids at locations throughout the Republic.

Tom Murphy, accompanied by Tony Dart, general manager, Strategic Business Group, and Colin Chitty, general manager, Teesside Services responsible for the FCS, said that he was delighted that the restructured FCS had won this first overseas contract.

In addition to the Irish contract, the FCS, now an SBU, had retained most of the major calibration contracts, including those for all the BAA airports and for Birmingham, Luton, Leeds/Bradford, and London City airports. With confidence high, the Flight Calibration Service was now looking at restarting some of the overseas work given up in the past.

Captain Watson, deputy manager FCS, said,

> *Marketing our services and meeting our customer needs are very important to us. These things were always there but now there is a special emphasis. I am confident that we*

can meet the challenges that lie ahead and continue to be a professional and successful service.

Capt. John Oliver, the IRE/TRE CAAFU training inspector on Concorde since 1976, retired, his place being taken by Capt. Gwynn Williams of Flight Ops at SRG Gatwick.

1994

The FCS had now attained a British Standards Institution accreditation, all attempts directed at being a competent commercial flight inspection team.

In spite of the break-up of CAAFU, the CAA Doc 640 for this year, in describing the quality of approach of its calibration service, again set out the experience of its pilots; over ten thousand flying hours (doubled since the previous year's document) with experience of many types of aircraft including Concorde.

Essentially the effective art of calibration requires an understanding of every link in the chain—and that requires plenty of experience.

One concludes that this not only meant crews at the front of the aeroplane but also included the NAIs and engineers at the rear and on the ground.

Ken Chapel, Tels ground engineer, was now asked to do contract work for two weeks a month until the 748s retired.

Government proposed the privatisation of NATS. It had already formally agreed to them being a wholly owned subsidiary of the CAA as a precursor to any privatisation.

Although the CAA was not directly a government department, one could not help feel the association from these comments made by *Flight* International in July:

The UK Government's obsession with trying to run traditionally funded public services as commercial businesses has, justly, received far more criticism than praise. That is not because its primary aim (to reduce the cost to the taxpayer of providing those services) is wrong, but because it does not understand the nature of the services and the effects of what it is trying to achieve.

In April, FCS spent three weeks in the Republic of Ireland as part of its contract to calibrate navigation and landing aids. The first week was spent inspecting the instrument landing systems at Dublin, Shannon, and Cork airfields. The second week was spent on DVOR navigational aids at Baldonnel, Shannon, and Connaught, while the last week entailed calibrating non-directional beacons (NDBs) and the Waterford and Connaught ILSs.

In August, the FCS received a call from the Dutch Authorities to urgently calibrate one of their CAT 3 systems at Amsterdam, Schiphol, one of Europe's busiest international airports. Runway 06 was due for a scheduled flight inspection, but their calibration aircraft had become unserviceable. Tony Dart, general manager, Strategic Business Group, said,

This is a perfect demonstration of the flexibility and professionalism of Flight Calibration Service, and underlines the growing international recognition of FCS's skills.

In September, the FCS HS748, G-AVXI, was on ground display at the Farnborough Air Show. In an effort to promote the FCS, clients and potential customers were invited aboard the aircraft to see its facilities at first hand.

1995

Highland and Islands Airports Ltd. was transferred to the secretary of state for Scotland.

In March, it was reported that the Norwegian CAA had purchased a DH Dash 8-100 for calibration purposes.

Christopher Chataway, the CAA chairman, was knighted in 1995 for his services to the aviation industry.

The college where Telecommunications staff were sent to do their training was moved from Bletchley to Highfield park, not far from Farnborough, and this was a very different prospect. The technical facilities, such as there were any, were discreetly hidden away among the trees. It was much more of a management/conference centre, with a small technical annexe. It was probably what the CAA needed as it changed from being a provider of equipment to a manager of facilities and change. One engineer remarked, "Certainly modern systems are very different animals to the hardware intensive environment that I was trained for in the seventies and eighties. The decision was definitely the right one, although it was the end of an era."

Later still, it became part of a new Whitely setup (the Corporate and Technical Centre [CTC] of NATS) not far from the Swanwick ATC Centre. Even later, engineer training would be outsourced altogether by the CAA.

A final story related by David Lacey (ex-CAAFU Tels engineer) tells of the time after his graduation when he moved to the Scottish and Oceanic Area Control Centre (SOACC) at Prestwick:

My boss there was Ian Jess who had also spent some time at CAAFU, probably in the mid-1960's. In contrast to me, he had hated it and spent most of his time re-wiring Doves!
Here I worked mainly on the Oceanic Systems supporting the Shanwick (Shannon & Prestwick Oceanic) operation. There was an unusual operation (in UK ATC terms) which was very procedural and where the controllers had no direct verbal

interface with pilots, in other words ideal for the application of data link technology. It took us a while, but in 2003 this became possibly the world's first airspace where a flight could make all the necessary ATC interactions without a word being spoken on the radio. The pilots love it. I consider this to be the pinnacle of my career and that it would not have been achieved without the experience and knowledge gleaned from my time at CAAFU.

Flight Ops at SRG Gatwick was still using a leased HS125 at Luton with Magec Aviation using the specially registered G-OCAA. The computer program created by CAAFU in the early eighties was still used by them when asked by NATS to do radar trials. These flights were probably charged at an advantageous rate.

1996

At the end of May, Christopher Chataway stepped down as chairman of the CAA and was replaced by Sir Malcolm Field. Sir Malcolm had previously sat on the Army, Navy, and Air Force Institute for twenty years, chairing it for seven. At the end of 1995, he had retired as group executive of W. H. Smith Group.

Surprisingly for me, there is a dearth of information between 1994 and 1996 to record about the FCS, so no wonder it came as a sudden shock when the CAA announced that the strategic business unit, Flight Calibration Services, was sold to the private sector. It was sold on October 22, 1996, to Flight Precision Ltd. (FPL, although called Flight Precision Services), a joint venture company formed only in 1993 and owned by the FRAviation Group Ltd. (UK) and Aerodata AG, whose purpose was to carry out the calibration of airfield and en route navigation aids. (FRAviation Group Ltd. was a 100 percent subsidiary of Cobham PLC and Aerodata, a privately owned company). Flight Precision Ltd. was contracted by the CAA to conduct all the civil calibration flights previously undertaken by CATFU/CAFU/CAAFU/FCU and FCS over the previous fifty years.

The livery of the two HS748 aircraft remained much the same; only the white CAA name on the fin, together with the white crescent moon CAA logo, was changed, with the letters "FP" and a small logo just above. The logo is interesting because it was shaped like a mating dragonfly, slightly above and joined to another below it. It was the logo for the FR Aviation Group, a subsidiary of Cobham—a flight refuelling (FR Aviation) company. Presumably FP stood for "Flight Precision," yet the title on the fuselage, surprisingly, remained the same, FLIGHT CALIBRATION SERVICE. Perhaps this strategy would leave customers with a feeling of continuity—that nothing had changed.

Having acquired the assets, staff, and contracts of the Civil Aviation Authority's Flight Calibration Service, FPL now became a major UK flight inspection service provider.

So finally, after twenty nine years registered to the Ministry and CAA, the two HS748s, G-AVXI and G-AVXJ, were deregistered on October 22, 1996, closing a period of history, which began in the 1940s, conceived by a perceptive government that instituted a new Ministry during wartime, and born immediately after World War II had ended.

CAA FCS Aircraft:
DEREGISTERED

| HS748 | G-AVXI | CAA | OCT 1996 |
| HS748 | G-AVXJ | CAA | OCT 1996 |

Now that the Flight Calibration Service was sold, it was the point at which, under CAA direction, the National Air Traffic Services Ltd. was formed.

FCU Staff wave Goodbye at Stansted, 1993
Photo: Peter Moon/Jan Jenkins/JF

HS748 new FCS livery at Jersey, June 1994
Photo: Copyright Rolf Wallner (Airliners.net) 0233599[2]

VXJ at Glasgow, November 1997 in Flight Precision Ltd. livery
Photo: Copyright Fred Seggie, (Airliners.net) 0129823[1]

CONCLUSION

This book started out enquiring how, why, and when did CAFU come about. Just as important, I wanted to know how it could have disappeared.

CAFU emerged politically. The mystery for me as to why or how and when lies between the chapters.

The ending is far more cloudy, though the when is also within the chapters. But only after assembling the history can one discover the why and how of its enigmatic disappearance.

Why, was simple and straightforward: cost.

How, was a long evolutionary process caused by events; some accidental, some by chance, and others deliberate. It is strange how events can shape.

There was no single event that caused CAFU to disappear. I can count about a score of events that, combined, gradually brought about the end of CAFU. The list is too long to go into fully. But it is worth running through the half dozen or so that led the way towards its finalization.

> 1961 The formation of the Flight Operations Inspectorate. With Kilner and Chouffot.
> 1966 Captain Gurr sent to the Flight Operations Inspectorate on level transfer as principal.
> 1968 The Edwards Report, strengthened by the BoT recommendations.
> 1970 Gurr returns to CAFU as commander.
> 1972 Formation of the CAA

1974 Mr. Chouffot is made the director general of the Operations Division, which includes CAFU, FOI, and FCL.
1976 May, an OSAP conducted on CAFU
1976 July, the Phillips Review.
1977 CAFU advised of changes: No commander and Flight Inspection placed under the control of NATS.

Captain Gurr's transfer to the Flight Operations Inspectorate in 1966 allowed the then CFOI to realise the importance of CAFU inspectors within his fold.

The Edwards Report in '68 set exactly how the construction of air safety should be.

It was then another political foresight, a new body, the CAA that brought to the forefront one man, Geoffrey Chouffot, who had the vision to use earlier events to enable changes to fully integrate CAFU with the FOIs.

CAFU was never a political unit. It stood for expertise and set standards. Power is formed at the centre where Stansted never stood.

The OSAP on CAFU in early 1976 and the appointment of the CFOI to the Phillips Review panel, probably at the suggestion of the director general of Operations, could not be a coincidence. By the time the report was announced, the CFOI had retired, and an ex-CAFU deputy (then a principal) working within the Flight Operations section was announced as the new CFOI.

Captain Gurr, the man whose position was removed as commander, could have been greatly influential in future events. Yet his previous experiences nudged him into retirement at the age of just fifty-three.

With no commander, the three deputies at CAFU became principals, primarily concerned with their own directorate tasks. At first though, working practices remained the same, but the split was accomplished. All that was left was for the CAA to finalise their goal, to provide a new working centre.

For the Telecommunications Flight Inspection side, now under NATS, it was a precarious time. NATS as a customer perhaps welcomed the opportunity to influence its new charge. But the expense of operating aeroplanes would not be welcome, and they would need to be free of this burden if they were ever to achieve a long-standing ambition and become independent.

With flight inspection of all aids later contracted to outside agencies, two questions for me remain:

In the event of the CAA Flight Inspection contractor collapsing, is the CAA still legally obliged to be responsible for the service?

If so, then what is the contingency plan? For the CAA would surely not be in a timely position to take back what has been given away.

In 1972, the CAA staff paper *Airway* wrote about CAFU:

Since 1944 CAFU had gained a world wide reputation in aviation safety. Any pilot whose instrument flying ability had been approved by CAFU and any radio navigational aid which had been tested and cleared by the Unit had met the highest standards of flying performance and safety . . . . the work it carries out supports the claim that the operation of British Navigational systems and the pilots who fly them are among the world's best.

Though CAFU is now in the realms of history, the standards and functions remain mainly within the CAA.

Perhaps it would be fitting, as a final word on the history of CAFU, to take a story Charles Marchant tells from his talk to the Institution of Navigation, when he talked of the early days in the fifties, when he and his boss, Mike Whitney, were puzzling their way into solving improved methods of calibration. Of Mike Whitney, he said, "He was a truly talented man who played a major part in the development and refinement of ILS and VOR systems. He cleared the way for ILS to become the fundamental part of CAT 2/3 operations worldwide, and was much involved in the specification for MLS." Mr. Whitney (the CAA's UK representative on the ICAO All Weather Ops Panel to decide a new landing aid in the late seventies) died in 1992 at the age of seventy-one.

In a final conclusion, in Charles Marchant's paper to the Institution of Navigation, he remarks how at Gatwick Airport, the place where

CATFU was born, the Safety Regulation Group of the CAA has a "glass palace," whose entrance has a notice declaring "Safety Is No Accident." Charles suggests that his double entendre, with tense modified, would also make an appropriate epitaph to any account of the history of the Civil Aviation Flying Unit:

"SAFETY WAS NO ACCIDENT."

AFTERWORD

There will be a number of people interested in what happened next. Even I could not resist taking a peep at some of the happenings after 1996.

In 1997, Flight Precision Ltd. (FPL) was awarded a major ten-year follow-on contract to provide flight inspection services to all UK Ministry of Defence (MoD) flying establishments. This contract also included, under special arrangements, those airfields belonging to Qinetiq (one of the world's leading defence technology and security companies), formerly DERA.

FPL had only provided flight inspection services to the MoD since 1996 when they won the contract, against competition, from the existing service provider (the RAF). So successful was this outsourcing exercise in cutting costs and improving efficiency, the MoD devolved the task fully to FPL before the contract was barely two years old.

In May 1998, FPL acquired the assets, staff, and contracts of TRACE Worldwide in the United Kingdom, Belgium, and Germany. FPL now held approvals/permits from the following organisations: CAA Safety Regulation Group (CAP 670); Holding British Standards Institute, BS EN ISO 9002; NATS Ltd. (airport services and infrastructure services); UK MoD DEI (formerly the Royal Air Force Signals Engineering Establishment); Irish Aviation Authority; Directorate of Civil Aviation; and the Republic of Lithuania.

In January 2008, Flight Precision Ltd. became part of Cobham Aviation Services, and is now called Cobham Flight Inspection (CFI)

Ltd. Its Internet site states that Cobham Aviation Services has been providing flight inspection services, through its various guises, since 1947, and was able to use its extensive knowledge base and expertise to deliver a highly professional solution to all of its clients, working with all from the smallest airport to the largest in Europe and prides itself on its ability to develop a partnership relationship.

Up until 2008, CFI were using Beech Super King Air aircraft; while in Germany Aerodata, another subsidiary of Cobham Aviation Services providing flight inspection, upgraded to the Beech 350 King Air.

For me, the whole story of CAFU, in particular flight inspection, began when *Flight* magazine quoted Alan J. Cobham, KBE, AFC, in February1943, favouring the setting up of a separate Ministry of Civil Aviation. How extraordinary that the flight inspection of UK navigational aids should, at this stage, end in the hands of Cobham Aviation Services and be known as Cobham Flight Inspection (CFI) Ltd. A better story could not have been made up in my Hotspur reading days.

The DECCA system ended as a flight navigational aid in the United Kingdom on March 3, 2000, after fifty-six years' use, to be taken over by the global positioning satellite system (GPS).

In 1998 Ken Chappell, ex-CAAFU and CFU, was asked by FPL to help strip the flight inspection equipment out of both HS748 aircraft, G-AVXI and VXJ, at Exeter airport. Then early in October 1998, both 748 aircraft were reregistered to Emerald Airways. Although they were ready stripped, they were so heavily modified they were unlikely to be of any use for airline work and, consequently, never put into Emerald's colour scheme, being used primarily for spares.

According to *Wrecks and Relics*, says David Lacey, G-AVXI was at Southend awaiting the axe, which fell in November 2001. However, G-AVXJ can still be seen—as a diving attraction at Vobster Quay! It was at Exeter when the airport donated it to an inland diving centre, Vobster Diving Ltd. at Radstock, Somerset. With the help from Army Royal engineers, it was laid to rest in three separate sections. The cockpit, which still has many flight controls in place, and tail section are on a twelve-metre underwater plateau. The centre section is placed much deeper around twenty to twenty-six metres.

On January 30, 2001, Flight Operations, using the leased HS125, G-OCCA, conducted their last radar trial on behalf of the National Air Traffic Services, flying the Mount Gabriel radar head in West Cork, Ireland.

During 2001, the National Air Traffic Services Ltd. is part privatised. It is now 49 percent government owned, and the rest by a group of seven, including British Airways, Virgin, and Easy jet who have 42 percent. The airport operator, BAA, has 4 percent, and employees own 5 percent. The CAA is then restructured to become the UK specialist aviation regulator.

In 2008, ICAO produced its latest Eurocontrol Navigation Strategy for airport landing aids:

> 2008-2015: ILS to be maintained as a primary approach aid.
> 2015-2020: ILS maintained as the primary landing aid. Implementation of a microwave landing system (MLS) as a global landing system (GLS)

It seems as if ILS is still having a good run.

The European Aviation Safety Agency (EASA) was established in 2003. It started in temporary accommodation in Brussels on September 28. The agency was organised into four directorates: Certification, Rulemaking, Quality and Standardisation for Certification, and Maintenance.
In the "EASA system," both EASA and National Aviation Authorities (NAAs) have their parts to play.
In 2003, EASA moved its operations to a new building in Cologne to "promote the highest common standards of safety and environmental protection in civil aviation." It is intended to be the

centrepiece of a new cost-efficient regulatory system in Europe and a reliable partner for equivalent authorities throughout the world.

In 2008, EASA extends its remit to cover operations and licensing, plus oversight of non-EU airlines.

In 2009, First female CAA chairperson appointed, Dame Deidre Hutton CBE. For those who are perhaps a little unclear as to the relationship between the government and the CAA, in October of this year, the secretary of state for the Department of Transport, Andrew Adonis, wrote to the new CAA chairwoman, formally welcoming her and setting out her priorities in the role.

Finally, to go back to the very, very beginning, it may be of interest that one of the first aircraft used by CAFU and its predecessors, given a civil registration by the Air Ministry back in 1944, one of the Austers, G-AGLK, can still be seen flying today—and still with its Civil Air ensign. It seems some things do go on forever.

END

Safety Was No Accident 369

Auster G-AGLK first registered to the Civil Operations Fleet August 1944
Photo: Copyright Jenny Coffee (Airliners.net) ID: 1112894

APPENDICES

A - F

Appendix A

ICAO International Civil Aviation Organisation

CHICAGO CONVENTION 1944
The invitations to the International Civil Aviation Conference held in Chicago, sent out by the US government, were extended not only to all members of the United Nations but also to nations associated with them during WWII, and to European and Asiatic neutral nations.

An official announcement explained that the participation of the latter is desired "in view of their close relationships to the expansion of air transport which may be expected along with the liberation of Europe."

Apart from Great Britain, Russia, and China, the following governments and authorities were also invited to participate:

>Twenty Latin-American states
>Bolivia, Brazil, Chile, Colombia, Costa Rica, Cuba, Dominican Republic, Ecuador, El Salvador, Guatemala, Haiti, Honduras, Mexico, Nicaragua, Panama, Paraguay, Peru, Philippines, Uruguay, Venezuela

>The dominion governments of
>Australia, Canada, New Zealand, South Africa, and the government of India

Eleven belligerent European states
Belgium, Czechoslovakia, France, Greece, Northern Ireland, Luxemburg, Netherlands, Norway, Poland, and Yugoslavia

Five neutral countries
Eire, Portugal, Spain, Sweden, Switzerland

Finally,
Afghanistan, Egypt, Ethiopia, Iran, Lebanon, Liberia, Saudi Arabia, and Syria.

ICAO Annexes to the Convention

All of these annexes would apply to UK operations, in particular CAFU would follow guidelines for annexe 1 and 10.

01. Personnel Licensing
02. Rules of the Air
03. Meteorology
04. Aeronautical Charts
05. Dimensional Units used in Air-Ground Comms
06. Operation of Aircraft—International Air Transport
07. Aircraft Nationality and Registration Marks
08. Airworthiness of Aircraft
09. Facilitation
10. Aeronautical Telecommunications
11. Air Traffic Services
12. Search and Rescue
13. Aircraft Accident Inquiry
14. Aerodromes
15. Aeronautical Information Services

Appendix B

NAVIGATIONAL AIDS

Aircraft are the only form of transport able to move in all three dimensions. As Sir George Cayley said in the nineteenth century, "The air is an ocean that comes to every man's doorstep."

Air navigation has still to take full advantage of this fact.

ACR (Airfield Control Radar)
Developed by Cossor, it provided air traffic with a continuous indication of aircraft flying in the vicinity of the airport. Similar to the search element of GCA, it was intended to assist the approach and airfield controllers in coordinated movements in their respective areas. The system embodied transmitting and receiving apparatus working on primary radar. A rotating beam illuminated in turn all aircraft within a radius of about thirty miles and at heights up to about five thousand feet.

Echoes from neighbouring hills show up clearly, and precipitating clouds can be observed especially on a wavelength of 3 cm. Wavelengths of 3 cm and 10 cm are used. Interference caused by echoes from fixed reflecting objects, such as hills, hangars, or clouds, could be minimized with a technique known as MTI (moving-target indicator).

ASMI (Airfield Surface Movement Indicator)
The Airfield Surface Movement Indicator (ASMI) is used to provide ATC with a display of ground-based aircraft, vehicles, etc. movements on the airfield. Its maximum range was in the region of six thousand

yards, with an accuracy of ± 20 yards. This equipment, together with GCA, provided controllers with information on aircraft position in the air or on the ground.

BABS (Beam Approach Beacon System)

A secondary radar approach aid developed in the 1940s working on 176 MHz to give alignment to and range from runway threshold.

It was a ground-based transponder, fixed or mobile, located on the distant extended centreline of the landing runway. The aerial pattern, derived from horn reflectors, was two switched alternating lobes, left and right of the runway, overlapping on the centreline. One lobe transmitted an RF pulse several microseconds wide, and in the other lobe a narrower pulse. The amplitude of the pulse in each lobe was identical.

In the aircraft, Rebecca (qv) equipment interrogated BABS and displayed the reply on a CRT (cathode ray tube) with a vertical time base down the centre of the tube. The pulses were superimposed on one side of the time base.

The leading edge of the displayed pulses along the time base gave range. Unequal amplitudes of the pulses indicated that the aircraft was off centreline. Equal amplitudes indicated the aircraft was on centreline.

There was no glide path. Usable range was about 20 nm.

CONSOL

Consol, a long-range navigation aid developed from Sonne, was still being used more than a quarter of a century after World War II. Three antennae transmitted MF signals phased and rotated in such a way that the pilot or navigator heard dots, dashes, or an equisignal. He interpreted these to get his bearing. By referring a number to a chart, overprinted with a Consol pattern, he obtained a position line. Several sectors of the Consol chart had an identical radiation pattern, and experience was needed to overcome ambiguities. The system suffered also from the ionospheric limitations of MF radio transmissions, though in good daytime conditions, range was up to about two thousand miles.

DF (Direction finding)

MF beacons, medium wave direction-finding system, were one of the original radio aids to navigation and were one of the most popular with air crews in their time. The ground equipment consisted of a simple transmitter together with a non-directional aerial, an identity call sign being given out automatically in Morse code. Previously, most beacons had an output power in the region of two hundred to five hundred watts, and whilst these had proved satisfactory in temperate climates, there were good reasons for higher power, say, about two kilowatts, in subtropical and tropical climates, due to the higher atmospheric noise level. Metropolitan Vickers made a small one-hundred-watt transmitter that could be used as a locator beacon.

MF direction-finding service was once in great demand in civil aviation.

HF direction-finding was used to some extent on the long-distance air route. Equipment manufactured by both Marconi and STC incorporated cathode ray tube presentation.

VHF DF dispensed with the MF DF ground operator having to manually swing the aerials of the equipment, becoming more widely used, particularly as it was well suited for the homing of aircraft to an airfield. A simple—but effective—piece of equipment for manual operation was manufactured by E. K. Cole, and a more elaborate automatic system with cathode-ray indication and with remote indication at a number of sites was manufactured by STC and Marconi.

DECCA

Decca, like Consol and Loran, was a hyperbolic aid that worked on the principle of phase-locked master and slave transmitters. The radio waves from these transmitters lay down an imaginary hyperbolic lattice. A Decca chain typically consisted of a master station with three slaves around it at intervals of about 120 degrees. The distance (or baseline) between the master and each slave is 80 km to 160 km, say fifty to one hundred miles. The lattice of hyperbolic position lines so created may be overprinted on a map. A phase-comparison metre displays the position of the aircraft on a roller map in the cockpit.

Manufactured by the Decca Navigator Co., Ltd., it is similar in conception to GEE and suitable for both short—and long-range position fixing. Both are hyperbolic fixing systems; GEE operating on pulse, and Decca using low frequency, operating on the continuous-wave (CW) principle, making it unique among the hyperbolic systems. Position determining with Decca is accomplished by measuring the phase difference between the transmissions from the ground stations, accuracy being extremely high. Further, the system can be utilized at all altitudes down to sea level.

The ground stations had a very high degree of reliability, with automatic changeover from one piece of equipment to another in the event of failures. Disadvantage was, at night, the system was subject to errors. Nor was it, at first, very suitable for pilot operation, as it required the reading of several metres with reference to a special map. Later Decca systems were improved by using the Decca Log that enabled the pilot to see his track being plotted.

The accuracy of Decca was such that a position fix could be obtained to within one mile at a range of three hundred miles from the chain during the day. At night, the accuracy was five miles at 300 miles range, or one mile at 150 miles range. There is no altitude limitation; neither was there effective terrain limitation.

DECTRA
An extension of the Decca system to the long-range case, as over the north Atlantic. The receiver equipment is the same as for Decca, and aircraft can transit from Dectra to Decca coverage or vice versa simply by changing frequencies. Dectra is merely an adaptation of Decca to cover a specific route, whereas Decca covers an area.

DME
Distance-measuring, yet another British wartime development. A system of interrogator beacons that respond in a characteristic manner to a signal sent out from an aircraft. The airborne interrogator was named Rebecca (qv); and the ground beacon, Eureka (qv).

DME UHF distance measuring equipment (DME) gives slant range to a fixed beacon. The aircraft interrogates a ground station, which receives the coded signal and transmits a reply after a fixed delay. Aircraft equipment measures the round-trip time and works out range to the station. A position fix requires range to two DMEs (rho-rho—intersecting circles), using air data or bearing to a VOR to resolve the ambiguity. Range is 200 nm. Accuracy is better than 0-2 nm.

DME/DME is the preferred option to update RNav or INS, with a consistent accuracy of 0.24 nm, provided the angle of cut between range circles is within acceptable limits. "Agile" DMEs can track up to five stations in foreground, plus ten in background, selecting those providing the best cross-cut.

DME is also now used for position and range on an instrument landing system (ILS).

DOPPLER

Is a "noncooperative" aid; that is to say, one that makes an aircraft independent of ground aids. The Doppler effect is best illustrated by the sound of a train whistle. As the train passes the listener, the decrease in pitch, the same thing as a decrease in frequency, is proportional to the speed of the train. Thus a radar wave transmitted by an aircraft at a certain frequency will be reflected from the ground and received back at the aircraft at a different frequency according to its speed. This difference—the Doppler shift—is proportional to the velocity of the aircraft. A Doppler aerial that transmits beams in four directions provides an integrated Doppler shift. This is displayed to the pilot as groundspeed and drift.

Doppler is limited over calm seas, which do not reflect well, which is one reason why it has not been developed into a primary navigation system, as has INS.

EUREKA

Was ground based operating around 230 MHz associated with Rebecca (qv).

It was developed in the 1940s, originally as a small portable device used in clandestine operations to home aircraft to remote sites for supply dropping, including delivery and pickup of agents. Also used for homing to airfields.

It was capable of replying simultaneously to several aircraft, each aircraft being able to distinguish its reply by using its own random PRF (pulse repetition frequency). If too many aircraft were interrogating, the weakest signals were disregarded (i.e., the longest-range aircraft).

It received on one frequency and replied on a slightly different frequency.

Developed in the 1950s to a higher-power equipment capable of 200 nm range. (For the technically minded, the RAF version had an unusual "push push" output stage.)

GCA (Ground Controlled Approach)
A precision radar system enabling the position of an aircraft in range, elevation, and azimuth to be determined from the ground. Air traffic controllers provided information on range height and bearing from the runway, with the pilot controlling the aircraft on verbal instructions only.

It was recommended as a standby landing aid and for monitoring ILS approaches. The advantage of this system lay in the fact that it did not require any cooperation from the aircraft pilot other than response to instructions that were given from the ground controller; thus the aircraft could be landed in conditions of poor visibility provided it had means of VHF communication.

GEE (and LORAN)
Determination of position by measuring range from two beacons.

During the latter part of WWII, the British invented GEE, a medium distance hyperbolic fixing system. It was more difficult for the enemy to jam than were the point-source dots and dashes. It was a position-finding system developed to enable aircraft and ships to find their position by radio means. The most widely used was manufactured by Cossor Radar Ltd.

GEE operating on pulse (and Decca on CW). The ground stations of these systems had a very high degree of reliability, with automatic changeover from one piece of equipment to another in the event of failures. Cossor Radar also manufactured a simplified form of GEE known as GEE track guides. These provided fixed tracks on which aircraft fly to a given destination and proved valuable where the expense of a full GEE system was not justified. It consisted of a master ground station and two slave stations sending out synchronized pulses of radio energy with extreme time-base accuracy. A cathode-ray tube in the aircraft noted the reception of the pulses from the three stations, the time difference between the three receptions giving the position of the aircraft.

The first development of GEE was an increase in wavelength to provide wider coverage at some expense in accuracy; this was Loran, largely used by the Americans.

GPS (Global Positioning Satellite)
A three dimensional navaid based on multiple satellites.

Developed by the US military, the accuracy was initially downgraded for civilian use. Since 2000, the accuracy of the basic system has been identical for both military and civil use. The military have enhancements to improve accuracy to a few centimetres horizontally and vertically.

For aviation use, it is available for all phases of flight, including approach and landing, and is being developed to replace ILS and MLS. Recent augmentations including multiple frequency and ground determined corrections to the signal allow CAT 1 approaches (c2011). Some US airports and aircraft are so equipped.

Wide Area Augmentation Systems (WAAS) (qv) coupled with local augmentation permit accuracies of the order of one to two metres H & V, leading to less than one metre to permit CAT 2/3 operations. However, ILS, VOR, DME are likely to be retained as backup for the foreseeable future.

ILS (Instrument Landing System)
Became the international-approved landing aid and installed at a number of UK airfields. It was a modification of the wartime SCS51. The British ILS system of instrument landing was developed by Pye and first installed, by Marconi, at a number of airfields in the United Kingdom in the 1950s. Subsequently much developed and in worldwide use.

It consists of a localiser radio beam on around 110 MHz to furnish directional guidance to the airport runway, a glide-path beam to furnish descent angle guidance, and markers to give accurate radio fixes along the approach course (now superseded by DME). The localiser is located on the extended distant centreline of the airport instrument runway and radiates a field pattern down the centreline towards the direction of approach. The transmitter provides an on-course signal for at least twenty-five miles from the runway at a minimum altitude of two thousand feet.

The glide-path beam is radiated from a second transmitter located at the side of the instrument runway close to the landing point. The upper and lower sectors are also modulated with different frequencies and give the aircraft's position relative to a predetermined fixed descent path (usually three degrees) to a point of contact on the runway. The frequency of operation is in the band 320-336 mc.

ILS CATEGORIES
CATEGORY 1

Recognised as a landing aid at most airfields, it has a decision height (the height at which an aircraft commander must decide if he can land or abort the approach) of no less than two hundred feet (sixty-one metres) and with a visibility of eight hundred metres.

INS (Inertial Navigation System)
Is a true area-navigation system that is totally contained within the aircraft. It is the first pilot-navigation aid, since the human eye, to make aircraft independent of the outside world. It is a "non-cooperative" aid; it needs no outside radio like VOR, though such aids may be consulted to check the accuracy of, or to update, INS.

INS consists of a platform, three gyros spinning at 20,000 rpm or more, two or three accelerometers, and a digital electronic computer. The platform is mounted on three gimbals whose axes are in pitch, roll, and azimuth. Like a coin held between the fingers, it can be rocked from side to side, fore and aft, and rotated. The gyros keep the platform stable or completely horizontal, whatever the movements of the aircraft.

The accelerometers mounted on this stable platform measure the movements—which mean accelerations—of the aircraft, however slight. An accelerometer works on the principle of a weight whose displacement is proportional to the force applied to it. Each accelerometer in an INS is precisely positioned in a known system of coordinates and remains thus throughout the flight, even in turbulence.

A digital computer keeps track of all changes of time, speed, and direction as sensed by the accelerometer. The computer has been given longitudes and latitudes and the required flight path or navigation "program." Before take-off, the pilot simply dials the coordinates of the required waypoints. The computer memory compares the required flight path with the actual flight path as sensed by the accelerometers. The pilot is presented—on a moving map if desired, or on his instrument panel—with a continuous display of position, heading, groundspeed, distance to the next waypoint, and so on. The computer issues commands to the autopilot so that the aircraft is automatically steered along the desired flight path. Before each waypoint, a light blinks; over the waypoint, the aircraft is turned automatically on to its new heading. New waypoints can be inserted in flight, when a diversion is necessary to another airfield, for example, or to avoid a storm.

Although INS is independent of radio beacons on the ground, and is duplicated or even triplicated, VOR/DME and other outside aids may be used to update it. The gyros and accelerometers of inertial platforms are highly sensitive, but no bearing is perfect, and friction leads to long-term inaccuracies. Left to themselves, inaccuracies build up, and the aircraft drifts off track. INS error is usually measured in km/hr. A drift of more than 1 km/hr is unusual. With it, an aircraft can fly "across-country" instead of from one beacon to another.

LOCATOR BEACONS

Used as an identification and homing device, a low-powered medium frequency and radiating a continuous signal. Used by aircraft with a radio compass receiver associated with a loop aerial able to align itself automatically to the bearing of any station to which it is tuned.

LORAN

An American hyperbolic pulse system, Loran (short for long-range navigation) was intended for long-range navigation over large sea areas. The principle is similar to GEE. Chains consisted of a master and two or more slaves. A Loran fix took longer than a GEE fix.

Loran has two or more transmitters up to 1,000 km apart, each pair forming a chain. One transmitter, the master, emits a number of uniformly spaced pulses per second. The slave transmitter emits a corresponding series of pulses at a different phase. The phases of the master and slave transmissions are precisely timed. A computer in the aircraft (or ship) measures the difference between the times taken for the master and slave transmissions to reach the receiver. It is then possible to plot on a chart a number of hyperbolae for known difference values. Loran charts are overprinted with the hyperbolic pattern, and the pilot or navigator refers the difference value to his Loran grid to get a position line.

Loran was a step towards "area" navigation as opposed to beacon navigation. At the end of the 1939-1945 war, Loran chains covered a quarter of the Earth's surface. Area navigation permits aircraft to fly off airways.

LORAN C

A pulsed low-frequency long-range hyperbolic navigation system, Loran C uses time-delay comparison between synchronised pulses from a master and four slave stations. Ground wave range is 1,000 nm; sky wave range, 2,000 nm. Accuracy depends on chain geometry but is 200 m at best and 460 m typically. World coverage is incomplete. Loran C was operational in Europe before the Second World War.

LORENZ

From the radio range, the Germans developed Lorenz, an ultra short-wave radio beam, to guide aircraft towards airfields for approach and landing. Dots and dashes in the pilot's headset told him whether he was to the right or to the left of the runway. This was operational in Europe before the Second World War as a more effective method of night navigation. A radio signal broadcast along a narrow path could be tracked by following the signal to find the runway in low-visibility conditions. The signal was generated by the Lorenz system in which two broad signals (one mile wide at 200 miles range) were broadcast, overlapping to form a narrow region of "equisignal" that could be followed. The "equisignal" was produced by having one broad signal transmit dashes and the other dots. A pilot following the "equisignal" would hear a continuous tone, as the dots filled the silence between the dashes.

With Lorenz, there was initially a glide path provided by following on a metre the constant signal strength of the lower boundary of a lobe of RF. This was virtually unflyable.

MARKER BEACONS (Fan Markers)

A transmitter on 75 mc/s arranged to beam signals upwards into the path of an aircraft to provide position. Used in conjunction with ILS, they provide specific points on the approach path, 4 nm out from the runway threshold (outer marker), together with a middle marker at 3,500 ft and an inner marker (rarely installed) situated close to the landing point. Higher-powered fan markers can also be situated on an airway to indicate an aircraft's position.

Fan markers have now been superseded by DME.

MLS

The older ILS system has a typical three-degree glide-slope approach and can only be received within a narrow band each side of the runway centreline; further it requires a flat area in front of its aerials and is sensitive to reflections from high buildings or moving vehicles in the vicinity.

MLS provides a wide approach path of up to fifteen degrees elevation and provides bearing information in an approach sector covering forty degrees either side of the runway centreline. These wider levels would be useful to airfields with terrain difficulties where ILS cannot be installed because of high ground in the vicinity. It is thought that eventually MLS could be used with a curved approach.

DLS (DMLS)-DME-based

The principle of distance-measuring equipment (DME) is used in this system. But extra elements are added because DME measures only one of the three dimensions required—azimuth, elevation, and distance. DLS interrogates in the same way as DME, and the response of airborne equipment is received by both the DLS-E (elevation) and DLS-A (azimuth) antennae. Antennae are located in the same way as conventional ILS aerials. Information is available through 360 degrees in azimuth and between 0 and 75 degrees in elevation. DLS-A has a circular array of thirty-two receiving elements; the DLS-E antenna, forty vertically arranged elements. Interrogation-response signals occur as pulse-pairs and are received in all elements of both aerials. Phase and amplitude measurements in the circular array provide azimuth location, just as elevation angle is derived by the vertical array.

DLS is a ground-derived system, and all location data are passed to the DLS-A aerial in which the ground transmitter is located. Azimuth, elevation, and distance information are transmitted as a pulse coded signal to the aircraft, where modified DME equipment can decode it for presentation on standard instruments. The airborne fit is only slightly changed from current DME equipment, making it considerably cheaper to convert from ILS to DLS than to other MLS systems.

MLS Doppler

The Doppler effect is well illustrated by the way the frequency of a vehicle-mounted siren or whistle rises and then falls as it passes an observer at speed. This frequency change affects all types of waves and, used at microwave frequencies, forms the basis of Doppler MLS.

A source travelling at a known velocity along a straight line and transmitting at a given wavelength will seem to an observer to be emitting at a frequency similar to that originally transmitted. The received frequency will however be modified, depending on the angle between the observer's location and a line normal to the source's direction of motion. In practice, a source cannot move along a straight line forever, and for Doppler MLS, the source is switched uni-directionally along a short array of closely spaced elements. This is known as a commutated Doppler source.

The British Doppler MLS proposal (rejected by ICAO in 1978) radiates two frequencies—one is a reference, and the other, offset by a small fixed amount, is called the commutated frequency.

Motion imparted by the aircraft causes the received reference and commutated signals to shift equally. These are cancelled to produce a shift measurement that relates only to the observer's angle normal to the aerial. The reference frequency also provides a phase datum that is used for multipath signal suppression. Azimuth and elevation guidance are derived from two separate arrays mounted perpendicularly and at different locations near the runway. Preamble instructions identify signals, and each "frame" can last either 100 m/sec or 200 m/sec, depending on whether the system is a simple ILS replacement or embodies back-azimuth and flare elements. Auxiliary data capacity is available within each frame interval.

MLS FRSB (Frequency-Referenced Scanning Beam)

Exemplifying the MLS state of the art at that time was the tactical instrument landing system (TILS) developed by the AIL division of Cutler-Hammer. It operated in Ku-band and had two mechanically swept beams scanning across the azimuth and elevation volume. Location was obtained by measuring frequency, the beams being frequency-modulated during each scan; this technique was known as frequency-referenced scanning beam (FRSB).

MLS TRSB (Time Reference Scanning Beam)

TRSB MLS (the American system chosen in 1978 as the preferred ICAO next landing aid) uses two narrow fan beams that are scanned rapidly to and fro in the azimuth and elevation sectors. In every scan-cycle, two pulses, one each during the "to" and "fro" scans, are received in the aircraft. An aircraft receiver within the coverage volume derives its position directly from measurement of the time difference between these pulses. Precise solid-state timing devices and integrated digital circuitry are used to determine each angle accurately.

The American TRSB proposals use four beams, or "elements" for azimuth, elevation, back-azimuth and flare measurements. These can be transmitted in any order—preamble instructions are used to identify each signal—but all four signals, plus any auxiliary data that are desired, are synchronised so that one time difference is measured on each signal in each 150 m/sec "frame." Reflected-beam reception is eliminated by time-gating and time-averaging techniques, and beam scanning can be achieved either by mechanical means or by phased-array switching.

NDB

Non-directional beacons operate in the medium frequency (MF) band. Non-directional means that the beacon is not limited to fixed beams but emits radio waves equally to all points of the compass.

NDBs have limitations; the headings derived from them do not allow for drift caused by the wind. Although by keeping the radio-compass needle on zero, the pilot will arrive over his selected station, he may have drifted way offtrack in doing so, using up time and fuel, and perhaps missing an air traffic control reporting point, or even flying into a prohibited area. Another disadvantage of the NDB is that their medium wave transmissions are distorted by mountains, coastlines, thunderstorms, and "night effect." At night, the Kennelly-Heaviside and Appleton layers (the E and F ionised layers) of the Earth's atmosphere weaken, allowing sky wave propagation and hence false reception of MF radio signals. After sunset, these approach the antenna from above.

MF non-directional beacons are used in conjunction with automatic direction finders (ADF) equipment on the aircraft. NDBs marked a position on the airway or were beacons that an aircraft could home to by following the needle of the ADF in the aircraft, typically airport sited.

Automatic direction finding (ADF) simply provides the relative bearing of a basic ground based non-directional beacon (NDB) to the fore/aft axis of the aircraft by using a directional antenna assembly in the aircraft.

In the United Kingdom, NDBs are not required to be flight-checked. However, NDB procedures to ILS approaches are routinely checked for operational acceptance.

OMEGA

A continuous-wave very low frequency (VLF) long-range navigation system, Omega provides position by means of phase comparison using one of three techniques—range to two ground stations (rho-

rho), range to three stations (rho-rho-rho), or range difference (hyperbolic).

Accuracy is theoretically 300 m, but typically 2 nm. Because it uses the gap between the Earth's surface and the ionosphere as a waveguide, Omega is susceptible to daily errors caused by movement of the ionosphere. This and other known errors caused by ground conductivity and geomagnetic effects are corrected by software in the receiver. Omega is also prone to atmospheric interference, solar activity, precipitation, and aircraft static.

RADIO RANGES

Medium-frequency radio ranges were used to mark an airway or position within a control zone, often associated with an airfield.

The first radio range stations housed a beacon that projected a split beam; one side of which was a continuous repetition of the Morse letter *A*, and the other side a similar transmission of the letter *N*. As with the Lorenz landing system, the pilot heard a continuous note when flying on a straight course along the centre of the beam. Where two airways crossed, a four-course range station was established emitting the A/N beam, in Morse (*A* on the starboard side and *N* on the port side) along the four airway routes leading from the station. If an indication of position was required along a leg of a radio range, it required the installation of a non-directional beacon (NDB) or a VHF fan marker.

The shortage of frequencies on the MF band seriously restricted the number and power of MF installations.

REBECCA

Developed during the 1940s and used extensively thereafter. It was an airborne radar operating on 176 MHz for (BABS) (qV).

The aircraft had directional receiving aerials directed slightly left and right of the aircraft and an omni-directional transmitting aerial.

In use with Eureka, the transmitter pulse was received on the ground Eureka that replied on a different frequency. The received pulses were displayed on a CRT with a vertical time base; Left Hand aerial to left of time base, and Right Hand aerial to right of time base.

If one pulse amplitude was greater than the other, the aircraft was turned until the amplitudes were equal, which gave the heading to the airfield (not allowing for drift!).

Range was given by distance of leading edge of pulses along the time base. The range of later versions was up to 200 nm.

RNAV

A system that allowed Area Navigation, RNAV, sometimes referred to as random navigation because it allowed an aircraft to choose any course within a network of navigation beacons, rather than navigating directly to and from the beacons.

The development of the airborne computer made possible area navigation using existing VOR/DME or VORTAC instead of master-and-slave chains. The Decca chains installed in Europe and elsewhere, notably New York, are used by suitably equipped aircraft—including off-airways light aircraft and helicopters—and by ships.

But the computer's adaptation of VOR point-source aids to area navigation—RNav—was to prove almost as important to the airman as the self-contained aids like inertial platforms and Doppler. The computer's ability to offset a waypoint—to "ghost" a VOR station—was an important advance in air navigation. So was its ability to estimate climb and descent paths to assist air traffic control. Point source beacons no longer constrained traffic to the airways "tramlines" between them.

SBA

The Standard Beam Approach (SBA) was developed from Lorenz. A similar setup to the radio range except the transmitter was placed several hundred yards beyond the far end of the runway, with the beam directed along the runway itself. The twin beams radiated As and Ns as before, the twin signals blending into a continuous tone over a narrow zone along the centreline of the approach path.

There was no glide path. The height on approach was determined by fan markers, enabling the pilot to associate his height with relation to distance from threshold. This system was replaced by the ILS (instrument landing system).

SONNE

During the Second World War, Lorenz developed a long-range navigation system based on dots and dashes. Known as Sonne, it was used with great effect by U-boats and Focke-Wulf Condor maritime-reconnaissance aircraft in the German antishipping and U-boat offensive. Though easily jammed, it was unmolested by the Allied air and naval forces, who used it themselves.

Sonne was the first long-range navigation system devised to require no more than an ordinary MF receiver in the aircraft. After the 1939-1945 war, Sonne was further developed by the British Marconi company, who named it Consol.

SURVEILLANCE RADAR

The functions of surveillance radar for approach control:

(1) to give aircraft navigational assistance in positioning themselves for final approach
(2) to monitor the terminal airspace against "intruders"
(3) to marshal aircraft from holding patterns to final approach in order to secure a well-spaced traffic flow
(4) to monitor aircraft on their take-off paths in order to reduce the separation required between aircraft outbound from an airport and those in the holding pattern or on final approach.

GCA equipment had serious limitations in that its vertical cover was cut off at about four thousand feet, and it was subject to interference from permanent echoes. The ICAO specification for what is termed Surveillance Radar Element (SRE) was based on the old conception that this should be primarily an adjunct to the radar approach system. The cover specified is not adequate for the application of this equipment to air traffic control, either in altitude or range. The specifications laid down for new British radar equipment (approach control radar) went further than this and provided for cover to extend up to ten thousand feet at about twenty miles.

TACAN

TACAN (tactical air navigation) is a bearing and distance radio aid sponsored by the US Navy as a result of a research programme begun in 1945. It operates in the 1,000 mc/s (UHF) band, using conventional interrogator/responder techniques for distance measurement, and rotating and reference signal phase comparison for the determination of azimuth. A single channel serves both bearing and distance functions. The maximum line-of-sight range is about two hundred miles.

Because Tacan has a similar function to VOR/DME but is not compatible with it (there are objections to its use in light aircraft and the VOR/DME and Tacan distance measuring frequencies conflict), comparative evaluations were carried out, to the accompaniment of much political wrangling, in order to determine the best system.

VOR

VHF omni-directional range (VOR) gives absolute bearing to or from a ground station. VOR uses phase comparison between an omni-directional reference signal and a rotating variable signal transmitted by the station. The signals are in phase when the aircraft is due magnetic north of the station. A position fix requires bearings to two VORs (theta-theta) or range and bearing to a co-located VOR/DME (rho-theta). There are en route VORs with 200 nm range and terminal area TVORs with a 25 nm range. Accuracy is ±2 degrees. Conventional CVORs operate in the very high frequency (VHF) band, radiating two transmissions. Both are of constant frequency, but one remains stationary as the other rotates.

The ground station radiates a rotating (360-degree) field so that any aircraft receiver within range is able to determine its bearing from (or to) the station. In addition to the navigational signal, the station is able to transmit a Morse identification signal as well as VHF communication.

The receiver in the aircraft compares the difference in phase, this being proportional to the magnetic bearing of the VOR beacon. The receiver in the aircraft is a phase comparison metre. In its simplest form, it drives a left-right needle on the VOR instrument that tells the pilot which way to steer to maintain the radial he has selected. Accuracy is of the order plus or minus two to four degrees. The range is optical line-of-sight plus 15 percent at vertical angles. Thus an aircraft at two thousand feet could expect adequate signals up to a distance of seventy to eighty miles from the VOR station. VOR signals are susceptible to "scalloping" at longer ranges, which causes an aircraft to wander if coupled to a VOR radial.

VOR/DME

VOR Aerials put out two signals sweeping through full 360-degree arcs in the horizontal plane, their relative phase varying with azimuth. Since VHF is used, transmission range is limited. The distance-measuring equipment (DME) is co-located with the VOR.

DOPPLER VOR

By the mid-1970s, experience was being gained with an improved beacon called Doppler VOR; the modulations are reversed (the reference signal becomes amplitude modulated), and electronic switching avoids the need for a rotating aerial. The wider-aperture aerial reduces ground interference, and the net result is a more accurate, more reliable VOR. It is less prone to siting problems and is more practical in crowded areas where there are tall buildings; however, it is a big structure—around one hundred feet in diameter.

VORTAC

An entirely civil aid is a short-range navigational system arising from the TACAN-VOR/DME controversy, which combines the direction-finding portion of VOR/DME (the omni-directional range feature) with the distance-finding element of Tacan.

WIDE AREA AUGMENTATION SYSTEM (WAAS)

The Wide Area Augmentation System (WAAS) is an air navigation aid developed by the Federal Aviation Administration (FAA) to augment the global positioning system (GPS), with the goal of improving its accuracy, integrity, and availability. Essentially, WAAS is intended to enable aircraft to rely on GPS for all phases of flight, including precision approaches to any airport within its coverage area.

WAAS uses a network of ground-based reference stations, in North America and Hawaii, to measure small variations in the GPS satellites' signals in the western hemisphere. Measurements from the reference stations are routed to master stations, which queue the received deviation correction (DC) and send the correction messages to geostationary WAAS satellites in a timely manner (every five seconds or better). Those satellites broadcast the correction messages back to Earth, where WAAS-enabled GPS receivers use the corrections while computing their positions to improve accuracy.

The International Civil Aviation Organisation (ICAO) calls this type of system a satellite-based augmentation system (SBAS). Europe and Asia are developing their own SBAS, the Indian GPS Aided Geo Augmented Navigation (GAGAN), the European Geostationary Navigation Overlay Service (EGNOS), and the Japanese Multifunctional Satellite Augmentation System (MSAS), respectively. Commercial systems include StarFire and OmniSTAR.

Appendix C

ILS and VOR inspection procedures

ILS ROUTINE FLIGHT INSPECTION

GLIDE PATH ONE-THOUSAND-FOOT SLICE
Flown from ten miles out to overhead localiser.

LOCALISER PARTIAL ORBIT
At five miles fly from thirty-five degrees across at one thousand feet.

PROMULGATED PROCEDURE
From beyond eight miles, then down the glide path (G/P) and localiser (Loc), recordings at outer marker (OM) and photographs of boards on the ground.
Localiser against lights on the approach.
Two more runs on G/P and Loc from eight miles.

COURSE STRUCTURE STABILITY APPROACH
BIASED 75 µA ABOVE and BELOW GP
Checking for stray signals outside the beam path, two more runs made at deviations of 75 µA either side of the localiser, and 75 µA above and below the glide path.

TRANSMITTER CHANGE
Repeat—plus one approach instead of three.

Six runs made against each transmitter. The first is an alignment check of the ground tracking equipment, followed by three automatic approaches on the ILS beam.

MARKER BEACONS
Fly through times and coverage.

POSITION FIXING
Localiser alignment and glide path angles determined photographically sector width and range information achieved from visual pinpoints provided by the co-pilot from 1/50,000 Ordnance Survey Maps.

Where visual pinpointing or photography is impossible, i.e., approaches over the sea, Decca and/or theodolite fixing is employed.

MONITOR ALARM CHECKS
These were not normally carried out, as it was more convenient to ground check.

Exceptionally for glide path type M arrays, the checks were carried out at the request of ground engineers, the parameters checked by flying a succession of one-thousand-foot slices.

PERIODICITY
Routine flight inspections carried out at 120-day intervals with a tolerance of plus twenty days. Later routine flight inspections were undertaken every 180 days.

Categorisation inspections are carried out at twelve-month intervals, with a tolerance of plus four months.

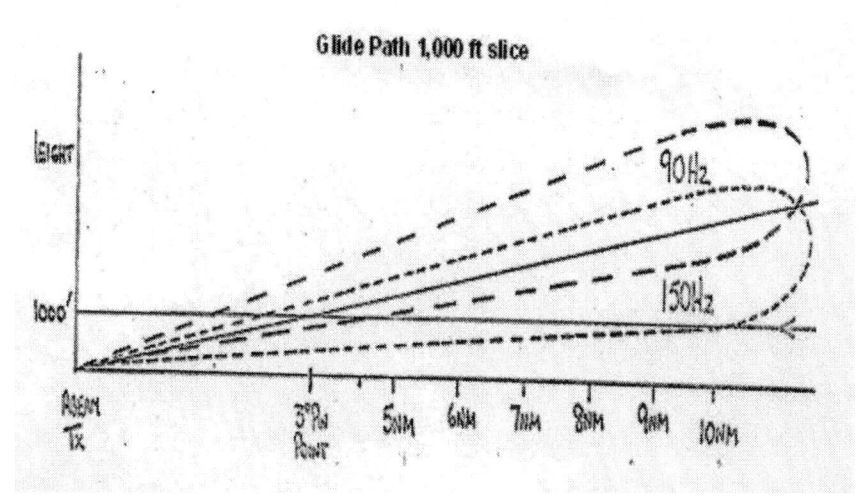

ILS G/P 1000 ft slice
Photo: Eddy Harris/JF
The glide path is where the two lobes overlap.

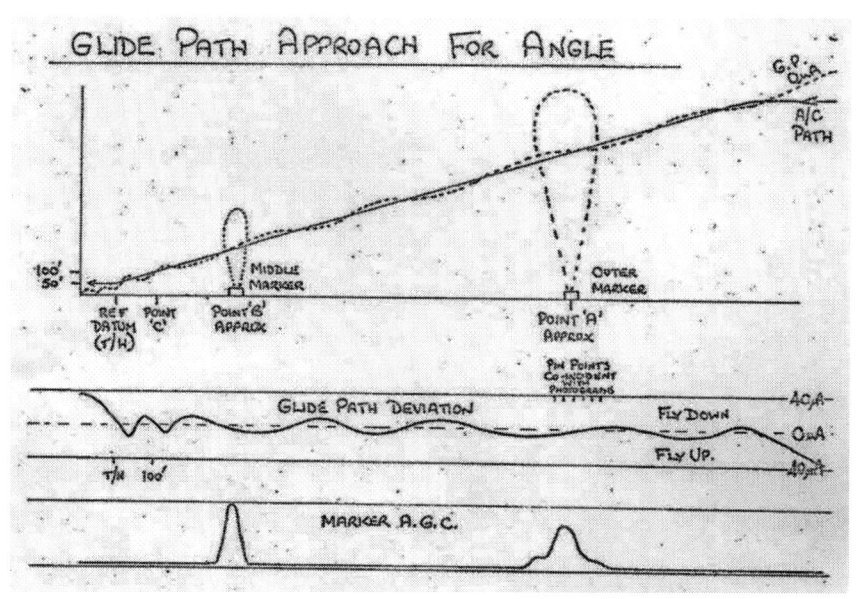

ILS G/P Approach angle
Photo: Eddy Harris/JF
The fan markers gave positional information on the approach to the runway. Outer marker about three miles, and the inner marker perhaps half a mile to touchdown.

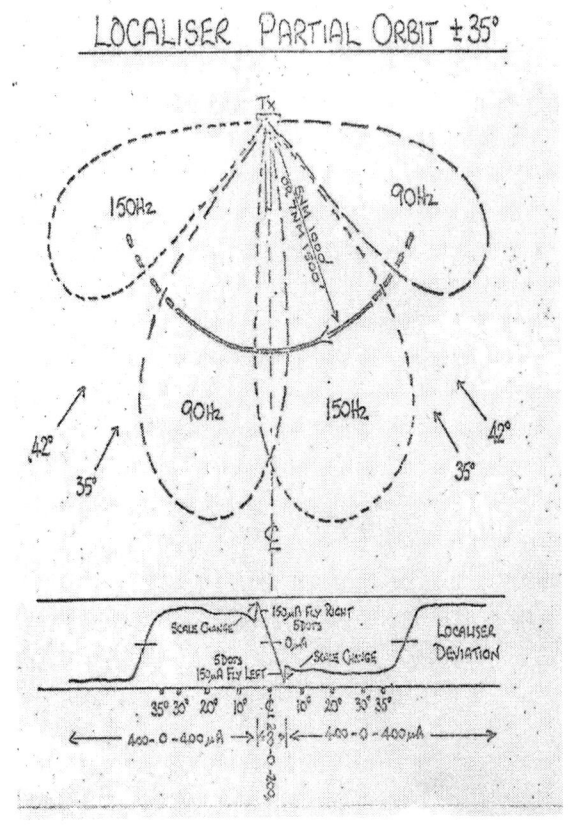

ILS Localiser Partial Orbit
Photo: Eddy Harris/JF

VOR ROUTINE PROCEDURE

Twenty-mile orbit at 2,500 ft, orbit to check both accuracy and coverage through 360 degrees.

In the London area, this could cause problems due to the number of aerodromes, as well as departing and arriving traffic at major airports, and is very much dependent upon weather conditions.

All the radials on an airway would be checked, although not necessarily at the same time, but picked off at intervals during any transiting flight.

DVOR

Gradually replaced VORs and due to their performance only checked every five years.

A 20 nm orbit flown at minimum safe altitude around the beacon.

Airways and reporting points, flown either to the limit of cover or the coincidence point of the next airway beacon.

All runway approaches based on the beacon are checked.

All SIDS (standard instrument departures) and STARS (standard arrivals) relying on the VOR are flown.

PERIODICITY

Checked every six months in the 1960s.
DVORs now flight checked every five years.

Appendix D

Leeds Letter

Attachments:

1. Letter from Leeds Bradford Airport
2. Internal Memo to CAFU staff

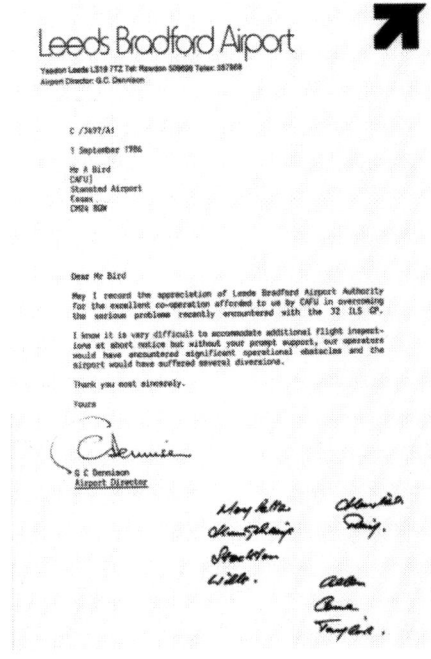

Leeds Letter
Photo: Eddy Harri /JF

Internal Memo — CAA

Mr N Aylesbury
CE CSM
CAA House

Our ref: 10B/32/19

LEEDS/BRADFORD AIRPORT

On the basis that flight calibration leads to more brickbats than compliments, I thought this letter merited your attention!!

I will circulate this plus the letter from Dennison to the staff concerned who are listed on that letter.

D R REIFFER
Manager FCU
CAAFU

5 September 1986

cc: Mr Moylette
    Mr Humphreys
    Mr Stockton
    Mr Wills
    Mr Norman-Allen
    Mr Cone
    Mr Taylor
    Capt Hawkes
    Capt Ray

Internal Memo
Photo: Eddy Harris/JF

Appendix E
CAFU FACTS

Over the period of its existence, CAFU and its predecessors were located at four airfields, with operations starting in 1945, ending with all three strands of work: flight inspection, "pre-airline" examining, and "post-airline" inspection at Stansted in 1988, ending with flight inspection in 1996.

AIRFIELDS
08 months 1944-1945 Croydon
04 years 1946-1949 Gatwick
43 years 1950-1993 Stansted
03 years 1993-1996 Teesside

OWNERS
CAFU had twenty-eight years directly under the control of various UK government ministries, before being handed over to the CAA. Starting with the Air Ministry, it then spent
08 years 1945-1953 MCA
06 years 1953-1959 MTCA
07 years 1959-1966 MOA
04 years 1966-1970 BOT
02 years 1970-1972 DTI
24 years 1972-1996 CAA

MANUFACTURERS

Over the period, CAFU had thirteen aircraft types, from seven separate manufacturers, five British, one Canadian, and one American. In total, there were forty-nine aircraft registered.

MANUFACTURERS

Airspeed
Avro
De Havilland/Hawker Siddeley/British Aerospace
DH Canada
Miles
Piper
Auster

AIRCRAFT

Single Engine

TYPE	No.	TASKS
Austers	02	Communication & Refresher
Proctors	02	Communication & Refresher
Tiger Moths	02	B Licence. Instructor Rat, Ref
Chipmunks	02	GFT, Instructor Rating, Ref.
Total	**08**	

Twin Engine

TYPE	No	TASKS
Anson	13	Flt Insp, Comms, GCA, OS, Ref
Gemini	03	Communications, Refresher
Oxford	05	IR, Comms, GCA
Dove	04	Flight Inspection, GCA, OS
Dove	05	IR, VIP, Comms, GCA, OS, Ref
Prince	03	Flight Inspection
President	01	Flight Inspection
HS125	03	Radar, VIP, Comms, Ref
HS748	01	VIP, Comms, Educ Flts, Lease, Refresher

HS748	02	Flight Inspection
PA31	01	Communications, Refresher
Total	**41**	

CAFU REGISTERED AIRCRAFT

Aircraft	Reg.	WITH	From	To
Auster	**G-AGLK**	AM/MCA	Aug-44	Aug-52
Auster	**G-AGLL**	AM/MCA	Aug-44	Jan-50
Proctor	**G-AGLJ**	AM/MCA	Aug-44	May-51
Anson XI	**G-AGLM**	AM/MCA	Oct-44	Feb-46
Proctor	**G-AGPA**	MCA	Jun-45	Jul-48
Tiger Moth	**G-AGRB**	MCA	Jun-45	Aug-52
Tiger Moth	**G-AGRA**	MCA	Aug-45	Aug-52
Anson	**G-AGPB**	MCA	Sep-45	Nov-50
Anson	**G-AGWE**	MCA	Dec-45	Jan-53
Anson	**G-AGWF**	MCA	Dec-45	Nov-51
Anson	**G-AGWA**	MCA	May 46	Jan-54
Anson	**G-AGZS**	MCA	May-46	Jan-52
Anson	**G-AGZT**	MCA	May-46	Jan-53
Gemini	**G-AIRS**	MCA	Oct-46	Oct-52
Dove	**G-AJLV**	MCA	Apr-47	Apr-72
Consul	**G-AJXE**	MCA	Jun-47	Nov-55
Consul	**G-AJXF**	MCA	Jun-47	Sep-55
Consul	**G-AJXG**	MCA	Jun-47	Jan-56
Consul	**G-AJXH**	MCA	Jun-47	Jan-56
Consul	**G-AJXI**	MCA	Jun-47	Aug-56
Gemini	**G-AJZL**	MCA	Sep-47	Mar-51

Gemini	**G-AKDD**	MCA	Sep-47	Sep-55
Anson	**G-AGVA**	MCA	Oct-47	Jul-54
Anson	**G-AHID**	MCA	May-48	15.05.50
Anson	**G-AHIH**	MCA	May-48	21.07.54
Anson	**G-AHIJ**	MCA	May-48	21.11.51
Anson	**G-AGUD**	MCA	Jul-48	Jul-54
Anson	**G-AHIC**	MCA	Jul-48	Oct-54
Dove	**G-ALFT**	MCA	Dec-48	Feb-77
Dove	**G-ALFU**	MCA	Dec-48	Apr-72
Dove	**G-ALVS**	MCA	Oct-49	Nov-72
Prince	**G-AMKW**	MCA	Aug-51	Jul-71
Prince	**G-AMKX**	MCA	Aug-51	Jul-71
Prince	**G-AMKY**	MCA	Aug-51	May-71
Chipmunk	**G-AMMA**	MCA	Sep-51	May-63
Dove	**G-ANAP**	MCA	Jul-53	Aug-73
Dove	**G-ANOV**	MCA	Mar-54	Jul-81
Chipmunk	**G-ANWB**	MTCA	Feb-55	Apr-71
Dove	**G-ANUT**	MTCA	Feb-55	Feb-77
Dove	**G-ANUU**	MTCA	Mar-55	Feb-77
Dove	**G-ANUW**	MTCA	May-55	Jul-81
President	**G-APMO**	MTCA	Apr-58	Jun-71
dH125	**G-ATPC**	BOT	Feb-66	May-71
HS748	**G-AVXI**	BOT	Nov-67	Oct-96
HS748	**G-AVXJ**	BOT	Nov-67	Oct-96

HS125	**G-AVDX**	BOT	Jun-70	Jan-83
HS748	**G-ATMJ**	CAA	Dec-72	Jul-78
PA31	**G-BFBH**	CAA	Apr-82	c 1987
Bac125	**G-CCAA**	CAA	Dec-82	Sep-87

Appendix F

Papers by A. C. Marchant

CONTENTS
1. 1966 *Flight* article—Charles Marchant
2. 2006 Paper—Charles Marchant

The 1996 *Flight* article, "The Work of the Civil Aviation Flying Unit" by A. C. MARCHANT

PRACTICALLY EVERYBODY knows that radio transmissions—like light—travel in straight lines. And practically everybody is wrong. Radio navigation "beams" can be refracted, reflected or otherwise distorted, so that the information they are intended to convey is considerably modified. In the early days of aviation this was not a matter for deep concern, but as airlines began to depend more and more upon radio guidance information, the relationship between accuracy and regular, safe flying operations became an important consideration.

The science of instrument flying using radio guidance progressed rapidly. Within a comparatively short time the "Instrument Landing System" had begun to simplify the pilot's task of interpretation of guidance signals, by turning the radio information provided for runway approach into easily assimilable visual data which could guide the pilot to a height of about 200ft above touchdown, at which point he would need to overshoot if he had not made visual contact with the ground.

Use of ILS below this height was originally not permitted, mainly because of inadequate system reliability; and thus, in spite of its name, ILS was really only a runway approach system. However, developments now in hand will enable the ILS to become part of a truly automatic landing system.

In theory, pilots had only to fly their aircraft accurately in response to the information displayed by the instruments. But, however carefully they flew, pilots could find that their aircraft somehow managed to deviate from the straight and narrow path or alternatively that the instrument information varied too quickly to be followed. Sometimes aircraft strayed too high or too low, or were so far displaced from the correct approach path, when decision height was reached, that pilots would have to indulge in unacceptably coarse manoeuvres in order to land. Thus, even as an approach aid, the ILS performance was inadequate at some locations and its use was inhibited by various promulgated restrictions.

These difficulties can be caused by local geography, building structures, etc., which can severely affect the quality of the information radiated from a ground transmitter. Since the position of the runway absolutely determines the location of the transmitter aerial, such errors might be very difficult to eradicate. Other difficulties caused by the presence of service vehicles or overflying aircraft may be more amenable to control once they are identified. In order to maintain ILS as an approach aid to 200 ft and in order to plan its further development so that it can become part of a true automatic landing system, it is therefore essential to know several things about each installation: firstly, is it accurate and stable? If not, exactly what is the nature and extent of the errors and what can be done to mitigate them? Similar problems arise with other radio navigational aids but ILS inherently poses the most difficult problems.

The answers to these questions can only be completely established by "flight inspection" techniques. So much for the aids themselves, but accurate aids lose their point if pilots cannot use them safely. Flight inspection of radio aids is only half the problem; how can we ensure that the pilots using them could reach a standard of instrument flying good enough to take full advantage of the facilities? It is the responsibility of the Civil Aviation Flying Unit (part of the Board of Trade) to tackle both sides of the problem. Its fleet of aircraft is specially equipped to test and inspect radio and navigation aids throughout the United Kingdom. Its staff of specialist pilots is entrusted with the flight testing of initial entrants to commercial aviation, with the training and periodic inspection of authorised renewal test-examiners and with the inspection of approved pilot training schools. The combination of a pilot whose instrument flying ability has been passed by CAFU, and a radio navigation aid inspected by the same unit yields the highest standard of safety in this field to be found anywhere in the world.

Today (1966) the unit has a fleet of nine HS Doves (four for telecommunications, five for delegated examiner training, communications flying, and competency checks), three Percival Princes, one Percival President, one Chipmunk (for pilot checks) and one HS.125 jet executive aircraft for VIP transport and special investigation of surveillance radar problems at high altitude.

The pilots are encouraged to be versatile. General flying over and above a pilot's specialised activities yields a useful cross feed of experience and information and helps pilots to evaluate developments in approach and navigation aids. Naturally, as aircraft become more complicated, it is less easy to switch pilots between tasks, but the policy is followed as far as possible.

When pilots join the unit they first qualify on the Dove aircraft. The next stage, a fortnight or so later, is flight inspection of approach and navigational aids. After about four months of this, the pilots begin to train as examiners for general flying tests. Eventually they become qualified instrument rating examiners, but it is not until they have flown with the unit for another 18 months that they become qualified to examine operators' check captains. These check captains themselves are specially trained and tested by CAFU before they are authorised to carry out instrument rating renewal tests of their own companies' pilots, with the approval of the Director of Aviation Safety.

FLIGHT INSPECTION REQUIREMENTS

ILS provides a good example of the way in which flight inspection requirements arise and techniques are developed to meet these requirements. For landing in IMC (instrument meteorological conditions) the minimum requirements for visibility (runway visual range) and the height at which a decision to land or overshoot must be taken (decision height) have gradually been reduced, and are being reduced still further as techniques and facilities improve. The following table gives an indication of the various categories of decision height and RVR requirements as defined by ICAO:

Instrument Landing Category Standards

Category	DH (ft)	DH (mtrs)	RVR (ft)	RVR (mtrs)
CAT I	200	60	2600	800
CAT 2	100	30	1200	400
CAT 3A	100	30	700	200
CAT 3B	12	3	330	50
CAT 3C	0	0	0	0

The fulfilment of CAT 2 and CAT 3 was a threefold exercise demanding:

(1) adequate airport installations
(2) adequate aircraft equipment and performance
(3) the attainment and maintenance of a high standard of pilot proficiency.

As far as the first was concerned, the most important consideration was the quality of the standard ILS.

Until recently ILS was only expected to meet CAT 1 standards and was thus "an approach aid." The above table shows that with the introduction of the CAT 2 and CAT 3 concepts, ILS would become an inherent part of the landing manoeuvre. Aircraft like the Trident (engineered for fully automatic landing, using ILS) will soon be landing—on scheduled services—in conditions of visibility which would now stop flying altogether. In a year or two's time, automatic landing on ILS will be standard procedure—whatever the visibility.

Understandably, if a ground approach aid is going to be used in this way, ICAO requires much smaller margins of error in the ground system than have been tolerated hitherto. In the past, course structure was evaluated by simply flying down an approach course-line and assessing whether or not the approach and eventual landing was reasonably comfortable. This is far too coarse and subjective a method of assessment to register the very small errors that must be detected if fully automatic landings are to be made safely. CAFU has had to devise new ways of fixing the position in space of an inspecting aircraft, not only continuously, but with great accuracy, so that a sufficiently true picture of bends in an ILS course structure can be obtained.

ILS FLIGHT INSPECTION METHODS

The obvious way to measure course structure of an approach system would be to endeavour to fly the course-line, with the greatest possible accuracy, and then compare the resultant approach path with the path that the system is intended to enforce. In theory, the procedure is a simple one; but in practice it becomes complex, since (1) the aircraft cannot fly the course-line perfectly and (2) permissible errors in measurement are less than one minute of arc. During the whole of the approach, the ILS course has to be analysed by comparison between the data available from instrumentation and navigational systems within the aircraft and that derived by direct optical measurements from the ground.

It often happens, when some new and specialised job is to be done, that the equipment for doing it simply does not exist. So it was, when CAFU found that it needed an automatic tracking facility. The unit therefore took over an instrument originally developed for military purposes and modified it for their own use. This instrument is known as the telecroscope. It is basically a precision infra-red telescope which is set up on the extension of the runway centre-line (for localiser measurement) or at the side of the runway, in the same plane as the glide-path (for glide-path measurements). The aircraft flying the ILS carries a high-intensity narrow-beam tungsten lamp in the nose adjacent to the ILS aerials. The telecroscope measures the angular displacement of this light from the nominal axis of the centre-line or glide-path, and translates the displacement into electronic signals which are processed and recorded by equipment contained in an adjacent motor vehicle. It is important that the airborne lamp should point directly at the telecroscope. The lamp mounting is therefore servo-controlled by the gyro compass and vertical gyro unit in the aircraft so as to compensate for changes of aircraft attitude during the approach.

A more elegant, servoed system (the Eltro tracker) is also available for this work. It uses similar principles to those of the telecroscope and has similar accuracy and greater range, but is considerably more expensive. However, it has a servoed traverse of 360° in azimuth and is thus suitable for VOR as well as ILS flight inspection work.

At the moment the tracking data from the telecroscope, together with data from the aircraft, is analysed by a computer on the ground; but CAFU hopes soon to be able to transmit telecroscope signals to the checking aircraft by telemetry. When this is done the signals will be recorded simultaneously with the ILS signals and a preliminary analysis in the air will be possible, using simple analogue computer techniques.

OPERATIONAL ASPECTS

The flight inspection of one ILS installation—perhaps hindered by poor visibility or traffic problems—may occupy several days. In addition to ILS, CAFU undertakes the flight inspection or evaluation of VOR, TACAN, PAR, marker beacons, VHF and UHF direction finders, primary and secondary surveillance radar, DME, and VHF communications, all represents a considerable commitment which has at times proved difficult to satisfy with the inadequate payload and endurance of the units present aircraft; icing conditions have also presented a serious operational restriction at times. These operational difficulties were borne in mind when it became necessary to plan the replacement of the Prince aircraft, which are now obsolescent. It would obviously be a great advantage if some of the airborne electronic equipment could be duplicated (so that unserviceability would be less likely to interrupt the programme).

It is also desirable to divorce specialised flight inspection equipment from the aircraft's own navigational and radio aids. A larger aircraft could also carry enough equipment and crew to run two separate checking programmes simultaneously, as well as carrying the telecroscope ground crew and their equipment. If the aircraft were big enough and well enough equipped, it would be able to operate as a unit largely independent of its base, carrying its own standard signal source (for calibrating its flight check equipment) and an APU which would enable calibration work to be done, on the ground, when away from the home base. A bigger aircraft, too, should be able to generate enough electrical power to run all the increased services on board simultaneously—both domestic and specialised—and still have a payload and power resourcing in hand for future developments.

Thorough market research showed that the most suitable aircraft would be a specially developed flight-inspection version of the HS.748. Apart from its suitable size and capacity—the flight inspection version of this twin turboprop aircraft will carry all necessary equipment with full fuel endurance of more than nine hours, and with a reserve payload capacity of 2,000lb—the HS748 has a relatively low approach speed, good stability, docile handling qualities, particularly on the approach. It can operate economically at altitudes up to 25,000ft, and it can be equipped with a coupled autopilot and full CAT 2 facilities.

Hawker Siddeley Aviation and CAFU have been working together for the last three years to plan a version of the aircraft specifically for CAFU work. The standard version of the 748 uses Rolls-Royce Dart 7 Mark 531 engines which give an operational cruise at 25,000ft. An alternative version will have Dart Mk 550-2 engines, which will increase the cruise height to 30,000ft. Endurance at that altitude will be three-and-a-half-hours. The recommended approach speed, depending upon weight, varies around 105kt, and drops by about 10kt at the threshold.

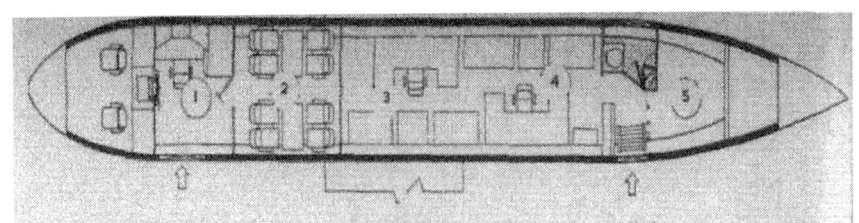

The proposed interior layout for CAFU's HS.748 aircraft which will be extensively used for the calibration of navaids. Key as follows: 1, Navigator's position. 2, 8-seat passenger compartment. 3, VOR/TACAN inspection console and racks. 4, ILS inspection console and racks. 5, 190 cu ft baggage compartment

HS748 Flight Inspection planned interior
Photo: Eddy Harris/JF

The flight inspection compartment (3 and 4) is at the rear of the aircraft. It contains two flight inspection consoles—the forward console for ILS and the rear console for VOR/TACAN—with the associated equipment and test racks.

The aircraft can carry equipment for flight inspection of the following aids: ILS; PAR; VORs (up to four simultaneously); TACAN (up to two simultaneously); marker beacons (airways and ILS); VHF and UHF communications and direction finding; NDBs; surveillance radar; secondary surveillance radar; and DME.

Apart from this work, the aircraft can be used for investigating radio interference with the aids being tested, for aerial photography, and for carrying up to eight passengers in a separate compartment.

The flight inspection work can be split broadly into two phases: first, the traditional pen recording and "manual" analysis of flight inspection data; secondly, recording of digitised data on magnetic or punched tape, followed by analysis using a computer. This second phase can be run in two different ways, by analysing the recorded data at base, or by using automatic control of the whole inspection operation and analysing the results in flight with the help of an airborne computer.

It is perhaps a wry comment on the comparison between two internationally competing position-fixing systems that CAFU often finds that the most accurate way of checking VOR/TACAN is to fix the checking aircraft's position by the DECCA Navigator system—which has accuracy in the order of ± 0.125n.m. Initially, an auto-observer will record position fixing data by photographing sets of

Decometers. In the second phase, a Harco D equipment will probably be used as a source of digitised position fixes. Not all areas, of course, have adequate Decca coverage; in some areas the aircraft will have to fix position by other systems—e.g. Loran C. Other possibly suitable position fixing methods still under investigation are inertial navigation systems or Decca Seafix—a portable Decca chain using transmitters sited by ground survey in suitable locations. VOR/TACAN could also be checked, if necessary but with rather less accuracy—by the very stable Sperry CL-11 compass system, combined with Doppler radar.

Photography offers a fairly accurate position fixing system and will be used when checking approach and landing aids (as a supplement to the telecroscope) or for identifying permanent echoes on surveillance radars; there is therefore provision for mounting a vertical camera in the aircraft.

However good the checking aircraft's approach handling characteristics, it would clearly be illogical to fly the aircraft manually to check an approach system designed for coupled or automatic approach procedures. An automatic system must always yield a more accurately controlled approach speed and flight path than a human pilot can achieve. The 748 will therefore carry the latest automatic flight control system developed by Smiths. This includes the SEP-6 autopilot, the STS-6 autothrottle, and SFS-6 flight director system. The initial certification aim is to clear the aircraft to full ICAO CAT 2 requirements with a special extension to remain coupled down to 50ft during flight inspection in conditions of good visibility.

Basic Electronics

Apart from the automatic flight control system, the aircraft will carry the following basic electronics: HF, UHF and dual VHF communications; dual VHF navigation; dual ADF; weather radar; radio altimeter; transponder; DME; Decca navigator; Doppler, and flight data recorder.

Although most of the aircraft's operational equipment will be independent of the specialised flight inspection gear, some of the communications and ADF equipment and some of the aerials will be used for both purposes. As far as possible, the operational equipment will be of the same type as the Specialist equipment. This will not only simplify spares provisioning, but also allow interchangeability in flight.

The designers of the aerial installations have to take particular care to make sure that the signals received from an aid under inspection are not modified by the presence of the flight inspection aircraft. In particular, the localiser and glideslope aerials in the nose are being specially developed to ensure as far as possible that the received signal is not modified by propeller modulation and "shift of phase centre" effects will be avoided.

Electrical power supplies are: 12kW dc from engine-driven generators at 27.5V; 3kW dc from transformer rectifier unit at 27.5V. For flight inspection requirements: 6kW dc from engine-driven generators at 27.5V; 6kW dc from transformer rectifier units at 27.5V; lkVA a.c. at 400 c/s, 115V, from the inverters driven by the basic dc system. An Auxiliary Power Unit (APU) can be installed, in the starboard engine nacelle, to provide electrical and hydraulic power and air conditioning when the aircraft is on the ground.

The significance of the work of the CAFU must inevitably increase considerably in the next few years as the trend towards fully automatic landing continues. The introduction of the two specially equipped HS.748s to the CAFU fleet will greatly increase the unit's capacity and flexibility.

PAPER 2

Author Charles Marchant

SPEECH PREPARED FOR INSTITUTE OF NAVIGATION c2006
This was taken from a paper written by Mr. Charles Marchant who was a Telecommunications superintendent at the Civil Aviation Flying Unit (CAFU) during the fifties and sixties. Mr. Marchant prepared this paper for a speech to be given to the Royal Institute of Navigation, Historic section, around 2006. By then, he would have been eighty-six years of age!

LANDING AID FLIGHT INSPECTION

ILS (instrument landing system) that, by 1955, had been adopted by ICAO as the instrument landing aid for civil airfields within the United Kingdom and overseas.

INSPECTION OF RUNWAY AND APPROACH AIDS

The most difficult flight inspection tasks faced by CAFU were those of checking an ILS and GCA (ground controlled approach) radar used as a landing aid.

ILS

The ILS system provides guidance in azimuth from a localizer transmitter placed at the far end of the runway (normally seen as a red and white caravan), and guidance in elevation from a glide-path transmitter (also a red and white structure) placed beside the runway about one thousand feet from the runway threshold. The carrier waves are amplitude modulated by two low frequencies of 150 Hz and 90 Hz and, the aerial systems arrange that one frequency predominates on one side of the approach path of the runway, and the alternative frequency predominates on the other side.

In the airborne receiver, the tones are turned into DC voltages, which are compared with each other and the difference in the level. Difference in Depth of Modulation or DDM is a measure of the aircraft displacement relative to the desired course line and glide path. A zero DDM should mean that the aircraft is on the correct path.

The ILS display on the flight desk looks like this:
- The vertical needle gives guidance in azimuth.
- The horizontal needle gives guidance in elevation.

The needles are centralised when an approaching aircraft is on the correct course and glide path.

Eventually, these DDM voltages have been used to drive automatic flight systems whilst the flight deck display remains as a monitor. Recording DDM involved recording of the small voltages that operate the ILS instrument.

ICAO annexe 10 prescribed tolerances that implied the need for a recording system capable of handling very low DC voltages. The system would have to be stable and reliable in an airborne environment.

In America, the Federal Aviation Administration (FAA) had introduced a type of pen-and-ink recorder, named the Easterline Angus recorder, and made these recorders available on a worldwide basis. At CAFU, they had already been fitted in some aircraft and were seen as being hopelessly inadequate for airborne use; they were unstable and as much ink was deposited on the navaid inspector (NAI) as on the recording paper. (Uncharitable as it may seem, it was wondered if, at that time, the FAA generosity was occasioned by a desire to be rid of a stock of dubious equipment, or perhaps an attempt to secure favourable votes for USA interests at ICAO meetings. Such was the depth of competition and suspicion at that time—ed.)

CAFU did plan to acquire its own recording system based on the use of Kelvin Hughes recorders in which the stylus passed an electric current through a conductive paper chart. However, DC amplifiers involving the use of thermionic valves were unstable, semiconductor equipment was not yet available and eventually CAFU devised its own DIY system to circumnavigate this difficulty.

Vibration of thermionic valves and various resistance in plugs and sockets were sources of instability when equipments were being moved between the calibration laboratory and the aircraft. To minimise these problems, the aircraft installations were left undisturbed, and aircraft were parked adjacent to the calibration laboratory (known as the CAL BAY) to allow direct cable connections to be made between aircraft and the Signal Generators in the laboratory.

UK STANDARD FOR ZERO DDM

Because CAFU's idea of what constituted zero DDM was imposed on all ILS installation in the United Kingdom, it was important to get the standard right in the calibration laboratory. Commercially available signal generators were not sufficiently accurate, and so a system was devised to provide a CAFU reference standard for zero DDM. The nominal zero DDM was determined by an oscilloscope display viewed under a microscope. This special apparatus was referred to the National Physical Laboratory each year for confirmation of its accuracy.

DETERMINING POSITION OF FLIGHT INSPECTION AIRCRAFT

Measurement of the angular accuracy of approach aids had to be associated with aircraft position, which itself had to be determined with an accuracy that was substantially better than that of the system being checked.

In the early days, this aspect had not been satisfactorily dealt with. For example, to make a flight inspection self-contained and to avoid the complications of using a theodolite on the ground to determine glide-path angle, a method was developed using a conventional air pressure altimeter. The aircraft would fly horizontally towards the runway at one thousand feet, and when the aircraft reached the glide path, map reading was used to determine distance to the glide-path origin. Then trigonometry enabled glide path angle to be calculated.

The questionable nature of this method was recognised by CAFU's Mike Whitney who proposed to derive height by photographic markers on the ground that were a known distance apart. With knowledge of the distance between the markers images on the film and of the camera's focal length, it was possible to calculate the aircraft's height above the markers.

Allowance had to be made for roll, pitch, and yaw, and these factors would be derived from instrument displays in a "photo box," which were photographed in synchronisation with the air/ground camera's operation. The photographs of the ground also would determine distance to touchdown and lateral deviation.

The author, Charles Marchant, says it was one of his first tasks at CAFU to evaluate the accuracy of this proposed system of height measurement. This involved simulating the aircraft rig on the ground and with it photographing white stripes painted on the side of the hangar. The results were statistically analysed by the Ministry of Civil Aviation Operational Research Branch who produced a satisfactory report. This conclusion was reached after the paper, which described the experiment, engaged in mathematical complexities, which was felt likely to deter any lawyer who might contemplate questioning the method.

CAFU navigators handled the implementation of the system by undertaking the film readings and calculations and by organising the provision of markers on the ground.** It took some time to implement the system throughout the United Kingdom.

CAFU felt they were following the right policy when after an accident involving fatalities at an airport where the old altimeter method of checking glide path was still in use, it was said that "flight checking cannot always be relied upon to test the Glide Path with complete accuracy" and that "it was gratifying to learn that a new and improved system of flight checking by photography was being tried out and hoped in due time to be completed."

As far as existing navigational aids were concerned, at last satisfactory standards were being set. But a more demanding task was in prospect.

*** Charles tells the story of householders under Heathrow's approach (who one supposed might have been hostile to the suggestion), who were charmed into having the tops of their gate posts painted white.*

SEEKING ALL WEATHER OPERATIONS FOR CIVIL AIRCRAFT
(The problem of ILS "Bends")

By the late 1950s, a problem in the case of ILS became greater as the pressure grew to achieve All Weather Operations.

In the real world, the path defined by zero DDM is rarely a straight line. The basic signals are modified by signals that have arrived by indirect routes, i.e., reflections from airport buildings, vehicle movement, etc. This results in the zero DDM path having "bends." If the frequency of the bend is low enough for a pilot to follow it rather than regarding it as noise, then it could be very upsetting to his "tranquillity of spirit." Whether or not a bend was acceptable called for the subjective judgement by CAFU's very experienced pilots.

In the 1950s, the problem of bends was such that many people thought that despite its name of instrument landing system, ILS would never become acceptable for civil All Weather Operations down to the runway. Different systems were being envisaged by the USA, the blind-landing experimental unit, and by others to replace ILS, at least during the landing phase below two hundred feet.

In the early days, ILS was not used below two hundred feet. If the airfield approach lighting was not visible when an aircraft had descended to that height, then the landing had to be abandoned, and the aircraft had to overshoot the runway. This situation became known as a category 1 operation. However, in the 1960s, various improvements were made to the ground equipment, to the control of the ground environment at the airport, and to the reliability and integrity of equipments both in the air and on the ground. These allowed use of the ILS down to fifty feet (category 2 operation) and eventually down to the ground (category 3 operation). In 1972, a world first was achieved when a BEA Trident on a scheduled flight made a category 3 landing at Heathrow airport.

CAFU played a part in these developments by evolving a system for the measurement of ILS bends. This consisted of using an optical missile tracking device called a telecroscope, sited near the glide path transmitter or at the end of a runway. The telecroscope followed and recorded the angular deviations from the ideal path of a narrow beam stabilized lamp carried on the nose of a flight inspection aircraft. A radio link synchronised the telecroscope measurements with the DDM and aircraft position measurements that were being made in the air, and thus it was possible to reconstruct the bend pattern. In the era, a computer became available to CAFU in the shape of "Apollo," a large second-generation affair that had been installed at the Prestwick Oceanic Traffic Control Centre. CAFU used it for ILS bend calculations, but feeding it involved turning analogue recordings into punched tape. This laborious task was performed by CAFU clerical staff using a machine specially designed for the purpose. However, this method played a significant part in ICAO eventually being able to prescribe acceptable criteria for ILS bends.

BIBLIOGRAPHY

British Aerospace—Air Britain publication, F. G. Barnes & R. J. Church

Airway—Civil "Current and Future Trends in Flight Calibration of Radio Aids"—Civil Aviation Authority 1991

DOC 340 1993/94—CAA Publication

Annual Report of the CAA 72/73, 74/75, and 76/77—Civil Aviation Authority

The Forgotten Pilots—Lettice Curtis. Publisher G. T. Foulis & Co. Ltd.

Hawkeye—Gatwick Aviation Society magazine via Tony Doyle

"Role of the Pilot in Flight Calibration"—J. Dunn, CAA c1994

Wrecks and Relics—annual publication, Ken Ellis, Publisher Crecy (Midland Publishing)

Flight magazine—for the period 1943 to 2010.

"Work of the MCS Flying Wing"—*Flight* magazine, 1952

Photographs—J. Fuller collection (via Eddy Harris)

Photographs—J. Fuller collection (via Jean [Jan] Jenkins)

A Testing Time—Capt. G. B. Gurr, self-published

HS748 series 2A for the Flight Inspection of Radio Navigational Aids—Hawker Siddeley Ltd.

The Stansted Experience—John F. Hamlin, Publisher John F. Hamlin

Hansard via Internet for the period 1943-1996

Guardians of Air Safety—Eric Jeffs, HAS Ltd. 1970 (reprint from "Engineering")

Stansted Airport—Nathan Kosky, Sutton Publishing Ltd.

"Work of the Civil Aviation Flying Unit"—A. C. Marchant, *Flight* c1967

Paper on the Civil Aviation Flying Unit—Charles Marchant c2000 (rewritten c2006)

Hunting Clan Review—Molly Neal BSc DIC AFRAeS Pub HC c1966

Radio and Television Engineers' Reference—Molloy Pannett (via Alan Richardson)

CAFU Booklet, unsigned, loaned by Capt. Peter Ray c1990

Radio and Electronics—Edited by J. H. Reyner, Pitman. (via Alan Richardson)

Essex and Its Race for the Skies—Graham Smith, Countryside Books.

Lecture notes—G. W. Stallibrass (published in *Flight* 1951)

Flight Calibration Unit Aircraft on Display—Chris Tyler, FCU c1992

Early Ringway—Ray Webb

Photograph: Copyright Derek Fergusson www.abpic.co.uk & Airliners.net 0600444[1],

Photographs courtesy Jan Jenkins

Photographs courtesy Peter Moon

Photograph: Copyright Peter Moore, www.abpic.co.uk [1317297[2]

Photograph: Copyright R. B. Johnston www.abpic.co.uk & Airliners.net 2006-2012

Photograph: Copyright Rolf Wallner, Airliner.net 0233599[2]

Photograph: Copyright Fred Seggie Airliners.net 012983[1]

Photograph: Copyright Jenny Coffee, Airliner.net. ID: 1112894

Photograph: Copyright Steve Williams, Airliners.net 0291111[1]

ABBREVIATIONS

A/C	Aircraft
ACR	Airfield/Approach/Area Control Radar
ADF	Automatic Direction Finder
ADL	Avionics Design Laboratory
ADSEL	Address Selective secondary surveillance radar
AE	Authorised Examiner
AFB	Away from Base
AFC	Air Force Cross
AGL	Above Ground Level
AFIS	Analogue Flight Inspection System
AIB	Accident Investigation Branch (BoT)
AIS	Aeronautical Information Service
AM	Air Ministry
AME	Aircraft Maintenance Engineer
ANO	Air Navigation Order
AOC	Air Operator's Certificate
APU	Auxiliary Power Unit
ARB	Air Registration Board
ATC	Air Traffic Control
ATCC	Air Traffic Control Centre
ATEL	Aviation Traders Engineering Ltd.
ATIS	Air Traffic Information Service

ATOI	Air Taxi Operator Inspectors
ATPL	Airline Transport Pilot Licence
ATS	Air Traffic Services
ATSS	Air Traffic Standards Services
ATSSD	Air Traffic Standards Services Department
AWD	Air Worthiness Division (CAA)
AWOP	All Weather Operations Panel
AWRE	Atomic Weapons Research Establishment
BA	British airways
BABS	Beam Approach Beacon System
BAC	British Aircraft Company
BAe	British Aerospace
BALPA	British Airline Pilots' Association
BEA	British European Airways
BEAH	British European Airways Helicopters
BFS	Bundesanstalt Fur Flugicherung
BLEU	Blind Landing Experimental Unit
BOAC	British Overseas Airways Corporation
BOT	Board of Trade (1966-1970)
CAA	Civil Aviation Authority (UK 1972)
CAA	Civil Aviation Agency (US)
CAAFU	Civil Aviation Authority Flying Unit (1972-1987)
CAFU	Civil Aviation Flying Unit (1949-1972)
CAL	Calibration
CAP	Civil Aviation Public
CATFU	Civil Aviation Telecommunications Flying Unit (1946-1948)
CAVOK	Clear of Cloud and Visibility OK (i.e., flying on instruments not necessary)
CDE	Central Data Exchange
CFI	Cobham Flight Inspection (2008-)
CFOI	Chief Flight Operations Inspector/Inspectorate

CNATS	Controller National Air Traffic Services
CO	Commanding Officer
C of A	Certificate of Airworthiness
C of C	Certificate of Competence
COF	Civil Operations Fleet (1944-1945)
COM	Communication/Commander
C of T	Certificate of Test
CPL	Commercial Pilot's Licence
CPM	Computer Programme Management
CRT	Cathode Ray Tube
CSE	Central Signal Establishment (RAF)
CTC	Corporate and Technical Centre (NATS)
CVOR	Conventional VOR
CW	Continuous Wave
DABS	Discrete Address Beacon System
DAS	Directorate of Aviation Standards
DC	Deviation Correction
DD	Deputy Director
DDM	Difference in Depth of Modulation
DE	Delegated Examiner
DERA	Defence Evaluation and Research Agency
DF	Direction Finder
DFC	Distinguished Flying Cross
DFICS	Digital Flight Inspection Calibration System
DH	Decision Height/De Havilland
DLS	DME-based Landing System
DME	Distance Measuring Equipment
DMEP	Precision Distance Measuring Equipment (associated with VORs)
DMLS	Doppler Microwave Landing System
DoA	Department of Aerodromes
DOS	Disk Operating System (pre-Windows)
DRDF	Digitally Resolved Direction Finding

DTI	Department of Trade and Industry (1971-1972)
DTL	Directorate of Training and Licensing
DVOR	Doppler VOR
EASA	European Aviation Safety Agency
ECG	Electrocardiogram
EFIS	Electronic Flight Instrument System
EGNOS	European Geostationary Navigation Overlay Service
EIB	European Investment Bank
ER	Engineering Regulation
ETOPS	Extended Twin (engine) Operation Standards
FAA	Federal Aviation Administration
FI	Flight Inspection
FCU	Flight Calibration Unit (1998-1993)
FCS	Flight Calibration Services (1993-1996)
FCS	Flight Crew Standards
FE	Flight Examiner
FIS	Flight Inspection system
FM	Fan Marker
FPL	Flight Precision Ltd. (1996-2008)
FOI	Flight Operations Inspector/Flight Operations Inspectorate
FOF	Fred Olsen Airline
FO(T)I	Flight Operations (Training) Inspector
FRSB	Frequency-Referenced Scanning Beam (MLS)
FSTS	Fire Service Training School
GAGAN	GPS Aided Geo Augmented Navigation
GCA	Ground Controlled Approach (Radar)
GEE	Medium Range navigational system
GFT	General Flying Test
GLS	Global Landing System
GP	Glide Path (ILS)
GPS	Global Positioning Satellite

GPWS	Ground Proximity Warning System (see also TCAS)
HAL	Hunting Aviation Ltd.
HAS	Hunting Aviation Services
HQ	Headquarters
HRW	Heathrow
IATA	International Air Transport Association
ICAO	International Civil Aviation Organisation
IF	Instrument Flying
IFALPA	International Federation of Airline Pilots' Associations
IFATA	International Federation Air Transport Pilots' Associations
IFR	Instrument Flight Rules
ILS	Instrument Landing System
IM	Inner Marker (ILS)
IMC	Instrument Meteorological Conditions
INS	Inertial Navigation System
INST	Instructor Rating
IPCS	Institute of Professional Civil Servants
IR	Instrument Rating
IRE/TRE	Instrument and Type Rating Examiner
IRR	Instrument Rating Renewal
IRS	Inspectorate of Radio Services (RAF)
IRT	Instrument Rating Test
IT	Information Technology
ITRU	Installation Test and Repair Unit
ITT	Invitation to Tender
JAA	Joint Aviation Agency
JAR	Joint Airworthiness Requirement
LAA	Light Aircraft association
LAP	London Airport
LCZ	London Control Zone

LOC	Localiser (ILS)
LORAN	Long Range Area Navigation
LTS	Licensing and Training Standard
LTSD	Licensing and Training Standards Division
MCA	Ministry of Civil Aviation (1945-1953)
MDS	Manager of Design Services (Tels)
MEL	Melbreak Aviation Ltd. (formerly Melbreak Engineering Ltd.)
MF	Medium Frequency
MFDF	Medium Frequency Direction Finding
MITRE	Massachusetts Institute of Technology Research Engineering
MLS	Microwave Landing System
MOA	Ministry of Aviation (1959-1966)
MOD	Ministry of Defence
MM	Middle Marker (ILS)
MOR	Mandatory Occurrence Reporting
MOS	Ministry of Supply
MOT	Ministry of Transport
MQA	Manager of Quality Assurance (Tels)
MSAS	Multifunctional Satellite Augmentation System
MSBLS	Microwave Scanning Beam Landing System
MSSR	Monopulse Secondary Surveillance Radar
MTCA	Ministry of Transport and Civil Aviation (1953-1959)
MTI	Moving Target Indicator
MTOW	Maximum Take-off Weight
NAA	National Aviation Authorities
NAI	Navigational Aid Inspector
NAMU	Northern Area Maintenance Unit
NATO	North Atlantic Treaty Organisation
NATS	National Air Traffic Services

NAVSTAR	18 Navigational Satellites
NDB	Non-directional Beacon (MF)
NCAA	Norwegian CAA
NOTAM	Notice to Airmen
OC	Out of Cover (MLS)
OCI	Outside-Coverage indicator
OM	Outer Marker (ILS)
OO	Operations Officer
ORB	Operational Research Branch
OS	Ordnance Survey
PAPI	Precision Approach-Path Indicators (lighting)
PAR	Precision Approach Radar
PATE	Principal Air Traffic Engineer
PFE	Principal Flight Examiner
PFOI	Principal Flight Operations Inspector
PFA	Private Flying Association
PPL	Private Pilot's Licence
PICAO	Provisional International Civil Aviation Organisation
PR	Public Relations
PRF	Pulse Repetition Frequency
PSR	Primary Surveillance Radar
PRFE	Polytetrafluoroethylene
PWFU	Permanently Withdrawn from Use
QBI	Instrument Flight conditions (3-letter Q Code)
QDM	Magnetic course to steer
QUINTIC	Leading defence evaluation and research technology comp
QNH	Regional pressure setting
QV	quad vide (which see)
RADAR	Radio and Detection and Ranging
RAE	Royal Aircraft Establishment
RAeS	Royal Aeronautical Society

RDE	Remote Data Exchange
RDF	Radio Direction Finding
REF	Refresher (flying)
RETRE	Revalidation Examiner TRE
RF	Radio Frequency
RME	Radio Maintenance Engineer
RMS	Radio Measuring Station
RNAV	Random Navigation
RO	Radio Officer/Radio Operator
RTCA	Radio Technical Committee Aeronautics
RTSB	Time-reference Scanning Beam (MLS)
R/T	Radio Telephony
RVR	Runway Visual Range
SAGE	Semi Automatic Ground Environment
SAL	Scottish Aviation Ltd.
SAMU	Southern Area Maintenance Unit (Heston)
SAR	Search and Rescue
SARP	Standards and Recommended Practices (ICAO)
SAS	Scandinavian Airlines System
SATE	Senior Air Traffic Engineer
SBA	Standard Beam Approach
SBAS	Satellite-Based Augmentation System
SBG	Strategic Business Group
SBU	Strategic Business Unit
SC117	Standing Committee 117 of the RTCA(ICAO)
SCPL	Senior Commercial Pilot Licence
SDAU	Safety Data Analysis Unit
SFE	Senior Flight Examiner
SFT	Simulated Flight Training
SID	Standard Instrument Departure (airport procedure)
SMC	Scottish Area Maintenance

SO	Signals Officer
SOACC	Scottish and Oceanic Area Control Centre
SPL	Student Pilot's Licence
SRE	Surveillance Radar Element
SRG	Safety Regulation Group (CAA)
SSR	Secondary Surveillance Radar
STANA	Standardisation Agreements (NATO)
STAR	Standard Terminal Arrival (airport procedure)
STC	Standard Telephones and Cables
STL	Standard Telephones Ltd.
STNA	Service Technique de la Navigation Aérienne (French: Air Traffic Services Authority)
STOL	Short Take-off and Landing
TACAN	Tactical Area Navigational Aid
TCAS	Terrain Collision Avoidance System (see also GPWS)
TEE	Telecommunications Eng. Establishment
TFU	Telecommunications Flying Unit
TI	Training Inspector
TILS	Tactical Instrument Landing System
TMA	Terminal Manoeuvring Area
TOC	Top of Climb
TOD	Top of Descent
TRE	Type Rating Examiner
TRSB	Time Reference Scanning Beam (MLS)
TSV	Telesurveillance
TVOR	Terminal Area VOR
UAE	United Arab Emirates
UHF	Ultra High frequency
ULAA	Ultra Light Aircraft Association
US	United States (of America)
USSR	Union of Soviet Socialist Republics

U/VDF	Ultra and Very High Frequency Direction Finding
VGPI	Visual Glide Path Indicator
VAR	Visual-Aural Range
VASI	Visual Approach Slope Indicator
VDF	VHF Direction-Finding station
VDU	Visual Display Unit
VFR	Visual Flight Rules
VGPI	Vertical Glide Path Indicators
VHF	Very High Frequency
VLF	Very Low Frequency
VOR	VHF omni-directional Range
VORTAC	VOR and TACAN Combined
WAAS	Wide Area Augmentation System
WO	Wireless Operator
WT	Wireless Telegraphist
WWII	World War II